Kinship by Design

Kinship by Design

A History of Adoption in the Modern United States

ELLEN HERMAN

The University of Chicago Press
Chicago and London

Ellen Herman is professor of history at the University of Oregon.

The University of Chicago Press, Chicago 60637
The University of Chicago Press, Ltd., London
© 2008 by The University of Chicago
All rights reserved. Published 2008
Printed in the United States of America
17 16 15 14 13 12 11 10 09 08   1 2 3 4 5

ISBN-13: 978-0-226-32759-4 (cloth)
ISBN-13: 978-0-226-32760-0 (paper)
ISBN-10: 0-226-32759-0 (cloth)
ISBN-10: 0-226-32760-4 (paper)

Library of Congress Cataloging-in-Publication Data
Herman, Ellen, 1957–
    Kinship by design : a history of adoption in the modern United States /
Ellen Herman.
        p. cm.
    Includes bibliographical references and index.
    ISBN-13: 978-0-226-32759-4 (cloth : alk. paper)
    ISBN-10: 0-226-32759-0 (cloth : alk. paper)
    ISBN-13: 978-0-226-32760-0 (pbk. : alk. paper)
    ISBN-10: 0-226-32760-4 (pbk. : alk. paper)
1. Adoption—United States—History—20th century. 2. Orphans—United
States—History—20th century. I. Title.
    HV875.55.H47 2008
    362.7340973—dc22   2008002077

♾ The paper used in this publication meets the minimum requirements of
the American National Standard for Information Sciences—Permanence of
Paper for Printed Library Materials, ANSI Z39.48-1992.

The striving to make stability of meaning prevail over the instability of events is the main task of intelligent human effort.

JOHN DEWEY, *Experience and Nature*, 1925

CONTENTS

ACKNOWLEDGMENTS

I am not certain about many things, but I am certain I would not have been able to write a single coherent sentence without the many peole who offered moral support, material assistance, and the gifts of friendship and simple curiosity along the way.

My first debt is to the talented scholars who began making adoption history visible at the very moment I stumbled on the topic. Bernadine Barr, Laura Briggs, Wayne Carp, Joan Hollinger, Randy Kennedy, Barbara Melosh, Margaret Rhodes, and Nikki Strong-Boag have been unfailingly encouraging teachers and supportive colleagues. For generously agreeing to read drafts, sometimes more than once, I wish to thank Bernadine Barr, Betty Bayer, Laura Briggs, John Carson, Fran Cherry, Joan Hollinger, Jeff Ostler, and Margaret Rhodes. Wayne Carp, Robert D. Johnston, and Barbara Melosh read this book in manuscript for the University of Chicago Press. Their incisive questions renewed my determination to aim high at a point when my energy was low. That I could not follow through on all of their challenging suggestions suggests my own limitations rather than theirs.

Like those adoptees who struggle to recover documentary evidence of their life stories, we historians cannot pursue our craft without dedicated record keepers who guard traces of the past. Archivists Dave Klaassen at the University of Minnesota's Social Welfare History Archives, Steve Novak at Columbia Medical School's Archives and Special Collections, Jeff Flannery at the Library of Congress, and Brother John Sheperd at Catholic University's Department of Archives and Manuscripts were especially helpful. At the National Archives, Jim Hastings came to my rescue at a crucial moment. Historians everywhere are indebted to interlibrary loan, and I am grateful to the staff at Widener and Knight Libraries.

A million thanks to the individuals and organizations who granted me permission to use unpublished documents: Mrs. Joseph W. Walden and her son Rex P. Walden for materials from the Arnold Lucius Gesell Papers at the Library of Congress; Steve Boehm of the Child Welfare League of America; Columbia University's Rare Book and Manuscript Library for materials from the Dorothy Hutchinson and Jessie Taft Papers; the Schlesinger Library, Radcliffe Institute for Advanced Study, Harvard University, for materials from the Ethel Sturges Dummer, Martha May Eliot, and Justine Wise Polier Papers; Mildred Freeman of Hillcrest Children's Center; Julie Rosicky of the International Social Service–United States of America Branch, Inc. (ISS-USA); and Columbia University Medical Center's Archives and Special Collections for materials from the Viola Wertheim Bernard Papers.

Along the way, I received generous institutional aid from the Viola W. Bernard Foundation, the Bunting Institute (now the Radcliffe Institute for Advanced Study), Harvard Law School, the University of Michigan Advanced Study Center (now the Center for International and Comparative Studies), and the Science and Technology Studies Program of the National Science Foundation. Student assistants Sarah Geddes, Bea McKenzie, and Shannon Parrott offered help and company. Without a gentle push from the Center for History and New Media at George Mason University, I doubt I would have been bold enough to launch a public history Web site. The Adoption History Project can be found at www.uoregon.edu/~adoption. The hundreds of people who have responded to that online project since 2003 have reaffirmed my belief that history matters in the most profound ways imaginable.

I have been the lucky recipient of kindnesses too numerous to mention from people whose creativity inspired me, whose faith sustained me, and whose friendship means more than I can say. These people include Betsy Bartholet, Barbara Beltrand, Gerry Berk, Mari Jo Buhle, John Carson, Nancy Cott, Ellen Fitzpatrick, Karen Giese, Amy Hoffman, Carol Katz, Sue Landers, Ellen Lapowsky, Jill Morawski, Sandi Morgen, Terry O'Nell, Bob Quintero, Kate Raisz, Mike Sokal, and Judy Vichniac. Jim Goodman cheered me on through good times and bad.

Academic, professional, and community audiences provided practical deadlines, tough questions, enthusiasm when I did well, and patience when I did not. I would like to acknowledge invitations from the American Bar Association Center on Children and the Law and the Harvard Law School Child Advocacy Program, the Archway Interdisciplinary Adoption Study Group at Massachusetts General Hospital, Brandeis University, the University of British Columbia, Brown University, the CUNY Center for Lesbian and Gay Studies, the Ethical Society of Boston, Linn Benton Community College, the University of New Hampshire, Northwestern University, and Oregon State University. Special conferences at Boston University's Institute for the Study of Economic Culture, Manchester University, the University of Michigan, Pennsylvania State University, the Woodrow Wilson Center, Yale University, and York University offered intellectual stimulation and community. Material scattered throughout this book was published, in earlier and different forms, in *Isis*, the *Journal of Social History*, *Religion and American Culture*, *Society*, and *Osiris*.

No colleagues have been more loyal or long-lasting co-conspirators than the members of Cheiron and the Forum for History of Human Science, who made me a part of their family before I had anything to show for myself. During the past several years, it has also been a pleasure to witness the birth of a new, interdisciplinary community devoted to adoption studies. Thanks to the hard work of Joy Castro, Jill Deans, Emily Hipchen, Marianne Novy, Martha Satz, and Carol Singley, the Alliance for the Study of Adoption and Culture has been central to this development. I felt privileged to participate in that organization's first two conferences, at the University of Tampa in 2005 and at the University of Pittsburgh in 2007. These gatherings of creative writers, artists, and scholars demonstrated the potential of adoption to illuminate basic questions in the humanities and social sciences in utterly original ways.

At the University of Oregon, the College of Arts and Sciences, the Oregon Humanities Center, and the Wired Humanities Project all provided aid. Since my move to the West Coast in 1998, I have been surrounded by the smartest, most generous colleagues I can imagine in the University of Oregon's History Department, including Carlos Aguirre, Bryna Goodman, John McCole, Ian McNeely, Jim Mohr, Jeff Ostler, Peggy Pascoe, Daniel Pope, Lizzie Reis, Martin Summers, and Lisa Wolverton. I have shared wonderful meals, stunning hikes, and interesting conversations with so many other UO colleagues that to list them here would fill many pages. They know who they are. No words can adequately express my gratitude for their collective confidence in my work and in me. It made all the difference.

At the University of Chicago Press, my editor, Robert Devens, was an advocate from the beginning, and Mark Reschke, Emilie Sandoz, and Kathy Swain made a complex production process painless, at least for me. Natalie Smith designed the cover. Camille Walsh, one of my students, took time out from her own work to help me with the index.

During the past eighteen months, I have served on the Lane County Citizen Review Board, a division of the Oregon courts responsible for reviewing case plans and making recommendations for dependent children in foster care and youth offenders in state custody. In retrospect, my move from analyst to advocate came later than it might have, but it has nevertheless opened a new vista onto the institutional problems and possibilities of family making. My service on the Citizen Review Board has been very humbling, frequently disturbing, and always compelling. I will be satisfied if this book reciprocates even in small measure what I have learned from the children, parents, and professionals caught up in the terrible tangle of the child welfare system.

Having written a book about family making, I have more reasons than most to note the contributions of kin and the complicated relationship between the family that made me and the family I have helped to make myself. My partner in life, Lynn Stephen, and our two children, Gabi and José, have graced my daily life with a constant stream of delights and demands. More than seventeen years ago, it was the kinship of Alejandro de Avila that made possible our *familia muy moderna*. Lynn, Gabi, José, and Alex are my personal reminders of the effort, accident, and sheer luck that collide to make families. They have kept me company in striking my own balance between design and uncertainty. I love them for that, and for everything else.

Family Making in an Age of Uncertainty

Adoption tells uncommon stories about how children, adults, and families navigate the common experiences of love and loss, identity and belonging. This combination of uniqueness and universality makes adoption histori-cally interesting and important. Before states passed adoption laws in the mid-nineteenth century, an assortment of private, largely unregulated ar-rangements transferred children between adults and households for reasons of love, labor, and inheritance. After 1900, adoption was reimagined as a delicate practice requiring skilled management and specialized knowledge. Who surrendered children and why? Were children who needed new par-ents normal enough to qualify for adoption? Were adults who were willing to raise other people's children up to the task? How should these adults and children be brought together?

I call the operation that answered these questions *kinship by design*. Its historically unprecedented and ambitious goal was to conquer chance and vanquish uncertainty. Kinship by design set out to make families up safely and well by making them up in public, on purpose, and according to plan.

The first premise of kinship by design was that adoption was dangerous and its outcomes doubtful. Participants suffered from a host of defects and disadvantages, from bad blood to illegitimacy, that threatened to sabotage their family ties. Kinship by design promised to reduce risks so that families made through adoption would be safe, natural, and real. Children placed by design would turn out well, becoming good citizens and making parents and communities proud. In contrast, adults foolish enough to seek children through baby farms, commercial maternity homes, newspaper ads, or infor-mal networks of exchange were asking for trouble and heartache.

During the twentieth century, the ideal of kinship by design moved from the margins of family making to the center. State and federal policymakers worked with allied professionals, forging a consensus that adoption be made governable. Legislators endorsed new legal standards and safeguards to manage the process that turned strangers into kin.[1] Together, they hoped to professionalize adoption and drive out entrepreneurial baby brokers and sentimental amateurs. Researchers who studied and clinicians who worked with foster children and families brought technological innovations to adoption practice, and their findings guided placement decisions.[2] Leaders in psychology, social work, medicine, and law were crucial to all these efforts. Among these individuals were Arnold Gesell, the most famous child-rearing authority in the United States before Benjamin Spock; Jessie Taft, an influential social work educator; Viola Bernard, a maverick in psychodynamic and community psychiatry; and Justine Wise Polier, a brilliant jurist who made child and family welfare her lifelong cause.

Ordinary people also participated in kinship by design. Their responses to new family-making procedures ranged from resentment and resignation to enthusiasm. Not all twentieth-century adoptions were examples of kinship by design; alternatives persisted. But the core values of planning and prediction spread over time, shaping both professional and popular opinion of practices that distinguished good adoptions from bad.

The design paradigm advanced through *regulation, interpretation, standardization,* and *naturalization,* keywords that adoption reformers in and out of government used to describe their own goals. These four historical processes transformed adoption into a manageable social problem.

Policymakers in the U.S. Children's Bureau (USCB), a federal agency established by Congress in 1912, were determined to regulate adoption, by which they meant making adoption a process over which state laws had much greater jurisdiction than in the past. When states required child placers to be certified or prohibited mothers from surrendering children at birth, they imposed stricter controls over family making. Adoption history consequently illustrates a regulatory vision advanced by Progressives early in the century and championed by New Dealers during and after the 1930s. These policymakers invoked the state's obligation to anticipate the serious accidents and catastrophic risks that accompanied modern times and to protect vulnerable citizens from harm.

Practitioners aspired to interpret adoption. By the term *interpretation* they meant two different but related things. First, they believed in psychological interpretation. The children and adults who came together in adoption needed professional help. Their behaviors, motivations, and personalities needed to be investigated, adjusted, and normalized to reduce the risks of family making. Casework, tests, and home studies were preferred methods through which psychological depths teeming with mysterious meanings could be probed for the good of the children and adults involved. Psychological interpretation reached its zenith in the post-1945 era. Like regulation, it originated during the years around World War I.

Second, practitioners worked to inform a naive public about the risks and rewards of adoption. They also called this public relations activity "interpretation." Both types of interpretation exalted expertise and skill over common sense and everyday knowledge and warned that individuals and communities alike needed protection from the many things they did not know about family making. Interpretation in adoption history epitomized characteristic features of therapeutic culture in the United States: its tutorial tone, its emphasis on the strangeness and difficulty of familiar experiences, and its insistence on making a strenuous project out of selfhood and social relationships.

Members of the new, insecure, and female-dominated social work profession promoted standardization by detailing rules for child placing and family making and by calling for protocols to keep records confidential. National organizations, especially the Child Welfare League of America (CWLA), promulgated these adoption standards, first in the 1930s, again in the 1950s, and in every decade since. Fixed waiting periods during which families were supervised before courts issued adoption decrees was one example, but many other family-making routines positioned adoption outcomes to be evaluated and improved. Minnesota's 1917 adoption law transformed several such standards into legal requirements, and virtually all states followed suit by midcentury. Like regulation and interpretation, standardization represented an exemplary principle of modern government. Public procedures should be consistent and transparent, never idiosyncratic.

Finally, researchers in the human sciences attempted to naturalize adoption, convinced that their discoveries about nature, nurture, attachment, and identity would refine policies related to qualifications for adoption, placement timing, and failed adoptions. Few ideals have been more compelling in adoption than nature, and its hold over modern adoption is explicit in techniques that sought to mirror the appearance and feeling of "real" kinship. Naturalization affirmed allegedly stable biogenetic truths as the correct measure of authenticity for social policies, privileging arrangements that appeared "only natural" and demoting those spoiled by artifice.

These four processes changed the modern adoption world as surely as they extended far beyond it, reshaping the twentieth-century social and institutional order, from education and employment to citizenship, while reconfiguring the public and private divide. Regulation, interpretation, standardization, and naturalization were quintessentially *modern* developments. They gathered momentum alongside the increasing social and economic interdependence—and fragmentation—that characterized the United States after the Civil War, an era of large-scale industrial production, mass immigration, and unprecedented urbanization that contrasted with the small, self-sufficient communities of the agrarian past. These four processes animated the governmental strategies required to manage a newly modern, complex nation. They suggested numerous approaches to social problems. Few approaches mattered more than accumulating knowledge about the problems at hand.

All four processes sought to rationalize adoption through orderly documentation and empirical validation. All were premised on the belief that the distance between adoptive and natural families—the factor that made adoption different—was both dangerous and, fortunately, subject to systematic management. Difference might be handled in one of two ways. It could be concealed with matching, the adoption paradigm that lauded likeness and held sway prior to the 1960s, or it could be openly acknowledged, a strategy more characteristic of the recent past.

Historians have already started to tell this story, and I build on an expanding literature in adoption history and adoption studies.[3] This book seeks to explain when, why, and how regulation, interpretation, standardization, and naturalization changed adoption. The fact that they did suggests that kinship by design matters not only for adoption and family life but also for far-reaching efforts in modern U.S. history to administer the present and direct the future.

Adoption is a different way to make a family. This is surely the most obvious thing about it. Because both difference and family making are contentious issues today, these features of adoption explain why stories about an exceptional form of kinship are regularly reported by the news media, featured on television programs and in the movies, and circulated on the Internet, where an abundance of cybercommunities constitute a virtual adoption world. Adoption is as familiar as Angelina Jolie and Madonna, as poignant as baby girls arriving on planes from China, as dramatic as reunions between adult adoptees and their birth parents, and as intractable as debates over sealed records and transracial placements. The operations that turn strangers into kin have become visible features of the social landscape.[4]

In fact, nonrelative adoption has always been rare. As a result of legal abortion and greater acceptance of single mothers, it has become even rarer during the past several decades. Since the late 1980s, approximately 125,000 children have been adopted annually by strangers and relatives in the United States, a sharp decrease from the century-long high point of 175,000 adoptions in 1970. Because growing numbers of children are adopted across national, cultural, and racial borders—and look nothing at all like their parents—adoption is more visible than in the past, despite the decline in the adoption rate and the drop in numbers. Between 1990 and 2005, for example, annual adoptions of foreign-born children more than tripled, from seven thousand to twenty-three thousand, and now represent around 17 percent of all adoptions by U.S. citizens. Estimates suggest that five million Americans alive today are adoptees, 2–4 percent of all families have adopted, and 2.5 percent of all children under the age of eighteen are adopted. In recent years, relative adoptions (e.g., by stepparents and grandparents) and adoptions from public foster care have increased. These adoptions involve older children with powerful ties to natal kin and complex special needs, worlds away from an earlier era in which newborns and toddlers were placed with matching parents, as if by nature. What adoption is, what it does, and who is involved have all changed over time.[5]

Adoptive kinship remains as atypical as it is unusual. Families touched by adoption are more racially diverse, better educated, and more affluent than families in general. We know this because, in the year 2000, "adopted son/daughter" was included as a census category for the first time in U.S. history.[6]

Adoption's symbolic importance in American life far outstrips its statistical significance. Since the 1960s, adoption has factored in the national conversation about pluralism, suggesting that kinship takes diverse forms and has diverse meanings. To be connected to adoption is to participate in a changing family landscape marked by such demographic trends as the rise of divorce, remarriage, intermarriage, long-term cohabitation, single parenting, gay and lesbian households, and families made by new reproductive technologies. And although adoptive families are "made up," they are hardly alone. American families are continually created and re-created in ways that confound the demarcation between natural kinds and social kinds, adding to the turmoil about how to define families. Today, many Americans welcome family diversity, whereas others grieve the decline of traditional kinship, by which they mean families made exclusively through monogamous, heterosexual marriage and a patriarchal division of labor.[7]

Popular interest in adoption expresses concerns about difference and equality that emerged from the civil rights revolution after 1945 and accompanied dramatic new waves of immigration from Asia, Africa, and Latin America after 1965. Jim Crow persisted in family life longer than it did in transportation, education, employment, voting, or housing. Antimiscegenation laws, which prohibited racial intermarriage, were not declared unconstitutional until 1967, and state bans on transracial adoption persisted into the 1970s. Adoptions across lines of race, culture, and nation symbolize gradual acceptance of multicultural kinship. Heated debates about white families adopting African American children, and other children of color, reveal persistent resistance to it.

Like controversies over domestic transracial adoptions, international adoptions betray ambivalence about turning outsiders into insiders. For all the joyful stories about Guatemalan, Vietnamese, Russian, and Chinese children being welcomed into American homes, it remains the case that transborder migrations of young children are inseparable from the wars, natural disasters, and episodes of traumatic mass violence that structure parent-child separations in developing and conflict-ridden societies. Debates about immigration and national security, border enforcement, and terrorism that have raged since September 11, 2001, may seem distant from transnational family making. They are not. They link global orders to personal life, outline a geopolitics of kinship, and expose the great hopes and terrible disappointments that Americans associate with negotiating the difference between "them" and "us."

Adoption's emblematic status is nothing new. Since 1851, when Massachusetts passed the country's first modern adoption law, observers have attributed curiosity about adoption to its compatibility with cherished national values and traditions, going so far as to suggest that migration and mobility amount to adoption narratives on the nation-state level. Adoption experiences "form an illuminating chapter in American democracy," the *Saturday Evening Post* observed with satisfaction in 1930.[8] "America's very nationhood is adoptive," the *New Yorker* boasted in 1993. With its immigrant history and multicultural consciousness, the country "can be seen as a historical experiment in mass geographical adoption."[9] One recent commentator enthusiastically dubbed the United States "Adoption Nation."[10]

If the meanings of America and adoption have been historically linked, why has adoption been so rare? Why has it not been more easily accepted or considered more "natural"? Why has the struggle to make adoption look and feel as real as the "real thing" been a virtual obsession in law, language, and literary representation as well as in the social and legal practices that bring families into being?

Adoption history during the past century displays both profound upheavals and underlying continuities. Old family-making rules clearly gave way under the pressure of new ideas about sex, gender, and love. Feminism and the sexual revolution raised a host of questions about what families were and what they were for, prompting Americans to reconsider illegitimacy, infertility, divorce, disability, and sexual orientation. As a consequence, the stigmatization of difference decreased, variation in kinship became more visible, and controversies raged over family forms and functions. Young people may be surprised to learn that "out-of-wedlock" pregnancies and "sterility"—if they even know these terms—disgraced entire families just a few decades ago. They may be unaware that many white unwed mothers were sent away during their "confinements" and coerced to surrender newborns. They may be shocked that single parents were treated unequally in law and public policy. Because of its ties to nonmarital pregnancy and infertility, and because it forged bonds between previously unrelated adults and children, adoption made pluralism a fact of private as well as public life. Yet adoption also suggested that not all families were created equal.

The spectrum of relationships Americans call "family" has changed significantly, but it has coexisted with blood bias. The equation between blood and belonging suggests continuity in adoption history. Successive waves of reformers struggled to endow adoptive kinship with dignity and authenticity in the face of belief that blood was the only reliable basis for kinship. Making blood the measure of realness fixed the values defining families and reduced complex questions of identity and belonging to uniform recipes. It flattened the many meanings that infused words such as "love," "permanence," "choice," and "real," as they were actually used to describe family lives, dreams, and disappointments.

Blood bias refused the uncertainty that was central to modern life. It emphasized the difference between nature and artifice as the reason why adoption was flimsy and inauthentic—not just different, in other words, but deficient. Enduring beliefs in the power of blood, and widespread doubts about whether families could thrive without it, fueled ardent efforts to subject adoption to regulation, interpretation, standardization, and naturalization. These combined operations accomplished two related goals. They identified adoption as an important social problem and designated kinship by design as its solution.

———

This book's account of twentieth-century adoption offers new ways to think about what American modernity has meant. As a story about strenuous efforts to endow social relationships with stability and authenticity in the face of a stubborn equivalence between blood and belonging, adoption exposes one of the most paradoxical tensions in modern American culture: between liberalism, on the one hand, and conceptions of nature at odds with it, on the other. The same culture that prized individualism, freedom, and choice also made blood the measure of relatedness, eclipsing an assortment of scientific and popular definitions. This constrained individual freedom and enforced a single dominant kinship standard: "blood is thicker than water."[11]

In public spheres distant from kinship, the rhetoric of liberal nationalism elevated solidarities achieved on purpose over solidarities ascribed to blood. Unlike societies in which birth was destiny and national character was fixed, histories of social mobility, geographical expansion, and immigration have become the mythical pillars of the American story. From the first European settlers to the immigrant masses of the nineteenth and twentieth centuries, starting fresh, inventing oneself, and succeeding by dint of work and desire have been at once the country's most basic premises and its most alluring promises. To claim, as liberal nationalism did, that Americanness was forged by willing participants whose common creed and experiences were more powerful than their disparate ancestral ties was to imagine the nation as a metaphorical adoption narrative in which all citizens were adoptees. American national belonging was deliberately made.

For some observers the affinity between American democracy and adoptive kinship was as self-evident as the submission of traditional societies to the absolute authority of God and nature. Massachusetts passed an adoption law in 1851, for instance, whereas the United Kingdom waited another seventy-five years, until 1926. What more was required to prove that the egalitarian United States accepted adoption while countries saturated in aristocracy resisted it? In this official story, the rapport between adoptive kinship and American identity was axiomatic.

One goal of this book is to trace the shadow stories that haunt this celebration of liberal culture, in private and in public. To the extent that American culture has defined nature as a product of blood-based (now gene-based) identities that are fixed, unchosen, and beyond the scope of social arrangement, adoption illustrates the authenticity crises that plague many forms of voluntary belonging, including democratic citizenship itself.[12] Is citizenship born or made? Legally, most Americans are born. Since the ratification of the Fourteenth Amendment in 1868, citizenship has been a birthright for virtually all persons born within the territorial borders of the United States. Yet the citizenship of immigrants who enlist in the national community is revered precisely because it "makes" Americans. "The divided heart of American civic identity," as Rogers Smith has shown, exists because voluntary nationalism has proved thin and uninspiring in comparison to the illiberal, inegalitarian forms of peoplehood that also litter U.S. history.[13]

The tension between ascription and achievement affects family making as it has nation making, and these parallel processes merge when kinship is forged transnationally. The acts of planning and consent that make adoption exemplary have also branded it as a family form of last resort. Birth parents who surrender children are disparaged whereas others consider adoption as a viable path to parenthood only after the normal (and preferred) method of biogenetic reproduction has failed. Beyond kinship, qualms about the quality and equality of elective affiliation are painfully apparent. Since the end of the cold war, quests for thicker, more enduring, even unquestionable solidarities have invigorated resurgent national and global fundamentalisms.

In addition to illustrating the ambivalence surrounding choice—a keyword in American culture, economy, and history—adoption offers new insight into modern government. The scientific and professional resources deployed to modernize family making were deployed to solve other problems too. Design, the term I use to designate purposeful social planning and management, often but not only by the state, first took root during the Enlightenment, which held that social action was both intelligible and subject to rational organization. Even before the French Revolution, design revolutionized public and private schemes to improve human welfare.

Examples include housing the destitute, confining the criminal, curing the sick, and instructing the young. In poorhouses, prisons, hospitals, and schools, humanitarian aid has lived alongside repressive control. Michel Foucault is the most influential scholar to examine the rise of design as a governmental paradigm.[14] Since the 1960s, his work has inspired narratives in which classification, incarceration, and other strategies of rational management had unforeseen and insidious rather than benevolent consequences. Foucaultian analyses of the Enlightenment's dark side and stories of progress and improvement in social welfare agree that the contraction of the family and its functions helped make design possible. As households became more nuclear and shed responsibilities, they became at once more private and more dependent on outside assistance for survival. Many families in the nineteenth century, for example, were so eager to take advantage of new asylums that admissions almost always exceeded capacity. The

Worcester State Lunatic Hospital in Massachusetts opened in 1833 with 120 beds. Overwhelmed by pleas from desperate kin, it tripled in size in little over a decade.[15]

In *Haven in a Heartless World*, Christopher Lasch explored design's influence on kinship and famously propounded "the family besieged" as both historical explanation and cultural lament.[16] Interventions to benefit children and families, he argued, benefitted neither. Instead, they pried socialization away from parents, transferred it to peer groups and representatives of commerce and government, and corroded the necessary barrier between public and private. The impact of the "so-called helping professions" was so "shattering," Lasch concluded, that "the history of modern society . . . is the assertion of social control over activities once left to individuals or their families."[17] Jacques Donzelot, working contemporaneously in a Foucaultian mode, was no more favorably disposed toward design than Lasch. He considered the "policing of families" indispensable to the entire project of Western liberalism, which did not govern families so much as govern *through* families.[18] A "tutelary complex," radiating outward from clinics and schools, subjected kinship to new forms of surveillance. By 1900, Donzelot noted, the regime of liberal governmentality extended to spirit and psyche, controlling individuals from the inside out.

When the twentieth century began, design was already a basic tool of Western liberal governments. It was embedded in statistics, whose very name invoked a literal science of statecraft. Institutions such as the census enshrined public numbers as the currency of national and imperial rule and created the historical conditions for "seeing like a state."[19] By 1900 the U.S. census covered not only work and taxation but also place of birth, marital status, physical and mental disabilities, literacy, incarceration, children, unemployment, housing, and internal migration, among other factors. The association between accurate data gathering and effective government was taken for granted before Congress established a permanent Bureau of the Census in 1902.[20]

As mass institutions emerged, the case for design became more pressing. Many Progressive and New Deal reformers embraced rationalization and research as twin solutions to the moral and organizational problems of industrial labor, urban life, immigration, and war. From work and housing to the Great Depression and both world wars, the reformers aimed to use regulation, interpretation, standardization, and naturalization—the same processes implicated in adoption—to orchestrate responses to significant problems. Ordering economic competition, protecting citizens from the ravages of unemployment and old age, and vanquishing enemies abroad all rested on implicit understandings of how families managed (and mismanaged) the production of the nation's future workers, consumers, and soldiers.

Design had momentous consequences. It helped to bring an expansive federal state into being during the first half of the twentieth century. Embraced by the Democratic coalition that powered the New Deal through the Depression and World War II and into the Great Society of the 1960s, it survived the conservative ascendancy of the post-1960s era. Design was not a partisan project, nor was it limited to formal government agencies. Rather, it was an ethos and set of telltale practices: bureaucratic organization; disinterested, rule-bound professionalism; technical competence; calculability and measurement; empirical inquiry; normalization; and self-conscious planning.

As a creed, design offered concrete rather than abstract recipes for solving social problems. Poverty and illiteracy, disease, crime, and racial conflict could all be conceptualized as originating in children and childhood. Frequently, they were. Far-reaching twentieth-century efforts to manage war and welfare as well as love and reproduction set out to control the future by engineering the earliest years of life. In this real-world experiment, intelligent child rearing within families yielded normal selves and average citizens while intelligent public policies actively rehabilitated children whose delinquency, deviance, or dependence endangered others or themselves.[21] In the United States of the twentieth century, design-as-government echoed the promise of control that animated the Protestant ethic during the country's colonial and early national eras. Design was a confident discipline. The kind of mastery it offered corrected for facts of life made more unbearable by modernity: accident and error, mystery and luck, chance and risk.

Kinship by design made adoption modern by making it therapeutic. The term *therapeutic* designates a type of government that included the operations of the welfare state but extended to many forms of managerialism. It displayed the ethic of prediction and control, the drive to banish doubt, the technocratic confidence, and the promises of progress that were hallmarks of twentieth-century U.S. politics and culture. Therapeutic government transcended divisions of right and left, representing a commitment to statist solutions that coexisted with conflicts over the appropriate size of government.[22]

Therapeutic government was gentle. It managed people and populations through prevention, protection, instruction, and help rather than blame or punishment. It originated in Progressive schools, courts, and hospitals, where female reformers and public health crusaders envisioned a benevolent state devoted to shielding dependents such as children and unmarried mothers from harm, but eventually guarding the welfare of all citizens. Juvenile justice, for instance, was the brainchild of pioneers such as Miriam van Waters, a penologist who began as a probation officer for delinquent girls with the Boston Children's Aid Society and ended her career as superintendent of the Massachusetts Reformatory for Women. Van Waters believed that courts and jails should be factories of knowledge about children and adults. She favored a style of justice at once objective and empathic, featuring professional consultation, mental testing, empirical research, and specialized treatment. It is perhaps not coincidental that van Waters, who never married and whose deepest emotional bonds were with other women, adopted a seven-year old girl, Margaret Mary Butler, in 1929.[23] Her circle included many people involved with adoption.

The therapeutic government that van Waters championed eschewed moral judgments about people and their problems. It repudiated the moralism of the past and pledged allegiance to objectivity. Its advocates have been accused of paternalism, which is understandable, although maternalism expresses the gendered dimensions of this ethos more accurately. Therapeutic government transferred responsibilities for risk management from individuals to the state and a variety of legal and regulatory mechanisms charged with protecting people from their own ignorance and foolishness, as well as correcting for deprivations and losses that seemed all the more tragic for being predictable and, hence, preventable.[24]

A century later, therapeutic government continues to shape national debate on problems from obesity and violence to addiction. Americans today are regularly informed about "risk factors" and "at risk" populations. Few institutions are governed more therapeutically than families because few are equally fragile and formative. At home and at school, children's bodies and brains are surrounded by proliferating dangers, from cigarettes and sexual abuse to learning disabilities and obesity.

Therapeutic government has been government "for our own good," nourished by the forces that transformed so many other dimensions of culture, selfhood, and social administration during the twentieth century. Three overarching developments were implicated in therapeutic government: the consolidation of the welfare state, the spread of research in the human and biomedical sciences, and the expansion of psychological authority over sickness and health. Therapeutic government represented a watershed in the scope, methods, and purposes of power. It married discipline to help, narrowed the distance between individual and collective subjects, blurred the line between private and public, and made the choice between structural change and personality adjustment appear useless and outdated.

Kinship by design is a case in point. During the first two-thirds of the twentieth century, adoption was regulated, interpreted, standardized, and naturalized to make it safer and more authentic. Between 1900 and 1945, as design moved toward the center of adoption theory and practice, adoption remained a drastic step, suitable only after all efforts to preserve natal families had failed. Many children were excluded from adoption altogether during this period. Unqualified for reasons of mental or physical disability, race, or religion, children who did not satisfy expectations of normality were placed in institutions far more frequently than in families until at least midcentury. After 1945 the civil rights movement, the sexual revolution, the baby boom, and the second wave of feminism challenged segregation, the gender order, and the place of children and youth in American life. These developments made it conceivable that all children belonged in families, that occasional transgressions of matching made sense, and that adoption could be a positive choice for children and adults rather than a desperate final stop on the road to family making.

The decades after 1945 inaugurated an adoption revolution. Such basic questions as what adoption was and who it was for were reconsidered, revealing the stark discrimination that had structured regulation, interpretation, standardization, and naturalization before midcentury. This might have undermined kinship by design by blaming it for the bigotry and bias that were inseparable from matching. Before 1945, adoption ideologists, along with rank-and-file social workers, held adoption up to the mirror of nature. They hoped that simulating natural families might neutralize the risks of difference in a compromised institution. They accepted the exclusion of children and adults who failed to meet their criteria for realness easily, or at all.

Evidence that public protection and professional help had failed the most vulnerable children and parents in the country, excluding them because of color or culture, proved not to be fatal for kinship by design. Instead, the democratization of adoption after 1945 put the question of difference under the heading of "special needs" while offering new theories that made difference synonymous with damage. The adoption revolution after 1945 brought safety, naturalness, and authenticity within reach of more children and adults, at least theoretically, and accelerated the momentum of rationalized kinship creation by the state, the market, and individual actors.

Design still resonates as a positive value today. Rather than being dislodged by the waves of reform that have rocked the adoption world during the past three decades, its promises of choice and safety have attached themselves to openness rather than secrecy and exclusivity. Ironically, exodus from the adoption closet has created new opportunities to govern families because adoption is now envisioned as a lifelong experience rather than a time-limited event. The mantra of risk reduction remains constant too, even if defenses of well-intended adoptive parents, routine a century ago, have been rhetorically eclipsed by defenses of vulnerable, "at-risk" children.

What made risk the central challenge for modern adoption? Like so many other modernizing enterprises, kinship by design was a response to the erosion of absolute values that directed life in traditional communities and the emergence of chronic states of doubt and disorientation. This transition delimited modernity, and it inspired vigorous campaigns to ground ethical principles in the social arrangements that human beings invented themselves. Without timeless foundations, there was only experience itself, overflowing with confusion, variation, and change.

Scholars have probed the revolution we call modernity in economics, politics, science, and religion. Its chronology, definition, and appraisal are notoriously slippery, but rationalization, secularization, and bureaucratization have been repeatedly named as its trademarks. These ordering processes aspired to alleviate the existential severity of chronic uncertainty. Coming to terms with doubt and risk provoked numerous reactions and rebellions, from philosophical pragmatism to religious fundamentalism, cultural relativism, and the widespread skepticism in the arts and humanities called "postmodernism."

Kinship by design pledged to make families secure and knowable in the face of risk, often by normalizing people and relationships. To be normal was an imperative in families and in other spheres where selfhood was exhibited and shaped. Norms lived under the sign of scientific objectivity, but functioned as dominant moral standards requiring conformity, which is precisely why they appeared bloodless and boring to anyone who believed that spontaneity, mystery, and chance defined authentic experience. Kinship by design navigated the complexities of modernity, which included urgent quests to reenchant social life alongside practical designs for intellectual, institutional, and psychological mastery in a disenchanted world.[25]

Adoption in the twentieth century departed from earlier methods of child transfer, sharing, and exchange in the United States and elsewhere. Kinship by design promised to increase control, decrease danger, mirror nature, manufacture authenticity, and still answer questions at once ancient and modern. Who are we, and where do we belong? What makes a family? What are families for?

———————

I am often asked what I think about the modernizing project I call kinship by design. This is a legitimate question. As a scholar I try to conduct careful research guided by respect, even-handedness, and curiosity about lives like and unlike my own. History is not a confessional genre, but neither can it escape historians' standpoints. So here, briefly, is my view.

All Americans, not members of adoptive families alone, have been touched by the allure of design. By the turn of the twenty-first century, the conviction that "love makes a family" was commonplace. Thinking about kinship as a network of freely chosen relationships whose ultimate function is care, as I do, has added layers of nurture to reproductive nature in every-day definitions of relatedness and responsibility. Design has transformed marriage and parenthood from unconditional mandates or gifts into acts of mastery, which may be performed well or poorly. All families are adoptive in this important sense. All of us have been simultaneously liberated and burdened by design.

Design unites diverse families, but adoptive families have been plagued by the particular equation between difference and defect. At times, adoption was envisioned as so fragile that advocates argued that there was one best way to make a "normal," "natural," or "ideal" family. The result was discrimination, dogmatism, and the ironic perpetuation of adoption stigma by those most dedicated to eradicating it.

Arrogant designs that seek blueprints for kinship in the transcendent dictates of nature should be rejected. Nature is everywhere, always, within human beings as well as between and outside of them. The vast modern knowledge projects dedicated to understanding and manipulating nature have produced results too famous and numerous to mention. I hope they have also nourished an appreciation for human nature, the reproductive body, and our planetary environment as resources that are always in the making and, at the moment, in considerable jeopardy because of subordi-nation to social designs. However we conceive of it, nature cannot answer our ethical questions about how to live and love. Will kindness or cruelty guide our actions? Will we respond to uncertainty with denial and fear or courage? These are the questions that matter most to me.

I support the quest for intentional belonging that animates adoption and believe its future is as significant as its past. Adoption reforms of recent decades—critiques of matching, moves toward openness, and the evolution of adoption into a civil rights issue—are positive steps. But the battle against stigmatized difference remains. What direction should it take? I would like to see us concede what we do not know about family making, as well as what we do, and endow design with humility, generosity, and improvisation. Design can improve the lives of children and families as long as we do not forget that it is a contingent and changing resource. If this book has one lesson, it is this: we have campaigned for control, but we must also reckon with risk.

This book is organized chronologically and thematically. Part 1 highlights regulation and interpretation as forces in adoption history from 1900 to 1945. Chapter 1 begins at the dawn of the twentieth century and emphasizes the variety of child-placing mechanisms then in existence, from orphanages, baby farms, and commercial maternity homes to sentimental baby bureaus and newly invented adoption agencies. Chapter 2 describes the organizations that supported kinship by design after 1910, especially the USCB and the CWLA, and documents their efforts to make adoption governable through investigation, supervision, record keeping, and empirical field studies. Chapter 3 considers pioneers in social work and psychiatry who believed that therapeutic approaches, such as casework and counseling, would diminish adoption stigma and enhance realness. Jessie Taft, Dorothy Hutchinson, Charlotte Towle, Viola Bernard, and Florence Clothier collectively exposed the links among family making, maternalist reform, professional help, personality adjustment, and the normalization of children and families.

Part 2 covers standardization and naturalization from 1930 to 1960. Chapter 4 explores matching, the blueprint that made social kinship simulate nature, especially physical resemblance and intellectual similarity. The chapter traces two standardization campaigns conducted by the CWLA in the late 1930s and late 1950s that resulted in influential policy statements about adoption law and practice. Chapter 5 considers the history of adoption tests and research. It includes a case study of psychologist Arnold Gesell, whose Yale clinic evaluated many potential adoptees, and explores the evolution of research about how adoptees turned out. Technological innovation and outcome studies joined standardization with naturalization.

Part 3 considers the era of adoption revolution from 1945 to 1975, which reconsidered the question at the heart of adoption history: difference. Chapter 6 explores the emergence of special-needs adoption, which radically expanded the terms of adoptability by transforming minority children and children with disabilities into candidates for permanent family belonging, at least in theory. It follows early critics of the matching paradigm—Justine Wise Polier, Pearl Buck, and Helen Doss—and surveys the beginning of organized intercountry adoption after World War II. Chapter 7 reviews the adoption history of children of color and details the controversial practice of domestic transracial adoption from the 1950s through the early 1970s. Chapter 8 tackles the attribution of emotional damage to adoption. It illustrates how adoption acquired an abnormal psychology of its own by documenting clinical perspectives on attachment and loss, as well as varied debates about "telling" children about their adoptive status. The literature on adoption and psychopathology was both new in the post-1945 period and deeply rooted in the enduring theme of adoption risk.

I will end this introduction with a note on terminology. Adoption language has been subject to historical revision, like family making itself. Terms common in the period before the 1960s, such as "bastard," "illegitimate" and "own" children, and the casual use of "natural" and "real" to refer to the kind of kinship that adoption was *not*, will strike many readers as antiquated and insulting. So too will "feeblemindedness," "Negro," and "sterility," words that have been replaced with developmental disability, African American, and infertility. Because vocabulary is embedded in deep patterns of culture and mentality, it stands to reason that words have changed in response to revolutions in how we think about adoption and the sensitivities and rights of people touched by it. That participants in adoption have sensitivities and rights is itself an index of social change.

Terminological reform and controversy are not inventions of the recent past. They have been crucial elements of adoption history. New words were eagerly sought by adoptees, family members, and allies who mobilized collectively against shame, silence, and discrimination. Their hope, understandable if not always realized, was that new language might help to rid adoption of its discrediting characteristics. Decades ago, saying that a child had "joined the family" was considered an advance over saying that a child had been "given away" or "adopted out." "Birth mother," coined in the mid-1970s, was considered more enlightened than "real mother." Recently, some adoption activists called for "mother" or "first mother" to replace "birth mother" because they view the "b" word as derogatory.[26] Vocabulary remains a battleground in adoption.

As a historian, I believe that grappling with the past means grappling directly with the words that people used in the past. We must not avoid them. Our predecessors, no less than we, struggled to dignify adoption in language and in life. Readers will therefore encounter outmoded language in many quotations in this book, and I have occasionally used vocabulary no longer in common use to reanimate the tone and values of earlier adoption worlds.

PART ONE

Regulation and Interpretation, 1900–1945

The Perils of Money and Sentiment (and Custom, Accident, Impulse, Intuition, Common Sense, Faith, and Bad Blood)

In the early years of the American republic, adoption did not exist as a legal method for forging family ties. Wills and indentures announced kinship between nonrelatives by specifying the inheritance of property and transferring parental obligations. Prominent citizens sometimes sponsored private bills that changed children's names: 101 of these bills were passed in Massachusetts between 1781 and 1851, and the transaction was explicitly called "adoption" after 1823.[1]

It was during the second half of the nineteenth century that states passed laws specifically to effect adoptions. The 1851 Massachusetts statute is typically cited as the opening bell of the modern adoption era.[2] These formal codes distinguished the United States from preindustrial societies in which adoption was one of many possible transactions between natal and non-natal kin that satisfied needs for labor, religious practice, and heirship. It also placed the United States considerably ahead of other Western industrial nations. France did not pass adoption legislation until 1923. England and Wales followed in 1926, Scotland in 1930, and Ireland not until 1952. In Canada, New Brunswick enacted legislation in 1873, but Ontario's Adoption Act of 1921 (revised in 1927) was considered the country's first important adoption law.[3]

In practice, few Americans used adoption laws or saw fit to enter courtrooms to formalize kin ties. Doing so was costly, embarrassing for parents who wished to keep adoption private, or simply too much bother for those who did not believe that legal procedures were necessary to bring families into being or make them real. Before the Social Security system provided material incentives to legalize family ties in the 1930s, reasons to adopt were not always compelling. Adopting a child was "an effort thoroughly formidable to families who have never in their lives had anything to do with 'the law,'" one keen observer of turn-of-the-century adoptions pointed out. "They naturally shrink from it and from the possible publicity entailed."[4] Legal adoption was extremely rare as a method for turning strangers into kin, and most Americans thought it should stay that way.

At the dawn of the twentieth century, many methods—formal and informal, commercial and sentimental, deliberate and impulsive—existed to acquire children. It was against this chaotic child-placing landscape that a novel family-making paradigm, kinship by design, emerged in the years around 1920. It promised to improve adoption by ridding child placement of money and sentiment, regularizing the practice of family formation, and ensuring that the welfare of vulnerable participants was protected. The watchwords of kinship by design were prediction, order, and control. These goals, historically unprecedented in adoption, were compatible with the simultaneous transformation of risk and uncertainty into intolerable yet manageable problems.

The Logic of Labor, Love, and Placing Out

Legal adoption was uncommon in 1900, but exchanging children was not. During a moment of great transition in the cultural meaning of youth and adolescence, children were transferred between adults and households for many purposes and by many means, formal and informal.[5] In the nineteenth century, child-caring institutions such as orphanages and infant asylums proliferated, but after 1900, the ideology of institutional care went into precipitous decline. A new imperative to place children in families was signaled in the very name of the National Children's Home Society (NCHS), a network of state organizations with home-finding missions founded in the late nineteenth century. In 1909, family life was championed by the first White House Conference on Children as "the highest and finest product of civilization," a famous declaration that obscured the stamina of institutional care.[6] In 1910 there were well over one thousand orphanages in the United States, and their average size (some housed more than one thousand inmates) had grown considerably since the late nineteenth century.[7]

"The passing of the orphanage" was more wish than reality. Not until the 1950s did the number of children living in temporary foster families exceed the number of children living in institutions, and the number of adoptive placements did not surpass the number of institutional placements until the 1960s.[8] Most children who were placed anywhere were white; until the post-1945 era, children of color in need of placement faced outright exclusion or segregation. By the 1970s, deinstitutionalization had either closed orphanages that had once cared for masses of poor children or transformed them into psychiatric treatment centers and group homes; the acceptable rationale for institutionalizing children narrowed from destitution to disturbance.[9] At the beginning of the twentieth century, however, foundlings (abandoned infants), illegitimate children (born to unmarried parents), and orphans (most of whom were "half" orphans with one living parent rather than "true" orphans with none) continued to be placed in orphanages because of poverty. The terms used to describe them, including "paupers" and "waifs," transferred to children the designations that branded adult need as deserving or undeserving. For many children whose own families could not provide for them, placement in others was a theoretical promise long before it was a universal practice.

"Placing out" was the term that designated all noninstitutional arrangements to care for dependent children. The terms of family care were more elastic than the rhetoric of home placement indicated. Agencies paid families to care for children in boarding homes, whereas in working homes, children earned their keep. Traditional indentures were still used in many states well into the twentieth century.[10] These contracts secured children's services for a period of years in exchange for food, shelter, and basic education. At their age of release, typically eighteen, indentured children were given a fixed sum of money, a suit of clothing, or other material resources specified in advance. Although many indentures amounted to apprenticeships, a study of 827 indentures in Wisconsin between 1913 and 1917 suggests that indenture was not an unusual means of securing children for adoption: 36 percent were eventually adopted, and those children indentured at young ages were far more likely to become legal members of the families in which they were placed. More than half of the adoptees had been indentured before age one.[11]

Free homes, in which children received care without monetary compensation, approximated a modern adoption ideal founded on love rather than labor or exchange. Workers who made such arrangements clearly viewed them in adoptionlike terms. "When we place a child in a free foster home we feel that if everything goes well he will be a member of that family for life."[12] Many of these children were never legally adopted, however, and free homes were always scarcer than homes in which board was paid.[13] Family life for children in need meant many different things socially and legally. Not until after 1945 was a terminological distinction regularly made between temporary arrangements (now called foster care and equated with the public system responsible for poor children) and permanent, adoptive placements. Before then, "fostering" encompassed most variations.

Placing out was grudgingly accepted by reformers who idealized families as the only acceptable place for children but also preferred children's own kin to strangers. Placement outside the circle of blood was, for many, an "abnormal arrangement."[14] Others praised its "normality," "economy," and "availability," at least in comparison to institutional alternatives.[15] Still, when older children were placed in families, the reasons had at least as much to do with labor as with love, and most of these placements were temporary rather than permanent, as they had been in the nineteenth century and earlier. Placing out offered material benefits to poor children whose parents often used the services of middle-class child savers to survive economic hard times and family catastrophes, such as death, serious illness, or desertion, and to provide their children with practical job skills and entry into the labor market. Boys were in demand as farm workers, whereas household services—cleaning, cooking, and child care—drove requests for girls. Placing out was a significant response to poverty in the era before state and federal governments provided meaningful support for children and families.

The orphan trains are the best-known episodes in the history of modern adoption, and they were emblematic of placing out (figure 1). As many as 250,000 children were transported from eastern cities to midwestern towns between 1853 and 1929.[16] Charles Loring Brace and the New York Children's Aid Society were the best-known but not the first or only sponsors of this movement. They aimed to permanently separate children, geographically and culturally, from their Catholic parents and communities by placing them in worthy Anglo-Protestant families that would Americanize them and salvage their civic potential while simultaneously reducing urban poverty and crime. Such disregard for natal ties was unusual, illustrating bias against immigrant groups (Irish or Italians) whose ethnoracial identities, although in flux, were considered inferior. Even so, the architects of the orphan trains often failed to achieve their goal. Poor parents had no intention of losing their children, and they usually did not, even in the case of very young children placed permanently for "adoption."[17]

Birth parents' periodic resort to placing out did not change abruptly after 1900. In 1901 Mrs. Soule, a hotel maid, applied to the Washington City Orphan Asylum (WCOA) in Washington, D.C., for temporary placement for her two little boys, David and Ezra, "so to bridge over this rough place in her life."[18] Any number of mothers at the time asked for such help because of impossible conflicts between paid employment and child care. Such a situation was especially ironic in the case of domestic servants and wet nurses, whose jobs made them responsible for other people's children while mak-

Figure 1. An orphan train. Used by permission of the Kansas State Historical Society.

ing it difficult for them to care for their own. Typical reasons that mothers offered for needing placement included "got to go work," "salary too small to keep house & care for them properly," and "have no one to take care of children while I am working."[19] "I am unable to give them the care and attention that children should have, having no means of support other than what I earn from daily employment as Salesperson at Woodward & Lathrop, inc." was the distraught plea of one working mother in 1916.[20]

Parents willing to surrender children for adoption were rare. No WCOA applications filled out by birth parents indicated that the "disposition of child" was to be permanent. The few parents who considered it typically changed their minds. In 1918 A.W. Sprinke, a domestic whose children had been under care for a considerable period, wrote: "If you know of any one who would like to adopt them and give them a good home, I would be willing to let them go. I want them to have a chance in life to make good Citizens and Honoreable [sic] Men."[21] Two weeks later, however, she sent the orphanage a money order and instructions to put her children on a train to Newark, New Jersey, where she planned to meet them.

At the beginning of the new century, customary expectations that children work and contribute to household economies were still alive and well. Inquiries about taking in older children frequently specified that children would work for wages, experience, or a combination of the two. E. E. Richardson of Chevy Chase requested an adolescent girl from the WCOA because his household lacked servants.[22] Families requested children from the New York Catholic Home Bureau "to help around the farm" and "to mind the baby."[23] Children, too, assumed they would work and protested when they believed their placements were not benefitting them fairly. "I would like for you to find me another place as I don't like this one," complained ten-year-old Earnest Fowler to the authorities who had arranged his indenture in 1910. Unless they could find him a home "with a man that keeps cows, horses, and chickens or a man that is a carpenter," Earnest intended to return to his natal home.[24]

Progressive reformers who declared war on child labor directed their energies chiefly against industrial employment, but the household and farm labor implicated in placing out also violated the emerging idea that children were innocent creatures whose value was emotional rather than economic. To treat children as producers or servants was to exploit especially weak human beings. "Binding-out" (a disparaging reference to indenture) was "a survival of the days when slavery and serfdom were tolerated."[25] Such a practice was bad enough when reciprocal obligations were carefully detailed and presumably known to all parties in advance. It was worse in cases where legal adoption obscured more personal forms of exploitation.

Preadolescent and adolescent girls, like their male peers, were desired for their labor, but they were less likely to derive educational benefits from the placing-out system, and they were vulnerable to sexual abuse. Men sometimes considered adoption an efficient means of securing sexual services. This was the case with one eleven-year-old Ohio girl who was infected with venereal disease and a fifteen-year-old in Indiana who took her complaint of sexual abuse to the court that had finalized her adoption without inquiry.[26] One sixteen-year-old Massachusetts girl finally confided in a neighbor that her adoptive father had started molesting her at age five and had been having intercourse with her since her adoptive mother died, when she was twelve.[27] In one Philadelphia neighborhood, rumors about the "indecent practices" of one adoptive father toward his twelve-year-old daughter were commonplace, and neighbors reported that they "had heard the girl begging the father not to touch her and not to turn down the light."[28]Another Pennsylvania case was so drastic that the adoptive parents were eventually tried on criminal charges: two sisters, adopted in 1923, were so "unaccustomed to decent living standards [that they] were not shocked by the lewd behavior of their foster parents but were merely resentful of their own forced participation in these orgies."[29] Thirteen-year-old Frances went personally to a local agency to ask for help. Her adoptive father had been having sex with her for two years. Her adoption, finalized in 1918, resulted from a transaction in which she was handed over by her birth mother "for a quart of whiskey."[30] "Bitter experience" with sexual abuse was common enough that some agencies would not place girls in homes where male boarders lived or might be present. It was understood that girls faced special threats and needed special protections because of their gender.[31]

The movement from productivity to pricelessness was a momentous economic and cultural watershed in the history of childhood, but it was also a gradual rather than an abrupt transformation.[32] Economic and emotional motivations for exchanging children were not necessarily antithetical at the turn of the twentieth century, and it was possible to consider children as recipients of adult affection or victims of adult abuse while also seeing them as agents who negotiated actively on their own behalf. Many adults who took children in temporarily for the labor or income they offered grew very attached to them. On the other hand, people who declared their intention to raise children born to others as "their very own" frequently required those children to work. Clara Curran, who had already raised one adopted daughter to adulthood, wrote to the WCOA in 1913 to request another girl and pledged that "I am in a position to give her a good home and education for which I ask but love and companionship in return." Curran added that her own mobility had been impaired because of a streetcar accident. She walked with difficulty "and feel I must have some one with me when going to church, calling, or shopping."[33] Love and labor were not opposites in this world where the meanings of childhood and family were in transition.

The adoption ideal popularized later in the twentieth century—an arrangement motivated by love for dependent children incapable of caring for themselves, involving the wholesale replacement of one family with another—existed only on the fringes of child placement in 1900. Childless couples were the first and most likely to seek out infants or toddlers who could not make immediate material contributions. Their vocabulary, common later in the century, figured children as investments into which parents selflessly poured their emotional and financial resources, expecting nothing but love in return. Emily McA of Baltimore, Maryland, wrote in 1920 of her longing for "one very small baby. . . . It does not matter if it is a boy or girl just so it is young, so it can never know who its father and mother were.

We would like to give it our name. . . . We are not rich people. My husband works every day for a living but we would sure give every attention to a little child."[34]

These adopters desired exclusive emotional ties, without interference from natal kin. In 1922 a North Carolina couple in their early forties with "no children to bless our home" asked for "an infant of not more than one month of age. . . . Yes, we have orphan children in our midst but we prefer one whose people are willing to release all claims to [it] and never seek it out in after years. We want it for ours, our very own."[35] In 1928 E. L. Armstrong of Virginia explained that she and her husband desired "to adopt an infant, prefer one that is illegitimate, as we feel that no claim can ever be made on a little one like that." They hoped to obtain a child far from home "as we want no one but our very own relations to ever think it does not really belong to us."[36] Contractual exchange by indenture or deed conjured belonging, too, but the modern adoption ideal rejected reciprocal economic obligations as a bogus basis for kinship and celebrated intimacy, emotion, and desire. In the rhetoric of modern adoption law and reform, "human values" trumped material considerations.[37]

Families made as if they were natural rather than social would eventually become synonymous with adoption. In these families, adults claiming to want children for their own sake used the power of love and law to turn other people's children into their own. But during the Progressive era, adoption was a way to preserve and re-create families (through grandparent and stepparent adoption) as well as make them from scratch.[38] In addition to the lingering emphasis on children's worth as workers, there was enormous reluctance to sever and replace the legal bonds that linked children to their birth parents. In comparison to other legal procedures that transformed kinship—divorce, for example—adoptions were rare.

Family preservation was the creed of early twentieth-century child welfare reformers. They believed that children should be separated from their own mothers and families only in the most dire circumstances. "Social conditions are not right in a community that year by year is agreeing to adoptions of large numbers of children," wrote J. Prentice Murphy of the Boston Children's Aid Society.[39] Extreme discomfort with adoption prompted another social worker to call it "abortion after birth."[40] "The yearning for blood kindred is a deep seated, natural instinct in every child," declared Rudolph Reeder, a New York orphanage superintendent. "It is a soul hunger which no foster home, whatever its type, can permanently satisfy."[41]

Reformers believed that sustaining natal families was as important for mothers as it was for children. William Henry Slingerland, a child welfare leader, worried that brokers who placed illegitimate babies "are panderers to evil passions and conscienceless abettors of illegal sexual relations. . . . These harpies do a thriving business with bruised motherhood submitting under protest to robbery in both finance and child life."[42] The placement of infants was "one of the most heinous crimes," cheating children out of the real mother love they deserved, denying birth mothers "what might have been a real incentive to right living," and saddling adopters with children genetically programmed to "develop traits which cause family heartache."[43] A survey of members of the CWLA shortly after it was founded in 1921 revealed that adoptions were arranged only as a last resort.[44]

Blood was much thicker than water in the 1910s and 1920s, and rapidly professionalizing child welfare agencies preferred natal kin to strangers when adoption was unavoidable. "Adoption by relatives at least has the merit of keeping the child with those of his own blood," one researcher noted. "He has the satisfaction of knowing the group to which he naturally belongs."[45] The New England Home for Little Wanderers, a leading regional agency, announced that "we do not care to be known as an agency for the transfer of illegitimate children from their mothers to waiting families."[46] Child-placing professionals took a variety of approaches to lightening the burden of shame heaped on unmarried mothers and their children, but adoption was not usually among them. "Where there is a spark of maternal instinct," insisted A. Madorah Donahue of the Henry Watson Children's Aid Society in Baltimore in 1915, "we cannot lend ourselves to any scheme of separation."[47] Like the evangelical women who founded maternity homes in order to keep unwed mothers and their babies together, until the 1920s, when attitudes toward adoption began to soften, professionals avoided permanent placements whenever they could.[48]

Anxieties regarding eugenics were a prominent feature of the antiadoption climate. The sexual immorality of unmarried mothers, the antisocial characteristics in children of certain backgrounds, and the heritability of mental defect (a widely used term at that time) were taken to be closely related by members of the emerging middle class, including child welfare professionals. "Unauthorized babies especially are not popular in the abodes of the wealthy," noted reformer Jacob Riis in 1890.[49] Even infertile couples, in the vanguard of redefining adoption as an operation that erased one family and substituted another, were frequently concerned about children's "stock." One West Virginia woman searching for a child to be "one of my family in nearly every respect" requested "a young foreign girl from 12 to 14 years of age to take into my home and train to help me. I prefer German, French or Scandinavian. The reason why I want a foreigner is that I think they are likely to have better blood in them than our American orphans, who have questionable parents usually."[50]

For a wide variety of potential parents, adoption coexisted with expectations that children live up to definite, detailed requirements. The mayor of a Louisiana town inquired whether a New York children's agency might send a "carload" of white babies for placement with local childless couples in 1918. "We do not care to know anything about their antecedents or parentage. All we want to know is that they are healthy. We would be interested in about one half Protestant and one half Catholic children, both boys and girls."[51] "Do you know anything about the stock?" inquired another man. "I don't want a girl whose parents are or was criminals[.] I want one I can be proud of. One thats intelligent & will take an education."[52] A married couple wrote, "We are very anxious to adopt a baby but would like to get one that we know about its parentage. Are there any homes or orphanages where a person can find out whether there is insanity, fits, or other hereditary diseases in its ancestors? We would like to have one from Christian parentage."[53] After a tragic shipping accident in Halifax, Nova Scotia, in December 1917, one Maine woman wrote to the Canadian Club of New York about adopting an orphaned child. She wanted "a good girl from that section rather than an American as they are more obedient and stable."[54] Such views illustrated the widespread belief that heredity mattered. They revealed that gender, racial, ethnic, and national preferences were linked to popular conceptions about characteristics transmitted intergenerationally. Race, religion, physical health, mental health, criminality, educability, sexual morality, intelligence, and temperament were all associated with blood.

The Varied Landscape of Child Placement in an Antiadoption Era

Some people did persist in their quests to adopt despite the period's ideology of family preservation and eugenic tone, facing down the "enemies of adoption."[55] These intrepid souls, mostly mothers, often told their stories anonymously, as if to acknowledge that adoption evoked as much dismay as curiosity.[56] One adoptive mother of five shrugged off the stigma. It was simply foolish to "shudder at the risks of inheritance" because "love-lines, not blood-lines, make motherhood."[57] Another adopted three siblings (ages four, six, and seven) shortly after World War I and explained that she and her husband willingly took in these children because their irresponsible birth parents had placed them in a state-run orphanage, in their view forfeiting any right to raise them. At first the children were exceedingly thin, sullen, slow, and wary of the adults who volunteered to be their new parents. But even their "very bad" family history could not stop these "unattractive" children from becoming "normal in tone, good-looking, and wholesome."[58] With good food, consistent care, and the expectation that they "blot out" all earlier family experiences, they flourished.[59] Adoptive parents rarely lost sight of how reckless their decision appeared to others. "I was trying hard to forget the mad impulse which made me take this particular step with all the odds against its being the right one or of its being even partially successful," one adoptive mother conceded.[60]

Journalist Honoré Willsie adopted two children after writing magazine stories about the hazards of adoption in the late 1910s. She admitted that it had taken her a long time to persuade her husband, for whom adoption "conjured up a horrid picture of discomfort, responsibility, and risk."[61] "It goes without saying that almost every one who knew us thought we were fools. . . . They considered me as a poor, well-meaning nut," she reported.[62] Willsie "reduced the gambling element" by availing herself of all the services and safeguards that professional agencies offered, "learning with my mind and not with my heart."[63] Her rational approach appeared rash to friends and acquaintances.

The means available for acquiring children illustrate that no single method or unitary paradigm of family formation predominated during the Progressive era. Among the most important sources of children were baby farms, maternity homes and lying-in hospitals, the first specialized adoption agencies, and institutions, such as orphanages. According to child welfare reformers, this chaotic child-placement landscape was overflowing with peril and tragedy. Through exposés of scandalous and botched adoptions, reformers began to make their case for an alternative to commercial, sentimental, and all other nonexpert forms of family formation. They wanted to modernize adoption, by which they meant instituting procedures that would make families up methodically, on a foundation of empirical knowledge, supported by protective bureaucratic machinery, disinterested professionalism, and technical competence. I call the enterprise that set out to make families on purpose and according to plan *kinship by design*. Its first promise was safety.

Baby Farming, Maternity Homes, and Commercial Adoption

The term "baby farming," common in late nineteenth- and early twentieth-century cities, referred to boarding infants for money and their transfer and sale for profit. Sherri Broder, who studied baby farming in Philadelphia, concluded that it was usually "a legitimate occupation which merely formalized the informal child care networks of single mothers and other laboring women."[64] Unwed mothers, prostitutes, domestic servants, and destitute or deserted wives forced to work for wages left their children in the care of women like themselves, sometimes by the week, often in conditions that were dirty and dilapidated even when children were not mistreated.[65] No matter how desperate mothers were, leaving babies in someone else's care violated the behavioral script of maternalism. Consequently, many reformers and members of the public suspected that paid child care was nothing but disguised abandonment and infanticide of unwanted children.

Exposés of baby farms confirmed these suspicions by uncovering shocking abuses and death traps. This was a "nefarious, murderous traffic,"[66] with evidence of "flagrant evils so insidious and deadly as to seem incredible; black wrong doing going on unhampered while would-be reformers watch hopeless."[67] "Put into plain English," Jacob Riis wrote in 1890, baby farming "means starving babies to death."[68]

Muckrakers invariably reported baby farming stories in lurid detail that relied on gender, racial, ethnic, and class stereotypes. Intended to elicit the outrage of a middle-class public, reports on baby farming scandals were part of the broad Progressive campaign to manage and eradicate vices—including prostitution, obscenity, and drug use—that proliferated when people of diverse backgrounds mingled in urban spaces that commercialized leisure and entertainment alongside production and exchange.[69] Because baby farms married economic exploitation to moral offense, exposés mobilized sympathy for vulnerable children and demands for new forms of government regulation (figure 2). State licensing and certification of child placers, like food and drug regulation, would protect an unwitting public from harm and abuse.

Baby farming was condemned for being simultaneously lethal and entrepreneurial. Its connections to death and money placed it at odds with emerging conceptions of public responsibility for child welfare. Because new ideals placed children's moral worth beyond material calculation, protests against baby farms served as sober warnings to anyone foolish enough to consider adopting from such places. During the first two decades of the twentieth century, public health research documented astronomical rates of infant mortality in poor, urban communities and congregate institutions, and pediatrics achieved formal status as a medical specialization with close ties to campaigns for urban hygiene, milk purification, and maternal education.[70] It came as no surprise that babies consigned to baby farms often died there. Causes of death included epidemic diseases spread by woefully un-

WAS IT WORTH WHILE?

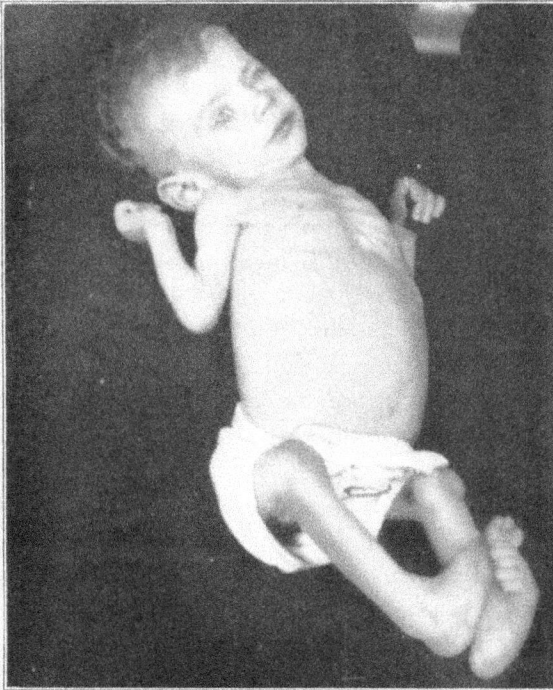

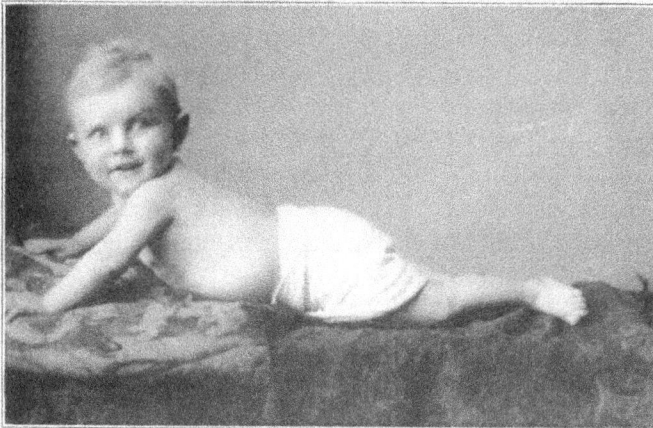

Figure 2. These before and after pictures of a child rescued from a baby farm in 1917 were typical of the movement to improve adoption by eliminating commercial placements and embracing design. Used by permission of the Child Welfare League of America.

sanitary conditions: inadequate space, unreliable infant formulas, unsteri-
lized bottles, dirty laundry, infrequent bathing, and flies and other pests.
Squalid conditions meant that perfectly healthy infants quickly sickened at
baby farms, where they were sometimes dosed with liquor or other drugs to
keep them quiet while they died.

At a time when breast-feeding was vigorously advocated by medical and
social welfare personnel as a life-saving practice, especially for illegitimate
children, separating infants from their birth mothers was considered deadly.
Hastings Hart, a national child welfare leader, lobbied for new laws regulating the most intimate relationships between mother and child. It should be
"obligatory upon each mother of an illegitimate child to care personally for
her child at least one year, and if physically able to do so to nurse it at the
breast for not less than six months."[71] In 1916 Maryland implemented such
a "six-months" law prohibiting the practice of mother-child separation. Its
proponents welcomed evidence that "some commercial agencies of poor
character have gone out of business on account of the restriction which the
law has placed on their activities."[72] The following year, a study of more
than one hundred Chicago baby farms revealed appalling conditions and a
mortality rate over 50 percent.[73] In Baltimore, mortality rates in baby farms
passed 70 percent, with children placed as newborns almost guaranteed to
die if they were not quickly removed.[74] State laws prohibiting infant placement aimed to prevent needless deaths by protecting women against their
own worst impulses. They also constrained mothers' freedom by criminal-
izing placements in the first months of life and stigmatized adoption by
equating surrender with abandonment and murder.[75]

In the 1910s forty states passed mothers' pension laws, adding economic
incentives to the moral obligations binding mothers to their children.[76]
These laws represented the success of women's organizations in arguing
for a state that assumed parentlike responsibilities, subsidizing home care
for poor children. Mothers' pensions rejected the institutional child-caring
arrangements that had prevailed in the nineteenth century, anticipated the
New Deal of the 1930s, and placed the United States on a clear path toward
a maternalist welfare state that sought to protect dependent women and
children from having to rely on the market for survival as much as it sought
to shield (male) citizens and workers from market failures. Mothers' pension laws deterred adoption by offering married mothers, especially wid-
ows, financial support when male breadwinners failed them through death
or desertion. By allowing these women to care for their children at home,
pensions made institutionalization or placing out less likely.

Mothers' pensions increased the stigma surrounding nonmarital pregnancies and heightened pressures on unmarried mothers despite the fact that before World War II, most children surrendered for adoption were probably born to married parents.[77] Aid to unmarried women and illegitimate children threatened the familial ideology that naturalized feminine domesticity and economic dependence on men while maintaining that dependence on public support was unacceptable. Recent scholarship has persuasively demonstrated that the American welfare state was rooted in such patriarchal premises. Efforts to bring a measure of security to impoverished female-headed families were marked by the class and cultural biases of the middle-class women's organizations that supported mothers' pensions and other reforms benefitting poor and working-class women.[78] Even as women's work was devalued and the family wage was celebrated as both an ideal and norm, poor, unmarried, unskilled immigrant women with young children were forcefully pushed into the labor market, where they earned little and worked extremely long hours. Their children were placed in the shoddiest child care arrangements, including baby farms, outside the circle of public protection and help.

The literal filth of baby farms was often equated with the metaphorical filth of baby farmers, made all the worse because these were women who repudiated nurture, allegedly so natural to their sex. They were almost always represented as uneducated and immoral individuals. Restrained portrayals cast baby farmers as "ungentle and unrefined."[79] Melodramatic descriptions turned them into inhuman monsters.

> The big, loosely-jointed woman lolled carelessly in the low chair, two great freckled hands on her wide-spread knees. The umber of long, unclean neck and arms foreboded ill for the cleanliness of helpless babies. A dreadful leer lay in the snakish green eyes, a tell-tale smile on the flaccid mouth, and between the two, accenting the significance of each, was that practically infallible stigmata of sensuality and cunning—a straight nose set crookedly on the face. A long life of dreary viciousness and secret tippling showed in the mottled face oozing with evil.[80]

Few baby farmers set out to murder unwanted children, but it is easy to understand why reports of organized infant death evoked horror. Eyewitness reports from Pennsylvania and New York in the mid-1910s described infant corpses left in alleys, dumped in pits, and burned by a "baby cremating Syndicate."[81] The New York Medical Association reported that on

New York City streets alone, approximately fifteen hundred dead newborns were found each year. One exposé offered readers a drawing of mass graves and photographs of bones excavated to make room for new corpses.[82] Even when not equated with homicide, baby farming spelled neglect and abuse. "Whippings, shakings, fussing and quarrelling" were reported by several neighbors of a Kensington, Maryland, baby farm called the Sunshine Nursery. One of them, Mr. Stubbs, "said it made his blood curdle."[83]

For-profit infanticide was an extreme crime, but it lived on a moral plane alongside the practice of commercial adoption, which was similarly motivated by money and was surely much more common. Reformers decried the traffic in children and denounced the dangers associated with greed. Baby farmers profited on both ends of child exchange, first extracting fees from desperate birth mothers and then demanding large sums from adopters. "The lowest I can take the child is $50.00," wrote one Nashua, New Hampshire, baby farmer to an undercover agent posing as a desperate unmarried mother. "I do not mind it being weak. . . . I could take it any time you want to come with it and no questions asked. . . . You would never have to take it back."[84]

An investigation by the Pennsylvania Society to Protect Children from Cruelty reported on "a drunken, worthless person" who received $10 for each child placed in an adoptive home in 1901.[85] One Philadelphia woman who purchased a baby for $15 from a local baby farmer tried to pass the child off as her own when her husband returned from a long trip. Its "Oriental" features made the man suspicious, led to the farm's exposure, and reinforced perceptions that untrammeled commerce would lead to intolerable racial mixing.[86] A survey by the Chicago Juvenile Protective Association reported that children were sold for up to $100 in the 1910s, with a percentage down and the balance in installments. No questions were asked, and children were frequently sent out of state.[87] One brash Chicago farmer used the following slogan: "It's cheaper and easier to buy a baby for $100.00 than to have one of your own."[88]

Closely allied with baby farms were commercial maternity homes and lying-in hospitals, where doctors and midwives served as brokers willing to place babies for a profit. Midwives sometimes extracted "surrender fees" from birth mothers and then dumped at baby farms the children they could not place with families. In one Philadelphia case at the turn of the century, a midwife earned $50 for her own services, $35 for her vow to locate a home, and $10 from a baby farmer, who was also hoping to gain from the exchange by identifying adopters.[89] Such midwives "have less feeling for a child than for an animal."[90] For some critics, midwives' immorality resided in their unseemly connection to abortion as well as to adoption. "They stand ready to kill the child any time before it is born; and after its birth their arms are stretched out for it to cast it to death."[91]

As men, doctors who practiced commercial adoption were less likely to be described as dirty or uneducated than baby farmers and midwives, but critics did not hesitate to accuse them of heartlessness and cruelty. In Tulsa, Oklahoma, in the early 1930s, a physicians' baby-selling ring equipped with a lengthy list of wealthy prospective adopters would "offer the baby for $100.00 down to $70.00 whatever they can get, but their desire is to get as much for the baby (they say their services) as possible. The baby goes to the one who has the money."[92] In Tulsa and elsewhere, surrender documents were sometimes signed under false names, making these adoptions fraudulent as well as callous. From Oregon to Illinois to Washington, D.C., and even Minnesota, a state in the vanguard of child welfare legislation, local officials complained about profit-hungry doctors who arranged adoptions of illegitimate children. Although some worked in connection with commercial maternity homes and hospitals, others proceeded quietly within their individual practices. As long as the cash that exchanged hands was payment for services rendered—and not the purchase of human beings—no laws were broken. Doctors who brazenly operated baby farms might be fined or placed on probation, but such cases were rare.[93] Reformers also suspected that doctors engineered many placements that birth mothers supposedly made themselves.[94]

Marketing was crucial in commercial adoption. Newspaper advertising was the primary means of reaching potential customers and suppliers. The text of adoption ads was typically short and to the point. "*For Adoption at Birth*, Full Surrender, No Questions Asked."[95] "BABY, expected March, offered for adoption to financially secure persons."[96] "For adoption to anybody who will give it a home, a healthy baby boy 2 weeks old."[97] "Who wants to take a little girl, three years old, the picture of health and a smart, handsome child? Only those who can give a comfortable home need answer."[98] Critics despised such blatant examples of the commerce in children and decried "advertisements in which babies, *tiny defenceless babies, sometimes still unborn*, are openly advertised as if on sale for the board that is due; or to be taken and disposed of '*in a happy home*' for the practically uniform charge of $50 a waif!"[99]

Efforts to ban ads or hold newspapers accountable for the unethical practice of publishing them were mounted in several cities in order to attack commercial adoption. In Boston, six child welfare organizations responded to more than four hundred ads appearing in local papers between

1912 and 1915 and found that adoption commerce was directly linked to illegitimacy, venereal disease, mental defect, racial mixture, and criminal behavior.[100] In Indianapolis, a six-month investigation of two local papers turned up fifty-nine adoption "want ads."[101] In 1921 the New York State Charities Aid Association investigated all the adoption ads published in local papers during the last six months of that year and discovered that an average of one baby a day was given away, or sold, by this means in New York alone.[102] The inquiry found that people responding to such ads overwhelmingly requested blonde babies; the desirability of whiteness was so self-evident that it went unmentioned. That ads specified details related to sex, appearance, and age (newborn, or as close to birth as possible) shows not only that adoption brokers were sensitive to the preferences at play in their trade but also that the market in children was like other consumer markets. Attacks on advertising envisioned a compassionate state drawing and then policing a bright line between vulnerable children and the morally indifferent world of commodities.

Some businesses marketed adoption aggressively. The Fairmount Maternity Home, based in Kansas City, claimed to advertise in four hundred papers around the country.[103] The Willows, another commercial maternity home established in Kansas City in 1905, used ads to attract unmarried mothers and adopters from many states. They were so successful that local officials complained to the federal government that the city had the highest illegitimacy rate in the United States.[104] In addition to newspapers ads, the Willows published a magazine that defended the home against accusations that commercial adoption was dangerous as well as unscrupulous. Accompanied by photographs of its attractive physical grounds and parlor, complete with piano, the magazine insisted that the home upheld the highest medical standards and boasted a very low mortality rate. The Willows existed "for those discerning couples whom Nature has forgotten or who wish to replace lost children."[105] Because the home allowed them "to obtain a child whose extraction, family background and physical characteristics match up well with that of their own, even the most exacting of applicants can be taken care of at The Willows."[106] Any skeptics with "mistaken ideas and notions" about the bad blood of available children were promised that the Willows offered only "babies whose family backgrounds bespeak refinement, intelligence, and clean health."[107] The Willows' chief goals were to save unmarried mothers "who are not habitual transgressors but the mere accidents of society" while giving adopters "an unusual selection of babies."[108]

The language of choice resonated not only with the commercial practices of a consumer culture but with cherished political values as well, including the right of citizens to form their families privately, as they pleased. Both types of choice were highly problematic for reformers. They opposed adoption transactions based on the crude calculus of the market, but they also mistrusted boundless personal freedom, which gave free rein to impulse, error, and prejudice. Advertising was a scourge not only because it commodified children but also because it facilitated family formation without the benefit of enlightened public oversight. Reformers argued that adoption ads consequently victimized adults and children alike. "Children of unknown history and family traits who are possibly feeble-minded, psychopathic or tainted with inherited disease, are being foisted upon ignorant, but in many cases well meaning foster parents."[109] On the other hand, newspaper ads were such an easy means of obtaining babies that adults who were considered undeserving—from single men and women to people with criminal records—had no difficulty acquiring perfectly normal children who were entitled to decent homes. "I gave 25 cents and a canary bird for it," one "unfit" woman explained.[110] Then she simply took the baby home.

Sentimental Adoption and the Invention of the Adoption Agency

Adoptions arranged through ads were objectionable because they reduced children's worth to money, sometimes transpired beyond the law, and ignored qualifications. The absence of oversight joined for-profit adoption to its humanitarian counterpart, sentimental adoption. Sentimental placements envisioned adoption as an altruistic and loving act, took parentless children and childless parents at face value, and assumed that family making would take care of itself. According to reformers, this displayed incredible naiveté and was no less misguided for being sincere. Benevolent baby brokers had a moral advantage over cash-hungry baby farmers, but their casual, intuitive approach was equally risky.

Sentimental adoptions were often freelance arrangements. Judd Lewis, a writer for the *Houston Post*, set up a baby bureau, "strictly a one-man affair," and placed more than one hundred children from all over the country by 1914.[111] Nothing was easier than placing parentless children in good adoptive homes, Lewis insisted, because all babies were loveable. He simply picked childless couples who were kind and clean to be their parents. Wealth was not required, only love. It is interesting that Lewis generally refused babies to couples who already had children of their own, a policy that anticipated the centrality of infertility to adoption theory and practice in later decades. Lewis explained that adoptees were less likely to get "a square deal" in a family where they had to compete with nonadopted siblings. Like baby farmers, Lewis resorted to newspaper ads, but his appeals were sentimental. He emphasized "the sound of baby laughter" and the "sweetness of dimpled arms about your neck."[112] His benevolent baby service earned Lewis praise and publicity. Stories about him lauded a "sweet-souled, talented, normal gentleman who beholds all that is beautiful in the world and whose heart is responsive to its sorrows."[113] Sentimental adoption contrasted with commercial adoptions, but like commercial adoptions, sentimental adoptions could be arranged by just about anyone.

Women were more likely to arrange adoptions than men such as Judd Lewis. The elite women who founded and financed the first specialized adoption agencies in the United States included Louise Waterman Wise, Clara Spence, Alice Chapin, and Florence Dahl Walrath (figure 3). They can best be described as philanthropic amateurs who had grown up with the model of the nineteenth-century "friendly visitor." That model posited social work as the job of everyone with the means to do it, not the exclusive province of a profession. Most were married to prominent men. Stephen Wise, for example, was a leading rabbi and Zionist involved in founding the National Association for the Advancement of Colored People and the American Jewish Congress. Henry Dwight Chapin was a well-known New York pediatrician and founder of the Speedwell Society, an organization that opposed institutional care and advocated home life for dependent children. "Miss" Clara Spence, on the other hand, adopted children with "her associate," Charlotte Baker.[114] Between 1910 and 1916, the two women placed fifty-eight babies in the homes of businessmen, physicians, and university professors.[115] After 1916, members of the Spence Alumni Society honored their benefactor by continuing her work from a ten-bed nursery in a brownstone on Sixty-second Street in Manhattan.

These adoption pioneers mixed benevolence and civic duty with self-interest and class interest. Frequently motivated to locate babies for personal friends, they elaborated a proadoption ideology that clashed with the antiadoption stance of eugenicists and Progressive loyalty to family preservation. In an era when blood was thicker than water, and illegitimacy was virtually synonymous with inferiority, agencies such as the Spence Alumni Society, the Free Synagogue Child Adoption Committee, the Alice Chapin Nursery, and the Cradle ventured to declare that heredity was not necessarily destiny, at least for white children. Such adoption optimism was rare at the time.[116]

Figure 3. Louise Waterman Wise, founder of one of the country's first specialized adoption agencies, with daughter, Justine, who became a New York judge and prominent child welfare advocate. Used by permission of the American Jewish Historical Society, Newton Centre, Massachusetts, and New York, New York.

These organizations openly acknowledged what commercial adoption made obvious: the transfer of children spelled upward mobility, moving children from poorer to richer parents who were likely to have exalted expectations about how those children would behave and what they would achieve in life. "Our purpose is to place children of unusual promise in homes of uncommon opportunities," declared the Spence Alumni Society.[117] The agency received orphans, foundlings, and babies whose parents simply could not support them. Flooded by requests from affluent families, the society took great pride in the high quality of children it placed. Selectivity meant that babies deemed unsuitable were simply rejected, a practice that betrayed the agency's lingering adherence to eugenic ideology.[118] Describing the adoption service his wife founded in 1910, Henry Chapin interpreted the divergent fertility rates of rich and poor as "not race suicide, but race homicide. Not babies merely, but better babies, are wanted."[119] One 1916 account of these privately founded adoption services bluntly described their purpose as "training babies for the 'golden spoon.'"[120]

None of the amateur adoption agencies placed African American children or other children of color, but all believed that white children from inauspicious backgrounds might be good enough to belong in families with material and social advantages (figure 4). This notion distanced them from their professional counterparts. Mrs. Sarah Van Alen Murray, who placed babies from her gracious home adjacent to New York's Central Park, thought children could be "made adoptable" by curling their hair and replacing their shabby clothing with fine apparel. After rescuing unsightly, sickly children from local institutions and caring for them in her nursery, she turned them over to friends and acquaintances. She claimed never to have had a child returned to her as unsatisfactory.[121] "In a large experience with adopted children," pronounced orphanage physician Charles Kerley in 1916, "I have yet to know one where the parents regretted the adoption."[122] "One may not pick over one's children," Kerley observed; "own" children "present a greater risk than the child who can be inspected and passed upon by competent authority."[123] Women who took it upon themselves to arrange adoptions were not only saving children's lives and bringing joy to adults. They were performing a great service to the state.[124]

Child welfare professionals and amateurs disagreed about more than the risks of adoption. Amateurs did not consider unmarried mothers and their babies to be complete family units and therefore did not see the point in strenuous efforts to keep them together. Why not turn to adoption instead, which offered "a thousand opportunities"?[125] Nor were they resigned to childlessness. According to Mrs. Charles F. Judson, a physician's wife who arranged adoptions in Philadelphia, "no family can be complete or normal without children and the happiness they bring."[126] Adoption offered clear social advantages while also making families whole. It might transform wretched children into people of substance and make honorable citizens out of human beings who would otherwise have been wasted or worse.

Figure 4. This illustration, which accompanied a 1910 article on the baby shortage, suggested
the upward mobility associated with adoption. In it, an orphan is transformed from a
"waif" (*left*) into "somebody to be considered" (*right*) in a single day.
Used by permission of *Cosmopolitan*.

Adoption was an act of civic power that simultaneously fulfilled the most
personal of needs; anyone who did it "shall have had a hand in the building
of the nation and of the world."[127] In this sense, amateur adoption agencies
anticipated by many decades the ethos of the post–World War II years. During the era of "the adoption mandate" after 1945, adoption became "the
best solution" rather than a dire last resort.[128]

Consider the case of Florence Walrath and the Cradle, the Evanston, Illinois, agency she incorporated in 1923. Walrath was the wife of William
Bradley Walrath, a prominent Chicago attorney. She arranged her first adoption in 1914 when she replaced a dead newborn belonging to her older
sister with a healthy infant.[129] After that, she received so many requests for
babies that her agency outgrew its space almost as soon as it opened. Like
the other elite women who began adoption agencies, Walrath embraced
adoption's potential to bring children and parents together to mutual advantage. Although she doubted at first that parents could love adopted children as much as their own, contact with adoptive families taught Walrath
that "true parenthood is a stewardship, not ownership; that its values are
spiritual, not physical."[130] Walrath's admirers considered her work a salu-
tary alternative to such practices as indenture and placing out, which by the
1920s suggested slavery rather than love to most middle-class Americans.

Walrath also celebrated the upward mobility, educational opportunities, and assimilation that accompanied the adoption of children born on
the economic margins of American society. The Cradle, whose board was
crowded with local luminaries, was known for catering to celebrities and
wealthy couples and earned a reputation in the 1930s as a "supply station

for Hollywood mother love."[131] George Burns and Gracie Allen, Bob Hope, Gloria Swanson, Barbara Stanwyck, Morton Downey, Frederick March, Pearl Buck, Donna Reed, and Al Jolson and Ruby Keeler, among others, adopted through the Cradle.[132] In its heyday the Cradle placed around 250 babies each year. By 1945 it had arranged four thousand adoptions.[133]

By the late 1920s, specialized adoption agencies, founded by amateurs, gravitated toward professional staffing and standards. The Cradle was known for being in the vanguard of pediatric care. It embraced "a new science of adoption" and implemented techniques to reduce death and disease.[134] With state-of-the-art equipment, sterile sanitary procedures, and top-flight medical services, Dr. Gladys Dick devised protocols for the Cradle, called the Dick Aseptic Nursery Technique, that were widely copied by hospitals and other institutions.[135] Considering the rates of epidemic disease and infant mortality in custodial institutions at the time, these protocols represented a considerable advance.

Her critics accused Walrath of having "a Messiah type of complex on physical care" that obscured glaring deficiencies in other areas of her agency's work.[136] In the late 1920s, babies spent an average of forty days at the Cradle before being placed in adoptive homes, an observation period considered dangerously short by social workers who stressed the enormous risks of "cradle adoptions" despite the clear preference by many adopters for newborns and young infants.[137] The Cradle was scrupulous about matching, never placing dark-eyed babies with blue-eyed parents, crossing lines of religion or race, or placing mentally superior babies with parents who were merely average. Even babies of mixed heritage went to intermarried parents. When Al Jolson (who was Jewish) and Ruby Keeler (of Irish heritage) adopted, they were given a half-Irish, half-Jewish baby.[138] Even so, the agency's methods relied more on intuition than careful investigation. "I question the mother," Walrath explained, "and I usually know whether she is telling the truth."[139] Professionals who believed that safety in adoption required the corroboration of all truth claims were appalled. High standards of medical care could not compensate for a lack of sophisticated attention to the human factors and social complexities in adoption.

Until she retired in 1950, Walrath remained "a thorn in the flesh" of child welfare experts.[140] The Cradle's physical plant was superlative, but social workers disparaged its casework. The agency resisted such basic safeguards as thorough paperwork, applicant investigations, and postplacement supervision, and it made too many newborn and interstate placements, made the placements too hastily, and brought them about without adequate legal protections. The Cradle also relied on funding strategies that left it vulnerable to charges of baby selling. Instead of calling on the generosity of community chests and the financial obligation of natal families, as professionally run child placement services did, the Cradle and other amateur agencies openly solicited large donations from adopters. (Professionals, in contrast, did not begin introducing fees until after 1940, and even then they did so gingerly.[141] Until 1945, they maintained that financial transactions between adopters and agencies were strictly unethical.) In 1945 the Cradle hired a respected social worker, Margaret Mink, to stave off charges that it was simply "filling orders of foster parents" rather than providing a valuable social service for children.[142]

Several of the other specialized adoption agencies were ahead of the Cradle on this score. The Spence Alumni Society, Alice Chapin Nursery, and Free Synagogue Child Adoption Committee (respectively consolidated as Spence-Chapin Adoption Service in 1943 and renamed Louise Wise Services in 1949) began reorganizing their social service operations around 1930. Originating in sentimental adoption, these agencies were soon on the cutting edge of professional practice.

First Steps toward Kinship by Design

Kinship by design was the answer to adoption as a social problem. In setting out to control the uncertainties of family making, its advocates defined it at first in negative terms, through concerted efforts to sideline commercial and sentimental adoptions and expose the risks of all haphazard and informal placements. Hastings Hart, who directed the NCHS before heading the Child-Helping Department of the Russell Sage Foundation, abhorred "cranks, sentimentalists, self-seekers, decayed preachers, quarrelsome men, or gossiping women" "who dispose of children with little more thought or conscience than they would give to the disposal of surplus kittens."[143] According to this view, individuals who negotiated child exchanges for entrepreneurial, humanitarian, or arbitrary reasons were thoroughly corrupted by interests that contravened children's welfare. They had no business placing children.

Money and sentiment were equally unacceptable as modes of family formation because they were equally biased, prioritizing adult desires over children's needs. Professionals promised that in the families they made, children would be protected and valued for their own sake, treated as beloved sons and daughters, and made into authentic members of real families. Their argument rested simultaneously on moral principle, new fears about children's vulnerability, and confidence they could deliver positive outcomes. Professionalism would yield better as well as safer and more ethical adoptions.

But what exactly was good for children? What designs produced permanent love and consistent belonging? The doctrine of children's interests had been elaborated in the nineteenth century, alongside efforts to enshrine maternal preferences and nurture in the law of child custody.[144] In the early part of the twentieth century, reformers concerned about adoption still defined children's interests in largely negative terms, as whatever was *not* contaminated by adult interests. New York's Catholic Home Bureau for Dependent Children, the first Catholic agency to use family homes rather than congregate institutions, condemned "boarding out" and "farming out" while defending "placing out" as an "attempt to give the dependent child the elements of a normal life."[145]

By counterposing enlightened placement against commercial considerations, labor exploitation, and impulsive acts that gratified adults, reformers began to formulate a new ideology in which they were the exclusive defenders of vulnerable children against a universe of threats and abuses. They also endowed themselves with a collective consciousness that helped to bring a newly imagined professional community into being: a community of adoption experts operating in state-sanctioned agencies on the basis of systematic training, empirical inquiry, and verifiable results. They vowed to make adoption safer by subjecting it to public regulation.

Such an effort was no small feat. Enormous resistance greeted the campaign to extend the family-making authority of governments and professionals, the first requirement of kinship by design. By virtue of blood ties, birth parents were accustomed to wide latitude in decisions about children, including decisions to place them with others temporarily or permanently. That children were still exchanged via contracts into the twentieth century suggests that parallels between children and property were not entirely outdated. Parents possessed something akin to rights of ownership, at least in regard to their "own" children. On the other hand, many adopters also resisted the constraints on their freedom that regulation represented. In a society being rapidly transformed by values and experiences associated with consumption, they preferred to be the agents of their own fate, pursuing preferences for girls or boys, younger or older, blonde or brunette, without judgment or interference.

Many religious and ethnic communities were also determined to retain control over children they considered their "own," much as birth parents did, and objected strongly to government regulation. Catholics vividly recalled the activities of nineteenth-century evangelical Protestants, regarding them as child-stealers operating under the hypocritical banners of humanitarianism and the public good. To preserve their religious community,

Catholics invested enormous financial and human resources in a sectarian social service system.[146] In the late nineteenth century, the Catholic Church built institutions at such a furious pace that by 1910, there were 322 infant asylums and orphanages serving almost seventy thousand children annually in the United States.[147] The essence of Catholic charity was to help while holding onto its own. Catholic children were cast as vital group resources rather than autonomous individuals whose best interests could safely be entrusted to experts charged with case-by-case judgments. This pattern would recur when other embattled groups—including Native Americans and African Americans—attacked legal individualism and professional child welfare as threats to the survival of minority communities and cultures.

The effort to regulate adoption also faced practical obstacles. Why should an ordinary process such as kinship creation be entrusted to government or supervised by professionals at all? This was the question pioneering social workers in the field of child welfare had to answer before they could claim legitimate authority over adoptive family making. They struggled to make the case for regulation as they established specialized child-placing and home-finding departments in social agencies, wrote training manuals, and wrapped their philosophy and practice in the meritorious mantle of science.

Whereas benevolent amateurs had invented the first agencies devoted exclusively to adoption, workers aspiring to professional status were concentrated in multipurpose child and family welfare organizations. The New York State Charities Aid Association was one of the first of these organizations to professionalize its home-finding services. It launched a placement program in 1898, and by 1922 the agency had found homes for more than thirty-three hundred children. Children were referred to the New York State Charities Aid Association because they had been abandoned or removed from homes deemed dangerous to their health or safety or simply because their parents and relatives were destitute. Although its practices evolved rapidly during its first twenty-five years, the agency kept written records from the beginning and took great care in exploring children's backgrounds and investigating potential foster homes. The period before 1910 was "a period when pre-placement information about the children was much less complete than it is nowadays," admitted agency official Sophie van Senden Theis in 1924.[148] She hastened to add that the agency had always taken full responsibility for each and every child it placed. Legally and practically, that duty was long lasting. Even children who were eventually adopted often waited years before their status was formalized.

Philosophically, the New York State Charities Aid Association was committed to making individual children's needs determining factors in home selection. According to Theis, this was the quality that marked the agency's work as superior, even in its earliest years. As it refined its methods after 1910, the New York State Charities Aid Association gathered as much data about children's personalities, mental abilities, and health histories as possible and treated foster applications in a manner "unique in its quality and thoroughness."[149] The agency required numerous written references and personal interviews and always placed children close enough to its offices to facilitate postplacement visits by experienced workers. Theis worked for the Child Adoption Committee of the New York State Charities Aid Association for forty-five years, from 1907 until her retirement in 1952, serving as its executive secretary for thirty-six of those years. She was a pioneer in professionalizing adoption practice and adoption research. A vocal proponent of technique, regulation, and study, Theis was the first adoption professional in U.S. history.

Other agencies, especially on the eastern seaboard, followed the model of the New York State Charities Aid Association. The Boston Children's Aid Society created divisions that separated home finding from placing out, treating each as specialized activities. The New England Home for Little Wanderers embraced scientific professionalism.[150] It hired its first social worker, Amy Clifton, in 1907, and by 1924, it employed twenty-four staff members, all trained by the country's first social work schools. A staff psychiatrist soon joined. In 1915 the agency opened a Study Home in which all children under care were carefully scrutinized by a "laboratory method . . . which will reduce the percentage of failure in the work of placing children in family homes."[151] All candidates for adoption were admitted to the Study Home "by way of precaution," along with much larger numbers of children slated for temporary placement in free or paid boarding homes.[152] Like most professional organizations during this era, the New England Home for Little Wanderers believed in family preservation. Adoptions posed grave difficulties, demanded great skill, and involved circumstances as dire as they were rare.

The first manuals for professional family makers were published in the late 1910s and early 1920s. They made the case for design by first emphasizing the hazards of making family placements without it. Mistakes were common and almost always due to a "lack of expertness," according to the first of these manuals, which described child placing as "exceedingly technical." With "expert agents and exact methods," placement by design "gives almost uniformly satisfactory results."[153] Until their procedures had been systematically scrutinized and measured, however, child placers would stumble along with little to guide them but guesswork. The variety of child-placing methods "emphasizes the necessity for some standardizing influence."[154] Although some workers broke up natal families without a second thought, others were reluctant ever to do so. Some studied children and foster homes and then supervised placements carefully, but many others did not.[155] Inconsistency was almost as much an enemy of design as amateurism. Hodgepodge defied the design credo: verify, improve, and then verify again.

At the same time that professional child-placing methods were distinguished by their uniformity and transparency, they also elaborated complex classification schemes. There were many different types of children and families, and many ways of working with them, according to William Henry Slingerland's 1919 *Child-Placing in Families*, published by the Russell Sage Foundation, a major patron of the new social work profession. One advantage of professional family making was sensitivity to subtleties that nonprofessionals ignored. Children who were neglected, deserted, needy, delinquent, defective, or orphaned might all need new parents, but they were hardly all the same. Each type required specialized treatment. Within each category, subcategories proliferated. For instance, disabilities might be mental or physical. Those with disabilities might have such conditions as feeblemindedness, insanity, physical abnormalities, epilepsy, or serious diseases. Within the feebleminded category, further distinctions existed between idiots, imbeciles, morons, and dullards. Even as they stressed such categorical differences, professionals called for new procedures that attended to the uniqueness of each child. One hallmark of design was its pairing of standardization with individualization.

Early manuals used case studies to illustrate significant differences between types of children and homes and to instruct social workers in the fine points of interpretation and discrimination.[156] Professionals who placed children in homes needed skills in interviewing, observing, recording, recruiting, and training. They needed to assess the truthfulness of references, reject unsuitable families, and discern hard-to-read signs that lurked beneath the surface of language, behavior, and physical environments. In bad placements, they removed children from families and re-placed them elsewhere. In cases that resulted in adoption—either because infants were placed with that goal in mind or because families decided to adopt children taken in for board—maximum professional skill was needed. Stakes were high because agencies' legal role ended when adoption decrees were entered.

In practice, individualized knowledge of the parties to adoption amounted to matching available children to homes considered appropriate to their intellectual, cultural, and social level. Placing children from humble backgrounds in materially advantaged families would exert too much

pressure on children, most professionals believed, resulting in disappointment and failure that might have been avoided. But because poverty was so
common a reason for placement, families willing to take in new members
almost never came from the same socioeconomic level as the children themselves. What should be done with a surplus of applications from "refined"
families? What should the financial qualifications for adoption be?[157]

> You must bear in mind that there are first class, second class, and third class
> children, and there are first class, second class, and third class homes. If a
> child is dull, stupid, untrained, or a bed-wetter, you cannot expect to secure
> as good a home as you could secure for a bright, attractive, well-trained child,
> and it is true that many humble homes of uncultivated people are permeated
> by a loving and faithful spirit, and will give conscientious care even to an
> undesirable child.[158]

To design kinship well meant not only placing children in the class to
which they belonged but also identifying children who really did belong
much higher up the social ladder than their natal origins indicated. The
engineering of upward mobility, which purposely disregarded class without purposely disregarding race, was a matter of pride as well as anxiety
among adoption professionals. They never tired of reiterating that love—
and children—could not be purchased, but moving children from modest
to wealthy homes was acceptable when knowledge about the child proved
that the placement was deserved.

Professional practices almost always took religion into account because
religious matching was legally stipulated in many states when adoption
statutes were first written or revised in the nineteenth century.[159] In the early
twentieth century, matching by race, ethnicity, and national origin was so
habitual that it occasioned relatively little comment, and it was presumed
that adoption applied chiefly to white children. When matching was mentioned, it was treated as only natural. Failure to match by race invariably
elicited horrified comment. Biracial children placed (wittingly and unwittingly) with white parents and white babies placed with intermarried couples were condemned as transgressions of the highest order.[160]

The advantages of identifying matching with natural facts and scientific
methods were recognized from the outset. Good matching, for example,
was a tricky operation that professionals finessed with the benefit of technologies and obscure but crucial information possessed only by them. The
term "modern" was invoked frequently in relation to scientific procedures
and truth claims, and the advocates of kinship by design embraced it, vigor-

ously defining themselves against primitive family-making paradigms that were neither modern nor scientific. "To differentiate social case treatment in the technical sense from the more or less haphazard, unscientific, but kindly and often very helpful 'influencing,' 'guiding,' 'helping out' process which goes on wherever human beings associate is a task in which case workers must make some headway if case work is to take rank with the professions which are firmly grounded in scientific method," wrote social worker Virginia Robinson in 1921.[161]

Robinson's life partner, Jessie Taft, was a prominent authority on child placement. In 1919 Taft called on her colleagues to develop "a scientific attitude towards child-placing," which was "the most experimental and delicate of tasks."[162] Taft eventually grew more sensitive to the differences between science and help and in 1941 warned against naive equations between the two. "We seek the best way of *working with*, not *experimenting on*, human beings and thereby, relinquish a priori all claim to be considered scientific, if by scientific one means emphasis on causes, experiment and laboratory control."[163] Taft cherished science because it eclipsed partiality and prejudice rather than because it engendered unambiguous truths about human motivation and behavior. Science, in sum, was a legitimizing language for professional leaders who wished to move adoption (and other helping operations) toward design. It aided their efforts to distance subjective from objective knowledge and separate interested from disinterested motives wherever children were concerned. But for many rank-and-file workers in the adoption field, science remained a foreign tongue.

Clearly the struggle to professionalize adoption mirrored the struggle to professionalize social work generally.[164] It was not easy to transform helping into something that experts did for clients or the state did for citizens rather than something that people did for one another in times of need and crisis. In 1915 Abraham Flexner famously declared that social work was "hardly eligible" for professional status.[165] It was, he argued, an idealistic occupation full of unselfish do-gooders who did too many different things in too many different ways. The advocates who set out to professionalize child placing appreciated the magnitude of the task before them. Commercial and benevolent motives for adoption would have to give way to exacting standards, regularized procedures, and empirical proof that the professional way was best.

Bold claims about the virtues of expertise in family making were made on the basis of a professional identity more imagined than real. Social work education barely existed as a formal enterprise in the second decade of the century. The first social work school in the country, the New York School of

Applied Philanthropy (later Columbia's School of Social Work), opened its doors in 1904; in 1915 there were only five independent and two university-affiliated social work programs in the United States. The American Association of Social Workers was not founded until 1921. Long after educational machinery was in place, however, amateur workers remained the backbone of many child welfare organizations, and the chronic shortage of trained personnel was a source of constant professional frustration and complaint.

In addition to the challenges that all rising professions encountered—putting credentialing mechanisms in place and making credible promises of verifiable, better-than-random results—would-be social workers had an additional problem: explaining why multitudes of merciful women should qualify for professional status. Although many child welfare pioneers were men—C. C. Carstens, Hastings Hart, and William Henry Slingerland, to name only a few—it was not always clear why women needed specialized training to do work that simply extended "natural" maternal responsibilities to other people's children. In the early 1910s, one agency official ruefully recalled, "almost any well intentioned woman, of any age, who had a 'love for children,' was thereby qualified for the work."[166] The view that adoptions could be easily and intuitively arranged by people who nurtured by virtue of sex was an impediment to a professional vision founded on skill. Replacing faith in commonsense maternalism with confidence in gender-blind specialization was challenging, especially in relation to work that touched ordinary and familiar aspects of private life.[167]

Considering the number of obstacles in their way, it is noteworthy that advocates of professional child placing made their case as persistently as they did. Commercial and sentimental adoptions were never eliminated. Campaigns to teach other professionals—especially lawyers and physicians—why they should cease arranging adoptions and allow social workers exclusive jurisdiction over child placement did not succeed, either. The constraints that blood ties, collective solidarities, family privacy, professional turf, and consumer values placed on adoption never disappeared. Indeed, they are with us to this day. The important question is not why kinship by design triumphed over all other methods of family making—it clearly did not. The principal question is, Why did a new paradigm that invoked state power, scientific knowledge, and expert authority become central to family making at all?

———

One reason kinship by design succeeded was that professionals in the early decades of the twentieth century promised to minimize the uncertainties of taking in other people's children as one's own at a time when uncertainty loomed as a disturbing and pervasive dimension of the modern experience. "Are you afraid to adopt a child?" asked the *Delineator,* a mass-circulation women's magazine in 1919.[168] A great many Americans undoubtedly were. They had heard of callous baby farmers and scandalous maternity homes. They worried about the bad blood and future delinquency of children born to poor, unmarried mothers. They suspected that defective children were unloaded on good-hearted adults, who were cheated out of the normal children they desired. They were also concerned that deserving children were being consigned to lives of debilitating maladjustment after casual transfer to unfit parents. Even people unconnected to adoption were warned that bad adoptions today would generate a tidal wave of costly social problems tomorrow.

Such problems were all the more heartbreaking for being preventable, according to advocates of kinship by design. Like other reformers involved in balancing progress against the new dangers of modern life, the advocates of kinship by design saw safety as their first and most important concern. They aimed to reduce risk in family formation by regulating adoption. Less than two decades after the *Delineator* reminded readers of their fears, *Parents* magazine assured its audience that it was quite safe to adopt a child. "Today the 'danger' of adoption has been largely obviated by scientific advance," it reported.[169] Making adoption safer was the first step toward transforming adoption into kinship by design. From the start, advocates championed increased regulation, expertise, and empirical inquiry as the surest signs of safety. They set out to make adoption safe by first making adoption governable.

CHAPTER TWO

Making Adoption Governable

Making adoption safe required making adoption governable. To manage adoption effectively, participants in the process had to become willing objects of knowledge and recipients of help, both characteristic features of welfare states bent on producing secure populations and protecting vulnerable citizens from harm. In practice, making adoption governable simplified complex, varied private transactions and made them "legible" through documentation, monitoring, calculation, and other forms of regulation.[1]

This chapter describes organizations that were key to the modernization of adoption in the early twentieth century: the U.S. Children's Bureau and the Child Welfare League of America. They envisioned a rationalized process, kinship by design, through which families would be engineered publicly, purposefully, and according to plan. This chapter also discusses the specific governmental practices that advocates of kinship by design equated with increasing safety in adoption: orderly information-gathering, investigation, supervision, and probation. Combined, these managerial operations would reduce the risks that children and parents would be unqualified, poorly matched, and prone to terrible, socially burdensome outcomes.

Child welfare advocates made regulation a high priority during the 1910s. These reformers aimed to standardize adoption law and practice because they believed that making families more systematically than in the past would improve family formation in the future. For decades, "standards" and "safeguards" were interchangeable terms, suggesting that oversight and routinization were synonymous with safety. Determined to protect dependent children and well-meaning adults from a host of dangers, reformers envisioned a regulatory apparatus that not only limited adoptions based purely on money and sentiment but also restricted all irregular placements whose logic involved intuition or accident, which is to say they involved no logic at all. Their efforts to expand governmental authority, create new professional jurisdictions, and promote empirical inquiry into adoptive family life took many forms, all sanctioned by the doctrine of *parens patriae*, which likened the state to a caring parent. Minimum standards were the most significant.[2] They made adoption more governable.

Standardized governmental practices were hallmarks of kinship by design. For advocates, they symbolized the superiority of this approach to adoption over all other family-making methods. From preplacement investigations and postplacement probationary periods to empirical field studies, proponents of kinship by design insisted that adoptive families should be made up deliberately and skillfully and on the basis of tested knowledge about what made families turn out well. Doing anything less amounted to a return to "that dark era when the child was sacrificed on the altar of ignorance, greed, and superstition," warned physician Douglas Thom, director of the Boston Habit Clinic.[3] That so many adoptions were arranged in a "casual, indifferent, haphazard way" rather than on the basis of "an intelligent, well-organized plan involving careful medical and social scrutiny of the entire situation" exposed the deplorable backwardness and irresponsibility of states at a moment when modern times raised expectations about what could and should be accomplished by and for the public.[4] Humane, modern government would make adoptive kinship safer by making it more visible and knowable.

Visibility and knowledge simultaneously simplified and complicated family making. Regularizing paperwork and procedures made the adoption process more uniform while ensuring that it was tailored to the needs and qualifications of the parties in each case. Individualization of this kind was a world away from the idiosyncratic child-placing landscape of the early twentieth century. How could reformers hope to know what worked in adoption if procedures were so erratic that comparisons were useless and conclusions impossible to draw? Field studies conducted in the late 1910s and 1920s gathered basic data about how many and what kinds of adoptions were taking place, making it possible to compare and evaluate adoptions. Control and comprehension went together. Governing families effectively was inseparable from learning more about them.

Institutions Involved in Kinship by Design

The U.S. Children's Bureau was the most important institution involved in making children and families governable. Established by Congress in 1912, it is located today in the Administration for Children and Families,

U.S. Department of Health and Human Services. The USCB was the brain-child of Progressive settlement house workers, the organizational capstone of the female reform tradition, and a harbinger of the welfare state that the New Deal created. Its famous campaigns to reduce infant mortality and its policymaking initiatives on illegitimacy and unmarried mothers have been widely noted in recent scholarship.[5]

The USCB provided a home for advocates of adoption rationalization within the federal government. During its early years, the USCB promoted state legislative reforms, disseminated massive amounts of original research, and sponsored periodic conferences on child placement issues and priori-ties. The first national conference on child welfare standards took place in 1919 under USCB auspices. Some agencies, such as the Illinois Children's Home and Aid Society, had already formulated their own child-placing standards by then, but the USCB aimed to bring consistency to the chaos of local practice and regional variation.[6] The published conference sum-mary, *Standards of Child Welfare*, included a resolution on child placing and supervision drafted by Edmond Butler, executive secretary of New York's Catholic Home Bureau, the first Catholic agency to use family homes rather than congregate institutions for placement. Proper placement, Butler noted tersely, "does not mean boarding-out, indenturing, baby-farming, the secur-ing of employment or the mere transferring of the custody of a child from one person to another or to an institution without regard to the object of each transfer."[7] In a paper given the following year, he also argued that "unless carried out in accordance with approved standards," child placing would add to the "thousands of human wrecks" already seeking public charity and "be responsible for destroying the future welfare of very many if not most of those intended to be helped."[8] Reformers' arguments for ratio-nalization invariably emphasized the dire outcomes of placements deemed "promiscuous."

Like other government and professional organizations devoted to child welfare, the USCB associated commercial and unregulated adoptions with exploitation and tragedy. Until midcentury, USCB field agents documented deplorable conditions in baby farms, maternity homes, and orphanages and oversaw investigations of placing out and interstate traffic. "Rascality in a considerable proportion of cases" was a lamentable fact, Emma Lund-berg reported in a 1915 memo to Julia Lathrop, the first chief of the USCB. Men casually adopted babies "because their wives complain of loneliness and want children as playthings." Illegitimate children were tools of black-mail and extortion. Unmarried women extracted money from their mar-ried lovers in exchange for silence. Birth mothers who made "scenes" could be "bribed into quitting the annoyance." Cases had been documented of "white babies falling into the hands of negroes," a possibility so shocking that it merited mention even as the wholesale exclusion of children of color did not.[9] If responsible government was obligated to monitor the production of pure food and drugs on behalf of citizens, it had an equally grave responsibility to monitor the production of families on behalf of children, reformers argued.

The USCB itself provided no adoption services. Still, hundreds of adults seeking children for love, labor, or a combination of the two wrote heartfelt letters to the bureau in hopes of realizing their dreams. Each inquiry was answered promptly and respectfully; references were provided to local or state agencies whose staff and standards were deemed reliable. Safety was the first concern of the USCB, and those who sought its help and advice suggested that adoption was risky. "Granted the home conditions are good is one taking a much greater chance than with their own?" inquired a woman who sought to adopt a companion for her only daughter. "I would also like to know what age is best."[10] Another couple wrote, "Please send me information concerning child-placing agencies. We are wanting to adopt a child and would like the service of reliable, experienced individuals in regards to same."[11] From its inception, the USCB recognized that public attitudes about adoption were "touchy" but also desperately in need of change. The life-altering character of adoption made "painstaking and thorough" study and social planning urgent in adoption, as it was in every aspect of child and family welfare that fell under the jurisdiction of the USCB.[12]

Another major force in adoption rationalization was the Child Welfare League of America, a national federation of public and private service-providing organizations. Founded in 1915 by fourteen pioneering organizations and supported by the Russell Sage Foundation and the Commonwealth Fund, the CWLA counted approximately seventy members when it formalized its constitution in June 1921. C. C. Carstens, already a well-established national figure and opponent of institutional care, was appointed the CWLA's first director. In 1938 the CWLA issued the first set of adoption standards to distinguish between temporary and permanent placements. By the late 1950s, several hundred CWLA members ranked adoptive and foster placements as a primary concern, and the CWLA initiated a far more ambitious program of standardization, resulting in *Standards for Adoption Service* (1958). This comprehensive family-making catalogue was intended to guide social work practice and legal procedure while also raising public consciousness. Today, the CWLA counts almost one thousand organizational members, and it revised its adoption standards bible for the fifth time in 2000.[13]

Most of the CWLA's founding organizations, including the New England Home for Little Wanderers and the Children's Home Society of Florida, were located along the eastern seaboard, but one-third were midwestern agencies. From its inception the CWLA worried that family placements across state lines made children especially vulnerable to shady operators and legal inconsistencies. Such officials as Ellen C. Potter, Pennsylvania's secretary of welfare, doubted that taxpayers would tolerate the future expense, in crime and dependency, of placement's "baffling problems."[14] To prevent children from being dumped within its borders, Pennsylvania prohibited any child who was "incorrigible," "mentally unsound," or "a social menace or unable to achieve self-support" from entering its jurisdiction without a significant bond.[15] (In 1918, Pennsylvania required $10,000.) Fiscal concern was the driving force behind such policies, rather than child welfare, because child exportation elicited very little state legislative activity in comparison to importation. Regardless of lawmakers' motivations, CWLA members approved such moves toward state scrutiny and pledged to oversee placements involving geographic distance. Standard setting was a major part of the CWLA's mandate. Its 1921 constitution named standardization as the single activity that would most enhance child welfare.[16]

The USCB and the CWLA forged a partnership cemented by overlapping personnel, a shared commitment to statism, and professional responsibility to "interpret" delicate social operations, the keyword "interpret" suggesting enduring awareness among professionals of their contradictory roles as educators of an unenlightened public and service providers who depended on public support. C. C. Carstens was a key source of inside information about adoption at the USCB even before he became the CWLA's first executive.[17] Edith Abbott, sister of the second USCB chief, Grace Abbott, served as a CWLA board member. So did Katharine Lenroot, a close colleague of C. C. Carstens, who was the third USCB chief and briefly served as acting executive director of the CWLA in 1953.

Standardization as Government

The CWLA firmly believed that child protection required "definite standards of efficiency" in record keeping, personnel training, and financial management; the new organization reacted in dismay to "very diverse" activities claiming to advance child welfare.[18] Home finding was an "old occupation" and one "enmeshed in sentiment that however kindly is ineffective or dangerous unless enlightened by knowledge."[19] Work done on behalf of children outside their own homes, the CWLA freely admitted, "ranges all the way from excellence to such a degree of inefficiency and malpractice as almost to justify legal prosecution."[20] C. C. Carstens's first report to the CWLA described the disorder he observed while traveling in the field. He noted, for example, that one "society has no family records," used "ministers of the gospel" instead of "real social workers," spent more time raising funds than supervising children, and "had very little appreciation as yet of their lack of good standards."[21]

The CWLA and the USCB agreed that minimal requirements had advantages over optimal ones. Minimum standards were more realistic given the heterogeneous practices at play in child placing. They encouraged improvement, but were not "so radical in their requirements as to provide discouragement" for organizations with a long way to go.[22] Advocating minimum standards solidified reformers' claims to new authority in family making while simultaneously acknowledging how tenuous those claims were.

Early standards included numerous specifications for kinship as well as more general criteria for an effective design process. Birth parents should be beyond rehabilitation; children should be "normal"; and adopters should be "industrious and thrifty," of the same religion as the child, and not too "advanced in years."[23] Adopters were presumed to be married couples—most surely were—but no states excluded singles from consideration. Before World War II, women succeeded in adopting by themselves, or with their female partners, but single male applicants, whose desires to adopt were "hardly normal," lived under a cloud of suspicion.[24] Religion was the only factor consistently singled out for matching by early adoption laws. Intended to guarantee "religious protection," matching provisions provoked heated controversies that prefigured debates about transracial and transnational placements after 1945. In fact, religion frequently intersected with racialized identities.[25] The formal invisibility of color in adoption laws paralleled the color-conscious consensus that race and racial matching were natural.

Setting, publicizing, and enforcing minimum standards of record keeping and preplacement investigation were especially important because both were necessary in selecting children and homes. Nevertheless, postplacement supervision and waiting periods prior to finalization in court were also considered urgently needed standards.[26] The "gross evils of careless selection of foster homes" were equaled only by "the disasters which attend the failure to maintain continuous and discerning supervision" as issues that galvanized the movement for adoption reform.[27] Agencies that examined their early child-placing practices knew that documentary and supervisory practices were hobbled by sloppiness, low salaries, and rapid turnover of inadequately trained staff.[28] Standardization epitomized professionals' efforts to articulate their own goals while making those goals harder for ordinary child placers to ignore.

Early in the century, the absence of standardized record keeping and other bureaucratic protocols made governing adoption challenging, if not impossible. Birth registration was not yet universally required, and states obviously needed to register births before they could mandate that adoptees' birth certificates be marked, altered, or sealed. Courts approved adoptions hastily, frequently on the same day that papers were filed. In Alameda County, California, for example, not a single adoption petitioner between 1895 and 1906 was turned down, and only a handful of cases took longer than two weeks to resolve.[29] Many of these cases were relative and stepparent adoptions, which, reformers agreed, merited less regulation, but casual family making between strangers appalled reformers, who argued that legal laxity facilitated fraud and abuse while denying children public protection. In 1917 Minnesota passed the first state law mandating that children's adoptability and prospective parents' suitability be investigated before adoption decrees were granted; in 1921 Ohio stipulated that adoption inquiries be conducted by duly accredited children's agencies.[30] Two decades later, more than twenty states had translated similar standards into law.[31] Revised statues typically contained provisions about the privacy of records.

By 1933, birth registration was universal, and the practice of amending original birth certificates so as not to indicate either illegitimacy or adoption was well established in many states. By midcentury, virtually all states required individual and organizational child placers to be licensed. Even agencies in rural states, slow to embrace new adoption protocols and policies, abandoned traditional ways. Bangor's Good Samaritan Home Agency, for example, had been known since 1902 for its staunch commitment to keeping impoverished birth mothers and children together. The agency had created a long-term residential program that offered women work and prodded them to take responsibility for their children so they could return to their home communities in the Maine countryside, where they might rectify youthful mistakes through marriage. By 1940 the agency emphasized confidential infant adoption, complete with testing and casework, and by the mid-1950s it had been "totally transformed" through professionalization.[32] Throughout the country, adoption policy moved in the direction of standardizers' constant refrain: investigate and supervise.[33]

Creating and enforcing minimum standards were the first steps toward making adoption governable. Equally significant, practices related to adoption information, preplacement investigation, and postplacement supervision also turned helping practices into calculable operations. Once standardized, the outcomes of kinship by design could be measured.[34]

Record Keeping and Information Management

The earliest surveys of child-placing procedures confirmed reformers' worst fears. Adoptions were sometimes so haphazard that family members unintentionally lost all track of one another. Either no paper trail could be found, or skimpy records lacked accurate names and addresses. "Will you please look up my birth record and find out who I am, who my parents are and if they are living and where they are located now," wrote one adoptee to the USCB in 1926.[35] Katharine Lenroot replied sympathetically, informing the letter writer that such quests for documentation were often fruitless. "Will you please look in the old records and see if you can trace up my father and mother," begged a former orphanage resident who, like many of his peers, was not an orphan at all, but a child whose family needed help weathering emergencies brought on by unemployment, desertion, or death. "As I grow up in manhood with no one to love but God I feel like a lost sheep. . . . I been searching for the last 6 yrs."[36]

Reformers were dismayed that sloppy or nonexistent records stood between adoptees and their natal kin. Not until after World War II was information about birth families placed off-limits to adoptees in most U.S. states.[37] Reasons to search also changed over time as birth records became more common requirements for employment, public benefit programs such as Social Security, and military service. Before World War II, agency workers often helped adult adoptees locate natal relatives.[38] Their best efforts were often stymied not by sealed records or opposition to reunion but by disappointingly meager information. Jennie Specter contacted the Washington, D.C., agency that placed her when she discovered her job as a nurse with the New York City Department of Hospitals depended on her locating her birth certificate. She had no wish for contact with her birth mother, but she found it "most embarrassing" to be an adult and know so little about one's origins, Specter explained in 1940.[39] All she wanted was documentation of her birth. After searching the files, an agency worker informed Specter that she had been received by the agency in 1909, when she was less than one year of age. Aside from the news that her year of birth was probably 1908 rather than 1913, as she had always thought, the agency was unable to offer Specter any assistance.

Cases where adult adoptees sought reunion for emotional rather than practical reasons were equally frustrating. One distraught Massachusetts man, adopted in the 1890s, pleaded for help from the USCB. "WHAT HAVE I DID AS A CHILD TO BRING this on myself. I had nothing to do with my coming into the world but yet afor 36 long years I have lived all ALONE without a MOTHERS LOVE FOR HER SON, and GOD KNOWS I LOVE HER WHOEVER SHE [IS] AND WHATEVER SHE MAY CHANCE TO BE."[40] USCB officials contacted a Boston court officer, Elizabeth Lee, who devoted considerable effort to tracking down the man's adoption before giving up, declaring that "it does seem to be a hopeless task. . . . I am very sorry indeed that I have not been able to do anything to help out."[41] The Russell Sage Foundation reasoned that poor recording methods were responsible for the many "instances [that] are constantly coming to light of boys and girls who cannot find out who they are."[42] The CWLA collaborated with the American Statistical Association to devise a system for uniform reporting intended to prevent such information calamities from recurring. The statisticians pledged to analyze all the data that CWLA member agencies could muster.[43]

Adoption could not be made governable without routinizing documentation. Not only did chaotic record keeping deprive children of background information that most people took for granted. It also denied policymakers and researchers the data they needed to study placement practices and outcomes, and most early empirical studies of adoption were thwarted, to one degree or another, by information gaps. This was true even in agencies, such as the New York State Charities Aid Association, that took pride in their information practices and stood ready to provide answers to children's questions later in life.[44] Few reasons for standardizing written records were more important than the mandate to evaluate individual cases in light of evolving knowledge and general principles.

By 1921 the CWLA supplied its members with standard forms specifying the information they should gather and the questions they should ask in evaluating children for placement and identifying prospective homes. According to Executive Director Carstens, slight modifications to forms were acceptable, but "if there can be a uniformity of essentials, we shall be making progress toward the standardization, not only of report but also of service, which we very much need."[45] Twenty years later, the CWLA launched a case record exhibit, which circulated hundreds of model files in order to extend documentary uniformity beyond facts to narrative style and interpretive commentary.[46] Typical record-keeping illustrations included intake, home investigations, transfers of babies from temporary into adoptive homes, and applicant rejections. More unusual were cases of children discovered to be biracial after their adoptions by white parents, cases in which applicants specifically requested older children or children with disabilities, and cases that showed how home studies might be used to block independent adoptions deemed harmful to children.[47]

Reformers argued that the quality, quantity, and accuracy of information gathered and recorded would determine the probable success or failure of adoptions long before children were actually placed. Facts loomed large, in contrast with the shoddy or nonexistent record keeping typical of nonexpert child placers. Information about children's backgrounds and the adults willing to take them became simultaneously a measure of professionalism and technical skill, a practical aid to placement decisions, and an entitlement for children themselves. Comprehensive records were the raw material for field and outcome studies that would improve practices in future adoptions by boosting knowledge about what had and had not worked in past adoptions. Adoptees also had a right to the information contained in their records. "Facts are a matter of justice to the child since adults have the right to know about themselves," the USCB pointed out in 1933.[48] The original architects of confidential adoption frequently functioned as agents of disclosure. They believed that "curious and unscrupulous persons" who were not "parties in interest" might reveal sensitive information and should therefore be kept away from it.[49] Adoptees, however, had every legal and moral right to recover whatever facts they wished in adulthood, including identifying information about birth parents and natal relatives.

Preplacement Investigation: Selecting Children and Parents

Preplacement inquiries aimed to select children and adults who were suitable for family making and for one another. In early twentieth-century adoptions, unearthing facts about the hereditary background of the child and his or her health and mentality was considered crucial to avoiding the error of placing unqualified children. Adopters and professional mediators alike agreed that only normal, healthy children were suitable candidates for adoption.

Before 1940, eugenic anxieties about the quality of available children surfaced openly. Some prominent eugenicists opposed adoption outright. Henry Herbert Goddard, director of the Vineland Training School and famous authority on "feeblemindedness" (mental retardation or developmental disability), was one example. Introduced to the study of heredity by Charles Davenport, a University of Chicago zoologist and influential founder of the Eugenics Record Office, Goddard defined heredity narrowly, as a collection of discrete traits that could be passed from one generation to the next. This simplistic Mendelian conceptualization was convenient; it made heredity measurable. In Goddard's famous study of the Kallikak family, for instance, feeblemindedness was transmitted from parent to child as directly as hair color and had an equally straightforward relationship to reproducing illegitimacy, poverty, crime, prostitution, promiscuity, and other social maladies.[50] That children inherited antisocial behavior from parents was, for many Americans, an article of faith bolstered by the new science of genetics.

To adopt children with mental defects, according to Goddard, was to contaminate the gene pool and spawn feeblemindedness and social disorder in future generations.[51] Adoption produced heartache by afflicting parents with children who were "a constant source of unpleasantness and unhappiness" as well as a chronic menace to life and property that was "an enormous drag upon society."[52] This was not the fault of the parties directly involved, Goddard hastened to add, because feebleminded women "can no more live in accordance with the conventions of society than the cats and dogs in the streets."[53] Rather than placing children of questionable mentality in good families, "they must be segregated, colonized . . . that they must never become parents."[54] A policy of permanent custodial care, combined with strict sexual regulation, would be financially as well as morally beneficial. It would bring relief to families who would gladly turn over their mentally disabled young to such ideal institutions. It would protect "feeble-minded" girls from the inevitable consequences of their own defectiveness: sexual exploitation and irresponsibility. At the same time, it would reduce the human toll of future crime and the cost of maintaining jails and reformatories.[55]

Not all Progressive-era professionals were as skeptical as Goddard. Many insisted that adoption could work in rare instances when it was unavoidable. They did, however, believe that it was a "social crime" "to place a feebleminded child in a home where one of normal mentality is expected."[56] Albert Stoneman, superintendent of the Michigan Children's Aid Society, warned that "there is no homeless child, no matter how bad his family history, but that some good man and woman will take him into their home and make him joint heir with their natural children without any question of future developments, if a certain sort of emotional appeal is sent out."[57] Pioneer Sophie Theis, more inclined to believe in the power of nurture than many contemporaries, suggested that children with bad histories should not be placed for adoption unless the family signed a binding agreement to return the child if and when abnormal characteristics appeared.[58] Her agency, the New York State Charities Aid Association, "naturally [made] no attempt . . . to place those who were known to be of low grade mentality, were epileptic or were for one reason or another in need of specialized institutional care," and it maintained this policy well into the 1920s.[59] In the late 1920s and 1930s, Paul Popenoe, a prominent eugenicist and founder of the American Institute of Family Relations, warned that children available for adoption "represent predominantly the inferior levels" and were reproductive time bombs.[60] As late as 1939, Florence Clothier, a psychiatrist affiliated with the New England Home for Little Wanderers, cautioned that "children who may be the bearers of the seeds of known familial or hereditary disease should not be offered for adoption."[61] Eugenicists urged parents to "be careful whom you adopt" and "take the child 'on approval' if this is possible."[62] Taking in a "bad seed" was one of adoption's most obvious risks.

Too many adopters, according to eugenicists, did not take this danger seriously. They were swayed by sentimental trivialities such as dimples and curls and did not appreciate relatively fixed genetic traits such as intelligence. Before Connecticut enacted a 1943 law requiring preadoption medical and psychological screening, "it was a rare family adopting independently who asked for any measure of the normality and fitness of the child they were taking as their own," lamented one widely publicized study of adoptions in that state, illustrating that eugenic fitness, mental matching, and inadequate standards were closely related concerns that divided professional from public opinion.[63] In the 1950s and 1960s, as racial exclusion and segregation were challenged and transracial and transnational adoptions attracted attention, miscegenation was added to the list of adoption risks. Normal children belonged in families. Subnormal children belonged in enlightened, well-managed institutions, where their reproductive sexuality could be contained. Identifying the former and disqualifying the latter were the first goals of child selection.

Careful preplacement screening could reduce the uncertainties of adoption and surround it with a new aura of safety. Cases used for instructional purposes often detailed the tragic outcomes of unregulated adoptions that ignored or overlooked facts pointing to terrible heredity. "Cradle adoptions," in which newborns and infants were adopted before anything could be known about their mental endowment, were especially perilous. Despite assurances that older children obtained through reputable agencies would not disappoint them, many adopters, blinded by "excessive desire," went to great lengths to obtain young babies.[64] Their reward, according to advocates of regulation, was sure to be heartbreak.

In 1923, for example, baby Billy was placed with wealthy adopters in Indiana. No one conducted an investigation. Later it turned out that his unmarried mother had been institutionalized for feeblemindedness and that Billy had been born with undiagnosed syphilis. The adopters had grown very attached to the child but were "naturally very much upset about not having known its inheritance possibilities before the adoption."[65] In a New York case, a young professional couple who adopted independently unwittingly took a baby with cerebral palsy and mental retardation and eventually turned in desperation to public assistance.[66] In Ohio and Illinois, adoption watchers condemned the "reprehensible practice" of birth mothers signing adoption consent papers even before the birth of their children, usually at the urging of unscrupulous physicians trying to "help" adopters determined to keep adoptions secret.[67] Such cases were emblematic of the "pure, undiluted torture" that awaited adopters foolish or naive enough to risk "well-intentioned but unscientific placement."[68] The mental and physical health of the child was the first risk. The second was adopting without professional guidance.

Reformers contended that thorough medical and mental examinations would reduce risk to a minimum and make adoption safer. Pediatric exams were sometimes cursory, and reformers called for more sustained attention to birth mothers' health during pregnancy, including testing for congenital conditions such as venereal disease and gathering as much data as possible about serious medical conditions among natal relatives. Dental exams were useful, too, along with good preplacement nutrition, even "fattening" children to improve their appearance.[69] Children's aesthetic qualities mattered to their chances of placement because how children looked mattered. Parents were known to dismiss children with crooked teeth or flat noses, sight unseen.[70] Reformers contended that appearances were a superficial, idiosyncratic, and unreliable guide to risk, although they could do little to dislodge tenacious preferences for attractive children. In contrast, standards that evaluated children in relation to abstract, statistical norms offered more assurance that real dangers would be detected before terrible mistakes occurred.[71] Such normalizing assessments, not coincidentally, made professional skill indispensable.

Mental measurement offers an instructive example. The first generation of adoption professionals suspected that mental deficiency and illness were hereditary conditions likely to afflict children born to poor and unmarried mothers, and they argued that psychological testing could reveal and manage risk. The records of professional child-placing agencies suggest that birth mothers were often tested during the 1910s and 1920s, but when it came to children, agencies had to be technologically flexible. The Stanford-Binet (or IQ) test, for example, was originally designed for school-age children and had to be administered creatively to anyone under the age of five or six. In 1915, when only the Binet was available, the report on mental examinations at the New England Home for Little Wanderers noted that "appearances are nowhere more deceptive than here. A good physique, vivacity, and fluency may mask serious mental defect, while physical disadvantages, languor, and reticence may conceal good ability."[72] By the 1930s, mental and developmental tests were available for infants and toddlers. Nature-nurture and outcome studies had also evolved to the point that science, safety, and technological innovation were presented as inseparable in kinship by design. Measuring intelligence was a technical feat that simultaneously served moral purposes: separating unadoptable from adoptable children and adjudicating legitimate belonging in families. These achievements promised to make adoption safer by making it more governable.

Closely linked to intelligence was family social history. Investigating the reputations of relatives suggested that children's eligibility for adoption was understood in moral terms even as reformers claimed it could be objectively assessed. Records of antisocial or criminal behavior in natal parents or kin indicated that subnormal mentality was probably inherited. Having too many relatives who were "vicious," "shiftless," "worthless," "ignorant," or "cruel" decreased children's chances of being judged adoptable. Clara Michaels, born in February 1915, was removed by court order from a violent, alcoholic father and neglectful mother at the age of eighteen months.[73] The father had been jailed regularly on charges of assault and disorderly conduct and utterly failed to support his family. The mother, who had no choice but to work outside the home to support her children, was sexually "immoral" and a "slovenly housekeeper" who never did laundry. Clara was a sickly child, and after a period of intensive nursing care, she was placed with a farm family who hoped to adopt her. But they returned her in exasperation after ten months, reporting that they "had no affection for her" and could not teach her to do even simple tasks. Clara drooled, had an abnormally large head, used meaningless words, and was "odd" and "silly." Suspecting feeblemindedness, the agency kept Clara under close observation. Mental examination convinced workers that the girl's retardation was mild, caused by neglect, and reversible, but Clara was removed from the agency's list of children suitable for adoption anyway. "She was too unpromising to be placed," her record concluded bluntly. Clara was expected to turn out as badly as her parents.

Negative social histories did not automatically disqualify children. Some children born into families like Clara's were deemed eligible for family love and belonging. Ruth Gibson was born to a white prostitute who "began living with a negro" after Ruth's birth on Christmas Day 1911.[74] Several years later, Ruth's mother was institutionalized, first in a reformatory and then in a state asylum, where officials concluded that she had the mentality of a "moron." Ruth's elderly father had murdered his first wife and was known to be an alcoholic. Her maternal grandmother was also a prostitute and "a big cow-like creature, silly, idiotic, who did not know enough to go in when it rained." Ruth lived a chaotic existence with her mother for several years before being committed to an institution. Once there, she was examined and found "attractive, teachable, and with no bad habits." Two different mental exams showed her IQ to be only slightly below average. Despite her inauspicious background, Ruth was placed at the age of five in a free home with a foster mother who wanted to adopt her legally and "did not care to know about the child's history, as she did not believe in heredity." Still skeptical about Ruth's background, her social worker wrote that "it is, of course, unusual to find a family willing to take a child purely on her own merits." Without proof that children such as Ruth were normal, the agency often decided against placing them, even when parents unconcerned with social history came forward. Luck was one reason that Ruth was adopted and Clara was not.

In addition to bringing the child into focus, documentation was thought to elicit desirable attitudes in would-be adopters. Paperwork might reveal subtle character traits that ordinary fact-gathering could miss. As one early text noted, "making a written application has a good moral effect upon the applicant."[75] This "moral effect" would, for instance, sensitize would-be parents to their own motives and needs in requesting children while providing child-placing organizations with meaningful facts for assessing potential parents: health; occupation; income; church membership and religious practice; quality and size of house or apartment; length of marriage; geographic location; age, sex, and nationality of the child desired; and so on. In the early decades of the century, applications still inquired about whether older children would be required to work and whether children would be treated as "members of the family."[76]

Facts were truthful in ways that people themselves were not, according to professional child placers, who noticed discrepancies between what people told them and what the documentary record revealed. The reasons that people offered for why they needed to give up a child or take one in were notoriously untrustworthy. According to the CWLA, "Only those should undertake it who are better qualified to judge the need than is the suffering family. The decision should rest, not on what applicants say they need, but on what the facts show."[77] "Only homes which can stand the test of a good probing are of any value in the work," noted Mary Doran and Bertha Reynolds in 1919.[78]

Uncovering relevant facts involved recording as well as gathering data. Useful forms had to be devised and filled out correctly and then placed in a record that tracked each and every child. Good case files included a complete record of the steps in the adoption process itself, from initial observations of children and investigations of families to conversations that occurred during postplacement visits. Just as forms required specific data about children and their natal relatives, they also required child placers to document "a minimum of fact information" about all potential foster homes.[79] "Because human beings may love and want a child as a child may want a toy or pet and still be neither capable of giving nor willing to give it the proper care, there are many chances for mistakes to be made," researcher Helen Pearson noted.[80] Independent references—character witnesses who had not been identified by the applicants themselves—had to be secured. Experienced investigators understood that such sources might offer difficult-to-obtain information leading to the disapproval of families that appeared otherwise acceptable.[81]

To avoid mistakes in parent selection, child placers were instructed to visit the prospective home, preferably unannounced, document the home's physical characteristics, and talk to family members. (Typical concerns included general cleanliness, the mother's cooking skills, the water supply, refrigeration, heating and ventilation, and the presence of a room specifically dedicated to the child, all of which offered "silent testimony" about the quality of family life.[82]) What about its geographic location? Were school and church located nearby? Did family members have experience caring for children? Facts about church attendance, income, and reputation with neighbors and community leaders were also gathered during home investigations.

Innovative child placers sought early on to dig beneath the surface of factual truths about adults, just as they had with children. What kind of people were these adults? What did they expect of the child? Would they be able to see things from the child's point of view? "Facts about these intimate traits of personality are quite as important as—one might say even more important than—the other information which is always secured," wrote Theis and Goodrich in their 1921 child-placing manual. "It is, moreover, very naturally the hardest kind of information to get."[83] Reformers dedicated to exposing the risks attached to children recognized that adults might pose risks, too. Dangers associated with "under-the-surface traits" that escaped ordinary notice simply proved that skill and training were essential for adoptions to succeed.[84]

Even well-documented home investigations could not always predict risk accurately. Cases of failed placements were useful for pedagogical purposes, figured prominently in child-placing manuals, and helped professionals learn from their mistakes. Mr. and Mrs. Peters were both thirty-nine, married sixteen years, and lonely without children of their own when they decided to adopt.[85] They had cared for two children belonging to Mr. Peters's sister for some years but had to give them up when the sister remarried. The agency worker reported that Mr. Peters had been thinking for a long time about adopting a child and preferred a girl "whose history he could know," "a foundling if he can get an attractive one." Mrs. Peters had been adopted as a baby by family friends after her father died and her own mother could no longer care for her. She considered her foster family her real kin. At the time of their application, Mr. Peters was judged "industrious" and "thrifty and temperate," and Mrs. Peters was described as "motherly looking" and "intelligent and sensible." Neither had much education. "Plain people" who lived close to church and school, their small six-room house was "exquisitely neat and clean," with carpets on the floor and pictures on the walls. The house was freshly painted and the garden carefully tended. Their income was modest but steady, they owned their home, and they had a life insurance policy. All of the named and independent references had good things to say about the couple. Theirs seemed "one of those simple homes of a familiar type, in which hundreds of adopted children are growing up happily and prosperously." The agent approved them for "a rather ordinary child."

The child they were given for adoption had to be removed from the home of Mr. and Mrs. Peters after Mrs. Peters became extremely quarrelsome and cruel. How could this unexpected turn of events have been anticipated? According to the text, the real danger lurked "in accepting the superficial instead of getting down further into the facts to see what underlies the promising surface." The worker had not asked enough questions about the two children who had previously resided with Mr. and Mrs. Peters. Nor had enough details been obtained from references. Although the original home investigation offered background information on Mr. Peters, Mrs. Peters's history was too sketchy. Because Mrs. Peters had been adopted herself as a child, the worker should have probed more deeply into "the effect of this irregular life on Mrs. Peters," a comment that betrayed doubts about adoption even by those most determined to improve it. Had the original investigation discovered what kind of person Mrs. Peters really was, "the home would certainly not have been used, as it was, with disastrous results."

Postplacement Supervision and Probation

The point of careful investigation and selection was to increase the chances that children would end up in appropriate families where provision would be materially adequate and emotionally satisfying. But only painstaking postplacement observation could confirm that a child's welfare was actually being served. "To place out without such supervision is a crime and should be treated accordingly," declared the earliest formal standards.[86] Professionals were keenly aware that their organizations retained legal responsibility for the children they placed until adoption decrees were issued, and legalization was sometimes very long in coming.[87] Long-term legal custody could last a decade or more; at least one-third of children placed in the early decades of the century were supervised for periods of five to ten years.[88] Agencies therefore had reasons to promote and to resist adoptions. Because adoptions ended agency responsibility, they were an ideal marker of children's formal belonging in a new family, the desired goal of child placers in cases where return to natal kin was impossible.

On the other hand, adoptions needed to be carefully scrutinized precisely because they ended the agency's oversight. One early professional manual even suggested that long-term foster parents be reinvestigated if they expressed a desire to adopt, a harbinger of the enduring perception that temporary placements involved different (and less desirable) parents and motivations than permanent adoption. Even children and parents who had been together a long time should be disapproved as an adoptive family if necessary.[89] The important distinction between the qualifications for temporary and permanent parents originated in the practice of paying to board children in temporary homes prior to adoption or awaiting their return to natal kin. In these cases, women who were paid to care for dependent children had to walk a very fine line between love, supposedly a natural expression of maternal instinct unconnected to money, and survival, which meant they could not volunteer to care for children without compensation.

"'Mothering' is definitely something which one would like to think should not be paid for," the CWLA noted in a 1942 study of board rates (a study prompted by a shortage of foster mothers resulting from new employment opportunities for women in defense industries after the United States entered World War II).[90] The CWLA directed agencies to defray expenses for children's food and clothing, but never to pay for maternal care itself.

Board payments tacitly acknowledged that temporary foster families had little to spare, yet payments could not be so high as to provide a genuine economic incentive to take children in. That would have blurred the ideological distinction between caring labor performed in families and wage labor performed in the market. It would have violated the assumption that only adults who accepted full financial responsibility for children were true parents and that adults who took payment to care for children were not prepared to consider them their own.[91] Some agencies rejected potential foster mothers who expressed curiosity about what they would be paid, required written promises that temporary parents would not decide to adopt, or took legal action against temporary parents who took steps toward permanence.[92] But these policies hardly prevented temporary parents from becoming very attached to the children they took in or convinced them that adoptive homes were better than their own.[93] They merely emphasized the hypocrisy of agencies that gave children to parents with more money while officially maintaining that money mattered far less than love.

One purpose of supervision was to police the border between temporary placements, where the agency remained in charge as the foster parents' employer, and adoptive placements, which eventually transferred complete legal and financial responsibility from agency to adopters. In theory, professionals insisted that all foster parents have similar qualifications, but in practice, payment differentiated nonadoptive from adoptive kinship. Cases in which temporary parents decided to adopt consequently troubled and confused adoption workers.[94] When Mr. and Mrs. Gutmann, paid foster parents, applied to adopt the girl they had cared for since infancy, the agency worker admitted that Mrs. Gutmann had undoubtedly saved the child's life; the baby had been critically ill at the time of placement. On the other hand, the adoption investigation noted that Mrs. Gutmann did not have the highest housekeeping standards and that Mr. Gutmann was "a little foreign looking . . . and acts very dull and stupid."[95] Their devotion to the child and time together had to be weighed against the defects of their home as well as their meager income. Paternal qualifications loomed much larger when making permanent placements. When the baby was first placed in the home on a temporary basis, Mr. Gutmann barely registered. But when it came to adoption, his inadequacies made all the difference. The Gutmanns' application was rejected.

Especially in preadoptive placements, board payments symbolized impermanence and agency control. Until agencies placed newborns directly into adoptive homes, a rare occurrence before 1945, one of the central purposes of preadoptive care was to ascertain whether the child was a good candidate for adoption. Permanent belonging, on the other hand, was meaningfully defined by adopters' eagerness and ability to assume the complete financial burden of children's care: "We know that homes that apply to board children are not necessarily good prospective adoptive homes. The reason seems simple. They do not wish to assume the responsibility implied in adoption."[96] The class divide between poorer foster parents and more affluent adoptive parents endures to this day.

Professionals worked to incorporate a standard probationary period into adoption law. The rationale for postplacement supervision was to observe the new family and offer assistance so that it could be trusted to function without supervisory authority after finalization. Even the most exacting methods of selection and investigation did not guarantee that new kin relationships would be problem free. Because placements "involve the most delicate yet radical adjustments," adoptive kinship was not automatic or effortless.[97] In some cases, difficulties dissipated quickly. Other families "achieve family unity by a more conscious, step-by-step development. Those who believe that after a child is placed in an adoption home he will live happily ever after, are simplifying life into a fairy story."[98] It was hard work to make adoptive kinship look easy.

Supervisory periods were mandated by most states by midcentury on the grounds that compatibility took time. Exactly how much time was needed, though? Some advocates called for periods of two years or more, but most states opted for six to twelve months. One observer termed this phase the "absorption period," whereas another favored "*adjustment* period."[99] The USCB reminded Americans that taking children "on approval" was a step designed for the protection of children and adults alike.[100] Probationary kinship epitomized several of adoption's most paradoxical tasks: making artificial kinship feel authentic, making deliberately constructed families appear spontaneous, and erasing from relationships founded on design and strenuous effort all traces of the deliberation and planning that had brought them into existence.

Foster parents often found the probationary period bewildering and stressful. Were they supposed to appear as autonomous as other families, or were they supposed to behave like dependent clients? Probation was "a rather grim term," one observer agreed in 1955, but there was really no reason for concern. "Most of the 'proving' has already been done," and all that was required was for parents to confirm that the adoption worker's decision to place a child in their home had been the right one.[101] Professionals tried to put adoptive parents at ease during this awkward time by "convinc[ing] them finally that she comes not to find fault, but to help."[102]

Supervisory methods included letters, visits, and telephone calls, and workers hoped that parents would use these opportunities to share the joys and problems of their new child's development. Agency workers called supervision "training" or "guidance" and reminded nervous new parents that children were rarely removed at the postplacement stage (although of course they could be). They emphasized that all persons in charge of children, including biological parents, could benefit from such assistance.[103] Professionals exulted in placements such as those of Philip and Helen, siblings placed for adoption in 1916 and 1918, respectively, at ages four and seven. "Everything about the whole situation seemed absolutely natural. It was hard to realize that the children had not been there always," wrote the satisfied worker who finally approved their adoption in 1920.[104]

Supervisory records continued the preplacement pattern of documenting empirical facts—from the child's appearance and condition of the house—alongside professional assessments of the child's degree of security and belonging. Were parents expressing genuine love and attachment, treating the child as their "own," or commenting happily on the uncanny resemblance between themselves and the child? Supervisory records also covered such topics as how and when to tell children about their adoptive status. In the early years of professional adoption practice, workers experienced enormous resistance to telling children, and anecdotal evidence and survey findings suggest that as many as half of all adoptees were never told, usually to spare them the knowledge that their ties to their families were considered inferior.[105] "Many foster parents object so strenuously to telling their children that it is impossible to insist on it," complained Theis and Goodrich in 1921.[106] Telling, nevertheless, was one of the few aspects of adoption marked by persistent professional consensus. Adoption's stigmatized difference from biological kinship was reflected in the imperative to tell, as it was in the probationary period itself. Surely this is why adopters hated them both.

When adoptive placements did not succeed, professionals owned up to their failures and tried to extract lessons that could be applied in the future to make families whose members would "fit" together smoothly. When children were rejected after placement, replacement was required. ("Disruption" was not a commonly used term until the 1970s.) Such cases were as common as they were awful. One study of child placing at the Boston Children's Aid Society before 1913 found that 129 children had been cared for by a total of 498 families—an average of almost four placements each—even though only half of the placements were intentionally temporary.[107] New

York's Catholic Home Bureau found that 65 percent of all children it placed remained with the families who initially took them in, the remainder requiring two or more placements before permanence was achieved. Until at least 1915, parents rejected children from the Washington Children's Home Society so routinely that in its newsletter the agency published a list of reasons not to return children; problems included trivial infractions—children who needed reminders to wash their faces—as well as more serious transgressions, such as stealing and lying.[108] Children adopted from the New England Home for Little Wanderers in the late 1920s and early 1930s experienced an average of 4.5 temporary placements before moving into their adoptive families, a pattern the agency's psychiatrist criticized for eroding the ability to love, "nipping in the bud the child's strivings to become a social being."[109] The damage that replacement did to "those who came back," like the happiness and stability that lasting adoptions created, could be appreciated only after adoption became governable and statistical approaches made its outcomes perceptible.[110]

Workers tried hard to locate new homes where subsequent placements would be happier and permanent, comforted by the thought that "replacements are usually made with much more knowledge of the child's capacities and characteristics than is possible in the first placement."[111] Worker error was sometimes blamed; better investigation or greater insight might have prevented disruption. Parents were also held responsible. Even under highly regulated conditions, with painstaking investigation and supervision, every eventuality could not be anticipated. Professionals could never be omniscient. Adoptions could never be perfectly risk free.

A good example is the case of Caroline, who experienced two disrupted placements before finally being adopted by a third family.[112] The first-born child of troubled and troublesome parents, Caroline and her neglected siblings were removed from their home in the mid-1910s. The four younger children were all judged feebleminded and dispatched to children's institutions, but Caroline performed normally on an intelligence test (her IQ was 103), and she was placed in a family by the New York State Charities Aid Association at the age of ten. The McMillans, a childless couple with substantial income, rejected her as unadoptable after three months. Although Caroline had been obedient and truthful, she was "too old and knew too much about her own family and circumstances." The McMillans despaired of making her their own and "said that they would not want to keep a child who would not amount to something."

The agency worker blamed the disruption on Mrs. McMillan's unreasonableness and unmotherly character, but could do nothing about the couple's decision to return the girl. After a three-week stay in temporary boarding care, Caroline was moved to a second adoptive placement. The Posts, with whom she lived for an entire year, were a very well educated couple who worried constantly that Caroline was not as bright as they had hoped. According to the record, the Posts "feel that Caroline is not developing as she should." Although Mrs. Post found Caroline "charming" and "attractive," Mr. Post "was convinced that Caroline had not the capacity for developing which he felt he must have in any child whom they adopt." Even after the agency arranged for repeated mental tests, proving that Caroline was mentally above average, the Posts were not satisfied. Disgusted, the agency worker blamed the Posts for the second adoption failure, just as the McMillans had been blamed for the first. Another agency official who reviewed the record concluded that the preplacement investigation had been inadequate. If the Posts' temperaments had been probed more deeply, it would have been obvious that no child could live up to their unrealistic standards, and Caroline would never have been placed in their home.

A third couple, the Andrews family, finally offered the love and belonging that Caroline and her advocates sought. More willing than the McMillans to acknowledge Caroline's natal family and less demanding then the Posts, the Andrewses were also less well off, described as "lower middle class" and "just natural, simple, unassuming people." "Mrs. Andrews said that both she and her husband loved her as if she were their very own." "Caroline says that she loves it here and wants to belong to Mr. and Mrs. Andrews completely." The upheaval and instability that had characterized Caroline's entire life ended in 1920, when she was finally adopted.

Early Field Studies: Making Adoption Legible

Selection, investigation, and supervision were skilled operations that defined kinship by design. They mattered precisely because they were absent in many adoptions during the early twentieth century, and the resulting risk reconfigured adoption as a formidable social problem. In addition to the challenge of judging the qualities, characters, and behaviors of individuals, moral controversies related to illegitimacy, adultery, alcoholism, desertion, and divorce added to the list of things that might go wrong. Only enhanced regulation and knowledge could prevent adoption failures, which were invariably blamed on the absence or inadequate enforcement of investigatory standards.

Adoption field studies, the first empirical inquiries conducted for the express purpose of promoting effective regulation, had several goals. First, they aimed to secure basic data on how many and what types of adoptions were occurring. At what age were children being adopted? By whom were they being adopted? Who exactly was involved? Second, they tried to discover whether states' regulatory requirements were being followed, or whether they amounted to nothing but "words, words, words."[113] Finally, the statistical findings they produced made the case for stricter regulation. Although field studies sometimes speculated about how procedures up to and including legalization might shape eventual outcomes for children and families, they were not outcome studies. They drew primarily on agency and court records to document the number, demographic characteristics, and typical procedures through which adoptions were arranged in the early 1920s. They did not conceptualize long-term outcomes in any meaningful way, trace adoptive families after decrees were issued, or correlate input and outcome measures. That would happen soon enough. What they did was link the state's promise of safety in adoption to an emerging consensus that adoption was a social problem whose solution was design.

The Children's Commission of Pennsylvania was one of the first public bodies to make an ambitious empirical study of legal adoption. It studied more than one thousand adoptions in thirteen counties between 1919 and 1924 (supplemented by another twelve hundred investigated by the USCB) and found that the total number of adoptions being finalized in the state was small, around thirteen hundred annually, with the vast majority involving children under the age of five. Of these, at least 62 percent were nonrelative adoptions in which unsupervised, independent adoptions outnumbered agency placements by two to one.[114] Data suggested that courts were exercising practically no discretion on children's behalf and that the casual movement of children between adults was not considered a problem in many communities. "Professional beggars and fortune tellers" adopted with ease, as did families supported entirely by charity.[115] Child abusers and criminals had no difficulty adopting, and families refused by the "higher grade" agencies simply turned to independent sources for the children they desired. Cases of perjury raised suspicions that birth parents might or might not be alive; the point was that no one seemed to know. Information contained in adoption petitions was as paltry as it was unreliable.[116] The commission nevertheless found that most adoptions were not abusive. The best cases bestowed on children "a tolerably good abiding place"; the worst cast them into the "deepest depths of misery and degradation."[117] Most adoptions fell somewhere in between.

On the recommendation of the Children's Commission, Pennsylvania's legislature passed a law that aimed to provide judges with many more facts to consider in granting or dismissing adoption petitions and required those judges, for the first time, to see the child and adopting adults in person. It stopped short of requiring judges to consider professional investigations and recommendations, but it did attempt to give agencies and interested parties occasional opportunities to protest objectionable placements. Because the study found that 29 percent of all adoptions were by relatives or stepparents (whose blood and marital ties presumably exempted them from supervision), the Children's Commission worried that a six- to twelve-month period of probation for all adoptions would have been too arbitrary, and it did not recommend one. The commission's outstanding finding was that regulation was required long before the family's day in court. Regulation might be better late than never in a few cases. But most adoptions needed to "be elevated to a very high plane of painstaking work" from the moment adoption was first contemplated. To regulate at the point where judges entered the process was to introduce "case work hind-side foremost" and "after a large part of the damage has been done."[118] To make adoption governable was to regulate it preemptively.

An Ohio field study conducted about the same time showed that unenforced regulation was not much better than no regulation at all. Adoptions were easily approved by courts without the detailed reports and recommendations that a revised state law required. Almost half of the adoptions surveyed included facts about why the child had been given up, the fitness of the proposed home, and the mental and physical status and heredity of the child, but more than half of the cases included no report whatsoever.[119] In Cook County, the most densely populated county in Illinois, Elinor Nims found that hundreds of adoptive homes were investigated only after children were placed in them, if they were investigated at all, and that far too little time passed between placement and legalization. Only those adoptions arranged by specialized child-placing agencies "deal with the question in a comprehensive, scientific manner," including documented preplacement study of the child, the home, and follow-up visits during a lengthy probationary period.[120]

In Indiana Helen Pearson found that the law required neither preplacement investigation nor postplacement probationary periods in 1923. As a result, fully 48 percent of the 636 adoption cases she studied were arranged by unqualified individuals, and 40 percent "are not reasonably satisfactory placements, although sanctioned as permanent by the state itself through its courts."[121] In Massachusetts, researcher Ida Parker painted an even bleaker picture after studying 852 adoptions. A majority involved illegitimate babies from families with very bad reputations and long histories of mental deficiency and criminality. These adoptions were doomed. "This is not the human stock which people contemplating adoption desire but many times, though by no means always, it is what they secure."[122] Courts, Parker argued, needed "some means of sifting the wheat from the chaff."[123] The crying need for "thorough investigation of the social facts which bear upon every adoption petition filed" was Parker's "outstanding conclusion" about how the epidemic of unsuitable adoptions might be curbed.[124] Her plea for comprehensive investigation and oversight was typical of reformers who stressed the urgency of reducing adoption's risks through regulation and standardization.

It was axiomatic among the Progressive architects of kinship by design, who labored to reveal the inadequacy of existing regulation, that increased governability would protect children and improve adoptive families. In the case of egregious abuses, their faith in minimum standards was surely warranted. One New York woman who adopted a little girl in the 1910s was not allowed to adopt another in the 1920s after an investigation revealed that she had casually handed the first child over to the Salvation Army. When the second adoption was refused, the woman complained bitterly about the unfairness and inflexibility of adoption standards, to no avail. "I could not get a child no matter how much better Home I have now. Is My past life got to be always throwed in my Face? I even tryed to talk with the Judge show hime where these things were being Held against me were False. He wouldnt even talk to me, slammed the door in my Face."[125] In other cases, a considerable gap separated regulatory rhetoric from reality. Few jurisdictions possessed the bureaucratic capacity to oversee adoptions as new laws stipulated, and many people working with unmarried women and dependent children heard the message of scientific professionalism dimly, if at all.[126] These facts illustrated "the possibility of evading the inquiry of the state" and consequently the shortcomings of rationalization itself.[127]

Acting through public agencies and private organizations such as the USCB and the CWLA, reformers promoted a family-making vision simultaneously standardized and individualized. New professional and legal regulations aimed to carefully select children and investigate parents and then supervise them during a probationary period. Theoretically, the entire process would be accompanied by record keeping that supplied relevant information while also making adoption visible as a social operation whose rules could be empirically surveyed and refined as new findings emerged.

The first promise of design was that adoption would be made govern-able to reduce its uncertainties and offer greater security and predictability to children and adults. Fears about the defective children and irresponsible parents who ended up in adoptive families arranged commercially or senti-mentally were prevalent at the dawn of the twentieth century. It made sense for reformers to argue that more attentive, consistent regulation would bring all the parties into clearer focus, lessen the probability of unwelcome surprises, and improve the results of family making. But what about the un-savory reputation of adoption itself? Stigma needed to be managed along-side risk. That is why kinship by design proposed making adoption real as well as safe.

CHAPTER THREE

Rules for Realness

Governing uncertain family-making procedures in the name of safety was the rationale for adoption regulation. Probing the uncertain psychology of all the parties involved, via interpretation, was another essential component of kinship by design. By exploring participants' personalities and motivations, adoption workers aimed to diminish the disgrace that linked adoptive kinship to sexual immorality and illegitimacy. They generated rules for realness, hallmarks of therapeutic government, that signaled the transformation of adoption into a full-fledged subject of casework and counseling.

Children and birth parents were often suspected, as we have seen, of being eugenic lemons, too risky to qualify for adoption. The kinship between children and adoptive parents was stigmatized because its social origins gave adoption a reputation as fragile and inauthentic. Adoption, like marriage, was a relationship formalized by law. But marriage promised to reproduce the biogenetic connection that children raised by nonrelatives lacked. This explains why adoption has been consistently viewed as less real than either kinship cemented by blood alone (which even law cannot eradicate) or kinship defined at once by blood *and* law.[1] Difference was the grounds for therapeutic interventions in adoption, which aimed to minimize and manage problems through skilled psychological analysis, adjustment, normalization, and guidance by helping professionals. When and how did adoption become an interpretive operation as well as a regulated one? That is the question this chapter answers.

The quest for authenticity has been one of the most consistent themes in adoption history—and modern culture—but definitions of realness and rules for achieving it have shifted significantly over time.[2] Until the late 1960s, efforts to dignify adoption, equalize its legal status, and enhance its cultural reputation all sought to make adoptive kinship analogous to kin-ship by nature. That analogy had two main components. Resemblance was one, and matching was the primary means of achieving it. But naturalizing adoption by combining children and adults who *looked* alike was not suf-ficient to make kinship real. Realness also required that children and adults *feel* like kin, and intimacy was not automatic with visible similarity.

Relational fit, like resemblance, was an ingredient of belonging that could be engineered. Consider the following testimony from one adoptive parent. "We couldn't possibly love her any more if she were our own flesh and blood. In fact, we don't even think of her as being adopted."[3] This was the sort of feeling that adoption professionals strove mightily to evoke. It capitalized on nature so closely that difference disappeared and undesigned realness emerged in its place. Mistaking adoption for the real thing was the point of design, of course. Realness was no accident. Artifice was the para-doxical key to authenticity in adoption.

Interpretation sought to instill the feeling of realness. The term *interpre-tation* referred to many things that agency professionals did for and with "clients" during the adoption process, along with public relations efforts to heighten community sensitivity to the difficulties of adoption.[4] In practice, workers explained agency policies, detailed legal requirements, conducted interviews with birth mothers, and investigated homes. They watched how children responded to temporary placements, informed applicants that a particular child had been chosen for them, rejected requests for children, and visited families after children had been placed. They compiled case files documenting the phases of surrender, application, placement, and proba-tion. These activities involved factual communication, but their ultimate purpose was to govern adoption by subjecting it to psychological inquiry and negotiation. Did birth mothers and adoption applicants comply meekly with agency rules? Did they ask for clarification, become impatient, or ex-press discomfort, nervousness, or anger? Interpretation was necessary for the same reason that regulation was necessary. Adoption was vulnerable to uncertainty and miscarriage.

Interpretation defined the adoption process as a series of psychologically demanding steps that most individuals did not appreciate, and could not adequately negotiate, by themselves. Because people possessed psychologi-cal depths teeming with forces that were intricate and baffling and resisted revelation, interpretation was imperative. It elevated psychology over biol-ogy, nurture over nature, and parent-child relationships over other deter-minants of adoption outcomes. It took training and skill to make adoptive families real.

These qualities were cultivated by professional helpers. Like translators working between languages, interpretation cast mediators in crucial roles. Professional help facilitated emotional transactions that exposed the ingredients of loving kinship and the obstacles to it: maturity, empathy, affection, fear, rage, conflict, loss, and all manner of human strengths and weaknesses. Most of the helpers involved in adoption were women, and interpretation was a gendered sensibility. Its preferred routes to realness were self-conscious introspection, candid talk about feelings, and willingness to display dependence and accept assistance. Helping was not merely a service provided by one person to another, but a unique relationship. Through this relationship the adoption process became an exacting project based on strict behavioral and emotional rules that, paradoxically, generated authenticity and naturalness.[5]

Psychologically informed adoption reached its zenith around midcentury, when therapeutic culture was most dominant in the United States, but the work of interpretation originated early in the history of adoption modernization. Pioneers included Jessie Taft, Dorothy Hutchinson, Charlotte Towle—all prominent social work educators—and psychiatrists Viola Bernard and Florence Clothier. Collectively, they represented the convergence of the female reform tradition, the movement from child welfare to child science, and the professionalization of human understanding and aid (especially in social work) during the first several decades of the twentieth century. They articulated themes that shaped helping professions, adoption, and child welfare policy throughout this period: personality as a category of analysis and object of adjustment, the normal and the abnormal, the responsibilities and burdens of "helping" roles, and the power of unconscious motivation. They believed that interpretation might deliver authenticity to adoption, an achievement no less significant than the safety associated with regulation. This chapter explores the rules for realness embedded in kinship by design, examples of the broader trend toward therapeutic government.

Historical Roots

Interpretive approaches to children and families originated in the child study movement, whose purpose was not merely to study children but to do so objectively. Initiated in the late nineteenth century by prominent developmental scientists such as G. Stanley Hall, an authority on adolescence, child study advocates aspired to draw a fact picture of children and childhood uncontaminated by sentiment and superstition. Amateurs and experts transcribed interviews, systematically documented their observations, took photographs, and compiled statistics all over the country. They also founded such organizations as the Federation for the Study of Child Nature (later renamed the Child Study Association of America), which was devoted to making childhood a resource for science and science a resource for children.[6]

During the first half of the twentieth century, new movements for parent education and child guidance were more professionalized and less collaborative than child study had been, but they kept the commitment to empiricism alive.[7] They converged on the notion that because children were complex, caring for them demanded expertise more than instinct or common sense. Parenthood, especially motherhood, was an intellectually demanding job that would benefit from more scientific methods. "The role now required of the parent is more that of psychologist than of disciplinarian," noted psychiatrist David Levy in 1928."[8] Levy was a well-known theorist of maternal deprivation and overprotection and often consulted on adoption cases. His work suggested that although psychologist-parents would do a better job of raising children, parental psychology could also be a source of terrible developmental damage. Foster parents no less than natural parents were a commanding presence in children's lives. That parents were powerful was one premise of therapeutic perspectives on adoption. That children were fragile and development treacherous was another.

Progressive reform also nourished the interpretive impulse. Women around the country mobilized to express their public concern for children and families and lobbied for maternalist legislation and policies in the era before the New Deal.[9] Women, observers frequently noted, were "leading the country in this field of understanding and interpreting behavior."[10] Their organizations favored research that was practical and problem centered. For instance, the University of Iowa Child Welfare Station, the country's first center to focus scientific research exclusively on "normal" children, was founded in 1917 through the efforts of Cora Hillis, a child-study enthusiast, lobbyist, and fund-raiser. During the 1930s, its famous studies helped to push the national nature-nurture debate away from hereditarianism, laying the foundations for a variety of early intervention programs, including early adoptive placement.[11]

The Iowa station's patrons at the Laura Spelman Rockefeller Memorial were also crucial sources of support for interpretive approaches to children, child guidance, and child welfare beginning in the 1920s.[12] Program officer Lawrence K. Frank directed the Rockefeller philanthropy's ambitious program to generate and disseminate new knowledge about human development that envisioned integrating psychology, medicine, anthropology, economics, and allied disciplines. Having worked closely with Frances Perkins in the 1910s, Frank shared Progressives' social values as well as their fondness for applicable, public-spirited knowledge. His most important asset, however, was the power he wielded to shape the institutional geography of knowledge about children and families through support of human science research. Frank's program provided seed money for the Iowa research station, Arnold Gesell's Yale institute, and university-based centers at Cornell, the University of Minnesota, and the University of California, Berkeley. Statewide parent education programs were mounted in connection with these new institutions, and agents employed by the federal Agricultural Extension Services brought the message of child science to thousands of mothers' clubs and parent-teacher associations. According to the foundations, reorienting academic knowledge was the surest way to change how Americans raised their children.

This view married the government of private and public. Simply put, to raise children was to make citizens. Frank consistently espoused this position during his long career, associating this point of view with the new sciences of childhood and touting its modernity and significance. What could be more consequential than an enterprise to direct the future of the country and even the world? To shape children and culture constructively, parents and policymakers had to appreciate the dynamic interplay between individual and society, psychological and social, family and nation. Subsumed under the heading of "culture and personality," these linkages grounded therapeutic authority in the anthropological sensibility of cultural relativism made famous by Franz Boas and Margaret Mead.

All American families were involved in the awesome project of social progress and reconstruction, whether they knew it or not. "The outstanding development" with respect to childhood and youth, Frank pointed out hopefully in 1933, "is the growing belief in the possibility of directing and controlling social life through the care and nurture of children."[13] Few family arrangements showcased the potential of child rearing more explicitly than adoption, because the child's socializing agents were chosen rather than given. In adoption, it was obvious that behind all developmental outcomes—accomplishment or disappointment, love, cruelty, or indifference—stood a series of particular, alterable social decisions about how families should be made. Designing American kinship was tantamount to managing American communities and culture because "the child is the bridge—biologically and socially—to the future."[14]

For children to become legitimate objects of therapeutic authority, their parents had to be drawn into the same orbit. Few modern narratives about personhood did more to fuse children and parents than psychoanalysis. In the world of child welfare and adoption, Freudian theories circulated through foundation-supported research that emphasized the role of sexuality, early attachments, and unconscious forces in human development. Its biggest boost, however, came from social work elites who embraced psychoanalysis as a doctrine offering both revelation and professionalization. Psychiatrist Marion Kenworthy of the New York School of Social Work was the patron saint of the mental hygiene movement, and she became the first woman to occupy the presidencies of the American Psychoanalytic Association, the American Academy of Child Psychiatry, and the Group for the Advancement of Psychiatry. Her Freudianism influenced social work's first generation of leaders, including proponents of interpretation in adoption, many of whom were her students and close associates.[15]

By importing new psychodynamic perspectives into human services for children and families, leading social workers hoped to disclose the causes of problems rather than merely assuage their surface manifestations, thereby transforming women's habitual care-taking work into something far more authoritative and analytical if not actually masculine and scientific. "Thou shalt not bow down to symptoms nor deal with them in isolation" was the first commandment of therapeutically oriented child welfare.[16] Once endowed with a body of knowledge and method it could rightfully claim as its own, social work would finally be liberated from charity and sentiment, free to enter the ranks of professions affiliated with science.

Psychoanalysis had the potential to transform social work into "casework." And casework elevated acts of help and understanding into feats of mental hygiene deserving the label "psychiatric."[17] Male psychiatrists had difficulties of their own persuading colleagues that their specialized knowledge was actually scientific. Freud's objection to the American requirement that psychoanalysts have medical training made it even harder. But that hardly stopped the female professionals who dominated social work and child placement from embracing science. Psychoanalysis was a revolutionary science that "provides a microscope whereby otherwise invisible psychic structures and processes come into view."[18] In the world of family making, the authoritative reputation of science promised to rewrite the rules. What had been informal and intuitive would become a systematic and skilled operation performed by professionals whose creed was design.

Child study, maternalist reform, foundation-supported developmental and behavioral science, and the spread of psychoanalysis were intersecting points of origin for interpretation in family making, which, in turn, was crucial in the expanding machinery of therapeutic government. Themes characteristic of adoption interpretation were the personality as category of analysis and target of adjustment, the normal and the abnormal, helping as a professional role and unique relationship, and the exploration and analysis of motivation.

Personality and Adjustment

Jessie Taft was the first prophet of the interpretive gospel in adoption. Born in rural Iowa in 1882, Taft attended Drake University in Des Moines and then took a job teaching high school before pursuing doctoral studies, one of few American women to do so in the early twentieth century. She graduated in 1913 from the University of Chicago with a Ph.D. in philosophy and a strong inclination toward social psychology. George Herbert Mead chaired her doctoral committee. "It usually takes a week or two of hard work to answer any of his questions," Taft reported to a friend at the time.[19] One of his queries was so rigorous that, in a moment of despair, she threw away all the work she had done on her thesis and started over from scratch.

She still finished her dissertation in a remarkably short two years. "The Woman Movement from the Point of View of Social Consciousness" probed the moving boundaries of private and public, subjects that galvanized new thinking about governing modern social problems therapeutically.[20] Her argument was that movements of women and industrial workers manifested conflicts understood (mistakenly) to be private, natural, and therefore immune from social influence. As "an effort to establish for herself her worth as a woman in the world of men," the dissertation deployed philosophers from Plato to Kant; surveyed how religious, political, and economic revolutions had shaped consciousness of self; detailed the excruciating conflicts that women faced in homes and workplaces; and concluded that the world needed many more social scientists.[21]

Unfortunately for Taft, a very good social scientist herself, the male-dominated academic world was closed to her. So like many other educated women at the time, she decided to make her way in a more hospitable women's world. For two decades, she worked in child and family services, maintaining her academic credentials by teaching psychology part-time. She finally joined the faculty of the University of Pennsylvania School of Social Work in 1934, where her life partner, Virginia Robinson, was a colleague. Taft and Robinson met in 1908 at the University of Chicago, where they established an intellectual and emotional bond that lasted for the rest of their lives. Both were feminists. They supported suffrage and avidly read Olive Schreiner, Ellen Key, Ida Tarbell, and Charlotte Perkins Gilman. Shortly after the two young women met, Robinson described Taft: "A joy to me. She's large and ungainly, and Western but with the kindest eyes I've ever seen. There is no escaping the appeal of her good, straightforward common sense and understanding of things. . . . I've never met such frankness in a mortal being."[22]

Shared formative experiences also cemented their loyalty to interpretive techniques. In 1912 Katherine Bement Davis hired them as interviewers for her study of women prisoners at the Bedford Hills Reformatory in New York, which used mental tests and personal histories to classify and analyze female criminality. Davis sent the pair to Charles Davenport's famous eugenics center on Long Island, where they were trained to create elaborate family charts, collect copious facts about mental illness and physical disease, and take a proper history. After a summer spent talking with drunks, prostitutes, and Davis, Robinson recalled, "Our choice was soon made to leave teaching and to stay in this field of work with people, a choice that included staying together and working together."[23]

By the 1920s, Taft had established herself as a national authority on child welfare and placement. Her career took her from the New York State Charities Aid Association to Philadelphia's Seybert Institution to the Children's Aid Society of Pennsylvania, where she directed the Department of Child Study. She knew Sophie van Senden Theis, who encouraged Taft and Robinson to consider adopting themselves. Like other women and female couples immersed in the professional world of child welfare, they did. The adoptions, arranged by Theis, were a matter of public knowledge within their social circle.[24] In 1921 they bought a house ("The Pocket") in Flourtown, Pennsylvania, where they raised two children, Everett and Martha, while participating in a close-knit community of like-minded women who shared meals, spent holidays together, and provided one another with lifelong mutual aid.[25] "You will be interested to know that Miss Robinson and I have enlarged our family by the addition of a little five year old girl whose name is Martha," wrote Taft to a colleague in 1923 (figure 5). "We feel very much like a family and some times wonder whether we are going to live through it."[26]

Taft is known today, if she is known at all, as Otto Rank's translator, biographer, and leading American exponent, although Taft was largely responsible for Rank's American fame.[27] She met the renegade Viennese psychoanalyst in 1924 at a gathering of the American Psychoanalytic Association, entered analysis with him in 1926, and eventually arranged for Rank's immigration to the United States and his employment at the University of Pennsylvania, where he lectured in her courses alongside Ruth

Figure 5. Jessie Taft and Virginia Robinson with the children Taft adopted and the two women raised together, at home in Flourtown, Pennsylvania, 1923. Used by permission of Roger Taft.

Benedict, Arnold Gesell, Karen Horney, Adolf Meyer, and Lucy Sprague Mitchell.[28] In Rank's ideas about the creativity of will and the healing power of emotional connection, Taft found encouragement for her own thinking about the helping process, the professional self, and the therapeutic activities of social agencies and schools. She rejected hierarchical and cure-oriented forms of therapy, preferring instead to conceive of help as a relationship in which the helper was "at once doctor and patient, experimenter and subject, scholar and healer, helper and helped."[29] Taft knew that perfect reciprocity was unattainable. In practice, the ability "to stand the inequality" and "to sustain the difference" was a never-ending challenge for professional helpers.[30]

Mutuality was the animating principle of the "functional school" in social work, which was strongly identified with Taft, Robinson, and others —almost all of them women—trained at the University of Pennsylvania's School of Social Work. Proponents championed agencies' "functions" of promoting growth, normality, and active participation by clients, even infants, anticipating the client-centered approaches of such well-known humanistic psychologists as Carl Rogers, who was influenced by Taft.[31] Although this philosophy contrasted with the orthodox Freudian emphasis on pathology and detachment, Taft was still emblematic of social work's conversion to psychoanalysis. For her, help that did not dive into the psychological depths was not worthy of the name.

Taft has been underappreciated as a theorist because sex discrimination forced her into social work and human service, locations rarely accorded intellectual respect.[32] No less than William James, John Dewey, or Jane Addams, Taft struggled to articulate a progressive scientific ethic and experimental method while maintaining that truth was tentative and partial, placing her squarely in the pragmatist tradition.[33] She too held "experience" to be the irreducible fount of meaning in a modern context that had shaken the foundations of knowledge, banished certainty, and cast traditional morality into doubt. Until her death in 1960, Taft mediated the important conversation between the male world of social inquiry and the female world of help, which is to say that she thought hard about what science could and could not offer people seeking aid and understanding.

No concept was more central to her thinking than personality. In the late 1910s and early 1920s, Taft set out the basic terms of interpretation in several manifestos and conference papers that identified psychologically sophisticated personality study as the premier responsibility of child placers. Detailed, individualized knowledge of particular children was mandatory for anyone trying to solve their problems, she believed, and making them members of new families necessarily invited interpretation. "For the child-placing agency," Taft pointed out in 1919, "*all children are abnormal* in the sense that no child is so simple that it is not worth while to become intimately acquainted with his personality."[34] Mental and developmental tests, extensive personal histories, prolonged observation, careful records, attentive supervision, and an abundance of empathy were all essential. Such social operations as family formation exhibited "a scientific attitude towards child-placing" only when they revolved around "the most important condition of the experiment, the personality of the child who is placed."[35]

The personality was a uniquely modern and social type of self.[36] From George Herbert Mead, Taft had learned that its origin was interpersonal, that the "I" existed only in and through relationships. This interdependent subjectivity made human beings problematic rather than depraved. If goodness and badness were not innate, but were elicited socially, then personality probes were distant from the harsh judgments of the past. Because the work of interpretation was based on awareness that "the self is a very complex, elusive, changing phenomenon," it was, Taft insisted, the antithesis of blame.[37] She urged her professional colleagues to abandon moralistic notions about vicious behavior and natural wickedness. However shocking the reasons for placement, workers were obliged to consider children's predicaments "with an humble spirit, an open mind and a desire not so much to judge as to understand."[38] By curtailing adoption stigma, advocates hoped to make adoption a no-fault institution.

Interpreting the child's personality was Taft's first priority. "Every child uprooted from its natural soil is a fit subject for the utmost intelligence and technical skill which sound case work, medical knowledge and a vital psychology can bring to bear."[39] Like most of her contemporaries, she initially believed that the foremost responsibility of professional child placers was to assess children's qualifications. These, more than other factors, would govern placement outcomes. But the rubric of personality study allowed for easy generalization to the adults involved in adoption, who quickly became targets of inquiry as well.

Personality assumed a central place in kinship by design as the object of therapeutic intervention. To place a child was to "analyze in detail the personalities and emotional relationships in a particular home and estimate their effect upon, as well as their reaction to a particular child."[40] By locating the causes of social problems inside the boundaries of troubled personhood, personality moved the terrain of social action from exterior to interior, from group to individual, and from general to particular. "All social problems are at bottom the inner problems of the human beings involved; . . . reform, if there be such, must come through inner as well as outer changes."[41]

Rationality was secondary when navigating the interior geography of personality, and child placers needed to unburden themselves of excessive regard for it. "We know that neither children nor adults are reasonable beings,"[42] Taft pointed out, but still "the world is full of grown people who are quite unaware of the underlying forces that drive them and who have no conscious use or control of those forces because they are unable to face them."[43] Emotion, on the other hand, really mattered, and child placers needed to face it squarely, without squeamishness or shame. "What we need, desire, want, not what we coldly think" was "the motive force in all of us."[44] This was the "vast, unexplored region" that demanded social workers' attention.[45] There was no getting around the psychological challenge of child placement, "no shortcut, no possible avoidance of the effort to understand personality in its emotional and impulsive aspects."[46] The embrace of personality was the first step in turning family making into an enterprise that involved interpretation as well as regulation. Not merely a traffic in people, child exchange was a traffic in personhood.

"Adjustment" described work performed deliberately on the personality. Ideally, it was the outcome of diagnostic intelligence so precise that it could be rendered as a blueprint for bringing the troubled self back into constructive social balance. To evaluate the personality and plan its adjustment catapulted social workers into roles as "working psychologists, not the laboratory research or clinical kind, but something more human, vital and practical."[47] According to Taft, adjustment was "that science or art of untangling and reconstructing the twisted personality, of changing human behavior so that it adapts the individual to his environment."[48] To do this well, the social worker had to become a "super case worker."[49] She had to learn the language of psychiatry and psychoanalysis while making adjustment indigenous to social work. Working with whole personalities as they coped with difficult situations was an entirely new way to practice psychology. Its laboratory was all of life.

Foster placement was a test case for adjustment because virtually all maladjustment later on originated in early experience. Foster homes that failed to appreciate the significance of children's personalities were unlikely to help because they did not act deliberately on the basis of interpretation. "More professional attitudes on the part of people who deal with our children day by day," infused with "scientific spirit," were favored.[50] The goal for every child placed by the New England Home for Little Wanderers in the late 1920s was "a true experiment in social living" that would reconstruct young personalities already bruised and broken.[51]

Adjustment involved knowledge and planning as well as sensitive care. Its ultimate goal was "perfecting the family patterns upon which the successful childhood and the adult happiness of all of us must depend."[52] In adjustment, the excavation of emotional meanings paralleled the professional critique of commercial placements and the dismissal of superficial, material qualifications in family making. Love and good intentions were flimsy and inadequate grounds for personal transformation after placement, just as they fell short when selecting children and parents in the first place. What children needed were parents and families who would understand and bind their emotional wounds. To adjust was, by definition, to design.

Normal and Abnormal

Adjusting personalities was part of kinship by design because placing children with parents other than their own was not a normal thing to do. "No one who is not willfully deluded would maintain that the experiences of adoption can take the place of the actual bearing and rearing of an own child," Jessie Taft wrote in 1929, years after she had adopted two children herself.[53] For unfortunate children and adults, she added, adoption could be a satisfying substitute for normal kinship.

To put something artificial in place of something real constituted a risk no less serious than the risks posed by commercial and sentimental adoption. Florence Clothier, a psychiatrist at the New England Home for Little Wanderers from 1932 to 1957 and an active member of the Boston Psychoanalytic Society, identified "the wound left by the loss of the biological mother" as "the core of what is peculiar to the psychology of the adopted child."[54] "It is to be doubted whether the relationship of the child to its post-partem mother, in its subtler effect, can be replaced by even the best of substitute mothers."[55] Ideally, adoption might be similar, but it would never be the same. Its very existence set it apart from nature and the family norm.

In the early decades of the twentieth century, the individual participants in adoption—as well as the institution itself—were frequently suspected of deviating from norms by falling below them. Fears that the children and adults involved in adoption exchanges were defective and unqualified were widespread, and eugenicists assumed that most children in need of placement were genetic lemons. At the time, families were considered appropriate destinations only for "normal" children, so developmental technologies were deployed to sort the adoptable from the unadoptable. Because normal children needed normal families, home studies eventually sought to distinguish between suitable and unsuitable parents.

Assessing children's adoptability and parents' suitability were interpretive feats that adhered to the logic of normalization. Normalizing judgments were important because they lived under the sign of science but defied the commonplace scientific distinction between facts and values. It was obvious that to be normal was good and to be abnormal was bad. Yet the "nonjudgmental" credo of psychiatric social work prohibited such explicit moralism. According to Dorothy Hutchinson at the Columbia School of Social Work, "Of all types of child-placing, adoption comes closest to normal."[56] This position was a way of saying that permanent, legal adoption was preferable to insecure, temporary placements or other family arrangements that denied children permanent belonging. It was almost as safe, natural, and real as biological kinship. It might approximate normality through intelligent design.

Hutchinson repeatedly emphasized this basic tension between normal and abnormal. "The great dilemma of placement is its abnormality," she pointed out. She then urged her colleagues never to forget that normality was the cardinal aim of home finding. "Although there is no such thing as a perfect home, there is such a thing as a normal family," she wrote in her 1943 guide, *In Quest of Foster Parents*.[57] "Normality is something that is hard to define, yet easy to feel and see."[58] Born in 1895, Hutchinson was a graduate of Smith College and the New York School of Social Work. A member of the Columbia faculty from 1935 to 1956, she trained scores of social workers and consulted with adoption agencies around the country, helping them detect the elusive yet crucial quality of normality while working with birth mothers, selecting parents, and placing and supervising children in homes. Social workers involved in adoption called her training sessions "invaluable."[59]

Practices of personality study and adjustment led to chronic difficulties in distinguishing normal from abnormal. Through the lens of interpretation, all the people involved in adoption became "cases," their dilemmas traceable to myriad abnormalities that were both unique and sufficiently patterned to be recognizable to the trained eye. Unmarried white birth mothers were a case in point. As early as 1918, when many still considered illegitimacy a moral failing or a consequence of male sexual depravity, Amey Watson, of the Philadelphia Conference on Parenthood, argued that "illegitimacy is the result of biological, psychological and social causes following definite scientific laws and there is a responsibility of the community as well as of the individual for its occurrence."[60] In 1921 Marion Kenworthy called for an end to condemnation in the name of assistance. "Illegitimacy," she claimed, "is largely a matter of maladjustment."[61] By the late 1920s the consensus in the mental hygiene movement was that unmarried mothers presented a "socio-psychiatric" problem whose roots lay deep within the personality. According to Henry Schumacher of the Cleveland Child Guidance Center, "Our aim should be the discovery of the motive that lies behind the act."[62] In adjustment, objective understanding replaced guilt and blame.

One theory popular during the 1920s was that unmarried mothers were feebleminded girls and women too lacking in intelligence to control their sexual behavior, and some agencies administered intelligence tests to birth mothers and evaluated the mentality of their babies.[63] But field studies and casework showed that such assertions were far too sweeping, perhaps entirely wrong. Alice Leahy's study of almost ten thousand unmarried mothers in Minnesota between 1918 and 1928 suggested that the minority of women who surrendered children for adoption were actually better educated and had higher IQs than the majority who kept their children.[64] Social workers encountered unmarried mothers who were bright, controlling, and sexually inexperienced as often as they were dull, impulsive, and promiscuous. Professional interpretation discounted simplistic accounts that made mentality, socioeconomic circumstance, or innate character categorically determining. Instead, interpretation produced narratives that explored emotional disturbance and need for help.

Through intensive casework, white birth mothers were reinvented during the 1920s and 1930s as unstable, neurotic, hysterical, narcissistic, or even psychotic. Rarely did they have any insight into the chaotic emotions that drove them or the unhappy familial experiences that had shaped their lives. They needed help but did not know it. In a professional climate that stressed individualization, this lack of self-awareness was perhaps the single tenable generalization about the unmarried mother. She was "an instrument out of tune for the time being with life, frequently with her family and most often with society."[65] The job of casework was "to know and understand her personality in all its richness and variety."[66] If unmarried mothers constituted any type at all, it was of a distinctly psychological variety. Desperate to obtain "gratifications desired but not received from the love objects within her family group," women became pregnant because of "destructive, regressive, infantile factors" they did not begin to understand.[67] Perspectives on nonwhite birth mothers were starkly racialized. That illegitimacy in African American communities was perceived as natural simultaneously excused racially exclusive placements and figured unmarried African American mothers as less deviant than their white counterparts, both culturally and statistically.

Maternal maladjustment sealed white children's psychological fate. Unless quickly surrendered and adopted by a happily married couple, the child of an unmarried mother was "practically foredoomed . . . to become one of the 'neurotic personalities of our time.'"[68] Florence Clothier agreed: "Unmarried motherhood in our culture almost always represents a distorted or unrealistic way out of inner difficulties."[69] As she saw the situation, "Unmarried mothers, with rare exception, are incapable of providing sustained care and security for their illegitimate babies."[70] By midcentury, most adoption professionals, whose goal earlier in the century had been to preserve natal families, believed that it was a mistake for unmarried women to keep their children. Childlessness and motherhood without benefit of marriage were both abnormal, but adoption was less abnormal than living in a female-headed family tainted by illegitimacy. Adoption protected children from troubled mothers and doomed lives, offering a positive solution for everyone involved.[71]

This position meshed with Hutchinson's view that adoptive family making brought together damaged materials, beginning with birth mothers' distorted personalities. "In my opinion, the majority of these mothers are unable, if not incapable, of making their own independent decisions without skilled case work service," Hutchinson noted in 1946. The causes of nonmarital pregnancy were comprehensible only by professionals. "To expect a severe neurotic or a pre-psychotic girl to use a six months' period of time to make up her mind alone is to expect the unreasonable if not the impossible."[72] Hutchinson's consulting files and case records described birth mothers as clueless about their own unconscious motivations, which typically pointed backward to unresolved oedipal relationships and emotional development stalled in childhood.

The "psychosocial diagnosis" that caseworkers formulated was that unmarried mothers needed help for themselves and surrender for their babies.[73] Not infrequently, they needed help *in order* to surrender their babies. In early 1945, having felt uncertain about her course of action throughout her pregnancy, S decided on surrender shortly after the birth of her son. "The definite release her decision has given her seems indicative of its rightness for her," her social worker recorded.[74] Yet this twenty-six-year-old woman from a strict, small-town family "was a very unhappy upset girl inside herself."[75] "I wouldn't be surprised to see her become very depressed and perhaps in the end take her own life."[76] For other young women, the prognosis was better. Discharged from the Women's Army Corps in 1943 because of her pregnancy, G presented her caseworker with "a fantasy picture of a home and security and a child which has very little to do with her reality feelings about men."[77] Yet she gave up her baby girl for adoption in 1944 with relative ease and fell in love a few months later with a man she hoped to marry. "I was very happy about [G,]" her worker commented.[78] In this case, surrender delivered hard-won self-knowledge.

Cases in which white, middle-class unmarried birth mothers resisted pressures to surrender were instructive. M, a Florida nurse who became pregnant while serving in the military, gave birth to a baby boy in 1946. She planned to give him up, but changed her mind. This was a tragic mistake, according to her social worker. M knew that adoption was the only way for her baby to have "a home and normal family life," yet decided to keep him, even if it meant he would "hate her for what she has done to him, by rearing him as an illegitimate child."[79] M's social worker speculated that "perhaps she is keeping the child as a form of self-punishment."[80] "She *enjoys* the suffering," commented Hutchinson.[81] "[M] was begging the worker for much more backing in this decision to give the child up."[82] After 1945, when unmarried white women such as M kept their children, the quality of the professional service was blamed along with women's own psychopathologies. They simply had not been helped well enough.

What defined good help for women whose disturbed personalities turned babies and young children into unrealistic fantasies or techniques for self-punishment? Good social workers were supposed to respond to such abnormality by "playing the role of the 'corrected' parent to the unmarried mother."[83] "It is clear that many of these unmarried mothers need to be dependent on workers and only in this way can they become independent," Hutchinson wrote.[84] Surrender was the ultimate sign of independence. Women who gave their babies to workers acting as symbolic mothers were tacitly admitting that helping worked: "positive transference" allowed the social worker to offer unmarried mothers "the kind of acceptance (as a person, and particularly with regard to her pregnancy) she undoubtedly has not known before."[85]

Not all unmarried mothers were equally reachable. "The healthy 'normal' unmarried mother" found it easier to surrender her child than "the psychotic unmarried mother," "the neurotic type," "the adolescent unmarried mother," or the "dull infantilized unmarried mother."[86] "Not all unmarried mothers will give up their babies for adoption, or should do so, but a large number will *want* to do this when they are given understanding of themselves by a mature and interested caseworker."[87] Unmarried women who chose adoption rescued their children and salvaged their own future psychological health.

Hutchinson's colleagues and students spread her gospel about unmarried mothers, which circulated freely in the pages of popular magazines during the postwar period, when psychoanalysis was at its height.[88] Social worker Leontine Young, perhaps the best-known exponent of the Freudian interpretation of unmarried mothers, was a close friend and colleague of Hutchinson.[89] This social-work generation also viewed the other major players in adoption—would-be parents—as "compulsive neurotics (these are hostile)" as well as "dominant & domineering."[90] Their needs were manifested in the very request for a child. Adopters' insight into the causes of their behavior was as flimsy as that of birth mothers.

To interpret was to normalize. Ironically, the quest to make adoption more ordinary frequently emphasized its strangeness, even its pathology. To become "normal" people, children needed nothing more desperately than to grow up with "normal" parents in a "normal" family. How exactly were adoption workers supposed to ensure this, inundated as they were with evidence of the mistakes that adults made, as well as their anguish and helplessness? Most social workers tried hard to make good decisions for children that would increase their chances of happiness. But their contact with families in trouble taught them that normality was a scarce resource. When Hutchinson pointed out that "the request for placement is merely the threshold to a family situation," she meant that families were inevitably mired in significant and debilitating psychological conflicts.[91] Well-functioning families were virtually impossible to find and harder to make. "Healthy and unhealthy behavior are quite close together, like the blood relations they really are," admitted Hutchinson.[92] The best that professionals could hope for was to balance their hopes for children against the all-too-visible evidence of abnormality surrounding them.

Norms had the enormous advantage of appearing objective in comparison to blunt moral assessments. Yet even strenuous, self-conscious efforts to evaluate situations coolly, with a "tough," "professionally disciplined mind" that "sees farther than the tender heart," could not shield adoption professionals from equating what was normal with what was socially expected and esteemed.[93] Hutchinson recognized that judgment was ever-present in home finding, but criticized an earlier generation of child placers who relied on such superficial indicators as cleanliness and material comforts. She chided them for negotiating family making as if it were a simple matter of selecting spotless, well-appointed homes and decried the error of equating bourgeois values with parental fitness. Because they lacked psychological sophistication, these earlier child placers "brought to their jobs a set of cultural and moral standards and a degree of enlightenment insufficient for an understanding of foster parents as people."[94] Yet Hutchinson herself did not hesitate to define parental normality in conventional terms. Her list of the most important qualities that social workers sought in adoptive parents suggests that heterosexual marriage and traditional gender roles were the lynchpins of normal kinship.

> A legal marriage.
> She likes being a woman.
> He likes being a man.
> She likes men; is glad there are men around; is not a man hater or an Amazon.
> He likes women while he enjoys being a man.
> He wants to give his wife a baby and she wants a baby which is a product of both of them; she doesn't have her children psychologically by herself.[95]

If Hutchinson and other advocates of therapeutic approaches found a silver lining in adoption's abnormality, it was design. Families that deviated from the norm had precious opportunities to adjust personalities on purpose. The adoptive parent, usually denied the experience of working with "untouched material," was "like an architect who remodels the old house and in so doing has to undo the old construction effort."[96] Purposeful parents also possessed uncommon strengths: "There is no special virtue in loving one's own child; such love is taken for granted. However, to love someone else's child requires really uncommon qualities of heart and mind. To love and nurture a child who belongs to you is a different thing from loving and nurturing one who knows he belongs to someone else."[97] Normal and abnormal were conceptual pillars of interpretation in adoption. They convinced social workers that their judgments of human worth were not really judgments at all.

Helping Roles and Helping Relationships

Assessing normality and abnormality was indispensable in family formation, but it placed enormous pressure on helping roles and relationships. Of all human service jobs, child placing was "surely the most dramatic and lonely," Dorothy Hutchinson reasoned.[98] It required the worker to harmonize warm empathy and cool interpretation, to exude acceptance while making painful adjustments to personalities. "She gets them to let their hair down and then passes judgement on them," Hutchinson admitted ruefully, "leading them on, only to chop off their heads."[99] It was almost always the case that the adoption worker was a "she." Women who placed children confronted the contradictory obligations that had plagued social work, a feminized profession, from the outset: to respect mutuality, on the one hand, and wield power, on the other. In adoption, there was no escaping the authority of the helping role, and its burdens were inflected by gender.

Adoption professionals responded to job strain, not surprisingly, by turning the interpretive lens on their own motivations, frustrations, and satisfactions. What kind of person aspired to make families? What made the job so emotionally taxing? Placing children required not only training but an uncommon mix of qualities: "a clear mind, a kind heart, and a scientific attitude."[100] Florence Clothier argued that the adoption worker had to love social contact, prioritize her loyalty to children above all else, and develop a knack for putting nervous, difficult people at ease while peering "around, beyond, and behind the facts into the deeper needs, impulses, and motivations of the personalities with whom she must deal."[101] She had to do all of this without ever condemning birth parents or championing adoptive parents. Nor could she lose sight of her own emotional reactions and motivations. She needed to "'clear the decks' of personal reactions" before meaningful help could be given.[102]

Why would anyone choose such a career? Clothier's Freudian sensibility led her to the unconscious. If child placing expressed maternal desires postponed or denied, this occupational choice might express resentment about workers' own unhappy family situations, satisfy their sexual curiosity, or compensate them for feelings of powerlessness they had experienced as girls, giving them longed-for opportunities to exert power over other people. Whatever the reasons, workers in the adoption field were obliged to interpret themselves in order to mobilize their own conscious insight to strengthen the helping role. "The social worker's success in the field of adoption depends upon her personality, her inner needs, and the feelings she has to project," Clothier wrote." "Successful functioning in the complicated fields of illegitimacy and adoption . . . must be aided by the tools that techniques, training, and experience can give."[103] It usually went without saying that adoption professionals were supposed to be mature and stable as well as skilled and knowledgeable. They had to be psychologically free and self-aware—"unlocked" was Hutchinson's term—before the work of interpretation could flourish.[104]

For all the conflicts that beset the helping role, the helping relationship was paramount. Because personality was interpersonal, originating in a social self, its comprehension and adjustment necessarily shared this same characteristic. Helping was not a one-way experience. It only worked relationally. Agency professionals established relationships—with birth parents, children, and adoptive applicants—and then used those relationships as a means of interpreting and adjusting the social universe that made clients who they were. "Caseworkers are human beings," Dorothy Hutchinson pointed out. "They are also instruments by which other human beings seek to work out their desires, their conflicts, their enmities, and their bad wishes."[105] Help offered the personhood of the worker as a means of enhancing the personhood of the client.

"Helping" was social work's answer to "treatment," its medicalized cousin. The term itself indicated hope that family formation would be a benign rather than pathological procedure. To help was not, strictly speaking, to cure. Although relationships were partially diagnostic—their point was to expose whatever was abnormal and in need of change—relationships were also a source of salvation whose goal was nothing less than "to establish a constructive love relationship between individuals who are strangers."[106] By accepting help, children and adults helped themselves.

The axiom of helping relationships was that everyone involved in adoption needed them, whether they knew it or not, and they often did not. Help was something that most people resisted, according to Dorothy Hutchinson. "It is not easy to be a client and *to ask for help,*" she taught her students, because requesting help could be as humiliating as it was necessary.[107] "The original need expressed by the client may be the *only* need but more usually is it [*sic*] one of a whole chain of needs, some of which the client may be aware of and some not."[108] To achieve a "professional attitude" about helping, Hutchinson concluded, one had to be "a genuinely accepting person" who acknowledged "the passing of *self-righteous reform.* . . . We *no longer impose services. We have let go judgement* and *moralistic condescension.*"[109] Workers were expected to defend clients' rights to self-directed, individualized services while underscoring how few clients understood the depth of their need for help.

Adults sought help from agencies because they were in trouble. In adoption, they wished to surrender or acquire children—not understand themselves better. Therefore, according to psychiatrist Viola Bernard, "the agency's clients are not patients, regardless of how great the incidence of personality and mental disorder among them."[110] Transforming adoption into a therapeutic opportunity for would-be adopters was the great challenge for psychiatrists who consulted to adoption agencies, as she did.

Bernard, a charter member of the American psychoanalytic movement, was born in 1907 to wealthy Jewish philanthropists in New York.[111] During World War II, she volunteered her family's large home in Nyack as a hostel for refugees from Europe. She served for forty years as chief psychiatric consultant to Louise Wise Services, where she oversaw the transition from amateur to professional agency (figure 6). She had no experience as a parent herself, but her lifelong friend, Justine Wise Polier, called Bernard the agency's "mother, godmother, and gadfly."[112] Through adoption, Bernard pursued a type of preventive psychiatry and applied psychoanalysis that she called "ecological." It acted through a social process, involved a range of social institutions, and depended on teamwork among professionals who agreed that well-designed kinship could bring about mental health, and better lives, for all the parties involved.

Helping Children

It was tempting to view children as helpless pawns in an adult game, their lives and circumstances dependent on decisions and circumstances entirely

Figure 6. Viola Bernard, 1950. Archives & Special Collections, Columbia University Health Sciences Library. Used by permission.

beyond their own control, but even the youngest children could chart their own destinies by taking advantage of professional assistance. Jessie Taft's "functional school" of social work was known for its theory that all participants in family making were active participants rather than passive observers of arrangements made by others. Even babies unlucky enough to be born to parents who did not want them or could not support them were, in theory at least, agents of their own psychological growth rather than tragic victims of accident and circumstance. Placement was not something that was done to children, according to Taft's *The Role of the Baby in the Placement Process* (1946).[113] It was an opportunity for participation that could be seized or squandered.

By conceiving of children as agents, Taft transformed helpers into facilitators of healthy, if painful, development. "The problem of the placement agency is how to make it possible for the child himself to choose placement," Taft wrote. "No agency can psychologically place a child who refuses to be placed, even though he remains in a foster home physically."[114] Decisions about where children met adoptive parents for the first time and whether children walked or were carried into their new adoptive homes could help or hinder children's own most vital resource, their growth-oriented self-direction. Through careful design and management of placement, professionals served as skillful extensions of infantile selfhood. They pledged allegiance to their partners in the helping relationship, no matter how young, and considered placement from the child's point of view.

Taft chastised Florence Clothier for stressing the analytic over the supportive role of helpers, as other theorists also did. Clothier was too quick to prescribe, too confident that she always knew what was best for the parties to adoption. This stance "implies fear of life itself," wrote Taft with uncharacteristic severity, "since all growth experience entails a continuous process of separation from the past and its love objects."[115] True helping could not relieve people of the excruciating decisions they had to make themselves. "All living is at bottom a matter of bearing the pain."[116]

Helpers who positioned themselves in between people and their difficulties exerted too much control. Denying clients opportunities to take advantage of respectful, mutual relationships was the opposite of helping. For Taft, squelching active selfhood was more irreparable than even the trauma of parent-child separation. Children who needed new families might suffer terribly, Taft believed, and still turn out well in the end if child placers defended their developing selfhood. Relational ability was a precious resource. Through it, helpers directed children toward new kin, and those children in turn established new bonds of belonging. The ability to trust in others was not fixed or unchanging, however. Too many separations early in life could erode and destroy it. Years before theories of attachment and loss became dogma among developmentalists, Taft and her colleagues relied on help as a proxy for love. Children who could use the former would be able to experience the latter.

Helping Birth Parents

Helping children was impossible unless birth parents and adopters agreed to helping relationships of their own. Birth parents were the first link in the helping chain. Although many adopted children were born to married parents, especially during the early part of the century, unmarried mothers always attracted a disproportionate amount of attention because of the problems associated with illegitimacy. At its height, interpretation cast birth mothers as individuals seeking to resolve developmental dilemmas through transgressive sexuality and stigmatized maternity. Pregnancies outside of wedlock were "symptoms" of ordinary psychological struggles that had veered sharply off course. In Freudian terms, they were "hysterical dissociation states in which the girls act out their incest phantasies as an expression of the Oedipal situation."[117] Familiarity with psychoanalytic terminology or concepts such as the oedipal crisis was hardly necessary to believe that women making decisions about surrendering children needed help, often very badly.

According to an insightful survey by Lilian Ripple, social work perspectives on illegitimacy shifted decisively away from "protective authoritarianism" and toward "psychodynamically based individualization" around 1933.[118] Whereas efforts in the 1910s and 1920s had equated children's needs with regulations tightly binding birth mothers to their caring obligations, interpretation concentrated almost exclusively on the disturbed psychology of the birth mother and her involvement in the casework relationship. Empirical and statistical research on illegitimacy during the interwar period took an interpretive turn that favored adoption by separating children's and mothers' interests.

Maud Morlock lived on both sides of this sea change. A staff member of the Connecticut Children's Aid Society in the 1910s, Morlock was steeped in the Progressive view that separating mothers and babies was no solution either for unmarried women or for their innocent children, whose lives and welfare were jeopardized by placement.[119] When Morlock moved to Washington, D.C., to work for the USCB as a consultant specializing in services to unmarried mothers, she received desperate requests for assistance from unmarried women around the country. By the late 1930s, Morlock's thinking mixed newer psychology with older beliefs about female victimization and the preservation of blood ties. For example, she suggested that unmarried mothers might benefit as much as children from living in foster homes. Foster home placement was welcome not only because it allowed unmarried women to retain custody of their children but also because it promised a more therapeutic environment than the typical maternity home. "If the girl has never experienced a satisfying relationship to her own mother, the foster mother may become a mother substitute to her," Morlock explained.[120] Exposure to normal family life was frequently a way to help women who came from "broken homes" that were tumultuous, irregular, and unhappy. Even brief residence in a normal family might have long-term benefits, adjusting women's personalities and influencing their decisions and behavior long after they left the shelter of casework.

Morlock understood that unmarried mothers faced tangible problems too, including lack of money, employment opportunities, and family and community support. The advantages and disadvantages of domestic service—which allowed some women to keep and care for their children while also isolating them in exploitive working conditions—were matters of constant debate, for instance. To really help birth mothers required addressing economic and psychological needs simultaneously. "Many unmarried mothers are not aware of the meaning of their behavior or of the influence of their life experiences," Morlock explained.[121] Whether the birth mother decided to keep or surrender her child, she had to "learn to know herself better."[122]

Birth fathers were shadowy figures, but interpretation accorded them new significance. To the extent that "putative" fathers had been noticed at all, they were targets of quasi-criminal legal proceedings designed to extract financial support and pressure them into marriage. The message of professional help transformed fathers' profile as it had mothers'. They represented a cross section of society and were united more by their psychological needs than by economic or social characteristics. Unmarried fathers were as neurotic, as driven by unconscious needs as their female counterparts.[123]

With personalities crying out for adjustment, these men too deserved a place in the widening circle of help. Although birth fathers were defensive and prone to denying paternity, Morlock knew that some would appreciate agency services. "When he realizes that the social worker's attitude is one of understanding rather than judgment," the birth father's attitude would change for the better, she argued.[124] Casework that used "mental catharsis" to help boys and men become more responsible would help those individuals and prevent illegitimacy from recurring.[125] Men needed to learn that their sexual behavior revealed feelings of inferiority, fears of homosexuality, and anxieties about their own virility. To be an unmarried father was to act out unresolved oedipal conflicts, just as women did.[126] In theory, men and women may have needed help equally, but in the era before DNA testing allowed conclusive determinations of paternity, men's needs were quite unequal in practice. The work of interpreting birth parents focused largely on mothers.

Helping Adoptive Parents

Of all the parties to adoption, applicants for adoptive parenthood, whose social status was likely to equal that of their helpers, were ultimately subjected to the most thoroughgoing interpretation. There were several reasons why. First was the turn toward nurture in the nature-nurture debate. During and after the 1930s, environmentalist theories overtook hereditarianism, suggesting that the qualities children brought with them into new families mattered far less than the interpersonal environments that surrounded them after arrival. Social workers occasionally noted that adoptees' new kin would include siblings, cousins, aunts, uncles, and grandparents, but parents were the font of nurture. They were the ones who created and maintained the relationships that determined developmental outcomes, children's happiness, and the success or failure of adoption itself. In adoptive families, adoptive parents were the architects of belonging.

Adoptive parents were also vulnerable to interpretation because, quite simply, they could be. Birth parents and their children were givens in the adoption process; their sheer existence demanded aid. Adopters, in contrast, were volunteers, selected and made into parents through the adoption process. Adults who wanted a child badly enough to request that an agency help them obtain one were unlikely to antagonize those with the authority to grant or deny their wish, especially when they believed the sort of child they wanted was in short supply. This situation gave applicants incentives to cooperate, but it also gave them reasons to resent the people who claimed to help them and hide anything they believed might prejudice their case. Adoption professionals were acutely aware of the pressures these adults faced: trying to make a good impression while fearing judgment. The unavoidable awkwardness of having to apply for parenthood, professionals argued, was really a boon. In psychoanalytic terms, it generated "transference reactions" that suffused the helping relationship with feelings of guilt and fear left over from the applicants' childhoods.[127] It placed personalities into sharp relief, exposed secret problems, and helped predict the quality that mattered most, aptitude for parenthood.

Exploitable therapeutic opportunities were conveniently built into every phase of the adoption process. Application, home study, placement, and supervision all facilitated inquiry and education. After requesting a child, would-be adoptive parents were supposed to display their qualifications and need simultaneously, a delicate feat. Adults had to prove their penchant for personal growth, on the one hand, while submitting to inspection for pathology, on the other. Doing so easily, calmly, and without discernable discomfort showed that they welcomed help and might be worthy of a child. So official was this interpretation that by the 1950s, national standards defined the adoption process as "an experience which may bring about change and growth in applicants' attitudes and expectations."[128] Through casework, would-be parents "can indicate their flexibility and adaptability to adoptive parenthood."[129] The work of interpretation prompted adopters to vacate roles as morally virtuous altruists and assume a new status as dependent clients.

Motives, Good and Bad

The problem of motivation illustrated how important interpretation became in adoption during the interwar era. Why adopt? Like many other questions, the answers that applicants gave could not be trusted, which is precisely why interpretation mattered. Social workers were charged with distinguishing good motivations from bad and examining the truths hidden beneath the reasons applicants gave for wishing to adopt. Interpretation implied investigation and discrimination. If couples possessed normal motivations, then chances were that their ability to be good parents would be normal too. But because abnormal motivations were unfortunately just as common, it was the responsibility of helping professionals to recognize them in advance, thus preventing children from growing up in families that endangered their developmental well-being.

Charlotte Towle, another leading social work educator, was among the first to identity the psychological salience of motivation in child placing. Towle was a little younger than Jessie Taft, but the two women's careers and lives displayed similar patterns. Towle was born in Butte, Montana, in 1896, and in 1919 she graduated from Goucher College in Baltimore, where she discovered that teaching was one of the only feasible options for educated women who wanted independent lives. World War I drew her into work for the Red Cross, and that led her to the U.S. Veterans Bureau in San Francisco in 1921, where she displayed such finesse that she was sent all over the state to train Veterans Bureau workers in history-taking and other casework techniques. By 1925, she was the director of Psychiatric Social Service at the U.S. Neuropsychiatric Hospital in Tacoma, and a Commonwealth Fund fellowship allowed her to enter the new field of social work. In 1926, she earned her degree from the New York School of Social Work, one of the first students granted a certificate in psychiatric social work under the direction of Marion Kenworthy.

Towle went on to direct the Home-Finding Department at the Children's Aid Society of Pennsylvania, where Taft had worked just a few years earlier. Towle knew Taft and Robinson and considered Taft's philosophy a dominant influence on her thought. After several years in New York, spent working at the New York Institute for Child Guidance with David Levy and other psychoanalytically inclined psychiatrists and supervising social work students, Towle joined the faculty of the University of Chicago's School of Social Service Administration. Its dean, Edith Abbott, a major figure in the history of social welfare, described Towle as "an extremely attractive, rather brilliant person."[130]

Towle taught at Chicago from 1932 until her retirement thirty years later and became a professional cause célèbre during the McCarthy era for suggesting that public assistance was the right of every citizen.[131] At a school better known for its commitment to social policy than casework, she made the study of psychology and psychoanalysis basic for all social work specializations. Her involvement with the American Association of Schools of Social Work placed her in high demand as an agency consultant. A specialist in marriage and childhood, Towle was remembered as deeply maternal, "in its best sense of nurturing combined with respect for the separate self of another."[132] She never married or raised children herself, but shared her life with another woman, "long-time friend and companion" Mary Rall, also a social worker.[133]

Towle's first publications explored the dilemmas of interpreting motivation in couples wishing to raise other people's children as their own. During the early years of professional child placing, volunteers for foster parenthood were commonly viewed as saints whose selflessness should be praised rather than "subjected to the objective scrutiny of science," except in cases of gross immorality or extreme poverty.[134] Such naiveté made Towle fume. "In this sentimental flight of fancy have been rooted innumerable maladjustments, which have wrought an injustice, not only upon the children, but also upon the parents involved."[135] Emotional diagnosis was the "raison d'être" of child-placing.[136] The children involved were scarred by deprivation and insecurity, but so were the adults.

The risk of selecting the wrong parents was not easy to control because the emotional geography of family life was difficult to assess in comparison to material welfare and outward conduct, both far simpler to observe and measure. Towle advanced the idea that the climate in which children were placed was heated and cooled by the emotional temperature of their parents' marriage. Simply put, Towle argued, good marriages produced families that were good for children. But because she also believed that "*well*-integrated marital relationships are rare,"[137] home finding became an exercise in locating emotionally healthy couples in a sea of maladjusted marriages.

Towle began her probes by collecting evidence about each parent's emotional history, dating back to childhood. Religion, occupation, recreation, and finances all offered clues not about such obvious things as how often they attended church or how much money they had but about how these issues influenced the intimacy between husband and wife. Relational detective work was indispensable when it came to telling motivational truth from falsehood and discerning the subjective meanings that propelled the desire for children. Interpreting and adjusting the marital situation in foster homes, according to Towle, could literally save children's psychological lives.[138]

Towle hypothesized that requests for children were attempts to establish or reestablish emotional equilibrium within marriages and families. Through adoption, adults hoped to fill voids created by children's absence, death, or departure. Husbands tried to fix wives' unhappiness or nervousness. Wives tried to compensate for husbands' physical and emotional failings. Men and women alike betrayed feelings—for example, loneliness, competition, anger, and inability to love—they sometimes did not even know they possessed. Not infrequently, oblivious couples resorted to adoption to salvage rocky or ruined marriages. This reason for adopting was extremely hazardous for children. Sexual difficulties also made the marital relationship unusually tricky interpretive terrain, and Towle admitted that a majority of social workers were as uncomfortable asking questions about sex as their clients were answering them. Sex nevertheless spoke volumes about the personalities under review and their mutual adjustment. Professionals with the right combination of detachment and warmth would never detour around the topic.

The point was to distinguish what people said from what their request for a child actually meant. In the language of interpretation, "professed" motives and "basic" or "real" motives were quite different things.[139] "Individuals present their rationale for wanting a child rather than the underlying reasons," Towle explained. "The observer with the trained eye to see will often discern the deeper purposes being served in the quest for a child."[140] When couples announced that they wanted a child because they could not have children of their own, or because they had one of their own who needed a sibling, or because they had room to spare, or because they hoped to rescue an orphan, the caseworker needed to ascertain the veracity of their motive and interpret the ramifications for any child who might be placed. After 1945, infertility became so synonymous with adoption that other motivations practically disappeared from view. During the early decades of the century, however, childlessness was only one of many possible reasons to adopt.

Towle used illustrative cases to show that interpretation was at once complex and consequential. One couple, apparently happily married, requested a child because of infertility, and a boy was placed with them. The new family relationships became extremely tense, the father began to drink, and he eventually deserted the family, leaving the child "an apron string boy, hypersensitive, withdrawn, who will probably always suffer through not having worked out a constructive relationship with his foster father—an emotional identification which is so essential to the ego development of every child."[141] According to Towle, the caseworker's fatal error was overlooking the mother's active and the father's passive role in requesting a child. Not only did the man harbor reservations about parenthood, but the mother's real motive was to replace her husband with someone who was smarter, more responsive, and more likely to meet her social expectations. The victim of this interpretive blunder, of course, was the child, left fatherless for a second time. Were wives and husbands sincerely united in their desire to adopt? In the decades that followed, this question was routinely asked. Women were frequently perceived as the driving force in adoption, but too-acquiescent husbands were a danger sign. Caseworkers might have no opportunity to interview unidentified birth fathers and little time to consider the men who resided in homes where agencies paid to board children temporarily, but they could not afford to ignore adoptive fathers. These men were expected to be conventional breadwinners and emotionally engaged parents.

Even husbands and wives who shared a strong desire to add a child to the family through adoption might be acting on destructive needs. In one case, a couple wanted to adopt so that their own ten-year-old daughter, an irritable and depressed child, would have a baby sister. On the surface, the family looked normal. The physical condition of the home was superior, the parents were healthy, and the mother, Mrs. X, was "a home-loving, faithful wife, apparently devoted to her husband and child."[142] But appearances were deceptive. The parents' histories revealed that they were "two individuals with infantile emotional reactions resulting from their respective family ties."[143] Mrs. X, Towle concluded, was already overly involved with the daughter she had. Far from wanting to provide a sibling for the girl, her request for another child actually satisfied her own selfish need for "a love object."[144] Mr. X, on the other hand, something of a child himself, would have bitterly resented another child. As for the daughter, a new baby in the family would have made things worse by introducing competition and eroding her security. Adoption always expressed adult needs, according to proponents of interpretation, but some were more normal than others. Adopting in order to solve the emotional problems of someone already in the family was a motivation to be regarded with skepticism.

Parents who wished to adopt for the sake of the adoptee could also do harm by investing too completely in the child. Eight-year-old Jackie was adopted at the age of six months and had never been left alone. The needy parents, who had not told Jackie about his adoption out of fear of losing his love, were "using him as a source of emotional satisfaction," centering "a veritable emotional orgy" on the parent-child relationship that unbalanced what had once been a well-adjusted marriage.[145] Jackie's domineering behavior and his propensity to swear and steal were outgrowths of his parents' overinvolvement. Interestingly, Towle did not dwell on the fact that Jackie should have been told about his adoption. Instead, she maintained that the family's problems could have been prevented if this couple had adopted a second or even a third child. Adopted children were always supposed to be wanted for their own sakes, but in this case adopting for Jackie's sake made sense. Not "having all their emotional eggs in one basket" would have helped him by dividing his parents' attention.[146]

Interpreting Infertility

Like normality and abnormality, good and bad motives were relative, not absolute. They had to be contextualized to be correctly interpreted. "Sterility" (a term used more frequently than "infertility" before the 1960s) illustrated this point. Inability to conceive was a common motivation for adoption that professionals also considered a sensitive barometer of marital adjustment and parental capacity. Infertility had not always been a decisive prerequisite for adoption, but childless couples were surely always attracted to adoption. By midcentury, infertility loomed so large that most agencies refused to consider applications from couples able to conceive children on their own. In 1943 Louise Wise Services began rejecting couples who already had or could have children of their own, even when they expressed a preference for adoption. The agency requested confidential medical reports from physicians to verify applicants' infertility and use as a diagnostic tool in the adoption process.[147] By the early 1960s, infertility was so well established as a qualification that adopting was tantamount to "an overt admission of biological failure," according to one Mayo Clinic psychiatrist.[148] If children made families and infertile couples could not have them, it was logical to privilege infertility as a qualification and allocate children to couples who would not otherwise be parents. Matching, which sought to bring adults together with children they might have conceived themselves, further cemented the association between infertility and adoption.

Translating infertility into a positive motivation for adoption paradoxically required that couples first work long and hard to correct their reproductive breakdown and have children of their "own." How long had they been trying to conceive? How many doctors had they seen? How much time and effort had they devoted to treatment? The more strenuously couples resisted their infertility, the more they appeared to want children, but the more strenuously they resisted their infertility, the further they were from "resolving" it. Many adopters experienced this kind of interpretation, unsurprisingly, as a double bind.

As infertility loomed larger, it became more apparent that adoption was a last resort, which posed impossible challenges for even the best-intentioned efforts to normalize and authenticate adoptive kinship. The poignancy of this paradox was best illustrated by couples who honestly admitted that they preferred to have children naturally and wished to adopt because they believed adoption would cure infertility and induce pregnancy. The probability that adoption might facilitate conception, hotly debated in the medical community, was sustained by anecdote, desperation, eugenics, and popular belief in the psychological forces at play in human fertility.[149] Although couples hoping that adoption would facilitate pregnancy were merely expressing culturally sanctioned preferences for natural kinship, they were often dismissed as neurotic by social workers.[150] Couples were expected to want their own children above all else, but they were also expected to want adopted children for their own sake.

Interpreting infertility reached beyond asking whether couples were infertile to asking *why*. According to Viola Bernard, who studied the psychosocial dynamics of reproduction for years at Columbia Medical School, childlessness might be "organic" or "psychogenic," and the difference made all the difference in assessments of parental capacity.[151] "Organic" causes

of infertility were medically explicable and figured infertility as a permanent state, located in the reproductive physiology of husband, wife, or both.
Couples afflicted with infertility of this kind were childless against their will.
Innocent victims of reproductively uncooperative bodies who negotiated
their infertility with emotional maturity "offer the most hopeful prognosis
for adoption and for adopted children."[152] In contrast, the causes of "psychogenic" infertility were lodged in the mind, and that made childlessness
mysterious and suspicious. Couples without children, but without any authoritative reason for not having them, might overcome their infertility at
any moment. Giving them a child might unfairly deprive another couple
with absolutely no hope of ever having their own. Even couples who had
experienced multiple miscarriages were sometimes denied children because
their reproductive potential was theoretically intact.[153]

The most serious risk was that psychogenic infertility represented hostility toward parenthood unknown to the applicants themselves. Would-be
parents whose childlessness could not be medically explained might be ter-
rified of pregnancy and childbirth, reproductively paralyzed by neurosis, or
unconsciously convinced they would make inadequate parents. "Psychogenic factors . . . may be far from evident to the casual observer," noted an
intake report for 1943, but they betrayed dangers "which we most desire to
avoid for the adopted child."[154] "This is one of the most difficult things to
get at," social worker Helen Fradkin admitted, "because the woman is not,
certainly, going to come to the adoption agency and say, 'I am afraid to have
a child of my own, I'd rather adopt one.'"[155]

There were occasional exceptions to the rule that psychogenic infertility
was impossible for clients to detect and ominous for children, and these
vindicated the work of interpretation by showing that no easy-to-follow recipes for kinship existed. One thirty-four-year-old social worker with experience in the adoption field worried that she had "no maternal feeling" and
sought psychiatric help over a period of years before applying for adoption,
admitting that "her infertility is probably emotionally caused."[156] In the case
of a sympathetic young couple from Ohio whose decade-long infertility
was inexplicable, the agency bent its own rules, allowing them to apply for
adoption in 1944 as a way of encouraging them to get pregnant.[157]

The difficulty of determining the underlying meaning of infertility led
some agencies to experiment with projective tests as an interpretive tool.[158]
Mr. and Mrs. W of New Jersey, for instance, were given a Rorschach test in
1947 and told that there were no right or wrong ways to respond, but Mrs. W
worried anyway that the test might spoil their chance to adopt. Nothing out
of the ordinary was discovered about Mrs. W, whose results suggested she

was a "'*normal*' subject."[159] Mr. W, however, turned out to be a "neurotic personality" whose sterility was linked to castration fears.[160] He was insecure, impulsive, and lacking in imagination, but, according to the Rorschach, without severe emotional disturbance. A decade later in New York, Mr. and Mrs. R were not so fortunate. Her test showed "many hysterical features intermingled with the obsessive tendencies" along with "the compulsive orientations and oral dependent attitudes.[161] "He expresses chronically frustrated passive receptive longings," noted psychologist Miriam Siegel, who administered the tests. "Mr. R expresses concern about his masculinity with emphasized homosexual inclinations."[162]

Even without resort to projective tests, the significance of infertility was apparent. Viola Bernard suggested that the first sight of a potential son or daughter could reveal all manner of unconscious reservations. At this crucial moment, seemingly ideal couples might have qualms that disclosed how much the prospect of adoption actually disappointed or disturbed them. Confronted with someone else's child, tangible evidence of their own inability to conceive, some couples panicked. On first seeing Joel in 1951, the Bs had an "extreme and unrealistic reaction": they called the child "moronic," proving only their neurotic wish for "a guarantee against abnormality . . . , behind which was the pain of their own infertility."[163] Such reactions proved they still harbored secret fantasies of having children of their own and remained mired in feelings of guilt and inferiority—all signs of "the unconscious rebellion against parenthood."[164]

In one detailed 1941 case study of psychogenic infertility, the wife's inability to conceive was attributed to gender trouble. Unable to rectify her own parents' disappointment at having a girl rather than a boy, Mrs. A was caught in a trap of "parental transference" rooted in childhood.[165] As an adult, her career symbolized the hopeless struggle to be like a man and reinforced the unconscious masculinity that sabotaged her achievement of true womanhood through pregnancy. Even though Mrs. A had undergone more than five hundred hours of psychoanalysis between 1932 and 1940, she was only dimly aware of the psychodynamic forces permeating her own reproductive life. The kind of infertility that menaced children would not announce itself. It needed interpretation.

Infertility illustrated how complicated it was for adoption to achieve authenticity. Infertile couples were expected to adopt, but preferences for adoption were no more normal or natural than infertility itself. Even when couples appeared to have resolved their feelings about infertility, the inability to have their "own" children could compromise their ability to create a nurturing family environment. Infertility left people less than whole, and the expectation that adoption might heal them or compensate for their loss was far from assured.[166] Childlessness could be remedied, but infertility was often a permanent condition. Giving children to infertile couples would make them parents, but adoption could not guarantee that they would perform normally.

––––––––

The establishment of child study and developmental science, the energetic sensibility of maternalist reformers, and social work infused with psychiatric and psychoanalytic insights were the historical sources of interpretation in adoption. They boosted professional confidence that adoptive families could be helped to approximate the interior subjectivity of real families and not merely their outward appearance. Like regulation, interpretation promised to reduce risk and increase certainty and success. The disquieting prospect in this case was that kinship would not feel or be "real." Adjusting personalities and appraising motivations were interpretive operations that might help adoption at least come close.

By emphasizing the deprivations that all parties to adoption experienced as deviations from norms, professional helpers ironically made it harder for adoption to contest the blood bias that stigmatized adoption. Children and adults who came together in adoption shared emotional histories that twisted their personalities, begged for adjustment, and turned them into subjects of professional casework. Interpretation sought to salvage, redeem, and compensate them. Such efforts could never achieve equality in the face of an enduring equivalence between difference and deficiency.

Therapeutic professionals prided themselves on detecting invisible emotional currents that imperiled adoption, an ability they trusted to prevent the formation of unhealthy families that were bad for adults and worse for children. But difference did not disappear after families were formed. The challenge of "telling" adopted children about their status, for instance, suggested that adoption was different not simply because children were given up or taken in but because it remained forever distinctive. It stood to reason that adoption itself—and not simply loss and pain preceding adoption—predicted trouble and trauma. The point of interpretation, like the point of kinship by design, was improvement. Yet interpretation saturated adoptees' development with an aura of abnormality and endowed birth and adoptive parents with ongoing needs for help. In theory, authenticity was cherished as an ideal. In practice, interpretation made getting to realness a never-ending project for children and adults afflicted by spoiled identities.

PART TWO

Standardization and
Naturalization, 1930–1960

CHAPTER FOUR

Matching and the Mirror of Nature

Kinship by design promised that a combination of expanded state power, professional oversight, psychological interpretation, and empirical research would lessen the dangers of adoption and make it more secure and authentic. Formal steps toward governing adoption, such as revised state laws, however, could not offer protection if basic safeguards such as investigation, supervision, and systematic record keeping were ignored in day-to-day practice. The earliest adoption field studies, as we have seen, revealed that regulations, when they did exist, were often not enforced. Design was more often an aspiration than an accomplished fact.

This chapter considers two key elements of adoption modernization: the matching paradigm and the evolution of professional standards in adoption practice. Their common goal was to predict and control the uncertainties of adoption. Matching held adoption up to the mirror of nature, and standards subjected adoption to systematic management. In both cases, families were deliberately made, even when design practices aimed to make them appear as if they were not. The idea of nature exerted moral authority over human social arrangements—to define them as appropriate, invariant, and good or as transgressive, contingent, and bad—that went largely uncontested in the early twentieth century in the United States.[1] Matching made kinship through effort-filled social operations that simulated the appearance, stability, and authenticity that were assumed to be effortless products of nature. Standardization made kinship according to plan so that its outcomes could first be made visible, then carefully measured, and ultimately improved. As rational methods, matching and standardization subjected family making to novel forms of scrutiny, discipline, and calculation. The paradoxical point was to design kinship so seamlessly that adoptive families did not appear to be designed at all.

The Matching Paradigm

Until the late 1960s, matching was the dominant paradigm in adoption; it promised to deliver naturalness and authenticity. According to the matching ethos, the best adoptive families never betrayed their adoptive status by declaring their difference. In practice, matching required that adoptive parents be married heterosexuals who looked, felt, and behaved as if they had, by themselves, conceived other people's children.[2] Exacting specifications aspired to create families that appeared to be authorized by nature rather than by society. Successful matching erased itself, making the social design of adoption invisible.

The disadvantage of social arrangements in comparison with natural ones was the rationale for matching, but emulating nature was paradoxical during an era when nature was placed in constant, unprecedented jeopardy. Far from reinforcing the power of nature, modernity made the social direction of both human and nonhuman nature tangible achievements to be feared and celebrated. Nature's moral and cultural power was magnified just as its material power was dramatically checked and challenged by capitalist economic imperatives and public policies that pursued the domination of nature for purposes ranging from agriculture and energy to reproduction.

The reproductive nature that matching copied was characterized by continuities of appearance and intellect. Its standard was sameness.[3] "There need be no question of superiority or inferiority raised in a rule to limit placements generally to similar personal, racial, or national types," pointed out one advocate of matching in 1919. "No good can come from, and much harm may be done by, wilful violations of customs and comity in the placement of children."[4] To deliberately place children with parents who looked nothing like them was not merely a violation of nature's aesthetic, according to this view, but an act of callous disregard for adoptees' primary need: to belong in a way that forged sturdy links between past, present, and future. Belonging depended on identification, identification depended on similarity, and similarity was tantamount to realness. So axiomatic were these associations that the ubiquity of discontinuity (physical, intellectual, and temperamental) in families made naturally was rarely noticed. When it was, it was deemed irrelevant to adoption. Variation might be tolerable in kinship stabilized by nature, but it constituted a direct threat to kinship founded on artifice.

Matching made many twentieth-century adoptions historically unprecedented, ambitious projects in which authenticity was achieved through simulating biogenetic kinship. Constructing complete and transparent substitutes for natal kin relied on matching visible characteristics—including eye, hair, and skin color—as well as more elusive qualities associated with mentality. Intellectual matching mattered because adoptive children and parents typically came from different economic and cultural worlds, where different expectations about intelligence and education prevailed. Especially before midcentury, the class backgrounds of surrendering and adoptive parents were likely to be very different. Transforming a child from "waif" to "somebody to be considered" consequently involved altering his or her outward appearance with clothing and hairstyle, both proxies for a dramatic shift in social opportunity.[5] Adoption moved children born at the bottom and on the margins of society into working-, middle-, and upper-class homes.

Beginning with Minnesota in 1917, many states moved to keep records of adoptions confidential, except to the "parties in interest and their attorneys and representatives of the State board of control," a policy that promoted matching by erasing the documentary traces of natal families and institutionalizing adopters' exclusive entitlement to their children.[6] The architects of confidentiality not only intended to shield adoptive families from unwanted publicity and stigma but also hoped that having states issue new birth certificates making it appear as if children had been born into their adoptive families would encourage autonomous and permanent kinship.[7] During the post–Word War II era, confidentiality was overtaken by secrecy, which prevented birth parents and adopters from learning one another's identities and precluded reunions, even after adoptees were adults. Matching made adoption real by making natal kin disappear, literally. It meant that the original families of adoptees ceased to have any legal standing or social meaning at all.

Physical Resemblance

In their simplest form, matching practices aimed to unite children with parents who looked like them because resemblance was only natural. Physical descriptions were standard features of case recording. "She is not a very attractive girl, has light brown hair, gray eyes, medium build," wrote one social worker on first meeting a birth mother in October 1944.[8] Adoption applications and home studies invariably included sections on "physical description."[9] "Mrs. A is a short, dark-haired, dark-eyed girl with a vivacious face. . . . Mr. A, also dark of hair, has blue eyes."[10] "She looks almost Italian," noted another social worker of a Jewish adoption applicant, and "has very olive but lovely smooth skin, dark brown eyes and smooth brown hair." Her husband "has dark curly hair, brown eyes and rather finely etched sensitive features."[11]

Preferences that would-be parents expressed about children's physical appearance were carefully documented, too. Desires to match could not have been more explicit. Adopters specified eye, skin, and hair color and explained their tastes in racial, ethnic, and national terms. "Your agent promised me a nice red-haired boy," noted one applicant early in the century. "I have a red-haired wife and five red-haired girls and we want a boy to match."[12] In 1925 one adoptive mother in Connecticut brought her two-year-old son into a clinic, complaining that he "awakens recurrent repulsion. . . . She dislikes his fair complexion and above all she dislikes his green eyes."[13] During World War II, the Gs of Arkansas rejected a girl they found "small and peculiar looking. This baby you offered us did not measure up to our desires at all," wrote Mr. G in a letter to the social worker; he explained that he wanted a "round-faced baby" with "mediumly-round features" to match his wife. "We still want a baby but I am not willing to take one when I am not satisfied with its features."[14] A few years later, a Connecticut couple explained that they were "not interested in J because they could not accept her coloring being darker than theirs."[15] Another couple agreed "they were willing to consider a child of Hungarian heritage or with an Italian strain, providing that their coloring was not too much of a contrast."[16] In New York, Mr. and Mrs. B explained that although they were Jewish themselves, they did not want a child who was "heavy Jewish looking" and therefore preferred one who was only half-Jewish.[17] In Orange, New Jersey, Mr. and Mrs. F rejected baby B out of hand in 1946 because he was half Italian. Their agency insisted that baby B "in no way resembled the 'typical Italian' . . . but was a rather large baby with fair skin, light hair and blue eyes," but Mr. and Mrs. F were adamant that his ethnic appearance was unacceptably different.[18] Physical resemblance was an obvious, popular feature of kinship perceived as real.

Even when parents were not choosy, overt differences in physical features were thought to make adoptive kinship riskier. A case used for teaching at the New York School of Social Work described the Marcuses, an average Jewish couple whose only wish was for a healthy infant. Although they insisted that coloring and features did not matter, the agency thought otherwise. Because "Mr. and Mrs. M. are fairly small people, a child of more fragile build would be most suitable," the worker concluded. "A good average child is needed since both Mr. and Mrs. M. seem normally keen and alert. Mr. M. reads a great deal and is particularly interested in books on psychology, Freud, etc."[19] Physical appearances not only mattered in themselves; they were also important because the feeling of kinship was contingent on resemblance. "A dark-haired, dark-skinned child in a family of redheads would stand right out as different. What he desperately needs is to belong. So agencies do try to match general coloring, and even bony structure. It isn't happenstance that happily adopted children grow to look like their adopted parents. They started out quite a bit that way—the agency saw to that!"[20]

The notion that resemblance expedited love and difference spelled trouble was accepted by adopters and social workers alike. On first meeting baby John, selected because he looked like his potential adopters, Mrs. Z said, "Oh what a beautiful child!" and "compared his appearance to that of her husband. . . . Further comments were made about the manner in which in his physical appearance, J. seemed to fit in."[21] Antonio, however, was an Irish-looking child in a family of Italian heritage. He became an "ugly duckling" and rewarded his adopters with bad behavior.[22] In theory, children were matched with parents who might have produced them naturally, and agencies were proud when "the baby's own mother and his foster mother are said to look so much alike that they would be taken for twin sisters."[23] In practice, matching was rarely so flawless. "All that one can do is avoid contrasts that are too glaring between the background of the true and that of the adoptive parents."[24] The closer to nature families looked, the closer to realness children got.

Religious Likeness

Matching was more than a crude mandate that children *look* like their parents. Its purpose was to ensure that children *be* like their parents, too. From the outset, adoption laws stipulated that children and adults should be matched on the basis of religion. In a country where religious freedom was a cherished value, adoption laws treated religion as a birthright, not an individual choice. "Religious protection" statutes required children be placed with foster parents of their "own" religion (meaning the religion of the child's birth parents) "when practicable." In the nineteenth century, when public child welfare services were often delivered by private, Christian organizations and public agencies were typically dominated by the Protestant evangelical spirit, children tended to be matched with the preferred religion of the placing organization rather than that of natal kin.[25] Cases of Catholic children placed in Protestant homes (the orphan trains were the most notorious example) were especially egregious. Many of these children were of school age, with established religious identities and affiliations.

Protestants made these transreligious placements in the name of child rescue, but Catholics considered them child stealing. Thus immigrant communities in the late nineteenth and early twentieth centuries embraced matching laws, which promised to retain custody of children, preserve corporate religious identities, and stave off the corrosive force of assimilation. Progressive child welfare advocates agreed that religion was a bright line, never to be crossed, blurred, or erased when making adoptive placements. Scrupulous religious matching distinguished expert services from commercial and amateur adoptions, which disregarded children's spiritual interests whenever commerce or sentiment exerted a more powerful claim. Agencies went beyond requiring foster parents and children to be of the same religion; they expected regular church attendance and considered religious education a parental charge as basic as temperance, industriousness, and good moral character.[26] Adults who adopted through agencies typically signed forms pledging to send children to church; only promises to send them to school were equally common. Especially vigilant agencies, such as the Pennsylvania Children's Aid Society, actually tried to verify families' habits of religious observance independently by sending inquiries to clergy. But religious behavior would certainly have been difficult to monitor or enforce. Most child placers collected little or no postplacement data about the religious lives of children entrusted to their care.[27]

Violations of religious matching occurred despite the consensus that it was necessary and natural, and they provoked repeated controversies during the first half of the twentieth century. Judges were considerably more lenient than agency professionals about religious matching. Because laws mandating adoption investigations took decades to pass, and even then did not always require inquiry *before* placement, judges faced the distressing prospect of breaking familial ties that had already formed. Understandably reluctant to do this, they approved occasional petitions involving mixed marriages, atheists, and agnostics well into the twentieth century.[28] Cases that explicitly prioritized children's temporal and emotional welfare over their religious identities (and the preferences of birth parents) were rare, but they did occur, often because children had already lived with adopters of a different faith for many years.[29]

In other cases, religious matching conflicted with racial matching. When forty Catholic toddlers from the New York Foundling Hospital were sent to Arizona in 1904 for placement in Catholic homes, local Protestants responded with outrage and violence.[30] The orphans were white, and the local families designated to adopt them were Mexican, a racialized category that jeopardized the children's entitlement to whiteness. After the orphans were forcefully "rescued" from their Mexican families and placed where the vigilantes knew they rightfully belonged—in white Protestant homes—the case went all the way up to the U.S. Supreme Court. The Court let stand the Arizona ruling that removing the children was a humanitarian act rather than kidnapping, as the Mexicans saw it. Ideally, matching was a seamless operation in which axes of identity all pointed in the same direction. But in the competition between these children's skins and souls, race trumped religion. Matching controversies such as this one revealed how mutable identity was while upholding the allegedly immutable places of race and religion in the natural order of things.

Transreligious placements also illuminated the dynamics of adoption "supply" and "demand." Some faith communities made more and others fewer children available for adoption. Early in the twentieth century, Louise Wise, founder of the Free Synagogue Child Adoption Committee, concluded that "Jewish sentiment is peculiarly intolerant of an unmarried mother" and that Jews were hostile to children "not of [their] own blood."[31] "It is enough to make the heavens weep," she wrote after visiting New York's Hebrew Sheltering Orphan Asylum. "Poor helpless children except for powerless me!"[32] In 1910 managers of a new Jewish institution in Los Angeles called home finding "impractical" and resolved to build more asylums to house all the unwanted and neglected children who were "coered [sic] with vermin, have no manners, are lazy and unobliging."[33] In the 1910s and 1920s, child welfare officials throughout the country reported that they found it virtually impossible to locate homes for a substantial number of Jewish infants and young children.[34] By 1940 this situation had changed. Jews determined religious descent maternally, and children born to Jewish birth mothers were scarce. At midcentury, authorities conceded there were simply no Jewish children to adopt.[35] One estimate had would-be Jewish adopters outnumbering available children by a ratio of twenty-five to one.[36]

In comparison to the shortage of Jewish children at that time, children born to Catholic parents were abundant. (The balance between Protestant "supply" and "demand" was considered most even.) These realities pushed Jews toward incorporating non-Jewish children into their families and sent them beyond U.S. borders, most often to Canada.[37] Many Jewish couples turned to independent placements, which offered more flexibility than agencies about religious qualifications, but sometimes such arrangements produced unwelcome racial surprises. Sally was adopted independently by a Jewish couple in the 1950s. The Fishers took her home from the hospital when she was only four days old. By the time she reached her first birthday, her African American ancestry was quite visible even though the birth mother "was very blond, blue eyed, and had a fair complexion and it never occurred to them that Sally could be Negro."[38] The Fishers, who had adopted a white baby, David, before Sally, agonized over what to do. Pressured by friends and family, they agreed that one of the children had to be given away; raising them as siblings was simply unimaginable. They presented their dilemma to the Children's Home Society of California, where workers assured them that they were not abandoning Sally by thinking about giving her up. Sally was finally placed in a "Negro" foster family in hopes that adoptive parents might be found from among "her own people."[39] This case illustrates that demographic pressures to adopt across religious lines did not necessarily imply dissent from the matching paradigm or signal desire to acknowledge religious (or racial) difference openly. What the Fishers (and most Jewish parents) wanted was to convert white babies born to non-Jewish (usually Catholic) parents into Jewish children whose religious identities and skin color would be compatible with their own. They wanted to match.

By exposing the malleability of spiritual belonging, adoption contrasted the kind of solidarity that was achieved voluntarily with solidarity ascribed to fixed and unchosen natural givens. This was the most basic quandary of matching and adoption itself. Long before transracial and transnational adoptions became embroiled in conflict, religion raised thorny questions about identity, belonging, and the role of law in making or changing them. Was religious affiliation given by birth? Decided by parental authority? Chosen and changed according to individual preference? If so, at what age? Controversies about religious matching during the first half of the twentieth century anticipated and intersected with later debates about the place of race, ethnicity, and nation in kinship.[40]

Racial Sameness

Unlike the stipulations regarding religion, early adoption laws were silent on race, illustrating how naturalized that concept was even in the decades after 1890, when many European immigrants were successfully reracialized as white ethnics.[41] Alternatives to race matching may have been impossible to imagine, but racial sameness between parents and children was no more effortless or obvious than religious sameness. Both revealed the excruciating purposefulness—the design—of matching. In cases of nonwhite or mixed-race children, color confusion was not unusual. The need for unambiguous racial classification was most urgent at the racial borders, where ambiguous racial identities called the naturalness of race into question. Two cases from the 1920s illustrate this point. In the first, a dark-skinned girl was placed in an institution after no family could be found to accept her. Her ancestry was Italian, but white families interested in adopting perceived her as "colored" and therefore unacceptable.[42] The other involved a white-looking baby accepted for placement by the Cleveland Children's Bureau who was discovered to have an African American father. Horrified at the prospect that a white couple might adopt the child, only to discover the truth later, the agency boarded the baby temporarily and pleaded with his birth mother to take him back.[43] White professionals considered adoption all but impossible for nonwhite children. Placement across race lines was unthinkable even in cases where it might be invisible.

For every case of transracial adoption detected in advance, others were not. Because interracial sex was so violently punished and profoundly shamed, there was a good chance that white birth mothers who had ventured across the sexual color line would not admit to it. African American birth mothers, on the other hand, faced outright discrimination in adoption. The taboo surrounding interracial sex meant that adopters who believed they were taking in babies born to two white birth parents were sometimes not. Responses in these cases ranged from determination to keep children to willingness to have them removed and placed in nonwhite families. In 1945 a New York court urged a Jewish couple who had unwittingly taken a "half Negro and half Jewish" child to surrender that child to a "colored home," which they did.[44] Before 1950, transracial adoptions were so surprising and upsetting that they should probably not be characterized as transracial adoptions at all, but rather as accidents.

Even so, the potential for adoption to destabilize and transform racial status was significant enough to generate literary interest beyond the adoption world. In 1928 Charles Chesnutt, one of the best-known African American authors of the early twentieth century, wrote a novel, *The Quarry*, about an adoption mix-up that illustrated the social choices shaping racial identity.[45] The plot revolved around Donald, adopted as a baby from an orphanage by a prosperous white couple, the Seatons, who had no children of their own. When Donald was two, the orphanage physician discovered that Donald's father was "a light mulatto." The Seatons briefly considered keeping the fact of Donald's parentage secret in order "to give him a white man's chance in life," but decided to turn Donald over to a middle-class black family, the Glovers, who set out to "make a good Negro of him."[46]

They succeeded. Donald grew up handsome and brilliant. He attended a black college and then Columbia University, where he pledged his life to racial uplift. At the end of the novel, the first adoptive father, Mr. Seaton, learns that Donald's birth father was not a "mulatto" after all, but the son of a renowned New England family that had come over on the *Mayflower*, and that his birth mother traced her ancestry to the Italian nobility. When Donald is informed that he is white after all, he renounces his racial birthright in order to maintain his blackness, honor his family ties, marry the African American woman he loves, and pursue his political goals. Donald's story reversed the typical transracial adoption plot—in which nonwhite children passed as white when they really were not—but it made the same point. Racial status was subject to accident and legal change. Social rather than natural acts governed children's racial identities in adoption.

Racial uncertainty was at least as common as racial error in adoption, where adjudicating race required time and expertise. Casual disregard for the complexities of racial status was one of the many reasons why adoption needed to be regulated, according to early reformers. To increase profits, unscrupulous and commercial brokers ignored race matching when they could, and sentimental placements naively assumed that white-looking children were actually white. One 1915 Boston case involved a young unmarried woman, suffering from venereal disease, whose own racial background mixed "Indian and colored blood." She used newspaper ads to locate adopters for her "fine looking little boy" whose father was unknown. As reported, the child was "probably adopted by some unsuspecting family," and the "almost certain tragedy ahead is offspring combining Indian, colored and white blood—and syphilis."[47] In adoptions that crisscrossed racial lines, the prospect of future generations of mixed-race people was considered as dangerous as combining parents and children of different races. Eugenic concerns mingled with rules that segregated families as strictly as schools and neighborhoods.

Anthropologists and geneticists were consulted in cases of problematic race matching.[48] During the 1940s, Louise Wise Services consulted Harry Shapiro, of the Museum of Natural History, when cases of white-looking children born to Jewish mothers and African American fathers first came to the agency's attention. The goal was to determine whether these children could safely pass with Jewish parents.[49] This practice was continued by many other New York agencies through the 1960s.[50] In New Orleans in the early 1950s, Tulane anthropologist Arden King was asked to examine the skin, nose, lips, hair, and skull of a toddler born to a white woman but placed with African American foster parents after the girl's rapidly darkening skin provoked suspicions that "the child possibly was a nigger."[51] Sheldon Reed, director of the Dight Institute for Human Genetics at the University of Minnesota, frequently advised adoption agencies, too.

Agencies wanted to know two things: would mixed-race children be able to "pass for white," and would the future children of those children be "throwbacks," reverting to more racialized appearances?[52] Such concerns did not disappear after vulgar racism was repudiated. Sheldon Reed epitomized how anxiety about adoptees' racial status straddled two distinct eras in the history of eugenics: the pre–World War II movement, with its programs of sterilization and race betterment, and the chastened post-Nazi era of everyday hereditarianism, during which the horror of race mixing and degeneration transmuted into more polite forms, such as genetic counseling.

Adoption trends reflected these changes. After 1945, shortages in the supply of "blue-ribbon" babies (i.e., healthy white infants) pushed some white adopters to consider the products of "racial crosses."[53] These adopters were not necessarily volunteers for transracial adoption, and mixed-race children who looked that way remained notoriously difficult to place. Catholic Social Service of San Francisco tried desperately to find homes for children whose backgrounds were Filipino, Japanese, Chinese, Negro, and Mexican during the 1950s, but it did not receive a single application from any family interested in a child of a different race.[54] In 1958 a couple specifically applied to the Spence-Chapin Adoption Service for a mixed-race child but "was very definite in wanting to consider a part Puerto Rican or Negro child if there would be nothing in the appearance to suggest this."[55] In 1962 an abandoned baby was left in a New York institution for more than a year because, according to the social worker, "he is a fair skinned child with a broad nose, and kinky black hair, evidently the product of an interracial couple."[56] By midcentury, agencies knew that limiting adoptions to placements of white infants was limiting adoption severely. White families who refused children whose background included any Puerto Rican or Native American ancestry (African American ancestry was still largely out of the question) were becoming a problem.[57] Matching remained a powerful paradigm because the naturalization of sameness retained a powerful appeal.

Even in the small number of adoptions frankly acknowledged as transracial, matching was the paradoxical ideal.[58] At the Dight Institute, Reed and his colleagues saw "babies practically every week to determine whether there is actually an appreciable amount of Negro blood present and if there is, what type of placement would be likely to be satisfactory."[59] They inspected infants' sacral spots, finger smudges, nose widths, lip thickness, eye folds, genital coloration, and hair textures. Babies were placed into five categories— from most to least white—to facilitate matching.[60] Members of the first group displayed no evidence of racial mixture, were classified as white, and were recommended for placement in white families. In the second group belonged children with such slight signs of racial mixture that Dight staff predicted they would easily pass and recommended placement in white families. The third group included children with "swarthy skin and dark eyes and/or dark hair." Unable to pass as the children of fair parents, these children were recommended for placement in families with Mediterranean backgrounds. The fourth group consisted of children too obviously dark or "Negroid"-looking ever to pass, and the fifth group included all children who appeared to be Mexican or Indian.

Reed preferred not to conduct examinations before infants were six months old because of the tendency of pigmentation to darken and hair texture to thicken as babies matured.[61] Questions about skin color were particularly fraught with social significance and personal anxiety. How dark would this child become by the time the youngster entered school? How dark might the child's future children be? Reed maintained that such predictions were tricky, but his reassuring rule of thumb was that mixed-race adoptees would have children no darker than themselves, presuming they married white individuals, and that the chances of lighter children were good. One mother of a teenage girl, who had never told the girl of her adoption, became distraught when her daughter's hair turned kinky and a schoolmate called her "nigger." Afraid to tell the girl of her adoption and anxious about her prospects for marriage, this mother sought advice from Reed, who told her not to worry. As long as she married a white man, her children "won't look any more Negroid than she does."[62]

Adoptive placements that bent the racial rules slightly became more imaginable during the era of renewed civil rights mobilization after 1945. Although matching and passing remained stated goals, Reed insisted that parents who adopted children of uncertain racial heritage "must be informed of the presence of a dash of 'colored blood,' and it must be clear that they are capable of accepting the fact without emotion before the child is placed with them."[63] This acceptance of the child's background mattered because white families who expressed interest in African American children often refused "to adopt a child who was *visibly* Negro," preferring "children who were 'part-Negro' but looked Caucasian."[64]

In the early 1960s, the Dight Institute conducted a follow-up study of all the adoptees for whom it had made racial predictions since 1947. It found that "mixed racial ancestry makes original placement more difficult but it does not seem to have serious effects on later adjustments in the home and community, if the geneticist's predictions as to future appearances are correct, and placements are made accordingly."[65] Were the predictions accurate? Were matching placements actually made? Reed and his colleague

Esther Nordlie calculated that their predictions had been valid 63 percent of the time, better than chance. (Hair texture was the fickle feature that lowered the predictability rate the most.) As for matching, most agencies tried. Children in groups 1 and 2 had been placed in white families; children in group 3 were placed whenever possible with parents of Mediterranean background; and children in groups 4 and 5 were placed with mixed-race or African American couples. In some cases, agencies had not informed adopters about the child's mixed background. In other cases, telling prospective parents about children's ambiguous racial identity had proved an obstacle to any adoption at all or a source of shame so profound that adoptions were disrupted.

Beyond Appearances: "Fitting"

The belief that physical resemblance between family members was natural and necessary endured tenaciously through race matching. But as we have already seen, matching also entailed continuities beneath the skin. It aimed to make families feel as well as look natural. As early as the 1910s, professionals tried to place children with parents of roughly equal intellect. Mental matching probed aspects of identity inaccessible to visual perception but nevertheless crucial to adoption success. In the post-1945 era, a stronger emphasis on emotional readiness and compatibility emerged in the campaign to endow families with security and realness. It could be tricky to fit children into families where their belonging would be invisible, but fitting them into families where their belonging would be experienced required design skills of a different magnitude. "Fitting" involved interpretation.

Therapeutic practices sought to engineer families whose emotional relationships would be as subjectively real as those in natural families. Such emotional forms of design built on a growing literature about the salience of attachment and deprivation in development. Research conducted with institutionalized populations during the 1920s and 1930s, Anna Freud's work with displaced children in England during World War II, and Harry Harlow's famous monkey experiments in the 1950s advertised the evils of institutional child care.[66] Developmental science pinpointed the mother-child relationship—its presence and its quality—as the fulcrum of early life development. British psychoanalyst John Bowlby was perhaps the single best-known exponent of this attachment theory. Children "are not slates from which the past can be rubbed by a duster or sponge, but human beings who carry . . . the deep emotional significance of the parent-child tie which, though it can be greatly distorted, is not to be expunged by mere physical separation."[67]

Adopted children negotiated the traumatic separation common to all humans: birth. In addition, they endured painful separations from birth mothers and temporary foster mothers who had cared for them prior to adoption. In forming attachments that would make or break authentic kinship, then, adoptees began with extra counts against them. "Especially because he is adopted, he needs to know that he is wanted, that he is acceptable, that the kind of person he is, is a good kind to be."[68] Awareness of the damage that broken attachments could create encouraged the trend toward earlier placements after 1945, including newborns placed directly from the hospital.[69] Many adopters had always desired infants, but scientific validation of the emotional advantages of infant placement eclipsed earlier concerns about the riskiness of cradle adoptions. Not only did adoption early in life approximate the experience of natural families—by "starting from scratch" with the daily rhythm of baby care—but it minimized the number and length of separations for children.[70]

Matching incorporated this chronological orientation as sensitivity to early bonds increased. Professionals' new appreciation for the naturalness of infant placements encouraged the placement of younger and younger children while causing additional authenticity problems for parents whose children came to them later, sometimes years after birth. One result was that the definition of "older" adoptees became younger after 1945, and children were eventually classified as having "special needs" by virtue of age alone.

Policies that deliberately cultivated intellectual and emotional fit illustrated the social fiction at the heart of matching and helped to plant the seeds of a powerful critique of that paradigm. The shift from conceiving realness as something that could be objectively copied to something that had to be subjectively cultivated demoted blood bonds. The architecture of belonging was not, in other words, a simple matter of how families looked. Decades before the notion of "psychological parenting" influenced legal decisions about placement and custody, a thoroughly psychologized perspective on development stressed continuity of nurture over nature, love over blood.[71] "Fit" undermined resemblance as a barometer of realness, enshrined attachment as the true measure of kinship, and pointed toward a new authenticity strategy for members of adoptive families: acknowledging rather than denying difference.

The 1938 CWLA Standards

Matching was one adoption standard. Others also promised to manage the uncertainties of kinship between strangers. Between the late 1930s and the late 1950s, the standardization effort that took place under CWLA auspices represented the most ambitious effort to modernize the government of adoptive kinship. It went beyond stipulating how children and adults should be matched to account for every aspect of family making from start to finish. What was adoption for? Who was qualified to participate? How were those qualifications to be assessed and by whom?

The CWLA was concerned with placement policies from its inception, but it did not issue standards that distinguished between permanent (adoptive) and temporary (foster) placements until 1938. Reflecting the Progressive consensus that natal families should be preserved and adoption avoided whenever possible, CWLA director C. C. Carstens commented as late as 1936 that so few adoptions were arranged by professional child placers that no national list of agencies providing adoption services even existed.[72]

In the 1930s, however, the CWLA publicized adoption as a significant social problem, characterized by "shocking practices" and the deplorable absence of "intelligent public opinion."[73] "Infants and young children are given away without consideration of their best interests and in some instances are even given for cash."[74] Too many people had "unfortunate experiences with organizations for the adoption of children that are either on a commercial or a philanthropic basis," Executive Director Carstens informed the membership.[75] He singled out the Cradle, the Willows, and the Veil for special rebuke. As mentioned in chapter 1, the Cradle was the Evanston, Illinois, adoption agency founded by amateur Florence Walrath, and the Willows was a commercial maternity home based in Missouri. Like the Willows, the Veil, a commercial maternity home based in West Virginia, catered to the desperation of birth mothers and to the baby hunger of childless couples.

The best way to combat commercialism and to sideline sentimentality was to routinize family making and require that standards synonymous with safety be applied throughout the country. All the parties to adoption would benefit, according to the CWLA:

> Both family and child need protection from the hazards liable to be connected with the complicated readjustment of human lives involved in the social procedures of an adoption. The family should be safeguarded against receiving with high hopes a child who in the long years ahead will prove to be a disappointment to them. The child should be safeguarded, for instance, against becoming an artificial anchorage for an unsuccessful marriage, or against becoming the victim of a woman's desire for a baby that might be to her a plaything—when she should have acquired instead a poodle dog.[76]

The 1938 standards were publicized in a pamphlet featuring a baby positioned over the headline: "Don't Sell Us or Give Us Away" (figure 7).[77]

In the place of heartless sale, casual surrender, or impulsive acquisition, the CWLA emphasized safety over speed and superficial, material measures of quality, such as blond curls and healthy bank accounts. Trained professionals could probe beneath the surface of child development and adult motivation, averting "tragedy and disappointment."[78] Adhering to standards promised the candidate for adoption that that child would be "wanted for the purpose of completing an otherwise incomplete family group" and that "the prospective parents [would] be well adjusted to each other." Attention to standards ensured that "the identity of the adopting parents shall be kept from the natural parents" and that "the child [would] have the intelligence and the physical and mental background to meet the reasonable expectations of the adopting parents." It promised the public that adoption would "avoid encouragement of illegitimacy on the one hand and trafficking in babies on the other."[79]

Formulating adoption standards was "one of the most important pieces of child welfare work waiting to be done in this country," the CWLA declared, inseparable from regulations "as can be undertaken only by the state itself."[80] Horror stories of adoptions gone wrong in the 1930s recalled earlier narratives. Feebleminded newborns were given away without any investigation; "elderly" single women adopted babies to experiment with eccentric child-rearing theories; religious matching was disregarded; and even racial sameness was overlooked as white infants were casually transferred "to shiftless colored couple."[81] The 1938 standards warned Americans about "the countrywide scramble on the part of childless couples to adopt a child, any child, on almost any terms."[82]

To prevent couples from rushing headlong into danger, the CWLA seriously reconsidered its reluctance to place children permanently for adoption. During the economic crisis of the Great Depression, stories about adoption's growing popularity often suggested that family making was a sign of renewed faith in the noneconomic qualities that children and home symbolized.[83] John Murdock was an investment banker who lost all his stocks and bonds during the Depression but whose "investment" in two adopted children produced "dividends" that permanently altered his beliefs about wealth, demoting materialism and enshrining attachment as the true measure of value.[84] Money still mattered, of course, even during this period of struggle and scarcity. Professionals habitually inquired about potential adopters' employment and income, budgetary discipline, housing, insurance, and ability to pay for whatever education an adopted child might

Don't Sell Us

or Give Us Away

Figure 7. Illustration from a 1938 Child Welfare League of America
brochure about the importance of minimum standards in
adoption. Used by permission of Mrs. Rex Walden.

need. "A bank account and property owned are, of course, always points in the applicant's favor," one social worker wrote in 1937, stating the obvious.[85] What the precise financial qualifications for adoption should be was an enduring dilemma for professionals who recognized and even celebrated the upward social and economic mobility of adoption but who never tired of reiterating that love—and children—could never be purchased.[86]

Any evidence of a "big bull market" in "bargain-counter babies" elicited withering criticism from reformers.[87] They denounced "investors" in "baby securities" who preferred infants and toddlers over older children and, in a reversal of typical gender preferences, requested more girls than boys. One sarcastic observer even dubbed girls "market leaders" who "go like hot cakes; we simply can't keep them on hand."[88] Professionals did everything they could think of to explain to the public that curtailing consumerlike choices actually made adoption safer. Agencies did not allow applicants to look over the merchandise, "as if on a shopping expedition."[89] Wise selection of a single child fitted to a particular family was far more effective than the "poor salesmanship" displayed by independent operators who allowed parents to pick out children for themselves and then return them, for any reason at all, if expectations were not met.[90]

It was not an easy sell. Professionals were the first to admit that their negative reputations were an impediment to progress. Agency practices were "hard, cold-blooded, full of red tape, and unnecessary."[91] Long agency waiting lists and aggravating bureaucratic requirements alienated birth mothers, angered adopters, and drove them all toward independent adoption. "Are we so inflexible that we cannot find a way to serve this group in need and yet serve them in a socially safeguarded way? Before we attempt to tear down the commercial agency which is meeting their need, we must be sure our service can be made acceptable," the CWLA argued.[92] Agencies' timidity in placing infants and refusal to provide material assistance to pregnant women, professionals conceded, were partly to blame for the persistence of the black market.[93] By the 1930s, alarming "baby shortages" were already widely publicized.[94]

A study of community attitudes in New York in 1938 confirmed that public interest in adoption and complaints about professional practice were both on the rise.[95] Adopters viewed professional services not as "safeguards," but as "very trying" or even "positively inhuman" strategies for keeping adults away from the newborn infants they wanted. Until at least 1930, most agency-mediated adoptions in New York involved children over age two. Even in the late 1930s, when agencies began placing more infants, they considered a four- to six-month period of preadoptive placement an absolute minimum,[96] and many clients lost patience with "having to wait a year to find out whether the baby is going to be a blonde or brunette." Those willing to wait encountered social workers "asking the same questions over and over as though they were trying to trap them into a wrong answer."

Standardization and Its Discontents

The Market in Children

Angered by the investigations and delays that were trademarks of kinship by design, many Americans avoided agencies when surrendering and adopting children. Safety was not their first priority. Taking risks to make families was perfectly acceptable for those who expected uncertainty to accompany kinship. Adoptions that circumvented expert authority also satisfied needs that agencies dismissed or disparaged: to give up and acquire children privately, in ways that acknowledged both the rights of birth parents to do as they chose and the discretion of adopters to seek the children they preferred.

Even as standardization progressed, design was not the only family-making paradigm with passionate adherents. The market in children, which had pushed reformers toward rationalization in the first place, persisted. After several decades of standardizing and improving the services that agencies offered, baby-selling scandals still surfaced regularly. Stories about adoption commerce were, for professionals, object lessons in avoidable risk. They exemplified the commodification of children and advertised the practical and ethical advantages of the alternative, kinship by design.

On the other hand, every scandal underscored that design was not the only route to adoption. Relatively few cases described the straightforward sale of children, although publicity about the "black market" was always sensational. Many more described "gray market" placements in which birth parents, adopters, and mediators acted on a variety of interests and motives, not all reducible to profit. Some professional enemies of black market placements, convinced that gray market adoptions were too difficult to eradicate, set out to put only the most unscrupulous baby sellers out of business. Others echoed Progressive-era arguments that all independent adoptions, whether arranged by profit-hungry entrepreneurs or misguided philanthropists, were equivalent social evils. Americans continued to opt for independent adoptions, demonstrating the limits of rationalization and the enduring appeal of families made by means other than design.

The dramatic growth of a consumer society from the 1930s through the 1960s provoked anxieties about family-making fraud that originated in the market revolution of the nineteenth century.[97] Exposés of commercial adoption emphasized the folly of people who resorted to buying and selling children and the tragic rewards of resorting to a "growing racket that deals for profit in shame and fear."[98] Adoption commerce preyed on the desperation that accompanied unwanted pregnancy and childlessness. "We have dealt in black men, have shanghaied sailors, have run rum and hijacked it. . . . This year there's gold in selling babies."[99] This kind of adoption was denounced as the moral equivalent of slavery.

Yet commercial adoptions also showcased intensely popular images of child beauty and purity that were already staples of consumer culture. Photographs of adorable (invariably white) babies, complete with rosy cheeks, blonde curls, blue eyes, and winning smiles, were equally common in adoption stories and in the advertising culture that was rapidly emerging in the 1920s and 1930s. Girls were in heavy demand (figure 8). They were "more feminine, alluring; they are grand little self-advertisers and they know instinctively how to strut their stuff," especially if they were "pretty little picture-book girls."[100] Readers appreciated the appeal of such images. However sexist, they equated attractiveness and lovability with the innocence that defined romantic childhood. In the visual and literary vocabularies of modern culture, icons of childhood charm were ubiquitous as consumable representations on stationery, wallpaper, and china.[101]

Acquiring children as an act of consumption made sense. It violated the pricelessness of modern childhood to point out that consumers in the adoption market got what they paid for, to be sure, but some adopters, perhaps many, thought in these familiar terms. Jim Brown, proud new father of a baby boy in 1944, crowed that "he should be a winner—we paid a thousand bucks for him."[102] Sentiments such as these were treated as evidence of the ignorance of adopters such as Brown and his wife, Helen, and stories advocating design warned that people who purchased children as they did commodities could be easily duped and saddled for life with terrible problems. According to a 1939 article, "Normally intelligent people will pay 1,000 dollars for a baby bootlegged to them—without a scrap of authenticated history—rather than wait one or two years for a baby from an approved child-placement bureau which goes into all the ifs, ands and buts of each case. These foolishly emotional couples expect to obtain a precious human relationship out of a grab bag. They pay their money, they take their grab, and they hope for a miracle."[103]

Yet many birth parents and adopters surely did equate such private actions with freedom that ultimately benefitted adults and children. "Which is the bigger crime?" one Oregon woman scornfully asked. "To buy your

Figure 8. The adoption market was a persistent theme in the popular press.
In this 1939 illustration from *Collier's*, a couple shops for a baby
and finds that prices for girls are higher than for boys.

babies, or to have them left in these over crowded homes so someone has
a good job caring for them?"[104] Like many other people, this woman knew
a wonderful couple who had been waiting patiently for years to adopt. Unable to understand the awful delay, she castigated stingy, self-interested professionals and "unforgivable tight laws" for the growth of a black market.[105]
Relying on faith and conceiving of family making as a miraculous enterprise
could appear more humane than the impartial creed of risk management
that defined kinship by design.

The very risk taking that professionals condemned as unnecessary struck
many adopters as acceptable, even admirable, and certainly natural as they
journeyed toward kinship. In contrast, certifying children "fit for adoption"
and surrounding the adoption process with safeguards seemed calculated
and unfeeling. It "exaggerated out of all proportion" the dangers involved in
family formation, according to observers who lauded parents open to "the
great adventure of adopting a baby."[106] By the 1950s, even magazines that
had lauded agency adoption began to blame agencies for the suffering of

would-be parents. "Why You Can't Adopt a Baby" was the title of more than one account, ironically published at the moment agencies decided more children were adoptable than ever before.[107]

Complaints about kinship by design centered on well-meaning adults who were denied children and on needy children who were denied parents because of complex agency rules and unreasonable delays. One earnest young couple from suburban Chicago who got caught up in a baby-selling racket only gradually realized that what they had done left both them and their child in legal limbo. "Five years ago, Tom and I committed a shocking crime," their story began. "We have no right to parenthood except love of our baby. No proof except devotion. . . . We are trapped in a web of sham and deceit."[108] Religious matching laws, IQ tests, and arcane eligibility criteria were all blamed for situations such as this one, but professionals were the real villains. "Over and over again they have placed the observance of rigid rules above common sense and the welfare of children in their care," charged *Woman's Home Companion*, dismissing stringent standards as "bureaucratic nonsense."[109] "Social workers in the adoption field suffer from an almost total divorce from reality," concluded Rael Jean Isaac, espousing the "radical view" that standards cherished by professionals had little or no bearing on child welfare.[110] Agencies simply wanted to monopolize the adoption market and exert "the final godlike power to decree who shall be parents and who shall not."[111]

Adopters shared professionals' desire to make adoption as real as the real thing, but they sometimes advanced more lenient conceptions of authenticity. They were not as preoccupied with the risk of severe disabilities because children were placed independently before their disabilities could be known.[112] Most adopters wanted healthy children, to be sure, but the elaborate certification rituals favored by professionals were time consuming (hence an obstacle to adopting infants) and unrealistic in comparison to the premium adopters placed on obtaining newborns and infants. "Did your mother get a guarantee of perfection when you were born?" one woman snapped.[113] Who could blame adopters for seeking out children wherever they could? If anything, the willingness to assume risk proved their sincerity and tenacity.

The adoption market occasionally spilled over on to professional turf, illustrating that even child welfare agencies were not immune to the lure of money. Between the 1930s and 1950, with the assistance of juvenile court judge Camille Kelley, the Tennessee Children's Home Society arranged more than one thousand interstate adoptions.[114] Problems included little advance investigation, no probationary oversight, and the exchange of large amounts of cash. Established in 1914, the Tennessee Children's Home Society was suspended from membership in the CWLA in 1941, charged with violating the organization's basic standards. Complaints about the agency included boarding children in unlicensed and unsanitary foster homes prior to adoptive placement. As late as 1946, thirty to forty children in the society's care died in a diarrhea epidemic. The agency's director was Georgia Tann, an experienced child welfare lawyer with a national reputation as a critic of institutional care and champion of family placement. After the scandal surfaced in 1950, the society was taken over by the state's Department of Welfare. Tann died shortly afterward, but a $100,000 judgment was held against her estate nine years later. Such episodes were disturbing not only because of the obvious conflict between protecting children and baby selling but also because they exposed the tensions inherent in all forms of adoption commerce.

Changing Standards

Dramatic changes in adoption theory and practice challenged the CWLA standardization enterprise in the two decades after 1938. "Adoption as a professional service is still very young," CWLA members admitted in 1948 as they took stock of policies on infant placement, fee charging, infertility, and "hard-to-place" children.[115] In the late 1940s and early 1950s, a series of CWLA surveys and conferences revealed that professionals themselves had changed their minds about adoption basics. Which children and adults were eligible? What purpose did adoption serve? The consensus that commercial and sentimental adoptions were pernicious was firm, but professional practice remained inconsistent.

At midcentury, professionals were, according to a CWLA report, "fearful and perhaps, overly cautious."[116] "If we are going to do away with the black market or even diminish it, we must compete with it," one social worker concluded, resolving to marginalize independent child placers by outperforming them.[117] Professionals realized that many couples seeking children were willing to do almost anything to "get very young babies," and many birth mothers wanted to be "relieved of the responsibility of her child, quickly, cheaply, and easily."[118] In Florida, 74 percent of independent adoptions between 1944 and 1947 involved children placed under one month of age; 39 percent involved children under one week of age.[119] Adult desires to make the children they adopted feel "just as if he was really born to me" were powerful, and they sustained nonagency adoption and its attendant risks.[120]

To compete effectively, agencies had to deliver more of what adopters wanted—healthy white infants—faster. In 1953 more than half of all U.S.

agencies had one- to three-year postapproval waiting periods, but 8 percent of agencies required more than a four-year wait, and these long delays between application and placement were the chief complaints about agency adoption.[121] "We know that you have said we were not forgotten but we are very discouraged," wrote a New Haven, Connecticut, woman to her social worker a year after filing an application. "We certainly would like to know one way or the other how we stand. We are getting older and every year counts. If your agency doesn't want to be bothered with us, please let us know and we will try another agency. We want a baby and we are not going to give up."[122]

After consulting with leading psychiatrists and psychologists on the question of placement age, the CWLA revised its earlier position that early adoption would place unethical pressure on birth mothers, deprive infants of life-giving breast milk, and encroach on the time needed to assess and predict children's developmental potential.[123] Placing children in the first few months of life satisfied adopters' desires while shortening waiting periods. In the early 1950s, Louise Wise Services placed around 120 children annually, none of them less than three months old, but received 1,000 requests. In 1952 the agency responded by placing a seven-week-old and inaugurating a cautious program of early placement.[124]

As the perceived danger of children's hereditary taint faded, agencies relied more on the emotional resources of adoptive families as determining factors. Emphasizing emotional resources allowed agencies to justify placing children as young as possible because such early placement would faithfully mirror the natural family, blunt the trauma of separations and quickly provide babies with stable mothering figures, and construct new kin ties on the emotionally compelling basis of infant care. One authority described early placement as "more normal. It comes closer to having your own baby."[125] Even trends toward nurture invoked nature and naturalization.

If early placement was good, newborn placement might be better. It matched the chronology of birth and eliminated lengthy and expensive periods of temporary care during which children were observed and assessed. By the late 1940s, a number of agencies were experimenting with "direct placement."[126] By the early 1950s, the CWLA reversed its earlier position that newborns were especially chancy and some children innately unadoptable. Except for cases of medical difficulty or birth mother instability, babies should be placed by three months at the latest.[127] Adoption's dangers had migrated from children's bodies to familial environments. Over time, the burden of inspection and certification grew lighter for children while it grew heavier for adoptive parents, but risk remained central.

Did such shifts mark "a firm step forward in the march of human progress," as professionals argued, or merely suggest that standards were moving targets that could never be stabilized before reversing the policies that an earlier generation held dear?[128] A major national conference sponsored by the CWLA in Chicago in January 1955 captured the quandary of standards in transition. As a celebration of the "peaceful revolution" under way in American adoption, the event brought together rank-and-file social workers, leading figures in many scientific fields, and the small but growing body of investigators whose research focused on adoption itself.[129] Selected interviews, including one with child-rearing guru Benjamin Spock, were broadcast on the NBC television network.[130] Organizers produced an impressive published record of their work, including a comprehensive national survey of agency practice, a remarkable range of scientific papers, and a study of special-needs adoptions that portrayed the professionals who had formerly promised to exclude defective children as the proud authors of an inclusive definition of adoptability.[131] "Adoption is appropriate for any child without family ties who is in need of a family and for whom a family can be found to meet his need" was the mantra of the postwar adoption revolution.[132]

The main purposes of the conference, the survey, and other associated materials (called the Adoption Project) were to assemble reliable information about actual adoption practices and evaluate those practices against ideal standards. The national survey summarized the work of 270 public and private agencies in all forty-eight states as well as Washington, D.C., Hawaii, and Puerto Rico.[133] Pointing proudly to patterns of progressive agency practice far ahead of outmoded state laws and backward public opinion, the survey equated professionalism with child and family welfare and reiterated the argument that independent placements took unacceptable risks with children's lives. "Fines and imprisonment should be just as heavy as they are for practicing medicine without a license," concluded the authors.[134] Agencies envisioned a day when lawyers and doctors would stay out of adoption and all independent placements would be banned.

The "eager willingness of all adoption agencies in the United States to subject their practices to constant scientific scrutiny and to make continuous efforts to implement their services" was, according to the survey, the most noteworthy feature of adoption service at midcentury.[135] In contrast with independent child placers, professionals used the most current disciplinary knowledge from psychiatry, psychology, genetics, anthropology, sociology, medicine, and law.[136] Professional adoption services offered a reassuring combination of information, choice, expert evaluation, responsible documentation, insightful casework, confidentiality, and legal savvy.

Considering these advantages, why did independent adoptions persist? Of the explanations favored by survey respondents—bad laws; baby shortages; unscrupulous brokers; uneducated, impoverished birth mothers; and applicants who failed to qualify under agencies' high standards—"by far the most important single reason . . . was lack of public understanding."[137] Americans had to be educated to believe that agencies knew best, even if what agencies knew in 1950 was different from what they had known in 1935. This emphasis on knowing best was one of the things that adoption professionals meant when they invoked "interpretation."[138] The campaign to make adoption safer worked on two fronts. Publicity aimed to make adoption professionalism look better while also making its alternatives look worse.

Survey results illustrated that professional practice and philosophy were themselves quite variable in areas ranging from the quality of agency personnel to the services offered to children, birth parents, and adopters. Agencies agreed about the desirability of well-trained adoption workers and boasted that adoption attracted more skilled professionals than any other child welfare field. Yet in the 1950s only 51 percent of all agency staff had earned social work degrees; 22 percent had no formal social work education at all.[139] Caseworkers, more likely to be involved in day-to-day placements than either supervisors or administrators, were also short on professional credentials. The lowly salaries of adoption professionals surely reflected the gender composition of this labor force along with persistent doubts that family making required professional skill.

Variation existed from one agency to the next. For example, most agencies delivered temporary preadoptive care in the form of foster family placement, but 25 percent still placed infants in institutions such as nurseries, considered entirely unacceptable by many in the 1940s.[140] No discernable relationship emerged between the numbers of applications agencies accepted and the numbers of children they had to place; 19 percent of agencies promised to complete home studies in three to six months, but 33 percent took up to a year, and 15 percent took two.[141] There was no consensus at all about the information, if any, agencies should share with adopters about children's natal backgrounds. Some communicated nothing. Others insisted on "pertinent facts." "There is considerable disagreement on what constitutes information that is dangerous or not necessary to share," the CWLA survey found.[142]

Professionals' changing their minds changed how adoption's risks were calculated, but did not eliminate the fact of risk itself. "Adequate safeguards in adoption are possible only through accredited adoption agencies with responsibility for the entire process," the CWLA reiterated in 1948.[143] Their plea to the public was, Why risk the unknown when authorized adoptions delivered healthy children in exchange for a little extra time and trouble?

Managing danger had always been professionals' specialty, but adoption's growing popularity made consistent standards more imperative than ever. The surge in adoptions after 1945 was traceable to broad cultural developments, including the global defeat of racial purity ideologies and the equation between parenthood and responsible citizenship that characterized the baby boom era. Adoption seemed more compatible with democracy than ever—a socially as well as a personally meaningful act—and adoptions doubled in the decade after the war to reach approximately 100,000 each year.[144] Almost half were still arranged by freelancers, and professionals warned that more people than ever would suffer the ill effects of botched adoptions if standards were not respected. Babies were still being casually "offered for adoption to financially secure persons" in newspaper ads.[145] Parents risked disappointment. Children risked maladjustment. Citizens in communities around the country risked a tidal wave of costly social problems.[146]

If anything, hazards had multiplied with adoption's new vogue. The upheaval and geographic mobility of the war years separated family members, lured mothers into the labor market, encouraged couples about to be separated by the draft to apply for adoption, and generated requests for placement from married women whose husbands were overseas. These developments offered "all the evidence we need to prove that child placing is more than following an impulse, more than an amateur's prerogative, and more than sentiment or patriotic duty," noted Dorothy Hutchinson.[147]

The 1958 CWLA Standards

The ambitious push for kinship by design that took place during the 1950s was visible in America's adoption culture. In 1954 CWLA president Marshall Field predicted that new standards would finally "take the 'folklore' out of child care, substituting in its place the most scientific knowledge currently available" in "psychology, psychiatry, sociology, anthropology, genetics, pediatrics, child development and medicine."[148] Standardization was the CWLA's "Number One priority."[149]

The timing could not have been more auspicious. U.S. senator Estes Kefauver (D-TN), an adoptive father, was about to launch congressional hearings calling for stronger federal laws to combat the interstate black market. As part of a federal initiative on juvenile delinquency, the hearings warned that improperly placed children would become social misfits and menaces.

Kefauver expressed "nothing but contempt for certain unscrupulous individuals who are fattening on the emotional hunger of others and reaping sizable profits by placing children for adoption through highly dubious methods." He called on the federal government to strengthen the authority of professionals with "specialized social knowledge."[150]

Standards aimed to translate such specialized knowledge into quasi-legal entitlements. Zitha Turitz, a graduate of Radcliffe College and Simmons School of Social Work, managed the CWLA standards project, which mobilized large committees to discuss principles and make detailed comments on drafts of standards. The adoption committee was the first to be appointed because of "the pressing need for nationally accepted standards, and the fact that almost every aspect of child welfare appears in adoption."[151] The committee was chaired by Elizabeth Townsend of the Children's Bureau of Delaware, and the twenty-five members met monthly from December 1955 through June 1956 at the USCB in Washington, D.C.[152]

The result was *Standards for Adoption Service* (1958), a lengthy handbook used to guide agency practice, educate public opinion, and instruct attorneys and judges who handled adoption cases.[153] It illustrated how far professional adoption services had come since the CWLA was founded four decades earlier. Rather than underlining the risks to adopters and stressing the dangers of removing children from birth mothers and blood kin, the manual presented adoption as positively beneficial for many children. "Many young women who become pregnant out of wedlock have serious personality disturbances, need help with their emotional problems, and in most social groups encounter serious social disadvantages if they keep their children with them," the handbook argued.[154] Agencies were advised to accept surrenders whenever birth parents were emotionally ready, not when viable placements materialized.

Emphasizing the disabilities of unmarried mothers signaled a decisive shift toward proadoption attitudes. By the late 1930s, the Freudian worldview had already started to rewrite the old script of women sexually victimized by predatory men, replacing it with a new script of psychopathological maternity. Women who became pregnant outside of marriage were deeply troubled and filled with unconscious hostility. Whether they knew it or not, they were pregnant on purpose. The theory that nonmarital pregnancy originated in the twisted psyches of birth mothers helped to turn the dogma of social work's founding generation on its head: babies should be given away rather than kept.

Adoption workers pledged to help birth mothers make free choices, but most also embraced adoption by World War II, a turning point in the emergence of the United States as a psychological society.[155] In 1939 social worker Mary Brisley declared that babies born to unmarried mothers were automatically "deprived." Their resentful mothers were plagued by guilt and "an unconscious wish to eliminate the child altogether."[156] Without benefit of placement in normal families headed by married couples, children of single mothers were doomed to disadvantaged kinship.

If unmarried mothers were trapped in unresolved oedipal and pre-oedipal developmental dramas, then their manifold emotional confusions threatened their own as well as their children's prospects for psychological health. Once children's interests were refigured as more secure apart from their mothers' interests, adoption emerged as a positive good. In 1951, Miss L, a young woman from a small town who felt ashamed of her pregnancy, encountered a caseworker in a maternity home near New York City. Her caseworker wrote, "I did try not to rush her or force her in regard to planning for herself and her baby, and yet tried to help her be realistic. I gave her permission to feel as she wanted, and permission and assurance that she could surrender her baby and still love him (not being a 'bad' girl or a 'bad' mother). I think, in the end, she came to recognize that the baby was not an answer to what she was seeking, and also that the best thing she could do for him was to surrender him."[157] The risks accompanying placement now paled in comparison to the risks of leaving children in the care of unstable and irresponsible women who needed help far more than they needed motherhood.

Proadoption trends influenced the rationale for preplacement investigation of children. The new standards underscored the expansiveness of adoptability—"*there are no hereditary factors that should automatically rule out adoption*"—and warned against overconfidence—"*it is not possible within the first year of life to predict with a high degree of accuracy an infant's future mental or physical development.*"[158] Careful study of children remained crucial, but the goal of investigation was to gather information that might satisfy children's future curiosity about natal origins rather than prevent adoptive parents from assuming the burden of damaged goods. Identifying information was not included, however, because many states had sealed records laws by midcentury. Adopters also needed to be shielded from any background information that would "only arouse anxiety," a vague standard that left professionals bewildered about what and what not to discuss.[159]

The driving force behind these changes was the stigma of nonmarital sexuality and pregnancy. After World War II, relatively more unmarried birth mothers came from white, middle-class families; their mortified parents desperately wanted their daughters to have another chance at marriage and "normal" motherhood. To guard the identities of disgraced birth mothers and shield adoptees from information that might shock them, confidentiality gradually calcified into secrecy.[160] Narrow concepts of feminine respectability, fears of potential interference by natal relatives, and concern that children would be emotionally "disturbed by having two sets of parents" constructed the adoption closet.[161]

As for evaluating the ability of adult applicants, the 1958 standards directed caseworkers to select parents "who can provide the conditions and opportunities favorable to healthy personality growth and the development of individual potentialities."[162] To accomplish this goal, caseworkers needed to evaluate carefully a host of factors: "total personality," "emotional maturity," "quality of marital relationship," "feeling about children," "feeling about childlessness and readiness to adopt," and "motivation."[163] References to adult functioning reflected class- and culture-bound understandings of maturity and motivation, but that did not prevent these criteria from being widely endorsed and disseminated not only by child welfare professionals but also by organizations that had previously resisted cooperating with the CWLA, including the American Medical Association.[164] Expectations were that applicants would be legally married heterosexuals of childbearing age and that wives would be economically dependent on breadwinning husbands. Working mothers were generally considered ineligible to adopt.[165]

By the 1950s, infertility was inseparable from adoption. On the one hand, infertile couples were viewed as such logical adopters that it was hard for many adoption professionals to seriously consider applications from couples who already had children of their own or were capable of conceiving them. The logical fit between infertility and adoption was practical and philosophical. Fierce competition for healthy white infants made infertility appear an equitable criterion for distributing desirable resources among the most deprived adults. Giving children to fertile couples, in contrast, would be deeply unfair. *Standards for Adoption Service* noted only two "valid" reasons why a fertile couple might wish to adopt: "factors in heredity or serious risk to the life of the mother."[166] Built into the infertility premise, in other words, was a theory that poignantly and paradoxically underlined adoption's status as last-resort kinship. Only couples unable to produce children themselves could be expected to adopt, and those children had to match racially and religiously so as to obscure the fact that they had been born to others.[167]

Infertility offered proof that couples really wanted children and assurance that adoptees would not suffer in comparison to preferred "own" children. On the other hand, infertility was a source of difficulty if a couple's feelings about it were unresolved. Partly for this reason, the home study was reimagined as a therapeutic technique and not simply an evaluative one. Ongoing contact with professionals was both "an experience which may bring about change and growth in applicants' attitudes and expectations" and a method of determining "their flexibility and adaptability to adoptive parenthood."[168] For adopters, the journey toward parenthood involved a delicate and uncomfortable balance. They were expected to display a penchant for personal growth while also submitting to inspection for pathology.

The 1958 *Standards* defined adoption as a child welfare service for children "who would not otherwise have a home of their own, and who can benefit by family life, to become members of a family which can give them the love, care, protection, and opportunities essential for their healthy personality growth and development."[169] The point was to nurture children's personhood by placing them with parents who had the requisite emotional resources to help them navigate both ordinary and unique developmental challenges.

Cases from this period frequently interpreted unconscious signs of parental readiness. Rorschach tests offered caseworkers a supposedly objective aid while also providing applicants with insight. The Children's Aid Society of Newark began experimenting with the Rorschach in the late 1940s in order to achieve a "total personality picture" of couples wishing to adopt; applicants paid $50 to have the test administered.[170] Projective tests were no simple supplements to casework. They could locate the fault lines in a superficially happy marriage or mature personality by exposing dimensions of personhood that even cooperative applicants kept to themselves. "The Rorschach reveals underlying feelings of inadequacy, helplessness, fearfulness, and anxiety, and the attempts to control this anxiety," reported one study of the diagnostic tool.[171]

Two couples, the Martins and the Rhinehardts, who appeared equally happy and qualified for adoptive parenthood, turned out not to be after the Rorschach results came in. Mrs. Martin was mature and giving, but her husband had a "severe castration fear" that made placement of a boy very inadvisable. They were given a newborn girl instead.[172] The Rhinehardts, on the other hand, were rejected outright. Projective testing discovered "an unstable personality . . . with indications of obsessive compulsive defense mechanisms" in the wife and "practically no evidence of emotional freedom or spontaneity" in the husband.[173] Even though this technique evinced mistrust in applicants, some would-be parents welcomed it; others probably reasoned that they were in no position to object. One client of the Newark agency agreed that the Rorschach was wise and described it as "about the best scientific approach I have heard of in this whole adoption business."[174] His wife was not so sure. "I'm keeping my fingers crossed because if anything were found out about me that means I had better not have a child placed with me it would hurt."[175]

Louise Wise Services, one of the country's first specialized adoption agencies (initially called the Free Synagogue Child Adoption Committee, as noted earlier), employed sophisticated consultants in psychiatry, psychology, and social work, who conducted ongoing staff seminars in addition to advising in particular cases. After Louise Wise caseworkers agreed to place a baby with the Ws in the mid-1950s, psychiatric consultation reversed the decision. The Ws' superficial presentation as a happy young couple masked deep emotional difficulties. Mr. W, an economist, had an "obsessive compulsive defense structure" and "would rather deal with intellectual things than people." Mrs. W had a close relationship to her own mother that crossed the line between acceptable intimacy and pathological dependence. Her strong preference for adopting an infant girl betrayed a narcissistic desire to re-create the unhealthy symbiotic tie with an adopted child. The agency's psychiatric consultant reasoned that "if her child behaved in some frustrating way, she would totally reject it."[176]

In the postwar period, adoption assumed a thoroughly psychological cast, frequently based on loose readings of Freud's "family romance" theory. Adopted children were psychologically disadvantaged because the fantasy of being adopted—a fantasy Freud hypothesized helped most children gain independence from their biological parents—was not a fantasy at all.[177] "The reality factor" for adoptees meant that "the idea of adoption had woven itself into the framework of the child's personality configuration" where it "played a role in symptom formation and object relationships."[178] Their rejection by birth parents damaged children so deeply and caused such "severe narcissistic injury" that adoption became, for some professionals, a risk factor for the development of mental illness.[179]

Psychoanalytic interpretations of gender identity and reproductive behavior were also prominent. Women who had children out of wedlock suffered from masculinity complexes and personality disorders. According to Leontine Young, who wrote extensively on nonmarital pregnancy, "We know that the unmarried mother is an unhappy and neurotic girl who seeks through the medium of an out-of-wedlock baby to find an answer to her own unconscious conflicts and needs."[180] Finally, adults who wished to adopt might actually be unwittingly boycotting parenthood. "Psychogenic sterility" (as infertility with no obvious physiological cause was then called) was attributed to "resistance," a significant danger for any adoptee unlucky enough to be saddled with such abnormal parents.[181]

In sum, adoption standards looked quite different in 1958 than they had in 1938 or earlier. Adoption had been reconfigured as an act of intricate psychological engineering that demanded diagnostic sophistication. As a result, the 1958 standards went well beyond exhortations to keep orderly records, investigate, and supervise. *Standards for Adoption Service* offered extensive rather than minimal designs for kinship—they might be called "best practices" today—and added complex definitions of psychological well-being in childhood and adulthood as major components of kinship by design.

From the first efforts to regularize and study adoption in the 1910s, professionals bent on modernization were passionately devoted to their cause. They achieved policy reforms by warning that their vision of kinship by design was all that stood between child welfare, irresponsible parents, and the heartless values of a consumer society. Their theme song was risk. Adoption was a major social problem, but it could be managed rationally. Matching and reliable standards were two strategies that promised safety and security.

Standardization never succeeded fully for a number of reasons. First, agency professionals never achieved the bureaucratic capacity to enforce their new authority, even when states revised laws to encourage or require oversight. There were simply too few agencies to deliver all the adoption services that the country required.[182] Second, regulatory loopholes persisted. Birth parents or adopters who were unhappy with the legal climate in one state needed only to relocate to a jurisdiction more to their liking. Third, alternatives to kinship by design remained attractive and powerful. Blood gave birth parents the right to control where and how children were placed. Practices associated with the commercial, consumption-oriented culture of a modern market society suggested that adopters had the right to shop for exactly the sort of children they most desired. Deeply rooted beliefs in the right to privacy endowed Americans with the freedom to make and remake families beyond the intrusive reach of state power. As a result, independent child placers continued to serve people angered, rejected, or simply indifferent to agencies. Fourth, professionals' own changing approaches to adoption raised doubts that standardization was feasible. If the criteria for adoptability and parental fitness could be revised to include many more different types of individuals than had ever been included before, how reliable could standardization be?

The proponents of kinship by design never achieved the full scope of their ambitious vision. Model legislation, promoted by the USCB and passed by the American Bar Association in 1953, would have prohibited all nonagency adoptions, but this drive for legal uniformity failed. Only two states outlawed all independent placements—Delaware was the first to do so in 1952, and Connecticut followed in 1957—and these were largely symbolic moves because jurisdiction shopping was easy.[183] Even in 1970, when approximately 80 percent of all nonrelative adoptions were arranged by agencies, professionals did not control each and every adoption in the United States or ensure that family making followed standard rules for matching or anything else.

What was accomplished by advocates of kinship by design? They gained limited power of the sort that social engineers often achieved during the twentieth century. They carved out a place for themselves within the liberal state and then had to contend with competitors and critics whose ideas about family making were nothing like their own.[184] Measured against its own ambitions, kinship by design must be judged a failure. Measured against historical traditions that sheltered personal decisions from public interference and elevated idiosyncratic preferences over expert evaluations, kinship by design appears as part of a profound intellectual and cultural revolution in private life. By moving childhood and kinship into the public sphere, prying a significant measure of power away from parents, and transferring decisions previously considered beyond the legitimate reach of state power to representatives of government and allied helping professions, kinship by design altered how children were acquired and families made. It added new voices to an old conversation. What is a family? Who belongs there? Does adoption make one just like any other?

CHAPTER FIVE

The Measure of Other People's Children

The uncertainties that professionals and reformers were bent on control-ling through matching and standardization included two particular dangers related to the distance between adoption and nature. First, other people's children might prove unfit because of bad heredity. Second, the absence of natural ties in adoption made family formation vulnerable to errors even when all parties were well qualified. As we have seen, the advocates of kin-ship by design argued that adoption could be governed and safeguarded through documentation, investigation, and oversight by trained profession-als. They outlined standards to prevent kinship catastrophes and defended interpretation as the best way to make adoption real. Kinship by design entailed the expansion of therapeutic government.

Science was a significant resource for this project in risk reduction. Tech-nological innovation, experimental discovery, and empirical research were all essential to kinship by design. "Thinking people will surely want to em-ploy all the aids that science can provide to avoid even the remote possibil-ity of a tragedy," psychologist Barbara Burks pointed out in 1929.[1] Ten years later, two observers noted that "science has been uncovering facts that mean for the family, and particularly for the adoptive parent and child, a welcome emancipation from fear."[2]

As a privileged source of truth, science gave people new reasons to be-lieve that adopting other people's children was safe. More knowledge of nature and better methods for approximating it were logical ways to reduce risks associated with artifice. Certified agencies functioned "like a chain of laboratories" once "science had come forward to speak its piece."[3] Adoption would necessarily remain a social operation, but incorporating science and technology meant that it did not have to look or feel that way.

Kinship by design made matching, and all of adoption, scientific. Matching also endured because most adopters strongly preferred children who looked like them. Before 1970, matching was overwhelmingly popular, especially among infertile couples who sought to adopt after failing to conceive children of their "own." By midcentury, sterility had become a prominent qualification for adoption, reinforcing the notion that matching compensated for reproductive failure. Matching created relationships that could pass for the exclusive, authentic, and permanent bonds of kinship that were only natural.

Efforts to classify, measure, test, select, diagnose, evaluate, and predict aimed to make families turn out better by turning them out more naturally. Scientific approaches elevated intention over intuition in family making and elevated knowledge over love, faith, and impulse. The science of kinship rested on systematic studies of child development, adult motivation, and nature-nurture relationships. It advanced an ethic of objectivity and rational control that equated methodological rigor with superior results. This chapter examines adoption technologies that were incorporated into kinship by design and considers the origin of one novel genre of adoption research, the outcome study.

Putting Children to the Test

Tests that allowed mental and educational status to be individually measured against aggregate patterns were new in the United States at the beginning of the twentieth century. The Binet scale, imported from France in 1908, was first translated by Henry Goddard and administered to children at the Training School for Feeble-Minded Girls and Boys in Vineland, New Jersey. Goddard, a well-known eugenicist, is best known for adding the term "moron" to the vocabulary of mental classification. He enthusiastically promoted testing as the best means of distinguishing retarded children, who needed and deserved institutional care and special education, from normal children, who belonged in families. By 1915 Goddard had distributed more than twenty-two thousand copies of the test and four times as many answer blanks. In tests, Goddard glimpsed the possibility of therapeutic government. Mentally subnormal children would be objects of enlightened treatment, founded on scientific understanding, rather than punitive policies based on ignorance and shame.

Goddard's testing ethic was based on historically fluctuating premises that later became so axiomatic as to seem timeless. First, intelligence was a singular trait, not an assortment of varied talents, skills, and capabilities.[4]

Second, it determined behavior. Third, it was largely innate. Fourth, age was the key to assessing intelligence because degrees of mental normality, subnormality, and supernormality could be discerned on the basis of when—not whether—individuals succeeded in performing more or less difficult tasks. Normal children could do more challenging mental work at age fourteen, in other words, than at age ten or six. Their feebleminded counterparts, however, would develop at a far slower pace, displaying patterns of delayed or arrested intellectual development at odds with bodily maturation. Finally, mentality could be objectively measured by tests that revealed an individual's relationship to carefully standardized, age-graded norms. In 1916, Lewis Terman revised the Binet scale and incorporated the "Intelligence Quotient" (IQ) as a way to report scores. This handy ratio, calculated by dividing "mental age" by "chronological age," turned intelligence into a single number. The managerial efficiency of quantitative categorization promoted the rapid spread of testing in education, military service, social welfare, and employment during the decades that followed.[5] Until the post–World War II civil rights movement, the equation between measures of "native intelligence" and individual merit was not widely disputed.

It is not well known that mental tests were used during the early part of the century in family placements. Initially, tests served the crude purpose of separating feebleminded from average children. In this sense, mental measures were "qualifying tests" that marked the boundary between adoptable and unadoptable as the difference between children with and without the capacity for normal development.[6] Technical means of disqualifying children from kinship buttressed moral, social, and public health policies to discourage illegitimacy, redeem unwed mothers, preserve natal families, and reduce infant mortality. Tests did more than rule children in or out of families. They constructed mental typologies and profiles to aid with matching.

The ability to fine-tune mental discrimination mattered to Progressive child placers for several reasons. They were certain that the thoughtless placement of subnormal children—idiots, imbeciles, morons, and dullards—in family homes was a risk that could be reduced. "All too often in the past have children from sub-normal or questionable parents been placed for adoption in good families where later they develop traits which cause family heartache," wrote an official of the Cleveland Children's Bureau ruefully in 1926.[7] With the help of mental testers, placements could be arranged or refused on the basis of precise, quantitative knowledge about children's mental status and potential. When testing showed that children did not possess the intellectual credentials for family life, they could be placed in well-managed, benevolent institutions. When they qualified for kinship, parents could be found who matched them mentally. Because cultural understandings of reproductive nature emphasized intellectual as well as physiological continuity, placing children with parents who were their mental equals was necessary to make adoption work well.

The significance of mental matching in adoption was first articulated in terms of "under-placement" and "over-placement," two errors that were all too common in family formation according to advocates of naturalization. "Under-placement" referred to the practice of placing bright children with dull parents, and "over-placement" gave dull children to bright parents. Failure was the likely outcome in either case.[8] Mentally average children belonged with mentally average parents, but superior parents and children belonged together, too. In some instances even mentally retarded children on the cusp of normality might be successfully placed with simple, unassuming people whose expectations of children were low. The term "selective placement" designated efforts to design kinship on the basis of mental likeness presumed to mirror natural patterns.

In his classic 1919 text on family placement, W. H. Slingerland called on all child-placing agencies to use professional psychologists to conduct "a scientific study of mentality and personality."[9] This study would have two purposes: to identify those who were so "constitutionally defective" as to be unadoptable and in need of institutional care, and to pair adoptable children with parents who were like them. "To put a low grade mental defective in a family home where a normal child was expected is a social crime, once to be condoned because of ignorance, but now inexcusable in a well-ordered and progressive child-placing agency," Slingerland chided his colleagues in the rapidly professionalizing field of social work.[10] Few activities were more important to modernizing child welfare than scientifically assessing children's current and prospective mental status.

Like testers intent on detecting feeblemindedness among immigrants, soldiers, and schoolchildren, child placers embraced intelligence as a proxy for social status that could withstand the egalitarianism of American democracy. "You must bear in mind that there are first-class, second-class, and third-class children," Slingerland noted, approvingly quoting Hastings Hart, "and there are first-class, second-class, and third-class homes."[11] In a meritocratic society, intelligence was a defensible rationale for social distinctions. It produced legitimate hierarchy in schools and armies, and this was equally true in families. Mental matching would maximize children's future happiness by helping them take advantage of adoption opportunities without causing "an inferiority complex."[12] It would also prevent the problems of children whose potential would be squandered or who would disappoint their parents by failing to "measure up." By 1920, the testing ethos had penetrated the professional child-placing world to the point that leaders considered it almost malpractice to make placements without the benefit of mental measurement. Fifty years later, the ability of professionals to deliver children whose intelligence matched or exceeded parents' specifications was still considered a decisive factor in successful adjustment and adoption.[13]

Even before tests were specifically devised for infants and young children, some managers of children's institutions understood that one could test children under age three. Psychologist Frederick Kuhlmann, for instance, whose adaptation of the Binet scale became the most widely used version for young children, had put the scale into service by 1910.[14] Technologies designed for use with school-age populations might also answer questions about the future for babies and toddlers of questionable mentality. Tests' promise to predict was an important reason why a number of leading professional agencies, including the New England Home for Little Wanderers and the New York State Charities Aid Association, pioneered the use of intelligence testing in temporary and permanent placements. Psychologist Rose Hardwick instituted a comprehensive mental testing program for the New England Home for Little Wanderers in September 1915. Every single candidate for adoption was admitted to the organization's scientific Study Home "by way of precaution."[15] Intellectual normality was a routine item on forms used by child-caring organizations and promoted by the CWLA in the 1910s.[16]

Testing clearly promoted the interests of those groups most dedicated to kinship by design. Mental measurement helped to distinguish professional placement from independently arranged adoptions that lacked such scientific safeguards.[17] Normalizing technologies marked the adoption process as delicate, difficult, and distant from the transparency of material signs and symbols. Neither adopters nor independent child placers were equipped to recognize the authentic ingredients of kinship. Child placers who acted out of ignorance were all too prone to confusing love with money, and those motivated by money obviously overlooked love entirely. Adopters, on the other hand, were easily taken in by adorable infants and needed to be rescued from their own gullibility and faulty assumption that love followed directly from charming behavior or attractive appearance. "Uncouth, foulmouthed children of ignorant and disgusting parents" might be happily adopted after they were "tested and pronounced normal" and cleaned up a bit, observed one writer in 1922.[18] Only professionals were equipped to pierce the superficial veneer of development by turning every child into an object of inquiry and technique. Scientific adoption could guarantee that children would end up exactly where they belonged.

Matching and merit mattered, but eugenic alarm about the children available for adoption was the most important factor in the spread of placement-related testing. Children in need of new parents were, according to prevailing views, prone to very bad heredity. "The family contemplating taking in a foundling has a little better than an even chance not to regret the act," advised Paul Popenoe.[19] Defects, however, could be remarkably difficult to detect. Many mentally subnormal children appeared perfectly normal to the untrained eye, Goddard warned, but placing them in "good families" "run[s] the risk of contaminating the race by the perpetuation of mental and moral deficiency." Constant vigilance was required with homeless and dependent children, and Goddard urged that "no pains or expense be spared to get all the information that can possibly be had" about their mental status and family background.[20]

Elaborate genealogies—extending well beyond parents to grandparents and other natal relatives—were considered evidence of professional thoroughness, although they were spotty at best in the years before 1915. The Boston Children's Aid Society, for instance, made "eugenic charts" to assist child-placing decisions. These practical aids were "something every children's worker should do" because "the strains and taints of families when plotted out in such a way stand out strikingly."[21]

That results could be surprising was the whole point of implementing novel placement technologies. One girl, by all accounts sensitive and refined, had "a heredity strain of appalling extent, going back three generations, and showing that nineteen of her immediate ancestors had been alcoholic, epileptic, neurotic and sexually promiscuous."[22] Practices such as eugenic charting testified to beliefs that criminality, immorality, insanity, and antisocial behavior, from alcoholism to prostitution and foul language, were all heritable. If these alarming characteristics were passed from birth parents to their children, and if those children were unknowingly adopted by families with unblemished heredity, the chances that mentally subnormal adoptees would reproduce a generation of future degenerates increased. Tests promised to prevent familial heartbreak and social degeneration simultaneously.

Humanitarianism was laudable, but the desire to help children in need could not be allowed to overwhelm scientific knowledge about children's nature. According to Henry Goddard, "It is neither right nor wise for us to let our humanity, our pity and sympathy for the poor, homeless, and neglected child, drive us to do injustice to and commit a crime against those yet unborn."[23] Many Progressive medical and social welfare professionals shared Goddard's preference for enlightened institutions over adoption. Not only did they offer feebleminded children decent lives, but they had the distinct advantage of controlling their reproductive sexuality and hence the future quality of the gene pool.

The "scientific attitude" prioritized facts over values.[24] According to Amey Watson, "No child that is of diseased and no child of feeble-minded parents should be placed in any home for adoption until the foster parents know the full facts of the case and are ready to take every precaution to see that the disease is not passed on to others and that later in life the defective germ-plasm is not mated with normal stock, thereby passing on the defect and causing much preventable misery."[25] This investigation was especially imperative when it came to placing the children of unwed mothers. "Illegitimacy is the result of biological, psychological and social causes following definite scientific laws," concluded Watson.[26]

The great promise of mental measurement was that it might prevent family unhappiness in the present as well as the birth of defective children in the future. Organizations in the professional vanguard opted for testing early on, but few child welfare organizations provided such specialized services across the board. They lacked the financial and professional resources to do so. Adoption-related testing remained an unrealized ideal in adoption— a sort of maximum rather than minimum standard—for a long time after the 1910s. One close study of fifty-six New England adoptions in the late 1920s and 1930s, for example, concluded that testing had become a more common and reliable "precursor to adoption" over time.[27] But it also noted that "the saddest tragedies to be found in the history of past adoptions have resulted primarily from the error which psychological testing is devised to prevent—i.e., the under-placement or over-placement of children in relation to their capacity."[28] "By the use of modern methods of mental testing and observation," Sophie van Senden Theis wrote in 1924, "it is possible to tell with a fair degree of accuracy about the learning ability of the child."[29] "From the test results in frequent examinations, the child may be found fit for adoption if a particular type of home is chosen," another social worker explained in 1934.[30]

The benefits of testing were rarely achieved. Most children requiring adoptive placement were never tested once (let alone two or three times) during the early decades of the century. The Boston Children's Aid Society found that only four children in its care prior to 1913 had undergone mental examinations before placement.[31] Between 1918 and 1928, only 4 percent of all illegitimate children adopted in Minnesota were given mental tests, and most of these were related to postplacement adjustment problems rather than preplacement selection or matching.[32] For professionals, advances in testing technologies during the 1920s and 1930s made widespread failures to mentally match children and parents more galling than ever.

Even when measuring technologies were not used to pick or match children, judgments of mental potential, however unscientific, were considered crucial to adoption success. Agencies simply used such ordinary proxies for intelligence as family background, school records, appearance, and behavior. Children of parents with some college education were not transferred to parents who were manual workers. Test scores gave selective placement an aura of precision, but even without them, children were regularly placed in the type of families where they supposedly belonged.[33] Within the framework of upward mobility that structured adoption, "better" children were still destined for "better" parents. Selective placement was "proof of intelligent placement."[34] It matched nature.

Scientific adoption may have been fully realized in practice only occasionally before 1945, but it was increasingly visible—in mass-circulation magazines and newspapers, in government pamphlets, on the radio, and in professional literature of many kinds—as a benchmark against which all adoptions should be measured. In 1922 *Century* magazine declared that adoption "had become as nearly scientific as anything as intrinsically inexact as the handling of a child could be." "The old lines of stupidity and sentimentality" still prevailed in too many cases, but "all that science could do for the right handling of a child's body, mind, and soul was being done" in a growing number of adoptions.[35] The first popular book-length manual for would-be adopters, *The Adopted Child* (1936), contained chapters titled "Heredity and Environment" and "Intelligence Tests in Adoption." The author, Eleanor Gallagher, noted that publicity about scientific adoption had already changed the behavior of many adults in search of children. Prospective adopters from small towns, where professional agencies were scarce, were likely to travel to cities, where their demands for the scientific selection of children could be satisfied.[36] Respected child-rearing authorities such as Douglas Thom helped spread the word that "science can help 'parents' find just the child they hope for."[37] "Success brings joy, failure unmitigated sorrow," he added a few years later.[38] Adopters with tragic stories to tell warned others that "awaiting your turn for a child from a recognized agency is your best insurance of a normal, healthy child."[39] Science and technology distinguished good from bad adoptions.

Some couples understood that scientific adoption could not eradicate guesswork, whereas others considered it an iron-clad guarantee. One well-connected would-be adoptive mother in the early 1920s "asked two well-known scientists, a biologist and a Harvard psychologist, for expert advice. They talked profoundly about inheritance factors, environment factors, and much else, till I came away with a whirling head, unsure about anything except that I still wanted a baby boy."[40] In 1931 one couple distributed a circular to agencies up and down the East Coast to aid their search for "a little girl, one who comes from an American Protestant family, who is between five and ten years old, and who is in perfect health. They hope to find a child who possesses, besides these essential requisites, at least some of the following: New England ancestry; an I.Q. of at least 110; a happy, loveable disposition; some social and cultural background."[41]

One Depression-era adoptive mother who published her story admitted freely that "we wanted the best material available." Though "fatalistic" about the hereditary credentials of adoptable children, their agency obtained "a baby who answered most of our requirements," including a high IQ and birth parents who had graduated from college. The adoptive parents attributed the eventual success of the adoption—a deep love for their adopted daughter despite initial worries that they would not love her as they did their "own" son—to this "cold-blooded" approach.[42] At midcentury, a New York couple applied to an agency for a pretty girl "with violet-colored eyes, of pure Nordic background, and an I.Q. of a hundred and thirty-five or above."[43] Roundly criticized as inflexible by agency workers, such detailed orders for children illustrate that promises of scientific certification had not fallen on deaf ears. More than a simple hedge against the unknown, scientific adoption boldly ventured to compensate participants for membership in families labeled artificial, unnatural, and less "real" than the biological norm.

Science might even endow adoption with a measure of predictive certainty unavailable to people who acquired children the ordinary way. "Consider the interesting fact that the foster parent does not appear on the scene until someone else has run the early, major hazards of childbearing!" pointed out two observers of the adoption scene in the late 1930s. "He can choose, he does not have to take what comes along."[44] Their letters, applications, and stories over many decades make it apparent that many would-be adopters eagerly sought out children who met their expectations for background, behavior, appearance, and future educational potential and rejected those who did not.[45] Children were rejected or returned for a wide variety of reasons: "child seemed Japanese"; "child had light hair and family would not keep her"; "as hard to understand as a German . . . the queerest child"; "he is a backward boy"; "he [the foster father] was disappointed because the boy had not taken to books."[46] Such reasons struck many professionals as trivial and heartless, but considering their emphasis on risk, child placers should not have been surprised that parents demanded certainty. Parents were keenly aware of the gap between making families naturally and making them socially, and the control over nature that adoption represented could be an advantage. What did kinship by design offer if not choices?

The exercise of choice varied with class location because class sharply distinguished how people located children, at what age they were adopted, the legitimacy and fertility status of the parties involved, and other important variables.[47] Anecdotal evidence suggested that "social class position is inversely related to the capacity of couples to accept deviations from normal in adoptive children."[48] Blue-collar and rural adopters, according to one 1957 study of sixty agencies in nine communities, were relatively skeptical of scientific methods of selection and quality assurance, open to "special needs" adoptions, and "tolerant" of difference. In contrast, white-collar and professional adopters wanted babies who looked as much like them as possible and expected them to be intellectually and physically perfect, or at least normal.[49] Naturalization may be interpreted, at least in part, as a handy method of product certification and class maintenance in the very adoption market whose abuses and idiosyncrasies had provoked fervent efforts to replace commerce and consumption with science and technology.[50]

Arnold Gesell and Adoption Technologies

The career of Arnold Gesell tracks the history of efforts to naturalize adoption and make it more scientific.[51] Gesell articulated the central premise of kinship by design when he asserted that "nothing in the field of social welfare needs more deliberate and conscious regulation than child adoption."[52] It is worth quoting him at some length to emphasize the logical, causal link between professional expertise and positive outcomes.

> [Adoption] can not be intrusted altogether to good will or to intuitive impulse, or even to unaided common sense. There are too many opportunities for error and miscarriage. The combined critical judgment of the social inves-

tigator, the court, the physician, and the mental examiner should enter into the regulation of adoption. . . . Systematic psychoclinical examinations not only will reduce the wastes of error and miscarriage but will serve to reveal children of normal and superior endowment beneath the concealment of neglect, of poverty, or of poor repute. Clinical safeguards can not solve all the problems of child adoption but they can steadily improve its methods and make them both more scientific and humane.[53]

In this view, scientific adoption was the only realistic antidote to the unregulated placements that were too early, too late, or just plain bad because of "haphazard, under-cover, boot-leg, hit-or- miss adoptions."[54] In contrast, adoptions arranged with "intelligent social control" were such a "rich addition to human happiness" that Gesell encouraged his nephew to consider it.[55] "Every well-conceived child adoption is an asset to society," he argued.[56]

Gesell was a nationally renowned psychologist and physician. He was best known for devising scales of normative development widely used by clinicians working in medical and educational fields during the interwar period, paralleling the rise of standardized height and weight tables. Gesell earned a Ph.D. in psychology from Clark University in 1906 and an M.D. from Yale in 1915, and his career coincided with the formative years of developmental science and modern adoption.

Throughout his long career, Gesell championed professional child welfare and adoption practices. He worked with the most important national and local child welfare organizations of his day, including the USCB and the CWLA, often advising these and other groups on policies related to placement age, preplacement testing, and clinical supervision in adoption.[57] Gesell was the most famous child development expert before Benjamin Spock, and public renown was a hallmark of his career.[58] His defense of scientific adoption helped to establish its credibility with popular audiences.

Developmental Measurement: Minimizing Risk and Maximizing Matching

Gesell spent virtually his entire career at Yale University, where he was head of the Juvenile Psycho-Clinic (figure 9). The facility, founded in 1911, was subsequently known as the Clinic of Child Development.[59] From 1919 through the 1930s, he devised normative scales of child development in his carefully designed laboratory and observation dome. After observing and documenting hundreds of New Haven children, Gesell produced an age-graded atlas of normal development beginning at birth. He conceived of development

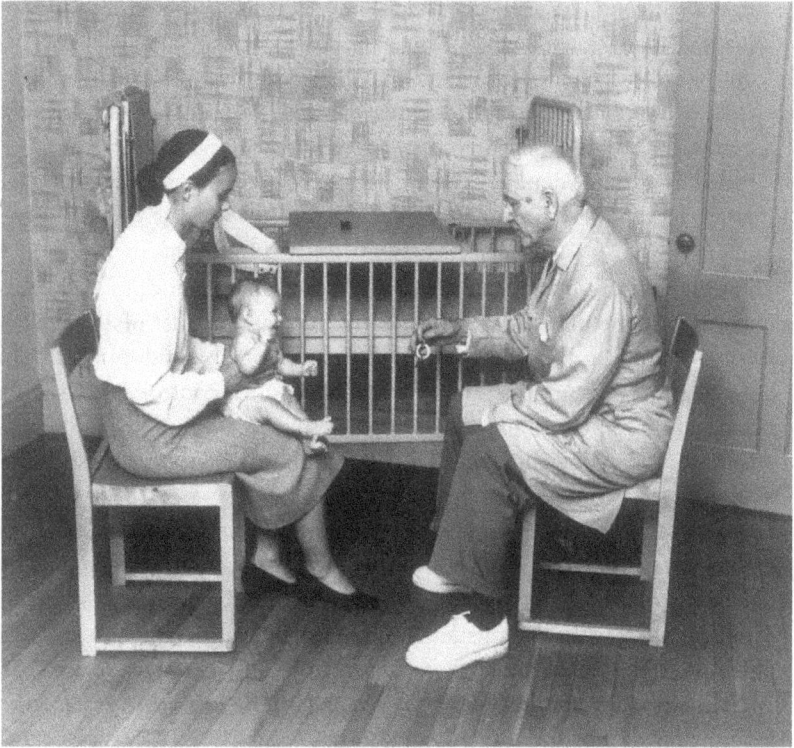

Figure 9. Arnold Gesell with a mother and child at his Yale clinic.
Used by permission of Mrs. Rex Walden.

as an orderly and visible process that unfolded progressively, from birth on-
ward no less than from conception to birth. Because most children moved at
roughly the same speed on the same path, aggregate measures—or norms—
became the yardstick for how any particular child should develop.

The technology that resulted from this scientific effort was a scale. The
scale translated developmental data into an instrument that gauged children's proximity to developmental norms at a series of key ages. Gesell defined norms as "a standardized tool for discriminative characterization," the
closest possible thing to a scientific unit of developmental measurement.[60]
He called his technology "developmental diagnosis" and envisioned it at
the center of an ambitious new clinical endeavor extending public health
regulation beyond bodies to minds, beyond preventing disease to promoting optimal growth. Developmental measurement was based on the same

intuitive linkage between age and growth that informed mental measurement, and psychologists who used the Gesell scale called its numerical results the D.Q., or Developmental Quotient, analogizing it to the IQ. As an aid to placement decisions, the Gesell scale was a major advance over earlier testing technologies, which focused solely on intelligence and relied exclusively on language and therefore could not be administered to infants or toddlers under the age of three without considerable improvisation.

The earliest mention of adoption in Gesell's published work came in 1923, when he reported that his assistant, Margaret Cobb, had evaluated the potential of 198 candidates for adoption. The results, based on the Stanford-Binet, equated adoptability with educability. Cobb concluded that only 2 percent had college potential, 7 percent could be expected to finish high school, 17 percent could do some high school work, 35 percent might benefit from vocational training after completing elementary school, 21 percent might finish the fifth or sixth grade, and 18 percent were unsuited for any kind of regular education but would benefit from special training.[61] Children available for adoption typically came from backgrounds full of drinking, immorality, and criminality. "Although it is a grave responsibility to prejudice in any way the opportunities for adoption," Gesell wrote, "we ought within judicious limits to attempt to forestall all the pangs and aggravations which may come from ill-considered adoption."[62]

In 1926 the USCB published a pamphlet, "Psychoclinical Guidance in Child Adoption," written by Gesell. It argued that "purely impulsive adoption should be discouraged and the whole procedure should be surrounded with clinical and supervisory safeguards."[63] Gesell spoke regularly on radio, gave public lectures, attended conferences, and otherwise publicized the advantages of scientific adoption, warning that only expert guidance could protect against the "the intense suffering" and parental heartbreak caused by "bungled" placements.[64] His devotion to standards established by systematic tests and carried out by duly trained professionals was typical of the pioneering generation of adoption reformers, as we have seen. Their commitment to children required that humanitarianism be put to the rugged test of rationalization.

Gesell never doubted that adoption was dangerous, even inappropriate for certain children, but he believed that the risks could be measured in advance and managed. This was the essence of kinship by design. By 1939 his Yale clinic had studied at least fifteen hundred adoption candidates; Gesell estimated that one in every ten was grossly defective and therefore unadoptable. Without assessment, he warned, many average and even superior children who should be placed would be passed over, and those who did find parents were likely to be placed where they did not belong.

Gesell's work was described in publications aimed at professional and popular audiences as proof that "science helps the adoptive family to approximate the biological family."[65] Adoption professionals from around the country responded by writing to Gesell.[66] One psychologist employed by a statewide agency in Kansas began, in the early 1930s, to administer the Gesell scale to the babies of mentally retarded mothers. By the end of the decade, the agency was routinely testing all babies in need of placement, confident that Gesell's technology had saved normal babies from wrongful institutionalization, accurately predicted children's future development, and guaranteed parents that children would "fit" their families and live up to their expectations.[67] Gesell's scale was also used by the Children's Aid Society of Boston and many professionally arranged adoptions in New York State in the 1920s and 1930s.[68] The Pennsylvania Children's Aid Society used Gesell's technology (alone for children under twelve months and supplemented by the Stanford-Binet for older adoption candidates) beginning in the 1920s. "As a protection to both the foster parents and to the child, and for the happiness of both, it is most desirable to know the intelligence level of the child, as well as his physical equipment, family background, and personality make-up," said one study.[69] The State of Iowa, concerned that retarded children might be accidentally adopted, began in 1934 to test all children who had been placed as babies prior to the finalization of their adoptions. These tests could be "a highly emotional experience for the parents, who understood that the psychologist's word was final in approving or disapproving completion of the adoption."[70] So much emphasis was placed on numerical results by some agencies and would-be parents that some psychologists reported only approximate Developmental Quotients, hoping to alleviate worry that a point or two differentiated superior, average, and feebleminded children.[71]

Occasionally, such agencies as the Boston Children's Friend Society provided parents with the IQ scores of children placed with them, but this was not a common policy early on.[72] The Menninger Clinic, one of the best-known psychiatric institutions in the country, established an infant testing service in 1944. Used mainly by adoption agencies, this service routinely administered the Gesell scale.[73] Sophie van Senden Theis not only supervised a program of infant and child testing at her own New York agency but also claimed that psychological testing was routinely used in agency practice around the country by the late 1940s to determine children's developmental baselines, ascertain developmental progress in borderline cases, predict

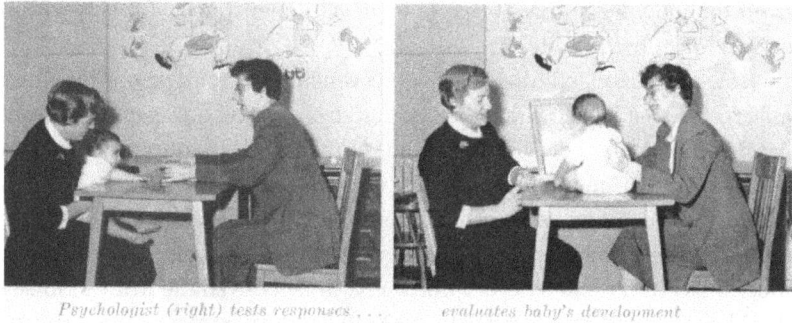

Figure 10. Psychological testing was an important feature of adoptive placement at Louise Wise Services. Archives & Special Collections, Columbia University Health Sciences Library. Used by permission.

future capabilities, and place children with parents who mirrored their mentality and expected neither too little nor too much of them.[74] Even rural agencies that were slow to professionalize, such as Maine's Good Samaritan Home Agency, incorporated professional testing into the placement process by the mid-1930s.[75]

By 1947 the Gesell scale was the most widely used developmental test in the United States, but other tests were also used in adoption: the Cattell Infant Intelligence Scale, the Buhler Test, the Merrill-Palmer Performance Scale, and the Kuhlmann revision of the Binet.[76] By the 1950s, most agencies in the United States employed psychological testing during the placement process, and it was not unusual for agencies to specify that at least two tests be administered during a mandatory period of preadoptive care, as the Children's Aid Society of Western Pennsylvania did.[77] Employed for many purposes, mental and developmental technologies helped to carve out new roles for testers and demarcated family making as fresh scientific terrain (figure 10).

Promises to predict the developmental future for children whose background was unknown or unsavory challenged the contentions that blood was thicker than water and that adoption was prone to disasters. Gesell's science helped by exposing the logic of maturation. "Growth *is* lawful and in no sense whimsical, fortuitous, or even wholly unpredictable in its nature," Gesell asserted.[78] No miracle or mystery, growth was a process "governed by laws and forces just as real as those which apply to an internal combustion engine."[79] Children about whom little was known, or about whom what was known was bad, could be comprehended more clearly and convincingly than ever before. People concerned about adoption could take heart from the knowledge that "because it [development] is lawful it is within certain limits predictable."[80]

However lawful, children's growth was neither automatic nor invulnerable to external influences. Gesell admitted that growth was more encompassing than mental development and more difficult to conceptualize than ability or achievement. He defined it as a sort of elastic potential for perpetual change. All growth was based on past growth, making it so reflexive that even the youngest baby was a "growing action system."[81] Technically, individuals never failed developmentally, because even the most seriously disabled children grew. But it was obvious that developmental patterns varied widely, with deviations traceable to prematurity, birth defects, accidents, disease, and malnutrition, among other factors. Growth potential, Gesell concluded, was innate; it "probably resides in the inherent protoplasmic plasticity of the individual."[82] Development was "for the most part hereditary in nature," its outside limits determined by "original equipment," especially the maturing nervous system.[83] But he never doubted that it was also conditioned by social institutions—families, schools, and communities—that provided (or withheld) opportunities and inspired (or stifled) motivation. Development was remarkably stable in aggregate terms, but individual differences proliferated within the limits of lawfulness.

Despite the tensions between Gesell's nature-oriented science and his nurture-oriented commitment to child welfare, he crusaded for new laws and policies to improve children's lives and often repeated that heredity and environment were reciprocal rather than antithetical forces in human growth. Committed both to exploring the forces that determined growth and to countering social fatalism, Gesell tried mightily to resolve the contradiction between nature and nurture and between determinism and government.[84]

Technologies such as developmental diagnosis suggested a revolutionary new level of social control over childhood. More hopeful about adoption than his lifelong friend and occasional collaborator Henry Goddard, Gesell believed that only some children made good candidates for family life. He was more concerned about bright children likely to be overlooked than dull children likely to be overplaced. "The more superior a child is, the more urgently does he demand placement in a home with optimum opportunity. The more defective a child is, the less he is harmed by institutional care."[85] Just as they would not consider adopting children with heart disease or tuberculosis, Gesell told would-be parents that they "should of course investigate the inheritance and mental status of the child; to make sure that capacity is at least normal."[86]

Gesell assumed that most potential parents would not want to adopt children who deviated from the norm by falling far below it. Was he right? Observers certainly reported cases where parents rejected or returned children who were "defective," "dull," unattractive, or simply not to their liking.[87] State laws frequently allowed for annulments of adoptions in which conditions (retardation, epilepsy, insanity, venereal disease, and so on) unknown to the adopters manifested later on. But instances also occurred when agency staff had to insist that parents give up subnormal children whom they had already grown to love, sometimes arguing that keeping an unworthy child selfishly deprived others "of good mental endowment."[88] With the movement toward earlier placement, some agencies offered adopters written assurance "that if the baby is not found to be properly developed the child is removed at our judgment."[89] In those rare instances where parents insisted on adopting despite Gesell's recommendation against it, he encouraged child welfare authorities not to block the adoption if the parents would promise to prevent the child from marrying and having children.[90] Figuring normal children as adoptable and subnormal children as unadoptable was a staple of the era's eugenic ideology. In contrast, discerning the boundaries of normality and establishing with certainty "the degree of normality required" for adoption were substantial scientific and technological challenges.[91]

Gesell's positions on adoption were somewhat unusual. For example, he believed that many unmarried birth mothers ought to surrender their children for adoption and that women unable to make definite decisions about placing their babies be given a two-year time limit. This stance ran counter to the eugenic sensibilities of many professionals. Gesell knew that many candidates for adoption were illegitimate; his estimate was 80 percent.[92] Many observers considered feebleminded mothers disproportionately likely to have out-of-wedlock children of subnormal mentality, although this was a contentious point.[93] Gesell considered the tendency to keep mother and child together "a sentimental idea" and urged that adoption be considered in order to "give a child a good home rather than a bad one."[94] Being born to a feebleminded parent was a burden and a liability; living with such a parent was acceptable to Gesell only "if it does not cost the child too dear."[95] Growing up in an institution and belonging to no one, he believed, was the most damaging possibility of all.

Gesell's nature-centered maturational narrative was compatible with the practice of kinship by design. He advocated placement even for some children on the border between mental normality and subnormality because for these children, even more than for others, social factors could push the developmental needle into the normal range.[96] "Mental hygiene, like charity, begins at home," he asserted.[97] His emphasis on the salience of social arrangements anticipated environmentally centered work on institutional retardation in the 1930s, the positive significance of attachment in the 1940s, mother-infant bonding in the 1970s, and even the articulation of "psychological parenthood" in the 1970s and 1980s.[98] He argued that "children need to take root, to attach themselves to someone, to have someone they can count on, someone they are sure of."[99] "We do not sufficiently serve the neglected child if we simply put a roof over his head," he noted. "There must be affection and understanding beneath that roof."[100]

Three-year-old Sarah seemed to bear this out. Mentally pegged as "low average" by Gesell's diagnostic staff when she was placed in an adoptive home, her test results quickly jumped to "high average." Gesell interpreted Sarah's progress as an "example of response to placing in *home of her own!*"[101] Meeting children's psychological needs for permanence and belonging might not guarantee normality or improved developmental prospects, but in some adoptions it made all the difference. The difficulty of recognizing such cases was another rationale for skilled clinical judgment based on science.

Improving Outcomes Scientifically

"The proof of the pudding" in adoptions was how children turned out.[102] Longitudinal data associated with developmental studies such as Gesell's made it more likely that adoptees would turn out well, becoming "sober, honest, useful citizens."[103] Gesell was sure he had reduced the risks of adoption by testing children's developmental status and predicting its future course. Technologies such as the Gesell scale turned matching from a clumsy moral theory that based love on simple likeness into a technical operation whose success could be calculated. Showing that kinship could be socially designed so as to approximate the results of biogenetic nature helped to mitigate adoption's reputation as second best and strengthened the case for design.

Gesell resisted pressures from parents and professionals to pinpoint an ideal age for adoptive placements.[104] Because children displayed broad growth patterns in unique ways, he believed that placement age should be determined on a case-by-case basis. Sound adoption policies and practices had to account simultaneously for very general and very individualized knowledge. Gesell considered placements before six months unwise, an opinion that reflected professional reluctance to endorse perilous infant adoptions. But adopters overwhelmingly desired the youngest possible babies. Gesell was willing to allow "early" placements, at four months, if detailed information about the infant's heredity and development suggested that the placement was absolutely safe. Such early placements, he admitted, had the advantage of maximizing affection between parents and child and minimizing public expense. In theory Gesell's scale was an equally accurate predictor at four months and beyond, but in practice he recommended repeated tests supplemented by a variety of other diagnostic techniques so that consistency of results would shape a reasoned prognosis.[105] When a life hung in the balance, patience and probability were more trustworthy than a single exam.

Caution was almost always more important than speed in making up families well. Older children, whose quantities and characters were already well established and known, had distinct advantages as adoption candidates. For example, Gesell advised parents who wished to know whether their adopted children would be qualified to attend college to consider no children younger than three.[106] No infant under six months should ever be legally adopted, he warned, because the chances were too great that adopters would take in defective children or even that white parents might adopt "colored" children.[107] Nor should babies be placed permanently after six months if any concern existed about the child's fundamental normality. "Hair-raisingly bad" family histories were all too common among children available for adoption, and they offered a good pretext to hold off, even if children themselves tested in the normal range.[108]

For Gesell, smart placements were wait-and-see placements. Delay was often the right course of action, and decisions could sometimes take years. One child, described by Gesell as "the most extreme case in our files," was a baby with a dizzying number of problems, from premature birth and syphilis to prolonged hospitalization for respiratory difficulties and fifteen months of institutional living. Her first exam indicated "a serious degree of retardation," but four years, several foster homes, and at least five developmental tests later, "she was an alert, attractive child, reaching almost a complete average performance on the developmental schedules—a remarkable realization of latent normality. . . . She was now in every sense adoptable."[109]

Just as developmental diagnosis could prove the adoptability of children who appeared too risky, so might it reveal the defects of normal-looking children. One telling case involved a "cute" baby girl who "was just the kind of child who would smite the heart of questing adoptive parents." But Gesell suspected that she would never even complete high school and predicted that "there may be genuine pangs of regret" in store for any parents foolish enough to adopt her as an infant, before her true developmental potential could be known with certainty.[110] Another child illustrated how easily physical appearance could mislead. Four-year-old Rose, brought to Yale for adoption assessment in 1923, "is physically attractive, of cheerful disposition, obeys readily and plays in a lively manner with the objects at the table of the clinic. Actual examination and analysis, however, clearly show that her deportment is much more in harmony with the 3 year level than with the 4 year level of development. . . . We feel warranted in classifying this child as definitely subaverage in spite of the general normality of the picture."[111]

Advocates made object lessons out of cases such as Rose, where serious parental disappointment might have been avoided if scientific procedures had been followed. Occasionally, however, parental disappointment was unwarranted. Such instances occurred in cases where people suspected that agencies promising to give them normal children had actually given them something less. In 1930 Alice Taylor, a psychologist for the Children's Aid Society of Pennsylvania, reported to Gesell that the new parents of thirty-five-week-old Matilda worried constantly "because her tongue hangs out a great deal of the time."[112] Taylor, who had put Matilda to the test of the Gesell scale on several occasions, assured the adopters that the baby was perfectly normal. In fact, her response on every testing item placed her well ahead of the normal growth curve. Children such as Matilda strengthened Gesell's conviction that developmental science offered more than technical progress. It was the soul of fair play, offering opportunities to all children who deserved them. "The best procedure is to study, as carefully as science permits, the child for the individual that he is," he argued.[113]

The democratic credentials of developmental testing cannot be taken at face value, however. Technologies that mapped children's current growth status and future potential were understandably perceived by some would-be parents as a means not only of knowing what they were getting but of ensuring that they got what they wanted. Had they not been told repeatedly that "children may be successfully selected with scientific precision for most worthy and particular families"?[114] Would-be adopters frequently expressed preferences for children with certain racial and ethnic backgrounds (light rather than dark), conventionally attractive features (blue eyes, blonde curls), educational potential (college material), and excellent prospects for physical and mental health. The rhetoric of systematic selection not only endorsed such preferences but surely led some adopters to view technologies such as Gesell's as scientific warranties.

Well-educated would-be parents who worried about whether adoptees could meet their personal and community standards were most inclined to credit the promises of scientific adoption. "I want very much to be unselfish and charitable in planning for the welfare of a child who needs help," one college-educated physician's wife wrote to Gesell defensively. The absence of information about available children made her "mentally panicky." She wanted a child who would fit into her upper-middle-class milieu, where children were expected to be bright. "I feel that I need impersonal advice from a properly trained person who knows what may and may not be expected of children. Will you try to help me? . . . I feel it is only wise to try to be sure that I am not being led by sympathy and sentimentality into a situation which is essentially unworkable."[115] One indelicate Yale graduate announced to Gesell that, even during the Depression, he had a very substantial income and was willing to "do everything possible to secure a child that will have the capabilities of making the most of a college education and all that goes with it."[116] "We can give a child a great many advantages," pleaded yet another questing parent. "Out of fairness to ourselves as well as the child, we desire to avail ourselves of the latest scientific achievements, to insure a happy outcome."[117] "We have understood from our reading on the subject that you are able to judge mental capacity of a child with fair accuracy even at such an early age," a Williams College physicist wrote in hopes of securing a highly intelligent infant boy with Gesell's aid. "We feel that adopting a baby is less hazardous if this is true."[118] The applied developmental science that Gesell trusted to legitimize kinship by design and promote child welfare was perceived by adopters as a method to identify the children they most desired.

Gesell and other adoption professionals were understandably uncomfortable with the expectation that they should infallibly predict how children would turn out. "Perfection of pedigree is a rarity," Gesell warned. "There is some danger that adoptive parents will go to extremes in seeking such perfection."[119] Requests for conclusive developmental forecasting were apparently common enough that Gesell had to remind would-be adopters regularly that biogenetic kinship had its own risks. "Normal parentage does not insure normal development of natural born children," Gesell patiently wrote to one Ohio man seeking ironclad identification of a child from fine stock with great potential. "A normal amount of risk and faith must enter into every adoption."[120] Picky parents who were "unreasonably detailed and exacting in their specifications" paradoxically believed both too much and too little in the power of science to deliver what they wanted.[121] Letters such as those quoted here exaggerated the power of developmental knowledge and simultaneously discounted its value, reducing it to one more service to be purchased in the course of adoption.

Outcome Studies

In addition to testing technologies that naturalized adoption, outcome studies sought to supplement individualized assessment and prognosis with data about collective patterns of success and failure over time. Knowledge about how children and adoptive families turned out, in the aggregate, offered another means of governing adoption by predicting probable futures. Probability was not absolute, but it was the only type of certainty available. Measuring outcomes transformed chance into a calculable risk. By reducing dangers to "standard deviations" from recurring norms, outcome research intimated that good results might be something close to a sure thing.[122]

Today, adoption outcome studies comprise a well-established research genre, especially in social work and psychology.[123] Early in the twentieth century, however, they were novel. These studies began when pioneering agencies set out to investigate the results of their own work by finding out what had become of children placed years earlier. Curiosity about the fate of these children was the starting point, but researchers also hoped to estimate the success of kinship by design and, they hoped, prove its superiority. Outcome studies offered a reflexive, systematic, and empirical research style, evidence of tangible results, and improvements to future family making. Ever greater knowledge spelled ever more refined design. Ever more refined design spelled ever greater control. Control was the key to positive outcomes, and positive outcomes spelled progress.

Outcome studies were important intellectual enterprises from the outset, and they complemented other strategies for governing kinship. Predictability, one researcher noted in 1951, was especially urgent in adoption "because of the irreversible nature of the adoption process and the fact that a child's whole life is at stake."[124] Outcome studies managed these high stakes by translating the knowledge derived from group patterns into the trustworthy language of numbers.[125]

Case studies never lost their appeal among clinicians and researchers, but outcome studies possessed unique advantages. They transcended the idiosyncratic details of personal narrative by producing statistical knowledge of entire populations. In this sense, the adoption outcome study typified the trend in public health and social welfare—also visible in efforts to combat prostitution, homosexuality, drug addiction, and juvenile delinquency during the 1910s and 1920s—toward using epidemiological concepts such as risk factors and social norms to assess and treat individual cases.[126] At the same time, the chronological orientation of outcome research helped to transform adoption from a temporally fixed transaction into an ongoing experience. Adoption was never over.

The managerial sensibility, normalizing tendency, and ambitious vision of outcome research made it exquisitely suited to the requirements of design. What made a person good or a family successful? What measures captured the human "inputs" or "outputs" of family making? Personal stories of dependence, love, conflict, happiness, and disappointment in adoption resisted quantitative reduction and had a way of reminding researchers how little they understood and how feeble their predictive technologies were. Taken one at a time, adoption stories made it impossible to calculate outcomes without appraising what particular people and their experiences were worth. Uniqueness, however precious, conjured incommensurability and uncertainty, and these thwarted the design impulse.

In contrast, the statistical representation of aggregate patterns promised that the ingredients of better and worse kinship might be more objectively discerned and their policy implications clarified. In practice, outcome research was not uniformly designed or conducted, nor did it always point in the direction of certainty. Outcomes were probed when children were still young and when they were adults and typically measured in snapshot fashion rather than longitudinally. Data sources were varied and inconsistent, including current and retrospective self-report, evaluations by external observers, and a host of documents. Samples ranged from just a handful to many hundreds of children and families. Because methodological requirements were in flux when this research genre came into being, and for a long time afterward, some studies compared adoptees to matched controls, and many did not. Time and financial constraints often made such comparisons impractical, but sometimes it was unclear to whom adoptees should be compared. Would it be appropriate to compare adoptees with children raised by their natural parents? Or would comparing adoptees with children who were not adopted and grew up in institutions or foster care be more suitable? What counted as an "outcome" also shifted decisively over time.

Despite this variability, all adoption outcome research tackled stubborn moral questions in a vocabulary that sidelined subjective judgments in favor of quantitative truths. In 1962 the CWLA published a report devoted to quantitative research on parent selection, and by 1965 its survey of trends in adoption research reported that "the prospects of moving toward a scientific base for child placement appear bright."[127] Outcome studies transposed value dilemmas into correlations suited to the ongoing reform of applied technique. They epitomized the dream of kinship by design as well as the project of the human sciences generally: to harness science to human betterment and mobilize knowledge for the effective government of social problems.

How Did Children Turn Out?

The most important purpose of the outcome study was to discover how children turned out. Did they become dutiful sons and daughters, good students, reliable workers, and upstanding citizens? Or did they lead lives of disappointment and failure at home, at school, and in their communities? Outcome studies isolated various factors that might influence success and failure: age at placement, sex, natal background, educational and socioeconomic level of the adoptive family, motivations to adopt, child-rearing practices, and awareness or ignorance of adoptive status. Many of these factors were equally relevant to the developmental outcomes of nonadopted children, of course, but the focus on adoptees as subjects underlined the conviction that practical research findings could directly alleviate adoption's special risks.

Studies aimed to identify the combination of variables that predicted certain outcomes. Which family-making practices and kinship configurations produced good results for children and families? Which led to trouble? Which seemed not to matter? With definitive statistical answers to these questions, the theory went, future adoptions could be more effectively designed.

The first significant follow-up on a large group of placements in the United States was published in 1924 under the title *How Foster Children Turn Out*.[128] The author, Sophie van Senden Theis, was, as mentioned earlier, a pioneering adoption professional and researcher who worked for the New York State Charities Aid Association for forty-five years. Theis's remarkable research into her agency's early placements was funded by the Laura Spelman Rockefeller Memorial, and the study became the prototype for adoption outcome studies in later years. Although it lacked some sophisticated methods that were incorporated into later studies—no effort was made to compare foster children to a matched control group, for instance, and little information about children's birth families was systematically gathered—the outcome study of the New York State Charities Aid Association was noteworthy for its size, detail, clarity, and confidence about the positive difference that practical knowledge could make.

Up to that point, only a few small and woefully unsystematic inquiries had examined the aggregated results of either professional or amateur child placing. One such effort by the Boston Children's Aid Society concluded that the organization had been engaged "in the task of fitting round pegs into square holes, and in some cases exposing communities to great dangers from the acts of exceedingly difficult children."[129] Other findings during the first two decades of the century dismayed advocates of kinship by design. "In all, we have pitifully little evidence to offer in arguing for our side of the case—we self-styled scientific social workers," complained A. H. Stoneman of the Michigan Children's Aid Society in 1924. "We must proceed to get facts and consequent enlightenment."[130]

How Foster Children Turn Out offered both. The project was "the first serious effort, to collect, at first hand, on a considerable scale, the facts as to the careers of an unselected group of foster children," noted Homer Folks, who introduced the study.[131] The study tracked 910 children placed in new homes after 1898, carefully documenting their family backgrounds, health status, educational careers, and work experiences. All subjects were at least eighteen years old as of January 1, 1922, and their fate as adults could be ascertained. Of the 910 children studied, 269, or 29.5 percent, had been legally adopted.

Using the straightforward measures of school success, self-support, and observance of law, Theis concluded that foster children turned out quite well: 77 percent were "capable," and 23 percent were "incapable," terms that linked placement outcomes directly to economic self-sufficiency and moral character.[132] In the "capable" category were "subjects who are law-abiding, who manage their affairs with good sense and are living in accordance with good moral standards in their communities."[133] "Incapable" was the opposite: "subjects who are unable or unwilling to support themselves adequately, who are shiftless or have defied the accepted standards of morality or order of their communities."[134] "Incapable" described children who were harmful to others, "definitely at odds with society," or in need of institutional care and protection as adults. "Incapable" also included children who turned out to be "harmless." They were not "harmful," but they were not "capable" either.

By defining outcomes as she did, Theis made the important point that children should be judged according to standards of "social adjustment" that prevailed in their communities. Because turning out well meant satisfying parents and agencies, Theis's outcome study (and many that followed) revealed as much about adult expectations and memories as it did about what happened to children. It also revealed problems that plagued all social research on stigmatized subjects. To secure data, Theis had to contact families long out of touch with the New York State Charities Aid Association. "Reopening connections after a lapse of fifteen or twenty years required tact and caution," Theis noted.[135] Enlisting adopters was delicate, and making contact with adult adoptees embroiled researchers in ethical dilemmas. Worries that birth relatives might want to reclaim children, concerns that parental authority might be questioned, and fears that family secrets would be exposed could easily bias the information and opinions adoptive parents and children chose to share. "No information was considered valuable enough to be secured at such a cost nor at the risk of disturbing a satisfactory foster relationship," Theis declared.[136] Knowledge was essential, but its pursuit could not trump the welfare of particular children and families.

Discretion therefore guided data gathering. Carefully worded letters were sent to locate families: no letterhead was used, and return addresses listed a post office box "so that if [the letters] fell into the wrong hands they would betray no confidential information."[137] Field workers were instructed to "relinquish any attempt to get information if it threatened the peace of mind of either foster family or child."[138] Families who agreed to cooperate were interviewed in person whenever possible. Most subjects—parents and grown children—were seen this way, but in 17 percent of cases, only foster parents were interviewed, and in another 15 percent, information was provided only by letter and not always by family members themselves.

Sixteen field workers used a standardized, uniformly administered questionnaire that included 143 items, supplementing it with the agency's original case files and occasional interviews with people from outside the family.[139] These data were eventually presented by Mary Augusta Clark, the study's statistician, in sixty-seven tables and six charts, setting out a variety of demographic factors and exploring their relationship to positive and negative outcomes in statistical form.[140] What was the child's age at placement? Was the child's family background good or bad? What level of schooling had the children reached? How many children had been legally adopted? How many had health problems? What were their present occupations and marital status?

The study's findings reinforced some prevailing views and challenged others. A majority of the children (55.2 percent) had backgrounds that were characterized as "predominantly bad"; another quarter (24.8 percent) were classified with histories that were "bad—unknown."[141] Indeed, almost one-third of the children had two living parents at the time of placement, and two-thirds had lived with natal kin for periods of more than five years.

These facts indicated at once how very chaotic the circumstances of the birth families must have been and how reluctant Progressive agencies were to separate children from natal relatives. The New York State Charities Aid Association, Theis pointed out approvingly, "has always stood for the principle that no children should be taken from their homes merely because of poverty."[142] Placements grew out of desperate circumstances, that is, not simply the death of one or both parents, but family violence, abuse, neglect, desertion, alcoholism, and severe mental and physical illness.

These findings confirmed the eugenicist position that available children were, by nature, very bad risks. Yet the study pointed toward nurture by indicating that bad backgrounds did not map neatly onto bad outcomes. How determining could natal family history be if 80 percent of the children had bad backgrounds, but 77 percent emerged as "capable" people? Eugenicists predictably disputed Theis's conclusion. Paul Popenoe was gratified to see the hard light of science finally shining on outcomes, but he accused Theis of sugarcoating her data. "This study can not be taken at its face value" because children's "'success' at the age of eighteen is not final," he argued.[143] Theis had not really reckoned with the power of heredity, Popenoe insisted. Blood was sure to tell later on, when the adult "loses his youthful ideals, ambition and self-confidence, and begins to think that 'the world has it in for him' and that it is no use to try to be a good citizen."[144] All Theis had shown, Popenoe wrote dismissively, was that "the worst parental home . . . is better than the best orphan asylum."[145]

Theis's data challenged the twin convictions that infants were especially risky whereas older children were safer candidates for family life. She divided the children into age-at-placement cohorts and found that age five was the most sensitive border between positive and negative outcomes.[146] Children placed older than five were far more likely to experience multiple placements, less likely to do well or go far in school, and twice as likely to become "incapable" people.[147] Numbers testified to the difference that age made, but Theis insisted that "human relationships cannot be literally stated in statistics."[148] The findings mattered because they suggested that age produced qualitative differences in parent-child relationships. Children placed early felt that their foster families were truly their own, she reasoned, and their parents reciprocated: "They are more tolerant of the faults of children who have grown up in their households than of children who come to them from a long stay in bad surroundings; they champion their children, encourage them, protect them and stand by them as parents stand by their own."[149]

Legal adoptions almost always involved children taken early in life. The New York State Charities Aid Association had not encouraged families to legalize kin ties, and less than one-third of the children studied had been adopted, yet adoption strongly correlated with positive outcomes. Adopted children invariably finished high school, and virtually all children in the study who had attended college were adoptees.[150] Adoptees turned out to be more "capable" than the study group as a whole, and even those who became "incapable" were likely to have satisfied parents.[151] The finding that "adopted children had better advantages and show better development than the rest" did not compromise outcomes for nonadopted children, Theis hastened to add.[152] Some parents felt so strongly "that the children belonged to them in spirit and fact" or "had accepted the children so completely as their own" that it seemed superfluous to legalize kin ties that were real in every meaningful sense.[153] For others, hiring an attorney was simply too expensive, or the publicity was too unwelcome. Legalization predicted positive outcomes and family closeness, but there were still practical and emotional reasons for families to avoid adoption.

How Foster Children Turn Out shaped the future of adoption research and anticipated the direction of adoption culture in several ways. First, its empirical portrait of placed-out children and their families over time implied that adoption was a process that transpired over many years rather than a transaction completed once and for all during childhood. Second, it established a statistical baseline for the numbers of children who did and did not make good. Finding 77 percent "capable" left Theis and her colleagues hopeful, "with a distinct impression that there exists in individuals an immense power of growth and adaptation. . . . Our study leads us to believe that there are tremendous latent powers within an individual awaiting development, and that under favorable conditions these powers may be developed and directed toward accomplishment."[154] The conditions of emotional nurture mattered most. "In so far as any statement is possible on so obscure a subject," Theis concluded, "it is that the human environment matters more than the material surroundings. Undoubtedly the child's adjustment to his foster family governs to a significant degree his adjustment to society, and his adjustment to his foster family has less to do with their standards of comfort and their place in the community than with their human qualities and their understanding."[155] From the beginning, outcome studies replicated the hierarchy of values embodied in modern ideas about children and child welfare. Children were priceless, and love was more important than money.

Making outcome studies authoritative was a significant step toward kinship by design. "The whole structure of child-placing rests on the success of the children who are placed," wrote one insightful mother in 1922.[156] Own children who turned out poorly caused their families anguish, but their failures were not used to disparage heterosexual marriage or reproduction. On the other hand, "if they [adoptees] stumble and fall, they cause to stumble that long procession of little bloody feet moving up from the children's hell."[157] The reputation and future of adoption itself hinged, in part, on outcome research.

Relationships as Outcomes: The Shift toward Parents

For decades after 1924, adoption researchers cited *How Foster Children Turn Out* and followed its lead. They used such straightforward indices as school grades, work records, and health histories, just as Theis had, to highlight the dynamic experience of adoption itself. This quantitative research genre gave qualitative factors, not easily reduced to numbers, enormous weight. The most important placement outcome was the feeling of the kinship it made.

How children turned out depended on complex, evolving relationships rather than reflecting raw inputs in any straightforward fashion. When children turned out well, it was not only because they had been suitable candidates for family life, matched well, and placed wisely but also because they were nurtured. What had brought parents to adoption in the first place? What did child-rearing practices and attitudes convey about their feelings about parenthood? How did parents account for their child's successes and failures and their own? Motivations behind placement became decisive factors shaping outcomes.

In its increasing attention to parents' perceptions and experiences, outcome research both reflected and promoted the significant trend toward understanding emotional interactions as the heart and soul of family life. Careful selection of children, a priority for eugenicists, receded as a factor in comparison to parent selection and skilled matching. Technologies such as the Gesell scale, which promised to assuage fears about children's quality by accurately predicting developmental potential, paradoxically became less relevant to adoption outcomes as they became more common features of the adoption process. One follow-up study of adoption candidates examined at Yale between 1942 and 1947, for instance, directly contradicted Gesell's claims that infant examinations would yield valid developmental predictions.[158] As fears of children with defects diminished, the conviction grew that parents could make or break kinship. Good parents made good children. Flawed parents ruined even the best children's chances for normal development, happiness, and success.

When Iris Ruggles Macrae studied all the adoptions arranged by the New England Home for Little Wanderers between 1926 and 1935, she found that virtually all the records after 1931 included significant information about the current and predicted emotional climate of the home, whereas earlier records were silent on the subject. The agency's new appreciation for the parents' role in children's development was visible in its records. After 1931, all files included notations that systematic discussions about "telling" had been incorporated into the adoption process.[159] Before 1931, files revealed that only about half of the agency's adoptions included any mention of "telling." The trend toward "a more psychiatric approach," according to Macrae, was "evidence of both a more scientific approach as well as better case recording."[160] Deliberate exploration of parental psychology was an improvement over cursory evaluation.

Outcomes rested heavily on parents' emotional qualifications. One early study of disrupted adoptions by a Buffalo, New York, child-placing agency identified defective parenting as the common element in all cases of "adoptions gone wrong." Worried about "tainted heredity" and insecure about their own status, adopters "had not been able to accept the child fully and wholly for himself."[161] Such anxieties might ruin children who "felt inferior and not a real part of the family group."[162] With outcome research blaming parents for adoption breakdowns, "determining the caliber of the adoptive parents themselves" became more important than ever.[163] This new emphasis placed a great premium on professional skill, insight, and "surer ways of evaluating people's motivations, their flexibility, their feeling qualities and the balance of relationships within the family."[164]

The move from (children's) nature to (parental) nurture was apparent in outcome studies from the 1930s through the 1960s. For example, a study of all thirty adoptions arranged by the Boston Children's Friend Society between 1932 and 1939 set out to reveal parents' perceptions of how children had turned out precisely because at the time the study was conducted, in 1950, such perceptions appeared to determine outcomes.[165] When the adoptions were first arranged, however, the agency concentrated on testing children's qualifications and provided adopters with details about natal background, preplacement developmental reports, and IQ scores. It did not try to anticipate adults' ability to be emotionally responsive parents. Outcomes that researchers defined and measured were in constant motion, along with the practices that aimed to predict and produce them.

In her study of Boston adoptions during the 1930s, researcher Georgina Hotchkiss considered parents' feelings about adoption synonymous with outcomes; she made no effort to confirm or compare their assessments independently against such measures as school achievement, test scores, or work records, as Theis had done. What Hotchkiss discovered was that 75 percent of parents were satisfied with how their children had turned out, almost identical to Theis's estimate of "capable" outcomes despite the huge difference in sample size. All the parents Hotchkiss interviewed reported problems, but only one-quarter used such terms as "poorly adjusted," "insecure," "difficult," and "baffling" or expressed real worry that their children's troubles might never end.[166] Parents who reported that others observed a physical resemblance between them and their children were especially pleased with the outcomes, suggesting, again, that matching mattered.[167] In only one case did parents judge an adoption a clear failure. Morris Quimby was institutionalized at age fifteen after spending eleven unhappy years with his adoptive family. His mother reasoned that Morris had never felt entirely at home, but Hotchkiss blamed the tragic outcome on his parents, "who never felt that he belonged to them."[168]

Hotchkiss found no meaningful correlation (as Theis had) between age at placement and outcomes and speculated that other factors tipped the balance between success and failure. Perhaps the agency's policy of sharing detailed information with adopters, unusual at the time, had made the difference. Because all the children were deemed average or above at the time of placement and "adoptive parents might feel a special need to rear 'successful' children when they had failed as biological parents," unusual pressure might have been placed on the children.[169] Whether such pressure was more likely to produce positive or negative educational outcomes remained obscure, but Hotchkiss did note that adopters with some college education tended to rate their children's school achievement more harshly than parents who had only finished high school.[170]

The study's analysis of parents' retrospective assessments ultimately circled back to two overriding factors: "the present tendency to blame parents for the inadequacies and failings of their children, rather than the children themselves" and adoption itself.[171] Even the most loving adoptive parents faced a difficult "compromise" because they lacked a biological connection to their children. "However closely the new family matches the natural setting, the child can never be the natural child of his adoptive parents, no matter how strong the wish on both sides. The fact of adoption remains."[172] By acknowledging that emotional realities could be distinct from more objective measures, Hotchkiss confirmed that research should probe subjective outcomes, including feelings about adoption itself. This therapeutic emphasis was fundamental to the interpretive approaches that reached their zenith at midcentury.

An outcome study of one hundred New York agency adoptions between 1931 and 1940 underlined how salient a factor adoption itself would eventually become in assessing outcomes.[173] The study, titled *How They Fared in Adoption*, was conducted in the 1960s, three decades after the adoptions had taken place. For authors Benson Jaffee and David Fanshel, the difference and difficulty of adoptive kinship were significant factors. Adopters were preoccupied with "resolving the psychological insult associated with the problem of infertility," they asserted.[174] Infertile couples might harbor conscious or unconscious feelings of hostility toward children who reminded them of their reproductive failure and would surely face a "primary task" not faced by natural parents: "developing a feeling of entitlement to his child."[175] One task of outcome studies, therefore, was to measure adults' "ability to undertake parental role obligations without neurotic conflict."[176]

How did Jaffee and Fanshel go about measuring this ability? They hypothesized that strict child rearing indicated decreased ability to handle normal separation and independence. In contrast, parents who rejected conventional modes of discipline, took more risks, and allowed children greater freedom had achieved nonneurotic parenthood. Jaffee and Fanshel conducted extensive tape-recorded interviews yielding "objective, categorized items which could be coded and treated quantitatively through use of an electronic computer."[177] Two additional sources of data were original case records and detailed interviewer ratings designed to assess parents' feelings about adoption, infertility, and their relationship with the adopted child. On the basis of this information, Jaffee and Fanshel examined outcomes in various "life-space areas," including school performance, quality of past and present child/parent relationship, health, vocational history, heterosexual adjustment, and parental satisfaction. The authors summarized the outcomes, calculated an overall adjustment score, and used the scores to divide the one hundred children in the study into "low-problem," "middle-range," and "high-problem" groups.

The researchers expected adoption to make all the difference, so they were surprised to discover that most parents they interviewed (73 percent) insisted that any problems they had encountered were unrelated to adoption.[178] Even among parents of the thirty-three adoptees categorized as "high-problem," few (only 21 percent) claimed that adoption was relevant to what had gone wrong. In correlating demographic, behavioral, and attitudinal factors with the final outcome measures, Jaffee and Fanshel found other surprises, too. Age at placement, which had declined steadily during the previous four decades, did not appear to influence outcomes as most people believed it did. Jaffee and Fanshel were astonished to find that the average placement age for children in the "low-problem" group was over sixteen months, whereas "high-problem" children had been placed earlier, at twelve months.[179] During the 1930s both of these groups would have been classified as early and risky placements.

A second shock came with the study's findings about revelation of adoptive status. Virtually all the children (90 percent) had been told about their adoptions by parents.[180] Aside from communicating the fact of adoption, however, families had made varied decisions about when to tell, how to tell, and how often (if ever) to return to the topic. Most parents did eventually say something, but no parents reported giving children honest information about birth parents' marital status or reasons for surrender, and many deliberately withheld sordid details.[181] Contrary to expectations that how parents managed telling would bear significantly on adoption outcomes, Jaffee and Fanshel found that no correlation existed with either favorable or unfavorable life adjustment. Children who had been told of their adoptions early in life did just as well or poorly as children told later on. The same held true for children whose parents discussed the adoption frequently and infrequently or who revealed or withheld information about birth parents. The data was poked and prodded so as to reveal exactly how "telling" influenced outcomes. Seven statistical tables tabulated "telling" data, but the researchers found only a single correlation with outcome measures. Adoptees who had expressed more interest and curiosity about their natal backgrounds were disproportionately clustered in the "high-problem" group.[182] This finding suggested to the authors that indifference to genealogy was a correlate of positive outcome. Such a finding confirmed a view frequently expressed in adoption literature at midcentury: well-adjusted adoptees were unconcerned about their natal backgrounds.

Finally, Jaffee and Fanshel's findings called into question their initial hypothesis that more- and less-controlling child-rearing practices reflected more- and less-neurotic parenting and would produce distinctive outcome patterns. The researchers tallied indices of child-rearing orientation that ranged from spanking and the gender division of disciplinary labor to babysitter use.[183] The latter was presumed to indicate a more relaxed child-rearing philosophy, but turned out on closer inspection to be an artifact of the family's socioeconomic standing. Parents with more disposable income, not surprisingly, hired more substitute child care. In any event, Jaffee and Fanshel found little evidence to confirm their theory that parents who vanquished the "psychological insult" of infertility would use more liberal child-rearing techniques that would in turn produce more successful outcomes. Only the data concerning mothers who were consistently absent from the home when adoptees were very young seemed to correlate strongly with adjustment difficulties, and these problems were concentrated in just a few "life-space areas."[184]

How They Fared in Adoption illustrates a noteworthy pattern in the evolution of outcome studies. As researchers used more sophisticated research design to compensate for uncontrolled sources of variance in their samples, and more rigorous statistical methods to isolate correlational significance, they also grew more reluctant to make causal claims. "There is no pretense of being able to make any causal inferences about the etiology of the various types of outcome," hedged Jaffee and Fanshel at the very outset of their study.[185] After hundreds of pages exploring carefully coded data, remarkably little could be known for sure.

Adopted children and families were the same as all children and families, the study concluded, but they were different, too. This made adoptive kinship a compelling research subject, but it did not answer questions about why adopted children turned out as they did. Theis's study, published almost five decades earlier, was more confident that knowledge produced through systematic research would shape future practices constructively than many outcome studies conducted in the second half of the twentieth century. Uncertainty increased even as techniques of probabilistic prediction were perfected.

Did Kinship by Design Produce Superior Outcomes?

One specific type of outcome study set out to compare the outcomes of agency and independent placements, typically to prove the superiority of the former. It deserves special mention because even after several decades of regulation, interpretation, standardization, and naturalization, research did not always vindicate the claims of kinship by design.

The most widely cited study of this kind at midcentury was by two Connecticut physicians, Catherine Amatruda (a colleague of Arnold Gesell's at Yale) and Joseph Baldwin.[186] They compared one hundred independently placed babies with one hundred babies whose adoptions had been arranged by agencies and discovered that each group of one hundred adoptions contained roughly the same proportion of "good" and "bad" babies and families: the ratio was three (good) to one (bad). Agency adoptions were not distinguished by access to better human material but rather by superior ability to match like with like, pairing good babies with good homes far more consistently than independent child placers. With matching itself as the index of success, Amatruda and Baldwin argued that "social agencies do better adoption placements than does the well-intentioned or expedient laity."[187] In professional adoption, design was paramount. In independent adoptions, "everything is relegated to chance and to luck."[188]

An ambitious Florida study of almost five hundred independent adoptions finalized between 1944 and 1947 explored why so many people relied on chance and luck when it was obvious to experts that agency adoptions were better. Desire for newborns and infants was the first reason. Almost 75 percent of adoptees were placed before one month of age; 39 percent were placed before one week, and 11 percent had new parents before they were twenty-four hours old.[189] Physicians, with privileged access to newborns, were the most common adoption intermediaries.[190] At the time, few agencies would have considered placing babies this young.

What became of these children and families a decade after legalization? The Florida study used original adoption records, extensive follow-up interviews with parents (mostly mothers), and a variety of school records and psychological test scores to measure outcomes. Researchers found that parents were significantly happier with adoption outcomes than observers who assessed their homes and their children. A full 85 percent of parents expressed unqualified satisfaction, whereas only 46 percent of homes were ranked excellent or good and only 70 percent of children were ranked well or fairly well adjusted.[191] These findings led the researchers to conclude that "the outcome of the independent adoptions was not as good as that which the law aims to achieve."[192] With less than half of the children "in homes that seemed fully up to standard," the risks of independent adoption were unevenly shared. Adopters almost always got what they wanted. Adoptees got what they needed only about half the time.

Like virtually all outcome researchers, the authors of the Florida study were deeply committed to kinship by design, yet their work hardly strengthened the case for it. Dismayed that less than half of the homes were considered adequate for raising adopted children, the researchers showed that 70 percent of adoptees turned out well anyway, no matter how they were placed or by whom. Instead of buttressing the authority of kinship by design, the Florida study undermined its main claims to make the decisive difference between risk and safety, between unfitness and belonging, between disregard and regard for children's interests.

Outcome studies of all kinds showed fairly consistent results over a period when adoption changed dramatically and professionals and agencies made significant gains. Increasingly sophisticated methodological approaches and findings that varied depending on sample sizes, the specific types of adoption under consideration, and shifting conceptions of what outcomes actually measured did not do much to alter average results, which had changed remarkably little since 1924. One meta-analysis of adoption outcome studies, beginning with *How Foster Children Turn Out* and ending with the Florida study of independent placements, arrived at the following tally: 78 percent of all adoptions were "unequivocally successful," 8 percent were in an intermediate category ranging from "fairly successful" to "some problems," and 14 percent were "unsatisfactory" or "poor."[193] This finding was close to Theis's tally: 77 percent "capable" and 23 percent "incapable" (the latter category included 11 percent "harmless" and 12 percent "harmful"). The adoption research enterprise had been transformed since 1924. Outcomes had not.

The vision of families made scientifically, hence more sturdily, made substantial gains by midcentury. By then, ironically, developmentalists' confidence in their own predictive techniques had diminished. A follow-up study of all the infants Gesell examined in the process of adoption between 1942 and 1947, for instance, showed no correlation between babies' original scores and their subsequent performance on the Stanford-Binet. "All our results are obviously contrary to the implications of Gesell's claims," lamented researcher J. Richard Wittenborn.[194] His hopes for the predictive validity of testing were dashed.

The quest to make adoption scientific endured nevertheless. At midcentury, most agencies in the United States used consultants who offered "the benefit of pertinent scientific evaluation" "in order to reduce . . . risks to a minimum."[195] Although 55 percent of agencies used mental testing to help determine children's eligibility for adoption, 75 percent called it an "integral part of the study of a child prior to placement," useful for matching children to families, even infants, whose scores were not reliably predictive.[196] Selective placement for mentality was considered slightly more important than matching by race or religion, not only because mentally similar children and parents naturally belonged together but also because of the emotional comfort that similarity of intellect engendered.[197] By midcentury, even most Catholic agencies considered "level of intelligence" the overriding factor in selecting adoptive homes; they employed psychological testers and consultants routinely, clear evidence that scientific adoption had spread to some child placers whose religious motivations had previously led them to advocate families made by God rather than by science.[198] The appeal of early placements, the promises of mental measurement, and vigorous public relations efforts to correct public ignorance blamed for the persistence of independent operators all helped adoption professionals. By the early 1970s, the high point of professional authority in adoption, only 21 percent of nonrelative adoptions were privately arranged.[199]

The history of outcome studies from the 1920s through the 1960s suggests how determined the advocates of design were to validate adoption quality through aggregate measurement. Like testing, outcome studies promised to govern and improve adoption by making it safer and more natural. They suggested that frightening uncertainties might be replaced with comforting probabilities, that other people's children could be adopted safely, and that dependent and vulnerable children might become responsible citizens rather than social misfits and menaces.

Outcome research also illuminated significant changes in the theory and practice of adoption. Initially, researchers approached the educational and occupational achievements of adult adoptees as the outcomes to be measured, expecting them to reflect qualities differentiating the relative goodness or badness of children's natal backgrounds. But evidence quickly showed that such inputs did not map neatly onto outcomes; most children placed for adoption had negative family backgrounds, whereas most adoptions had positive results. Beginning with Sophie van Senden Theis and *How Foster Children Turn Out*, researchers soon turned to the more dynamic and complex interactions that shaped adoption. As relationships became the most important outcomes, responsibility for the quality of kinship shifted from children to parents and from nature to nurture.

Testing practices and outcome studies embodied the managerialism of kinship by design and promoted a conception of adoption as an operation in which ambitious social engineering mitigated the presence of risk. Gesell was a vigorous advocate for this type of adoption process. For him—and for countless other clinicians and researchers in human science and human service—modernizing adoption meant standardizing, quantifying, and naturalizing it. Rationalizing processes were associated with scientific methods, practices, and personnel working cooperatively with a benevolent state. Scientific and technological resources were therefore crucial legitimizing forces in the history of modern adoption. Design promised to tame adoption, transforming other people's children into one's own.

PART THREE

Difference and Damage, 1945–1975

CHAPTER SIX

Adoption Revolutions

Adoption revolutions reflected upheavals in the history of modern American kinship that, in turn, originated in modernity itself. Older methods of defining and creating families gave way under pressure from novel ideas about childhood, adolescence, sex, gender, and the body that were articulated by social movements, incorporated as subjects of research, and nourished by sharp demographic shifts in patterns of marriage and divorce, childbearing and child rearing, and household formation and dissolution. American families in the twentieth century underwent constant change, resulting in a pluralistic patchwork of arrangements that simultaneously democratized kinship and increased the pressure to rank families on a hierarchy of more and less legitimate.

Within the adoption world, advocates strove to move adoption up that hierarchy. Successive waves of reform were greeted as unparalleled steps toward equality even when they overturned the most cherished achievements of the last adoption revolution. Early in the twentieth century, advocates set out to revolutionize adoption by governing its risks, concealing its artifice, and authenticating the experience of substitute kinship. They were confident that modernization would limit adoption to "normal" children, that only children old enough to be dependably knowable should be placed, and that children and adults should be matched on a host of visible and invisible factors. Then they changed their minds.

Sharp reversals in the design of kinship at midcentury revealed the historical and cultural innovations underlying all social operations, including matching, which claimed merely to copy nature. The invention of special-needs adoptions, the critique of matching, and the first glimmerings of organized intercountry adoption all changed the rules about who could be adopted by whom, how, when, and why, at least in theory. This chapter examines these adoption revolutions. The changes revealed that there was nothing fixed and foundational about even those policies and practices devoted to emulating a reassuringly fixed and foundational nature. The democratization of adoption that followed from considering many more children eligible for family belonging after 1945 revealed how limited the project of kinship by design had been up to that point and how allergic it had been to threatening differences. Instead of undermining the design project itself, adoption revolutions at midcentury resulted in extending regulation, interpretation, standardization, and naturalization to more people in more ways than ever before. Adoption revolutions, old and new, tried to reconcile difference with equality.

Special Needs and the Expansion of Adoptability

At midcentury, the special-needs revolution saw professionals alter their position on the appropriateness of family life itself for large numbers of children previously considered unadoptable because of disability, disease, race, and other background factors. Horrified by the spectacle of Nazi genocide, racism, and experimentation on human populations designated as inferior, Americans repudiated the crude eugenics that had made adoptive kinship as suspect as it was selective before World War II. The same professionals who had formerly patrolled the borders of adoption now campaigned to open them, celebrating the democratization of adoption services as a sign of enlightenment, progress, civil rights, and deinstitutionalization within the child welfare world.

That the architects of kinship by design changed their minds so fundamentally challenged their authority as well as the credibility of their vision. Some Americans perceived rapidly shifting agency standards as evidence that meddlesome do-gooders who acted in the name of children had excessive power, symbolizing the erosion of individual freedom by the liberal welfare state. "This is not supposed to be a socialist country," complained Percy Maddux of Seattle in 1944. "Parenthood is a natural, inherent, inalienable right. . . . When bureaucracy strides into the home telling people whether they may have children or not, democracy has flown out the window."[1]

Nor was it difficult to see hypocrisy in declarations to serve all children, no matter how hard to place. The pledge to make adoption widely accessible coexisted with markedly skewed patterns of service provision. Twenty percent of agencies, many representing communities where no other adoption agencies existed, offered no services whatsoever to nonwhite children or children of mixed race, according to a major CWLA survey at midcentury.[2] Total exclusion was less pervasive in 1950 than it had been twenty or thirty years earlier, but even agencies that did try to place minority children so often failed or placed so few that the survey concluded that "children of minority races do not have equal opportunity with white children for adoptive placement."[3]

This finding was an understatement. In some states with large African American populations, such as Florida and Louisiana, not a single African American child was placed for adoption by an agency for many years running in the 1940s.[4] The lower socioeconomic status and segregated housing of African Americans, supposed lack of adoption awareness in the African American community, and "cultural blocks" produced by "deep insecurity and prejudices" were all offered as reasons by agencies for why they arranged so few "Negro adoptions," as they were called at the time.[5] Even after a number of specialized programs were launched in the 1950s to combat the attitude that "adoption is a white man's luxury" and recruit African American parents, 40–70 percent of African American couples who filed applications with agencies dropped out of the adoption process, rates far higher than their white counterparts.[6]

During the special-needs revolution, mixed-race children posed unique dilemmas. At a time when racial intermarriage was both rare and controversial, almost any decision about where mixed-race children belonged required violations of matching. Some white couples were willing to accept children of mixed heritage, however, especially if they were trying to overcome eligibility disadvantages of their own. New, more expansive eligibility criteria, in other words, did not alter the hierarchy of characteristics that defined certain children and adults as more desirable than others. It simply matched less desirable children with less desirable adults and meant that "many agencies will have to lower optimum standards" to be "genuinely realistic" about hard-to-place children.[7] One 1950s study of special-needs placements in Wisconsin, a state in the vanguard of the special-needs revolution, found that some would-be parents disadvantaged by advanced age would compromise their racial preferences in order to adopt—but only to a point. White couples who wanted white babies might accept children who were part-Indian but would refuse to consider African American children, even if that meant living without children at all.[8]

Many couples who adopted Native American children at this time were motivated not by affirmative desires to adopt transracially but by eligibility disadvantages—such as being over age forty or already having their "own" children. Although the era's transracial adopters were frequently assumed to be political liberals and supporters of civil rights, this was not necessarily the case.[9] In fact, desire to avoid adopting children with any African American background motivated numerous white couples to accept Native American children. "It would be okay as long as the child would be light-skinned," one father recalled thinking when the agency first suggested an Indian child. "We did not want the child to be taken for part-Negro. The agency had said we would have a better chance of being accepted if we took an Indian child."[10] "They were very understanding," another parent commented, "and the agency was able to assure us that the child would not be too dark or have any Negroid features."[11] White adopters of Native American children in the 1950s and 1960s were far less willing to consider adopting African American mixed-race children (even in cases where the child's appearance did not testify to his or her racial background) than "Oriental" children, children older than eight, children with mental retardation, or even children with serious, uncorrectable physical disabilities.[12] Transracial adoptions frequently reflected, rather than transcended, the country's racial hierarchy. White remained at the top, black at the bottom.

Considering the durability of such preferences, worries that children would darken and display unpredictable, racialized features as they aged often made social workers reluctant to place them in white families at all.[13] Joe, born to Indian and Mexican parents, was "dark in coloring"; Marie, "Eskimo and Indian," looked "Oriental" except for her brown skin; Felix looked "more White than Indian," except for a single feature that betrayed his one native birth parent: "very thick coarse black hair."[14] Saul, born in 1949 to a white Jewish mother and a "partly Negro" father, "has a beautiful face, lovely blue-green eyes and long black lashes. His only features which indicate an admixture are his hair and his skin tone."[15] These children were difficult to place because of their appearance.

Unwilling to reject all such children as unadoptable, agencies sometimes followed a wait-and-see policy, resulting in later placement for these children than for their white counterparts.[16] They also consulted with scientific authorities in hopes of assuring themselves and jittery parents that their children would not grow up to have dark skin and other "Negroid features," especially kinky hair and full lips. Sheldon Reed of the Dight Institute for Human Genetics at the University of Minnesota made determinations about which babies might pass. When passing was not possible, agencies worried about the "extreme trauma that some parents may experience when racial characteristics in the developing child become markedly different from theirs," along with the "traumatic situation for the child."[17] In theory, new standards made virtually all children adoptable. In practice, old prejudices endured.

Placing mixed-race children with nonwhite parents also presented difficulties. Many African American adopters, who equated class mobility with sexual respectability and restraint, were as horrified by race mixing as whites. Others were determined to ascertain that their child's skin color would remain light, although judges could and did balk at allowing white-looking children to become legal members of nonwhite families.[18] In 1952 Louise Wise Services initiated an Interracial Adoption Program to place mixed-race children in African American and Puerto Rican families because Jewish adopters had proved unwilling to take these half-Jewish children. Even during this period of allegedly revolutionary change, race matching was so universally practiced that the CWLA included no questions at all about transracial placements in its midcentury survey. The only comment on this topic was a brief note that such placements never occurred.[19]

Social workers knew that rigid adherence to the material standards of white middle-class families amounted to a policy of racial exclusiveness. This became an increasingly pressing policy issue during the civil rights era. Some argued for standards that were more culturally sensitive and realistic about African Americans' socioeconomic standing, such as accepting maternal employment or relaxing requirements about income and age. To be flexible in these ways was not to lower standards or sacrifice the emotional welfare of minority children, they hastened to add. In the 1950s a number of pioneering projects around the country took practical steps to extend adoption services to nonwhite children, typically by mounting creative efforts to recruit nonwhite parents. But there was no getting around the fact that a large number of agencies simply refused to provide such services at all. Blatant discrimination necessarily applied to nonwhite birth mothers too, for whom services were often nonexistent.[20] In 1954, for example, few unmarried African American women who gave birth in Kansas City, Missouri, were offered any sort of professional casework during their pregnancies.[21] The geography of choice for adult women facing decisions about whether to become or remain mothers was as deeply marked by racism as the geography of eligibility for family life was marked for their children.[22]

Under the expansive new definition of adoptability, disability and age were in practice still reasons for excluding children. This was the legacy, in part, of an earlier standard that pledged to satisfy adopters' expectations for normal children (i.e., young, healthy, and as similar to the adopters as possible). The brave new adoption world, according to one description, marked a sharp turn away from thinking that adoption should involve "less risk than in natural parenthood" and provide adopters with a "gilt-edged guaranty, much like that of a purebred Holstein calf."[23] Professionals may have made "very rapid progress toward dropping the concept of the 'perfect child,'" but finding homes for school-age children, children with disabilities, and African American, Asian, Native American, and mixed-race children took a lot of extra time and money that many agencies did not have. "For infants we have a 'sellers' market," explained Martha Eliot, chief of the USCB, "but for older children the 'salesman' in the person of the social worker has to do an intensive job."[24] In the mid-1950s, 35 percent of all children who came to the attention of agencies were refused at the point of intake because of race, age, or disability, and one-third of these children were referred to other agencies.[25] These children were no longer shut out of adoption because they were considered unadoptable in theory, but they were shut out of adoption nevertheless. Agency officials conceded that implementing an expanded definition of adoptability was a major challenge in practice. It took time and money they simply did not have.

Children with mental and developmental disabilities represented an especially large portion of those turned away. More so than children with blindness, heart disease, tuberculosis, cancer, cleft palate, or diabetes, they were considered very difficult to place. Until the 1950s these children were more likely to be institutionalized than treated as candidates for family placement. Given the earlier equation between normal mentality and adoptability, this is not surprising. Social workers charged in earlier decades with identifying feebleminded and "defective" children so as to exclude them from adoption were now asked to find willing parents for them on the theory that all children needed family life. Adoption professionals understood that altering the standards for children's eligibility would also necessitate new thinking about what qualified adults to become parents. "If we no longer want the public to insist on rosy infants for adoption, we must also confess that we do not have a yen for handsome, 30-year-old parents and new ranch houses with home-made pies in the deep freeze," noted CWLA president Marshall Field, publishing tycoon, social entrepreneur, and grandson of the department store magnate. "At least, I hope we don't."[26]

Eligibility standards had been rewritten within a few years, but preferences in children did not change quickly. Most adopters requested healthy, attractive babies matched to their own race rather than older and disabled children.[27] Only 6 percent of agencies reported automatically excluding children whose natal backgrounds included mental defect, epilepsy, or incest.[28] Yet most continued to rely on a model of mental matching. When selecting parents for particular children, "level of intelligence and intellectual potential" were considered the most important factors, slightly more important than religion or race.[29] Even with placements being made much earlier and mental testers retreating from strong claims about predicting educational outcomes, adopters still wanted reassurance that the mental quality of the children they received would match their own.

Qualification Tests for Adults

As for the adult parties to adoption, practice at midcentury was also in transition. Agencies that had paid attention only to birth mothers were expressing new interest in the birth father, "a nebulous figure left largely unstudied."[30] Why? Some agencies sought contact with birth fathers to supplement information about the child's background or to solicit financial assistance for the child. Others contacted fathers only when their marriage to the mother gave them legal standing, preferring to ignore them when unmarried and legally irrelevant.[31] Not until *Stanley v. Illinois* (1972) did the informed consent of unmarried birth fathers become a major factor in adoption law and practice, and unmarried fathers have figured centrally in a number of high-profile adoption controversies since then, including the cases of Baby Jessica and Baby Richard.[32] Before 1972, the legal, social, and emotional concerns of birth fathers were frequently dismissed, if they were noticed at all. They were as putative as fatherhood itself.

Mothers were the most important people to children, even when they gave them away. Long the primary focus of professional help and scrutiny, birth mothers too had evolved in the minds of agency professionals. Although half of all children adopted in the United States in 1950 were born to married parents, unmarried mothers and their illegitimate babies were portrayed as the major players in the adoption drama. Unlike the first generation of adoption professionals, who held that unmarried mothers were likely to be feebleminded, sexually victimized against their will, or simply too immoral to heed society's rules, the view at midcentury was that nonmarital pregnancy expressed an underlying emotional problem rooted in women's own maladjustment and immaturity. Birth mothers at midcentury were not weak or helpless or bad. They were neurotic.

Because pregnancy had become "an unconsciously planned act" and a "result of a disturbed family life," surrendering the child for adoption became the responsible thing to do.[33] This new friendliness to surrender, combined with the desire to rid the country of independent adoptions, prompted agencies to reorient their services to white birth mothers. A national network of maternity homes (two hundred licensed homes in forty-four states after 1945, most run by the Florence Crittenton Association of America,

Catholic Charities, and the Salvation Army) served as an institutional symbol of a liminal space "behind the fence" from which white middle-class
women and babies could be returned, after adoption, to normal life.[34] The
goal of agencies in working with the birth mother was "to help her become
at peace with herself and become a happier person."[35]

Unlike the early twentieth century, when unmarried mothers were
scorned for abandoning their babies and many people believed that maternal redemption depended on family preservation, the second chance that
adoption offered after 1945 to young white women depended on releasing
the child for adoption. This decision, which promised to liberate the child
from a life with a disturbed mother and simultaneously put that mother
on the road to rehabilitation, was subject to enormous coercion. Mortified parents pressured or even forced their wayward daughters to leave their
schools and communities during their pregnancies in hopes that they might
return, magically restored to normalcy, nine months later. Professionals
were somewhat more subtle, but at a time when most social work studies
of unmarried mothers concluded that women who kept their babies were
more troubled than women who gave them up, it is not surprising that
they too supported the adoption mandate.[36] At midcentury, two-thirds of
agencies accepted relinquishments as soon as birth mothers were ready;
they also agreed that a warm, therapeutic relationship with a caseworker
was the single most important service they provided to this group.[37] Like
changing standards on placement age, pushing unmarried mothers toward
surrender represented a complete reversal in adoption philosophy and practice, sharply increasing the number of adoptions in the postwar decades.
This dimension of the midcentury revolution represented the triumph of
the therapeutic approach, which originated in the work of interpretation as
early as the 1910s and 1920s.

Applicants for adoptive parenthood were also subjected to thorough psychological interpretation at midcentury. The home study, as the investigation of parental worthiness came to be called, still compiled mountains of
facts about employment, education, religious and community affiliations,
and the physical features of the home itself. But motivation to adopt had
become more central to a process that moved away from simple discovery
and gravitated toward complex forms of help. The point was not simply
to accept or reject applicants on the basis of fixed standards but to evaluate the strengths and weakness of the applicants' not-yet-realized parental
abilities and "to help the applicants know whether they want a child, and if
they are ready to adopt."[38] Couples who requested children from agencies
"may or may not be consciously aware of their true motives."[39] They could

be fooling themselves about their desire to become adoptive parents, the reasons behind the desire, or both. No longer was the home study a naive procedure that "checked off the items on an outline and accepted families at face value."[40] In attempting to establish truths so slippery they eluded applicants themselves, social workers admitted they were "playing God."[41] Doing so was a moral and professional responsibility "to meet the child's right to have an emotionally secure family life."[42]

Financial stability remained very important in selecting parents, but emotional well-being ranked with physical health at the top of the agencies' list. What specific evidence of emotional welfare were home studies supposed to uncover? Agencies reported that they looked for such qualities as "personal adjustment," happy marriages, congenial relationships with family and friends, ability to love a child, and resolution of the grief that accompanied childlessness.[43] By midcentury, "sterility" was an eligibility criterion for adopters in most agencies, handy for the practical reason that it limited the number of couples eligible to adopt. Officially, using it as a qualification would "protect a child from placement with parents who do not want children or are fearful of parental responsibilities."[44] Vigorous efforts to overcome infertility typically indicated sincere desires for parenthood.

The CWLA's national survey showed that infertility was required by approximately 80 percent of agencies, and many did not consider an application complete without a doctor's report documenting the medical workup and length of treatment.[45] This practice masked ongoing disagreements about infertility's significance. Did it matter whether the infertile party was the husband or the wife? Was a pattern of miscarriages more or less auspicious for adoption than failure ever to conceive? What were agencies supposed to do when no medical explanation existed for a couple's childlessness? Was adoption ever advisable as a "cure" for infertility? Was it acceptable to give a child to a couple with secondary infertility, that is, who had one child of their own but could not conceive a second? Would children placed with infertile couples be adored as symbols of family completion or resented as reminders of reproductive failure? Most agencies agreed that infertility was a central qualification. Beyond that, answers varied.

Tests for psychological well-being and infertility limited the pool of applicants and were therefore most frequently applied to married couples requesting healthy white infants, who were in heaviest demand. What about single adopters? No state laws had ever prohibited single individuals from adopting children, and "spinsters" who took in children were recurring figures in adoption history before World War II and a staple of

Victorian moral fiction, although it is impossible to know how many single women or female couples actually adopted. [46]

The special-needs revolution after 1945 sparked the first systematic efforts to recruit single people into adoptive parenthood. The first agency to enlist single parents was the Los Angeles Bureau of Adoptions. In 1965 this public agency sought out single African Americans to locate same-race parents for African American children for whom married parents could not be found. Over the next two years, the agency placed a total of thirty-nine children with single mothers and one child with a single father, a small number considering the hundreds of children in care.[47] According to Los Angeles Bureau director Walter A. Heath, two parents were preferable, "but one parent is better than none."[48] By the time it revised its adoption standards in 1968, the CWLA conceded that married parents were an unattainable luxury for some children. Single-parent adoptions were permissible in exceptional circumstances where the child would not otherwise be adopted.

Matching provided the logic even for these unusual placements. Single-parent adoptions brought together hard-to-place children with adults who, by virtue of their marital status, existed outside the borders of normal parenthood.

The First Critiques of Matching

The adoption revolution at midcentury provoked new thinking about the qualifications of all parties to adoption. It also generated a sustained and thoughtful critique of matching, the naturalizing paradigm that deployed the social design of similarity to achieve authenticity in adoption. Three of the most important early critics of matching were jurist Justine Wise Polier, novelist Pearl S. Buck, and author Helen Doss. Their opposition to racial exclusions, along with examples of families that flouted matching, raised legal and moral questions about the legitimacy of denying difference in adoption and pointed the way toward reconsidering the difference that difference made, in nature and in kinship. The case against matching, which emerged against the backdrop of the early cold war and civil rights activism, paved the way for transracial and transnational placements, more open adoption arrangements, search and reunion, and records reform. By the late 1960s, all these trends had gathered momentum.

The critique of matching was inspired by the special-needs revolution within the adoption world as well as by the civil rights revolution outside of it. To challenge matching was to extend the racial liberalism that infused the southern movement from 1945 through the early 1960s.[49] Convinced

that "the American Negro problem is a problem in the heart of the American," in Gunnar Myrdal's famous phrase, racial liberals emphasized the
immorality of prejudice, encouraged intercultural contact and education,
championed the potential for species-wide solidarities, and suggested that
coming to terms with difference was a fundamental task of democracy.[50]
Racial liberalism was key to dismantling the most visible aspects of Jim
Crow: segregation in schools, public accommodations, and workplaces and
at the ballot box.

In comparison to such public segregation, many racial liberals felt almost
as ambivalent about integrating the private sphere of love and sexuality as
their opponents, but the despised color line made matching in adoption
look like an invidious form of segregation, no different from segregated
lunch counters, at least in theory.[51] What could realize the civil rights slo-
gans of "beloved community" or "black and white together" more literally than racially inclusive families? After 1965 the forces of nationalism
gained strength within the civil rights movement, placing racial liberals on
the defensive. The Supreme Court declared the color line in marriage unconstitutional in *Loving v. Virginia* (1967), and federal courts struck down
the remaining state bans on transracial adoptions by 1972. By then, other
developments had slowed movement toward integration in families and
renewed the old demand that parents and children match, especially by
race.[52]

Justine Wise Polier

Justine Wise Polier was born in Portland, Oregon, a child of privilege. Her
parents were Rabbi Stephen Wise, a founder of the National Association
for the Advancement of Colored People and leader of the liberal American
Jewish Congress, and Louise Waterman Wise, a gifted artist who established
one of the first specialized adoption agencies in the United States, New
York's Free Synagogue Child Adoption Committee. Polier lived in a Boston
settlement, the Elizabeth Peabody House, during college, where her thinking was deeply influenced by the female reform tradition. She attended Bryn
Mawr, Radcliffe, Barnard, and Yale Law School before launching a brilliant
judicial career. She was an ally of Eleanor Roosevelt and worked with Kenneth Clark, Thurgood Marshall, Eleanor Holmes Norton, Bayard Rustin,
and other civil rights leaders. She forged an unusually effective partnership
with her second husband, Shad Polier, an attorney also passionately devoted to social justice in child welfare.[53] Horace Kallen declared Justine Polier the equal of Jane Addams for "her endeavors to help make the American

Idea a fact of experience as well as a faith and a hope."[54] Polier was equally shaped by two traditions she believed were entirely compatible: her parents' Reform Judaism and American democracy.

In 1935, at age thirty-two, Polier was named to the Domestic Relations Court in Manhattan by Fiorello La Guardia, the mayor making the first judicial appointment in New York State that elevated a woman above the rank of magistrate. She ended up staying in that post almost four decades. "I had no idea it would be so gripping," she explained.[55] "I stayed there for thirty-seven years because I was challenged and fascinated, horrified at times, hopeful at other times. As case after case came up, I saw the vast chasms between our rhetoric of freedom, equality and charity and what we were doing to, or not doing for, poor people, especially children."[56]

As a family court judge, Polier presided over many adoptions. The enormous civic and personal potential of family making impressed her, as it had her mother, and she hated to see it squandered. The first adoption case she oversaw involved a young professional couple who had adopted independently and without adequate investigation, unwittingly taking a baby with cerebral palsy and mental retardation. Years of futile efforts to secure medical help exhausted their life savings and emotional resources, and they turned in desperation to public assistance.[57] Professional supervision, Polier believed, could save people from making such tragic mistakes.[58] She pioneered diagnostic and mental health services in her own courtroom in association with such close friends as psychiatrist Viola Bernard and such institutions as the New York School of Social Work. Polier's style of justice was intensely therapeutic.[59]

Polier remained active in the adoption agency her mother founded in 1916. Renamed Louise Wise Services in 1949, two years after her mother's death, Polier served as president of its board, transforming it from an organization devoted exclusively to Jewish adoptions into a national innovator in services for children of color in the 1950s and 1960s. In 1951 the agency began placing African American and mixed-race children in African American and mixed-race families. In 1952 the agency revised its charter to formalize its nonsectarian commitment and pursued a policy of deliberate religious and racial integration of staff that placed it in the social work vanguard. Polier was especially proud of the agency's professionalism. When risks were overlooked, placements were arranged for profit, or adoptions were botched because of naiveté, Polier blamed it on lackadaisical standards and inadequate enforcement. She trusted professional collaboration and worked to advance it. She followed research in the human sciences and sought to apply it.[60] She believed in kinship by design.

Like most other adoption professionals before World War II, Polier believed that matching was sensible and that children and parents should be made to resemble one another physically and intellectually.[61] Gradually, she changed her mind. By legitimizing mistrust of difference, she wrote in 1960, matching served to "institutionalize the results of prejudice and then rationalize them."[62] Her observations of New York's child welfare system convinced her that sectarianism and equality were at odds and that "religious protection" laws that required matching in families did little to protect children. In New York, public services for children had been monopolized by private, religious agencies since the mid-nineteenth century, but religious agencies were very prominent in child placement and adoption throughout the country.[63] The result was that some children were provided with care "as a matter of right," whereas others had to wait patiently, hoping they might be helped "as a matter of grace."[64] As New York's demographic profile changed in the 1930s and 1940s, religious distinctions increasingly mapped onto racial distinctions. Services that favored Catholics and Jews were inevitably services that favored whites over African Americans.

Polier's dissent from religious matching began right after her appointment to the bench. In a complex and much-discussed divorce and custody case in 1936, *Matter of Vardinakis*, Polier rejected the notion that children were the permanent property of religious communities, accorded them a measure of autonomy, and suggested that families encompassing differing religious faiths and practices were compatible with child welfare. The *New York Times* observed that Polier's assignment of siblings to different religions was an unprecedented move in New York. It got her into deep trouble with the Catholic Church, whose newspaper declared, "Daughter of Rabbi Wise Turns Over the Child of Christ to the Bearded Prophet Mohammet!"[65]

Polier was outraged by the dogmatism as well as the unfairness of sectarian rules surrounding placement. In one case, the city informed a Jewish agency that it could not place the child of a Jewish birth mother in a Jewish home because that mother had once been baptized (on a "whim"), and the Catholic Church claimed the baby as its own.[66] In another case, school-age sisters who had lived all their lives as Jews were removed from their adoptive parents when their birth mother appeared and revealed they had been baptized as infants.[67] For years afterward, they remained in the custody of the Catholic Home Bureau. Louise Wise Services had placed the girls in "an exceptionally fine adoptive home," but "it was obvious that the Catholic agency would stop at absolutely nothing in their attempts to get these children," concluded the agency director, Florence Brown, in disgust.[68] If any consideration of the environment in which children actually lived and grew was prohibited by matching, how could it possibly benefit children?

Religious and racial discrimination comingled. "Most religious institutions have drawn a sharp color line," Polier wrote in 1938.[69] Sectarian agencies rejected children with dark complexions out of hand, claiming that finding adoptive families for them was impossible. Prejudicial comments about skin tone, facial features, and hair texture were not only perfectly open in many court documents—"Brenda age 4 is light olive complexioned but has negroid features"—but explicitly requested by the Bureau of Child Welfare as an aid to placement planning.[70] Preferences for lighter, more Caucasian-looking children were taken for granted. Siblings were placed separately when agencies thought one child's color or features would make it impossible to keep them together.[71] Whether Puerto Rican children were "light" or "dark" was routinely noted through the 1960s.[72] For Polier, this was tragic and unjust. Matching imposed constraint in circumstances where children needed flexibility.

The legal crux of the problem with religious matching was the impermissible state sanction and funding given to the discriminatory regime of sectarian service provision. Polier did not seek to abolish agencies organized on a religious basis—indeed, her mother had founded one—but she insisted that discrimination denied thousands of children permanent homes every year and that secular services were therefore imperative. After years of agitation and research on the racial bias of New York placements, Polier called on the city to establish a public adoption service.[73] (It finally did in 1957.[74]) "No state has the right to say to a defenseless child, 'You have no home, but, because of your race or religion, you shall stay in an institution until you are sixteen or seventeen and then be turned out into a world in which you have no one to whom you belong.'"[75] Democracies that used public authority to monitor group boundaries and referee group competition were not democratic.

Polier's critique was influential, but it did not shake the foundations of New York's child welfare system until after her death.[76] During her life, representatives from Catholic Charities attacked her as "communistic and totalitarian."[77] Orthodox rabbis called her a "travesty" to the "sainted memory" of her father and consigned Louise Wise Services to the "rabbinical doghouse."[78] The agency's turn toward children of color steadily diminished the funding it received from the Federation of Jewish Philanthropies.[79]

Polier's critics often mistook her for an advocate of religion-blind and color-blind individualism. She was not. Polier never suggested that religion should be ignored in adoptions, nor did she consider children autonomous creatures unencumbered by collective ties and traditions. As a Jew, she believed in ethical teaching by religious communities and supported parents' freedom to express their religious beliefs by controlling their children's religious upbringing. But democracies respected the line between private voluntarism and public coercion. "No short cuts, bargain methods, and no indoctrination by compulsion have ever strengthened the true religious impulses of any man, woman, or child," she wrote.[80] Religion was secure only when it was freely chosen and when church and state were separated in practice as well as in theory.

In cases where the preferences of parents and communities of descent came into direct conflict with children's needs for protection and permanent belonging, Polier adamantly opposed sustaining parental or group rights at children's expense. The most fundamental right children had was a right to parents who would "accept the child as he is."[81] Love and security were not contingent on sameness; adoption was no "ode to Narcissus."[82] To deny that loving families could be formed across lines of race, religion, or nationality, she wrote in 1960, "has contributed to the tragic shortcoming of our services."[83] Matching perpetuated a "bulldozer approach to the newcomer or the 'different' child, which seeks to level the peaks of cultural differences in American life."[84] Adoption was clearly good for children, but it might also be good for the nation by advancing the civil rights movement where it had advanced least: at home.[85]

Pearl Buck

Pearl Buck concentrated less than Justine Polier on the constitutional dilemmas of matching, but her universalist anthem about the possibilities of love across the borders of difference reached well beyond Polier's circles in law and social welfare. As the recipient of both the Pulitzer and Nobel prizes, Buck was one of the most widely read novelists of the twentieth century. She was the child of Protestant missionaries and spent the first half of her life in China and the second half in the United States. She wrote prolifically about Asia for Western audiences, hoping to dignify Chinese history and make it intelligible for Americans. Remembered today for *The Good Earth*, she wrote many books (a number of which became major Hollywood movies or were adapted for the stage) and contributed regularly to mass-circulation magazines such as *Reader's Digest*, *Ladies Home Journal*, and *Good House-keeping*. Biographer Peter Conn has suggested that Buck's literary reputation suffered because she wrote popular books for a female audience at a time when most tastemakers were men who scorned mass appeal, especially among women.[86]

A childhood spent feeling she was "the wrong color" was only one of many reasons why Buck worked tirelessly on behalf of international and intercultural understanding.[87] After giving birth to a "feebleminded" daughter, Carol, in 1921, Buck had a hysterectomy and institutionalized the girl at Vineland Training School, where eugenicist Henry Goddard had honed his antiadoption views a decade earlier. At Vineland, Carol joined scores of other children with mental and developmental disabilities who were presumed unfit for family life. Buck kept Carol's existence a secret until 1950, when she went public with her painful story.[88]

Between the 1920s and the late 1950s, Buck adopted seven children.[89] In 1936 she adopted two infant boys with her second husband, Richard Walsh, through the Cradle, where no matching infractions were ever knowingly tolerated. In contrast, Cheiko, adopted in 1957, was the child of a Japanese woman and an African American soldier; Henriette was also an African American mixed-race child whose birth mother was German.[90] Like other Americans who moved toward transnational adoptions during the early cold war, Buck responded personally and politically to the U.S. military presence in Europe and Asia. Incorporating the world's children into the national family would be "a triumph of American democracy," striking simultaneous blows for humanitarianism and against international Communism.[91]

So dedicated was Buck to the cause of transracial and transnational families that she founded an adoption agency of her own in 1949.[92] Welcome House (whose children inspired Oscar Hammerstein's *The King and I*) began when Buck ran into the same pattern of discrimination that so incensed Justine Polier. Robbie, a fifteen-month-old baby of mixed white and East Indian background, was brought to Buck's attention, but she could find no agency willing to place him for adoption because his skin was brown. A "Negro" orphanage was the only institution willing to take him, and the possibility that this beautiful, intelligent child might languish there for years infuriated and galvanized Buck. "I was indignant, so I started my own damned agency!" she explained.[93]

Buck set up shop in a farmhouse next to her home in Bucks County, Pennsylvania, where she received a stream of children considered unadoptable because of their mixed heritage. At first, Buck worried that it might be hard to locate parents for these children. It pained her that prejudice might be as deeply entrenched in the United States as Communist propaganda maintained it was during a period when civil rights were a cold war battleground. She quickly changed her mind. "The real barrier to adoption of mixed-blood children was not that no one wanted them," Buck insisted, "but that adoption practice demanded child and adoptive parents to match. . . . Who really matches his parents?"[94]

Until the mid-1970s, Buck's dissent from matching attracted regular attention. She published stories about mixed-race children, children suffering in war-torn Asia, and her own growing family. In these stories, readers with little or no adoption experience encountered an ideology of family formation that reflected Buck's larger perspective on the world. It respected cultural difference while subordinating it to love, the common property of the human species. "I know," she wrote, "for I have tried it myself. . . . Parenthood has nothing to do with color, race or religion. It has to do with far deeper likeness of mind and heart and soul."[95]

Buck's universalism made her no more a simplistic individualist than Polier. At its best, love might be color-blind, but people certainly were not, so interracial kinship had to be fiercely race conscious. Parents unwilling to teach their children the value of their heritage, or confront bigotry directly, were not prepared to love across the color line, according to Buck, and they would not help to realize their children's potential to become bridges for intercultural understanding. Buck was a multiculturalist before the term came into vogue. She saw race, culture, and nation as resources, but she saw them as obstacles too. She conceded that prejudice made it more difficult to find parents for black children, such as two of her own daughters, than for other mixed-race children. White adopters were more open to Asian or Native American children, and even "Negro" adopters preferred "light" children. Studies during the 1950s, as we have seen, confirmed that white couples willing to compromise on racial matching were often willing to do so only after being reassured that no "Negro" blood was part of the child's mix. The stubborn racial hierarchy that branded blackness as uniquely unassimilable also explained the curious fact that many whites unwilling to consider domestic transracial adoptions were willing to take racially different children into their families as long as they were born in Asian countries.

Buck's belief in the transcendent qualities of love was generous and hopeful, even romantic, but it was not naive. It never led her to deny that adoption was a different way to form families, a way that frequently caused "a permanent wound" and much turmoil for adoptees as they grew up.[96] She recommended that parents not only tell their children about their adoptions but also help their adopted children if they wished to search for natal relatives. At a time when anonymity and authenticity were virtually inseparable, Buck moved against the grain by declaring that realness required acknowledging difference rather than denying it. Why insist on sameness or chase after nature? Children born to others would become one's own "flesh by love," but purposeful families would always have to live with the burden and blessing of difference because "society still forces them to remember and to inquire of themselves who they are."[97] Whatever difficulty came with adoption, in other words, was a by-product of stigma and suspicion. Discrimination—not nature—caused the difference that difference made.

Helen Doss and The Family Nobody Wanted

The kind of multiracial and multinational family-by-love that Buck defended and forged for herself was compelling during the 1950s because of the propaganda value of cold war civil rights.[98] Harmonious interracialism within American families might counter the accusation that anti-Communism hypocritically insisted on equality abroad while segregation prevailed at home. The Family Nobody Wanted, an adoption memoir by Helen Doss, brought to public attention the story of a "one-family U.N." that was ordinary and extraordinary at the same time.[99] The book was serialized, picked up by major book clubs, and dramatized in film (where Nanette Fabray and later Shirley Jones played Helen Doss). It went through two dozen printings, was translated into seven languages (Pearl Buck wrote the introduction for the Japanese edition), and remained in print for three decades. Its 1954 publication coincided with Brown v. Board of Education, the Supreme Court decision that ruled segregated schooling unconstitutional, ushered in a lengthy period of violent resistance to integration, and catapulted children and adolescents into a place of practical and symbolic importance in the civil rights revolution.

The Doss family story was appealing because it struck reassuringly common chords while offering a glimpse at difference still unusual within American families. Helen Doss and her minister-in-training husband, Carl, were a young California couple blessed by a surplus of Christian faith and love that offset their lack of money and material possessions. (Doss originally titled her book "All God's Children" and went on to write Bible stories and children's books.) Infertile at a time when motherhood was synonymous with female fulfillment, Helen wanted nothing in the world more than to have a "happy, normal little family."[100] That longing was the unstoppable force that propelled the Dosses toward adoption. What could be more understandable, ordinary, and natural than wanting a child? Their first adoption was improbably easy. A social worker told Helen about Donny, "a chubby little fellow with blue eyes, and a perfect match for you two," and the couple dashed right off to the local hospital to pick up their six-week-old son.[101]

Finding children to adopt got harder after that. Helen wanted a sibling for Donny, but discovered to her dismay that poverty disqualified them with agencies and independent child placers. Desperate for another child, Doss began begging agencies for the children of mixed background they found so tough to place. "I would rather see a child raised in an orphanage, than by parents who look so *different,*" one appalled agency official replied. "Crossing racial lines is against all our *principles* of good social-work practice."[102] After three years, the Dosses finally convinced a hesitant agency that color made no difference to them. So Helen and Carl Doss, whose only desire was to expand their family, ended up with twelve children: Filipino, Hawaiian, Balinese, Malayan, Indian, Mexican, and Native American, in various combinations (figure 11). The Dosses were exactly the good-hearted people that Pearl Buck counted on in founding Welcome House. They were white, but they were eager to raise children callously designated as different and unwanted.

The Doss children were afflicted by a host of "special needs"—one child had a tumor on her forehead, and another was described as mentally retarded—but the imperfections quickly disappeared as the young people blossomed under a regime of unstinting love and acceptance. Much of the story's charm is attributable to the normalization of these children. Separately, they appeared exotic, but the alchemy of togetherness transformed them into adorable, funny, mischievous, and very ordinary American siblings. The heartwarming message underlying this saga was that the love that bound them together was solid and familiar. It tamed difference and made the children so alike that "they took it for granted that this alikeness would show."[103] Nor were their parents unusual. The Dosses resented it when people asked about their motivations, "as if we had just gathered this family together as a cold-blooded social experiment, or a sort of laboratory of racial relations."[104] They were a typical couple who happened to believe that kinship had more to do with love than blood. Just as they never doubted their children's status as real Americans, they never doubted their own as a "really real family."[105] One sort of authenticity was linked to the other.

All the love in the world did not shield the Doss children from racism, but it did seem to protect them from its most toxic consequences. Teddy, whose background was Filipino, was taunted on the school playground by shouts of "nigger-boy." With his parents' encouragement, he confronted his tormenters assertively, but with a disarming sense of humor that stopped the bullying and increased Teddy's popularity among his peers. Other incidents

Figure 11. The Doss family looked like a "One-Family United Nations" in *Life*, 1951.
Used by permission of Wayne F. Miller, Magnum Photos.

narrated in the book also illustrated the potential of human commonality
to subvert prejudice. Taro, a Japanese American child who lived with the
Dosses for one year, initially epitomized the tragedy of racial fear. Almost
his entire family had perished in wartime internment camps, and the only
remaining relative, his father, had no choice but to place Taro in temporary
foster care when he could not find work. Brutally beaten by two angry white
men on the way to visit his son (because "the only good Jap's a dead one"),
Taro's father was rescued by Mike, a "big blond soldier."[106] Mike's own life
had been saved by a Nisei friend while they were stationed in Italy during

the war, a turn of events that put him on the path to marrying a Japanese American woman. Mike had been touched in the most personal way imaginable by the true meaning of brotherhood and citizenship. So were Taro, Taro's father, and all the Dosses. Prejudice was irrational, unpatriotic, and exclusive. Real Americanness, on the other hand, was generous, open, and undaunted by difference—just like a real family.

The Doss story pointed only obliquely to virulent racial animosities unsoftened by love. In all the years they adopted and raised children, the Dosses never once adopted an African American child. After they already had many children, Carl confessed that "I've had a secret hankering to adopt a child with Negro blood."[107] Yet their one effort to adopt a half-black German war orphan, four-year-old Gretchen, suggested that love was not always transcendent. Even close friends of the family balked at their interest in "pickaninnies," called the couple shockingly radical, and threatened to cut off contact if they proceeded with the adoption.[108] Carl's own mother swore that "no nigger will call *me* Grandma."[109] The Dosses reconsidered their decision in the face of such resistance. They helped to locate a "Negro" couple interested in adopting the child, and the story ended happily. Gretchen had parents "the same warm toast shade that she was, and she would know that her own color was just right for *her*."[110] In this case, even Helen Doss had to concede that love had a color.

Matching Transgressed: The Beginnings of Intercountry Adoption as an Organized Movement

Because matching practices were so closely identified with professional adoption, dissent from one frequently implied dissent from the other. In 1955 Pearl Buck bluntly accused professionals and religious institutions of standing between tens of thousands of homeless children and willing parents. Rigid insistence that children match the families in which they were placed preserved their jobs, she argued, at the cost of sustaining the black market. Buck's charges, published in *Woman's Home Companion*, received a lot of attention, partly because of her celebrity but also because she maintained that the very professionals who claimed to be disinterested advocates of child welfare were acting on distinct interests of their own. "The mediocre quality of the average social worker as a person" was to blame, compounded by the fact that "there is no leadership, worthy of the name, in child adoption."[111]

The leaders of the child welfare establishment, not surprisingly, were outraged. CWLA executive director Joseph Reid howled that Buck's views were "inaccurate and misleading," even "slanderous."[112] Most children in orphanages and temporary foster care were not legally free for adoption, and terminating parental rights could not be effected casually. Moreover, many children who were available for adoption were not the healthy, happy, pretty infants that so many Americans desired. "Public apathy, lack of funds, and lack of public understanding" hindered adoption, not selfish social workers.[113] "You have led the public up the blind alley of your prejudice," Reid wrote to Buck in dismay.[114]

Buck responded that the family-making designs professionals favored were nothing but racial, religious, and national prejudices in disguise and that the transnational and transracial adoptions they resisted might overcome these biases. The transgression of matching became more thinkable after World War II and during the early cold war, when the adoption market globalized and wars, refugee migrations, famines, and other natural disasters made the plight of dependent and orphaned children abroad more visible to Americans, beginning with U.S. service personnel and their families stationed around the world. Soldiers and sailors sent to Europe during the war, Germany and Japan after 1945, and eventually Korea and Vietnam produced significant numbers of children (many of mixed race) in those countries. Estimates suggested that four hundred thousand children were fathered by American service personnel after World War II, especially in England, Germany, and Japan; at least ten thousand children in Western Europe had African American fathers.[115] These were "the pitiful human debris of 15 years of war and occupation," wrote an observer in 1956, "a gigantic living time bomb ticking toward explosion."[116]

A few American men sought legal responsibility for the children they had fathered overseas, but most did not, and they were legally shielded by occupation laws that prohibited local women from bringing paternity or child-support suits.[117] Still others never knew of the children they had left behind. The story of these half-American waifs attracted the attention of journalists, who wrote about them in *Time, Life, National Geographic, Reader's Digest*, and elsewhere, prompting military personnel and civilians alike to consider intercountry adoptions.[118] ("Intercountry" was a more common term than "international" at the time.) Mass-circulation magazines reported that mixed-race children were cruelly stigmatized, subject to infanticide and slavery, and rarely, if ever, adopted in their countries of origin.[119] "Negro orphans are the most pitiful," wrote Susan Pettiss, an official with the International Social Service, American Branch, about children fathered by U.S. service personnel in Korea. "It is said that ninety percent of the children of mixed parentage perish."[120]

Humanitarian efforts to save the children of war characterized this phase in the history of transnational adoption, recapitulating the rhetoric of rescue and the religious fervor that had animated many nineteenth-century domestic placements while echoing the sexualized racial anxiety that accompanied episodes of imperial intimacy, such as the case of children produced in the Dutch and French colonies of Southeast Asia during the first half of the twentieth century.[121] For Americans, saving the "children of calamity" infused adoption with the particular patriotism of the cold war era.[122] Transnational adoptions after 1945 mobilized Lutherans, Catholics, and Seventh-Day Adventists, among other faith communities, and inspired the formation of such organizations as the League for Orphan Victims in Europe (LOVE), the U.S. Committee on the Care of European Children, and the American Joint Committee for Assisting Japanese-American Orphans. As with earlier phases in adoption history, displays of American benevolence conveniently dovetailed with pursuit of citizens' desires.[123] Coming on the heels of complaints that domestic agency adoptions were plagued by difficulties and delays, the search for children logically pushed beyond national boundaries. Several thousand white infants from Canada were adopted by Americans, many of them Jewish, who resorted to a profit-driven traffic in children because they were thwarted by religious matching laws that made it very difficult to adopt through domestic agencies.[124] American Jews also hoped that Europe and Israel might be sources of the Jewish children they longed for, but they were often disappointed.[125]

Other Americans found what they were seeking. Ireland was a "happy hunting ground" for the hundreds of American families who adopted illegitimate children from that country, with little if any regulation or paperwork, between the 1940s and 1960s.[126] One delighted American father described a "baby bonanza" in West Germany, the product of a "bumper crop" of children and looser laws. (One source estimated that American, British, and French soldiers had fathered ninety-four thousand babies in West Germany alone between 1946 and 1951.[127]) He called the German situation an adoption "El Dorado" for Americans: "The treasure is not gold or diamonds, but thousands of bright, healthy children."[128] Mobile military families could not satisfy domestic agency requirements for lengthy applications, home studies, and supervisory periods, so the armed services facilitated family-making quests.[129] During the occupation of Germany and afterward, the U.S. Military Adoption Board screened couples rather than turning over the adoption process to German authorities.[130]

From military families, interest in adopting foreign children spread to other Americans. Nor was it necessary to travel internationally or have contacts abroad to learn about these new adoption opportunities. Information moved quickly through domestic media. During the 1950s, "proxy adoptions" were the most widely publicized means of transnational adoption. They allowed U.S. citizens to adopt, in absentia, in foreign courts. Because children adopted this way entered the United States as the legal children of parents who had never met them, proxies circumvented investigatory and supervisory regulations and flouted the notion that child welfare was the dominant factor in adoption. After 1961, proxy adoptions were no longer permitted. Americans who adopted foreign children had to meet them personally during adoption proceedings in the child's country of origin or, in the case of adoptions completed in the United States, satisfy legal requirements in their state of residence.

Proxy adoptions revealed that the interests of U.S. nationals predominated in cross-border adoptions. They also illustrated the shortcomings of federal policy, a problem that the USCB and the League of Nations had identified as early as the 1920s and 1930s.[131] Until passage of the Immigration and Nationality Act of 1961, which incorporated transnational adoption, the migration of foreign-born children to the United States had no place in permanent law. It was governed by a series of provisional refugee and displaced persons acts, beginning with a directive from President Truman in December 1945 that envisioned the entry of "eligible orphans" from war-torn countries as a temporary emergency and set quotas for that purpose. Between 1953 and 1962, fifteen thousand foreign children were adopted by Americans, but concerns about immigration and unwillingness to interfere in the legal systems of sovereign nations meant that transnational placements were, in effect, exempted from the regulatory regime that had been laboriously put into place domestically.[132]

Proxy adoptions epitomized the problem, as professionals saw it, that foreign children were given unequal legal protection and accorded few, if any, safeguards (figure 12). Officials in the USCB, the CWLA, and the American Branch of International Social Service charged proxy peddlers with masterminding an unscrupulous "mail order baby racket" and sought to extend basic investigatory and supervisory regulations to children born outside the United States by proposing new and reformed federal legislation.[133] In addition to the regulatory basics—investigation, supervision, and probation—professionals pointed to special hazards in transnational adoption. Many foreign children—from Asia in particular—had spent lengthy periods in orphanages that were bound to produce developmental problems in need of clinical attention. Parents adopting foreign children needed additional preparation: basic education about children's home countries, rudimentary

Figure 12. This woman symbolized the danger of proxy adoption, a procedure that allowed
U.S. citizens to adopt foreign children, sight unseen. According to officials, she appeared
drunk and over fifty years of age when she arrived at the airport to greet her baby
in 1957. Used by permission of International Social Service—
United States of America Branch, Inc. (ISS-USA).

language skills, and enlightened attitudes about a host of factors from food and sleeping arrangements to neighborhood integration and—the most controversial issue of all—interracial dating and marriage.[134] One tip sheet designed for people adopting from Hong Kong included Cantonese translations of essential phrases including "Don't cry," "I love you" and "Are you hungry?"[135] The dream of "a human family in which the superficial differences are insignificant" was appealing, but until it was realized, family making required sensitivity to the problems that accompanied difference.[136]

Proxy adoptions ignored these problems. Child welfare leaders could barely conceal their contempt for the "self-styled benefactors" who arranged them and handed children out like so many "prize packages" to couples they suspected could not meet agency standards.[137] After meeting The Flying Tiger, a chartered plane that delivered one hundred Korean-born children to American families in Portland, Oregon, in December 1957, Arnold Lyslo described seeing cardboard boxes in which infants had been stacked during transit and a scene of general confusion. He was shocked and bewildered. "That this could happen to children and parents in the United States today!" he wrote.[138] Professional assessment was so obviously needed for the good of the children, to ascertain whether the parents had the ability to adopt at all or possessed the special sensitivity required to adopt Korean children. Lyslo added, "My worries for these children have never ceased."[139] Oregon state officials believed that much more stringent laws were needed to rein in proxy adoption. Extreme cases of proxy abuse, such as one in which an adoptive mother of a Korean child was indicted for murder in 1957, helped to spread the alarm.[140]

USCB chief Katherine B. Oettinger was diplomatic but extremely concerned. "All of us respond to the idea of rescuing helpless children from the dragon of deprivation. But the mere fact that we are in a hurry does not mean that we should speed the adoptive process so much that we are forced to by-pass the necessary safeguards. Human beings are too complex to be thrown helter-skelter into permanent family relationships."[141] "Most people who seek to adopt children do so out of love—but love alone is not always enough," Oettinger added, and "problems in adoption are infinitely harder to resolve in an adoption which spans the ocean."[142] Proxy adoptions too frequently ended in abuse, neglect, and disruption that could be avoided with less haste, more information, and the protective machinery of legal regulation and professional oversight.

Many Americans objected to this call for more design. Celebrating the deliverance of foreign children by American couples was the more attractive choice of two competing adoption narratives that had been well established

Figure 13. International adoption pioneers Harry and Bertha Holt and their fourteen children, including eight adopted from Korea in 1955. Used by permission of International Social Service—United States of America Branch, Inc. (ISS-USA).

in domestic adoptions in the nineteenth century: rescue and kidnap. After 1945 an evangelical couple from rural Oregon, Bertha and Harry Holt, suggested the enduring power of humanitarian appeals. Inspired by Bob Pierce, whose Christian organization, World Vision, allowed Americans to sponsor Korean War orphans, the Holts began making transnational placements after a special act of Congress permitted them to adopt eight Korean war orphans in 1955 (figure 13). They relied on proxies, swept aside the investigatory protocols endorsed by social workers, and became lightning rods for divided opinion about nonprofessional adoptions.[143] The Holts, middle-aged parents of six other children prior to the adoptions, became heroes in the press, in Congress (where Oregon senator Richard Neuberger called them incarnations of "the Biblical Good Samaritan, as of 1955"), and in faith communities around the country.[144] "We would ask all of you who are Christians to pray to God that He will give us the wisdom and the strength and the power to deliver his little children from the cold and misery and darkness of Korea into the warmth and love of your homes," pleaded the Holts' form letter seeking adoption applicants.[145]

Family making of this sort invoked faith, not regulation, presumed that childhood in America was unquestionably superior to childhood in developing nations, and found nothing terribly alarming in the idea of adopting a child sight unseen. It also took at face value the desires expressed by people seeking children. Many people found this refreshing. It undercut solemn warnings that good intentions were not to be trusted by insisting that good intentions were not only good, but good enough for adoption. In addition, many waiting families were heartened by the Holts' promises of speedy and uncomplicated placements. California schoolteacher Elizabeth Campbell wrote to public officials in her area in 1956 requesting two half-Korean children because "they are not well treated by the other Korean children, even to the point of being murdered."[146] Reading about the Holts' program had alerted her to the possibility that adoption could save children.

Such admiration for the Holts and lingering belief that adoption was an altruistic rather than selfish act recalled Pearl Buck's confidence in the decency and compassion of American citizens. Buck objected to the Holts' fundamentalism, but she admired their determination to solve the problem that social workers had failed to address.[147] Why couldn't all the children who needed parents simply be transferred, quickly and easily, to adults who were seeking children, proxy or no proxy? Buck's charge that social workers held children hostage to their own vested interests made sense to people whose anger fused genuine sympathy for children with resentment against decision makers perceived as arrogant and self-righteous.

It did not help matters that most of those decision makers were women, sometimes unmarried. During the golden age of psychoanalysis after World War II, social workers, earlier considered natural child placers by virtue of sex, came to be regarded as repressed, "narrow-minded spinsters."[148] Their own ignorance of marriage (perhaps even deliberate avoidance of it) made them inappropriate judges of normal, married couples, almost as inappropriate as placing children with single parents, who could not provide "normal family life" or a "real home."[149]

Privacy and Blood

The beginnings of organized transnational adoptions, the special-needs revolution, and early critiques of matching brought difference out of the shadows in adoption, prompting professionals, parents, and the public at large to ponder why shame and anxiety were so closely associated with it. The defense of privacy that facilitated adoption across a variety of borders was, however, far from new. Support for the freedom to form families without interference had hampered adoption regulation from the outset and sustained independent placements, notwithstanding periodic scandals. A few states in the 1950s still did not require that child placers be certified. Others had not criminalized baby selling or taken steps to monitor interstate traffic in children. Rationalizers had made considerable progress with legal mandates for investigation and probation, but even here resistance endured.

In Florida, for example, opposition to "the burden of bureaucratic control" was fierce, agency adoptions were scarce, and independent placements far outnumbered professional placements. Opponents of legal reform warned that firmer control over adoption would only anger "that great class of the good people of our state standing ready to open their homes to helpless and needy children," eliminating precious possibilities for permanent love and belonging "under the guise of serving the welfare of the child."[150] These arguments did not ultimately prevail; investigation and supervision were included when Florida revised its adoption law in 1943. As a practical matter, however, the post-1943 regulatory regime was exceedingly mild. Investigations were made by overworked and undertrained social workers reluctant to remove children from homes in which many had lived for considerable periods. Recommendations against granting adoption decrees were entered in only a tiny number of extreme cases: the figure was 2 percent during the three years after the law went into effect, and courts actually dismissed only half of these.[151]

It was not fondness for commercial child placing that prevented states from tightening the regulatory net. Fear of encroaching on the privacy and freedom of birth parents and would-be adopters was a powerful brake on legislative action. Many Americans were especially distrustful of state involvement when it came to matters of the heart. "The total involvement of public institutions" violated the spirit of "private efforts, motivated by love and kindness."[152] Marriage was also a highly regulated social institution, of course, and its impact was felt by infinitely more people than adoption, but the personal sphere of family and sexuality was still distinguished from the political sphere of state and economy. The bright cultural line between private and public, no matter how illusory, was also a major impediment to kinship by design.

Others simply expressed consumer preferences for "bootleg" over professional placements. Commercial brokers offered faster service and treated adopters like "customers," with warm appreciation rather than cool objectivity or suspicion.[153] Because of perceptions that extra "pull" was needed to adopt through agencies, the for-profit adoption world represented an even playing field, presuming, of course, that the requisite funds were available. Some suggested that would-be fathers were more supportive of independent placements than women, who were hell-bent on maternity and would do almost anything to adopt. Men found agency procedures especially intrusive and would not tolerate them. Women and men alike resented professionals who treated applications to adopt as unconscious cries for help disguised as generous acts. Although would-be adopters certainly wanted information and reassurance—especially about children's physical condition and background—they did not appreciate being treated as if their parenting credentials were on trial—which of course they were.

People rejected by agencies appreciated the existence of alternatives for the obvious reason that it offered them another way to acquire a child or children. Senate hearings in 1955 on interstate adoption practices revealed that some Americans exercised their choices foolishly, but that did not make family-making freedoms any less important. Testimony linked the scandal of unregulated and commercial adoption directly to a variety of social problems, including juvenile delinquency, but it showcased the values of privacy and autonomy just as clearly.

At the outset of the hearings, attention focused on an adoption ring centered in Chicago that exported children all around the country, thanks to lax residency requirements in Illinois. Otto Kerner, at the time a Cook County judge, testified that most adopters who showed up in his courtroom were "wonderful people . . . doing a grand thing."[154] But because adoption brokers such as Chicago's Bernard Brody cared only about money, Kerner's responsibility was to protect well-meaning parents from fraud and to shield helpless babies from being the pawns of greedy adults. Many adopters were unwilling to leave such sensitive decisions in either social workers' or judges' hands.

The hearings proceeded to describe adoption markets in Oklahoma, Texas, Minnesota, and elsewhere and offered a platform for lawyers and other brokers from Canada as well as the United States to explain how the services they offered met the needs of would-be parents. One New Jersey couple, for example, went to Montreal in search of a baby from entrepreneur Sarah Wyman, who was known for arranging high-fee, cross-border adoptions. The couple, who testified anonymously, explained that they had become terribly discouraged after waiting patiently on an agency list for four years. Their encounter with Wyman was harrowing. "She was a definite psychopathic individual with a diabolical mind for making money out of the situation" and "looked like a live character from the French Revolution," they testified.[155] But the couple got exactly what they wanted: a baby, a legal adoption, and a happy ending. If not for independent adoption, they could easily have remained childless forever. Some unscrupulous individuals were certainly taking advantage of adoption, but was that really so bad if the families that resulted turned out well?

Other inquiries into profit-oriented, independent adoptions during the postwar era revealed similar cleavages between the views of outraged professionals, on the one hand, and mediators and adopters grateful for a menu of choices, on the other. When the CWLA investigated a commercial adoption ring in southern California in the late 1950s, it vented its anger at the exploitive "illicit, under-the-counter," and "unchecked" placements that cost from $4,000 to $7,000 and placed babies all over the country. Chief investigator Ernest Mitler, a specialist in commercial adoption since his days as a New York City assistant district attorney, explained what was wrong with for-profit adoption by stressing the incommensurability of money making and family making. "The very same devices, the very same philosophy that is appropriate in dealing with mortgages, real estate, real and personal property are used unblushingly in dealing with unmarried mothers, adoptive parents and the placing of a child. Contract, options, deposits and trust funds are the tools of the trade," he reported. He argued that "child placement involves myriad of emotional problems that can only be solved by using the tools of human sciences—psychology, case work technique, psychiatry and even plain simple common sense."[156]

One of the California attorneys involved in arranging adoptions, however, proudly compared his operation to the underground railroad that had harbored slaves on their journey to freedom. He called it a "grapevine" and argued that professionals were jealous because they knew many intelligent people preferred private placements. Compared to agencies that insisted on "playing God," had impossible waiting lists, and established unrealistic requirements, the adoptions arranged in California met the needs of birth mothers and adopters alike.[157] Some adopters agreed. "The agencies sit there with all the power," complained C. Coleman Blease, an adoptive father, "and you have no recourse but to accept their decisions. I haven't met that many people in my life who know that much about other people. My wife and I wanted to make our own decisions."[158]

When it came to the lives of helpless children, professionals took a dim view of adult decision making and bristled at accusations that they were bent on monopoly control. According to CWLA executive director Reid, "We take the radical position that the individual has no rights here. . . . We base our stand on equity, equity for the child, not for the natural parents or for the adoptive parents."[159] Professionals insisted that adopting was a privilege rather than a right, but everyone conceded that birth parents had rights in their children by virtue of blood. The regulatory aspirations of kinship by design remained ultimately unrealized for this final, important reason: few people questioned birth parents' prerogative to place their children personally or to designate independent child placers to act on their behalf. The blood ties that adoption lacked legitimized birth parents' power over their children while severely limiting the authority professionals could wield. Birth parents acted on rights that adopters never possessed.

For birth parents the variety of adoption arrangements available outside of agencies had some distinct advantages. One was the promise of complete secrecy. Nonprofessional mediators who placed babies were especially aggressive in playing on the combination of shame and financial need that surrounded white unmarried mothers and their families, as the following Wichita advertisement suggests. "ADOPTION—Upstanding responsible childless couple desires to adopt infant at birth. Will pay necessary expenses and provide seclusion. Completely confidential."[160]

On the other hand, not all birth parents wanted secrecy. In the era before open adoptions were deliberately arranged, independent adoptions allowed birth parents to select adopters themselves or at least to be certain that their children would grow up in families that met with their approval. One study of almost five hundred such adoptions in Florida in the late 1940s found that a full 38 percent of the adoptions included some kind of contact, however brief, between birth and adoptive families, an especially notable fact because the doctors who arranged many independent placements were known to favor anonymity.[161] One in four cases of adoption arranged directly between adopters and birth parents used the old strategy of newspaper advertising.[162] In other cases, birth parents already knew the adopters as neighbors or friends or through community networks. Even when they did not, placing children directly indicated a willingness to have their identities revealed.

In comparison to birth parents' reasons for wanting openness, adopters tended to tolerate contact with birth parents, but they rarely welcomed it before the 1970s. Most adopters preferred to know little or nothing about the people who had produced their children. For example, fewer than one in five of the Florida couples studied expressed the desire to know as much as possible about the child's natal background; most wished to know nothing at all or to obtain medical background information only.[163] Fears that birth parents would return to reclaim their "own" children, or otherwise disrupt the life of the adoptive family, shaped attitudes toward direct contact between natal and adoptive parents for a very long time.[164] Worries about future interference by birth parents may have pushed some adopters toward agencies and their promises of secrecy, but others were more than willing to risk contact with birth parents, if only for the sake of acquiring a child.

Birth parents were probably always more interested in openness. This was the case even in the early 1960s, when anonymity was an ironclad rule not only in agencies but also in most independent placements. At a time when the families of pregnant white teenagers frequently pressured them to surrender babies in secret and then resume "normal" lives, numerous "open adoptions" were arranged by San Francisco attorney Philip Adams. These types of adoptions satisfied the desires of birth parents for ongoing contact with the children they surrendered and prefigured reforms of later years. Independent placements did not always flout the rules of agency adoption, of course. Many were scrupulous about matching, confidentiality, and testing because these measures were frequently expected by adopters. But that was not always the case. What most distinguished independent adoptions was that "they enable the people involved to make their own decisions and not have them made by other people," according to Adams. "That's the important thing."[165] Where kinship by design held out the prospect of reducing risks, the alternative promised something that was valued as much or more: increasing choices.

After midcentury the lessons of the Holocaust and the pluralistic formulations of identity and solidarity that accompanied the civil rights revolution made their mark on the adoption world. Public figures, including Justine Wise Polier and Pearl Buck, insisted that matching was antithetical to Americanism long before diversity and multiculturalism became keywords in American political culture. In arguing that difference produced discrimination, they argued that difference was not merely an empirical description of natural facts but a prescription for inequality that distorted social life. Claims about children's adoptability and the importance of resemblance consequently appeared to be not simply antiquated but unjust.

The result was an era of adoption revolution that made special-needs, transracial, and transnational adoptions more imaginable while undermining the authority of matching. In retrospect, these developments in kinship by design symbolized changes already under way in adoption. Beginning in the early twentieth century, matching promoted naturalization as the best way to design adoptive families, supplemented by techniques of regulation, interpretation, and standardization that would help adoption correspond to all that was secure and authentic in family life. Yet the cultural direction of modern life made it clear that very little about family life was secure or authentic. After the 1960s, matching looked more like a lie than the truth. Secrecy and simulation seemed dishonest and exclusive whereas openness and celebration of diversity offered the real thing at long last. Nature had become "nature" and was not what it used to be.[166] Difference, on the other hand, was forever.

CHAPTER SEVEN

The Difference Difference Makes

What were the adoption histories of children who faced discrimination and exclusion from placement on the basis of race? When and why did white Americans deliberately begin to violate matching by incorporating mixed-race children, minority children, and children born in foreign countries into their families? This chapter begins to answer these questions. It describes efforts to locate adoptive homes for children born into minority communities, continues the story of transracial and transnational adoptions after 1945, and suggests that by the mid-1960s, a new strategy for achieving authenticity had emerged. Denying difference gave way to acknowledging it. This shift was especially controversial in the case of race, where matching continued to seem logical, natural, and absolutely necessary to many parents and professionals. Realness never lost its power as a goal for adoption, but the rules for getting there started to change.

Matching and Adoption for Children of Color

Before the 1960s, love invariably had a color. The critique of matching that emerged in the 1940s and 1950s seems prophetic in retrospect, but it departed dramatically from majority opinion at the time and influenced adoption practice only on the margins. The civil rights movement after 1945 incorporated a range of political views, but racial liberalism predominated, demanding an end to the color line in education, public accommodations, politics, and employment. Few were willing to consider the family a key locus of struggle over racial equality, however, or endorse intimate forms of integration, whether between marital partners or parents and children. Even as the attack on public segregation gathered momentum, family-making practices upheld the idea that, in private, like belonged with like. Racial matching mattered for children of color just as it did for their white counterparts, and most professionals assumed that recruiting parents in minority communities was as necessary as it was challenging. Nonwhite children were hard to place because nonwhite parents were hard to reach.

For a good part of the century, few bothered to try, and adoption was "the least likely of all child welfare services to be extended to Black children."[1] Adoption services were simply denied or offered on a token basis that placed the systemic racism of services to children and families in sharp relief. Many believed that out-of-wedlock birth was not severely stigmatized among blacks, as it was among whites, frequently justifying neglect of African American birth mothers and making it impossibly difficult for most black women who wished to make adoption plans ever to do so.[2] The notion that it was as "natural" for blacks to keep their children as it was for whites to give them up revealed how racially differentiated conceptions of nature rationalized unequal social services and choices.

When dependent children of color did come to the attention of child-placing organizations and institutions, such as orphanages, they were refused services outright, sometimes (as Justine Polier had observed) because they were of the wrong religion, but often because of their color. This situation prevailed nationally, not in the South alone, well into the 1960s.[3] From its founding in 1921, the CWLA saw the color line as an obstacle to its goals. The organization dismissed facile assertions that home finding for "Negro" children was impossible, but admitted that finding "colored homes" was extremely difficult.[4] The favored solution was to encourage black community leaders to establish services of their own.[5]

Maternity homes and hospitals catering exclusively to "Negresses" were noted occasionally in the late nineteenth and early twentieth centuries.[6] The existing orphanages for "colored children" were frequently sponsored by churches such as the Society of Friends. Those established by African Americans themselves tended to be less institutional in character than many traditional orphanages, more like large boarding homes. Individuals rather than organizations established them, and they were often kept afloat on such shoestring budgets that they collapsed after founders died.[7] Cleveland's sole black orphanage, for instance, was founded privately in 1895 on the rural outskirts of the city. It did not last long. After officials objected to the presence of black children in the local school and neighbors complained to county commissioners about conditions at the home, it closed in 1903.[8]

Adoption flourished among African Americans despite the discrimination that kept them out of the child welfare system and the poverty that placed parallel services out of reach. In 1909 W. E. B. DuBois commented that child-care traditions among African Americans, originating under slavery, included a "habit of adoption" that was "still widespread and beneficent" under postemancipation conditions of migration.[9] In the 1930s sociologist Charles Johnson noted that African Americans in Alabama routinely took in the children of friends and relatives because of divorce, separation, desertion, illegitimacy, death, migration, and the fact that childless couples lacked the social standing that came only with children. "We jest tuk her as one of the family," one of Johnson's informants declared about an orphaned child they were raising, "and don't sho' no difference. We don't tell no difference."[10] At midcentury Mildred Arnold of the USCB wrote that "there are many Negro families who have 'adopted' children for all intents and purposes but who have not taken any legal steps to accomplish this."[11] Clearly, African Americans responded to children in need. In large families where membership was fluid, distinctions between natural and adopted kin were not accentuated.

Informal family making among African Americans was considered both meritorious and inadequate by the child welfare establishment early in the century. "No house is too small or family too large but that a needy child brought to the notice of a neighbor will find a snug harbor of safety," C. C. Carstens noted admiringly in 1927. "The provision that is made may be unsanitary, ill-considered, or unsafe, but the spirit is there for genuine help."[12] African Americans protested discrimination in adoption and child welfare services during the 1910s, 1920s, and 1930s, but the suggestion that they might forge a separatist solution, as Catholics had, met with resistance among many civil rights activists. The Cleveland NAACP, for example, opposed establishing a private, black-only child welfare institution but also feared that expanding public child welfare might result in segregated all-black agencies. Integration was their goal, and racial exclusion could not be countenanced, even to offer desperately needed services to children in their own community.[13] During this era, children made do with scanty and punitive public and nonsectarian services—detention and penal facilities that did not even pretend to offer children the prospect of home—or with nothing at all.

By the 1940s Lucile Lewis, of the Child Welfare Association of Fulton and DeKalb counties in Georgia, estimated that thirty thousand to fifty thousand "Negro" babies in the United States needed new parents. Few would find adoptive homes. "Negro" adoptions were uncommon and, even more, rarely supervised by agency staff, who invariably took longer to place the few African American children in their care, even though the babies in question were healthy, charming, and had average mentality or better.[14] Deeply frustrated, Lewis called on her colleagues to eradicate the discrimination that pervaded their services by first integrating their own ranks.

Segregation was just as firm when it came to providing for children of Asian descent. Three California orphanages that cared for most of the state's Japanese American orphans, for example, were shuttered and moved whole-sale—along with their Japanese American staff—to the Manzanar Reloca-tion Center during World War II. The Children's Village, a stigmatized camp within a camp, was home for more than one hundred children (newborn to age eighteen) from June 1942 to September 1945. At war's end, the vast majority rejoined their natal kin (having been made "temporary" orphans by the internment process) or were parceled out to wage homes.[15]

In 1948 the USCB finally incorporated race into its adoption reporting system.[16] Before that, national statistics on African American children sim-ply did not exist. Leading professionals had long known about the racial disparity in adoption, however. The New York State Charities Aid Associa-tion placed a total of forty-nine "Negro" children in "Negro" family homes beginning in 1898. After a quarter-century, it found only seven had been young enough to be likely candidates for adoption.[17] The number of "Ne-gro" children actually adopted during the first two decades of the century was so marginal to the agency's mission that it was never recorded.

As we saw in the last chapter, after 1945 the special-needs revolution expanded the terms of adoptability and posited belonging as a vital resource for all children in need of parents, including children of color. Services to nonwhite children also attracted attention after important national surveys and conferences revealed how inequitably adoption opportunities were dis-tributed. But the presumption that matching should govern adoptions did not change. Around the country, a number of important experiments set out to recruit nonwhite parents for nonwhite children. What they had in com-mon was a commitment to improving services through programs of com-munity education offered by racially representative professionals in racially sensitive agencies. Minority adoptions could be encouraged by undoing agency racism.

Outreach to members of minority racial and ethnic communities was the first order of business for these programs. This effort took the form of citizens' committees bringing white social welfare professionals uneasily together with minority elites. Typically initiated by adoption agencies, the committees sought to mobilize publicity and increase applications rather than share power. Agencies retained all authority over parent selection, in-vestigation, and supervision. The Interracial Committee on Adoptive Home-finding was founded in 1939 in New York, for example, and it began its work on Long Island. Sophie van Senden Theis of the New York State Charities Aid Association was the force behind this project. She believed that targeted media announcements and posters might produce a groundswell of interest from adults who might not even know that scores of babies desperately needed parents. An essay contest on "How to Interest More Colored Families in the Adoption of Children" brought in 250 entries from twenty-one states. The committee succeeded in placing a maximum of twenty African American children annually.[18] In Chicago the advisory board of the Negro Adoption Project brought together black business leaders and professionals, representatives of sizeable black organizations, delegates from the local bar association and medical society, and adoption service providers.[19] Such efforts assumed that African American couples, even if they were childless, avoided agencies because of ignorance.

Churches and the press were key to publicizing adoption in minority neighborhoods. *Ebony* did its part in 1948 to advertise the pathetic plight of "10,000 brown orphans," "their only crime, that of being brown."[20] An article in the *Afro-American* about German children fathered by African American men generated mountains of letters.[21] These articles suggested an extreme humanitarian crisis. Abandoned as foundlings in boxes, sold for small sums, or rejected by white adopters when they discovered the babies had "Negroid features" or showed evidence of "Negroid admixture," these children were doomed unless suitable adopters could be found to match them.[22]

In Los Angeles, advocates placed hundreds of posters in street cars and busses, disseminated radio and television announcements in English and Spanish, and generated stories for the minority press, including six local Mexican, one Chinese, ten African American, and five Japanese newspapers. Pictures of attractive children looking for homes, they found, were especially effective, far more so than pictures of children already placed.[23] In Maryland, agencies enlisted the support of black ministers and circulated sample radio and television spots as well as newspaper stories.[24] In Lake County, Indiana, the Citizens' Committee on Negro Adoptions succeeded in getting several mayors to declare a Negro Adoption Week in fall 1954 and used radio spots to announce that "you don't have to be a Joe Louis or a Jackie Robinson to adopt children."[25] In 1957 a San Francisco Bay area project, MARCH (Minority Adoption Recruitment of Children's Homes) produced a film, *Eddie Gets a New Name,* and two half-hour NBC telecasts to spread the appeal for homes into Mexican American as well as African American communities.[26]

Urban areas with significant African American populations, such as Chicago, Cincinnati, Los Angeles, New York, and Washington, DC, took the lead.[27] The Los Angeles County Bureau of Adoptions, the first public adoption service in California, recruited African American and Mexican parents from its establishment in 1949; in 1954 it placed 394 children for adoption, and in 1965, it was the first agency in the country to recruit single parents, a move aimed at finding homes for black children.[28] San Francisco's MARCH had a caseload that encompassed not only "Negro" children but numerous "Spanish-American," Chinese, Filipino, Hawaiian, Japanese, Korean, Samoan, American Indian, and other children.[29] Social workers who had rarely encountered African American (or any nonwhite) families, such as Theodora Allen of the North Dakota Division of Child Welfare, were so stymied by cases of "Negro" or mixed-race children that they had to make strenuous efforts to locate nonwhite homes.[30] Perhaps this explains the curious fact that such overwhelmingly white states as Washington, Oregon, and Minnesota launched "Negro" adoption initiatives. The Minority Home Finding Committee of the Children's Home Society of Washington recruited parents for black children in the mid-1950s, and "Operation Brown Baby" of the Boys and Girls Aid Society of Oregon began in 1957.[31] Parents to Adopt Minority Youngsters (PAMY) in Minnesota also started in 1957, when two social workers—one from a local private agency and the other from the Urban League—discussed the urgent need for adoption services among children of color. Funds to hire staff and place children were not set until 1961, and the project lasted only two years.[32]

Hiring more African American social workers was a high priority, but the color line in social welfare separated professionals as it did the children they served. After placing a few "Negro" children for adoption between 1940 and 1944, the Illinois Children's Home and Aid Society hired two black caseworkers and found that "the applicants seemed to feel much more comfortable talking with a member of their own race than with a white person."[33] Spence-Chapin Adoption Service hired a black social worker in 1948, even before setting up a committee to investigate why the agency received so few applications from "Negro" couples.[34] Louise Wise Services established an Interracial Adoption Program in 1952 alongside a staff interracial committee. Annie Lee Davis, a consultant to the USCB on minority groups, suggested that agencies without "Negro" staff consult local chapters of the Urban League for help in identifying qualified personnel.[35] The Adoption Unit of the Washington, DC, Department of Public Welfare made "Negro" adopters part of its recruitment strategy on the theory that others in the African American community would find a "satisfied customer" the most persuasive advertisement for adoption.[36] If racial difference between staff and clientele hindered adoptions, racial rapport might facilitate them.

Diversifying agency staff and publicizing services would accomplish little without heightened cultural sensitivity. Attitudinal, behavioral, and policy changes were needed for several concrete reasons. Many African Americans believed that adoption was entirely beyond their reach, that it was "a white man's luxury," and all too many white professionals simplistically assumed that whites believed in adoption and blacks did not.[37] When the occasional African American contacted an agency, white workers often suspected that he or she "consciously or unconsciously expects to be rejected."[38] Offering a sincere welcome to "Negro" applicants was therefore required. Self-consciousness, embarrassment, and anxiety stood between too many children and permanence. So too did the imperiousness of agency professionals. "Giving up our delusions of omniscience" was the first step toward finding more homes for minority children, according to PAMY.[39]

The aesthetic preferences of African Americans also deserved respect. African American adopters were as specific as their white counterparts about the details of children's appearance. According to Bernice Daniels of Spence-Chapin, African Americans were "much more exacting about color-matching," and "this cultural emphasis on color" had to be accepted before adoption services would improve.[40] White social worker Catherine Oberholtzer recalled that caseworkers in 1950s New Orleans routinely constructed color charts to assist black adopters to specify the (typically light) skin color and hair texture ("good" rather than "kinky") they desired.[41] Responses to the 1948 *Ebony* article about parentless black children suggest that African Americans were as interested in physical attractiveness as whites who specified blond curls and blue eyes. "I read in the paper where homes are wanted for Brown Babies," wrote Mrs. Joseph Samuel of South Carolina. "We both want children so badly, hoping this will be an answer to our prayer. Our choice of color will be brown (light)."[42] Virginia Beaton, from South Carolina, thought the *Ebony* article might bring her the baby daughter she longed for: "We would like for her to [have] brown skin not dark or too light with pretty good hair."[43] For her part, Mrs. Thomas Jones "prayed to God that some day I would care for some one's baby if not my own. . . . We would like for the baby to be huskey brown skin light."[44]

In her letter, Mrs. Jones promised that she could afford a baby as well as love one. The details she provided about her employment, bank accounts, and dream of owning a home displayed awareness that financial qualifications might be obstacles to adoption. These too needed adjustment. Research conducted by David Fanshel in Pittsburgh suggested that socioeconomic and educational disadvantages were significant reasons why African American applicants dropped out of the adoption process at disproportionately high rates (almost 60 percent compared to 40 percent for whites), and he called on agencies to rethink and revise standards of material well-being that too often placed legal family making out of reach.[45]

Adoption fees placed a disproportionate burden on poorer applicants, regardless of race, but age requirements and expectations that adopters prove their infertility deterred far more black than white applicants.[46] In circumstances that reversed the supply-demand situation—African American adoption was a "buyer's" rather than a "seller's" market—agencies scrambled to rationalize differential treatment of white and black applicants. One approach, taken by the Children's Aid Society of Pennsylvania, was to rename paid foster care by black parents as "quasi-adoption"—effectively instituting a program of subsidized adoption without benefit of legal finalization.[47] In the case of formal adoption, however, recruitment efforts had to be flexible. They had to maintain the validity of race-conscious standards without provoking suspicion that the services or children that African American adopters received were inferior.

The National Urban League Foster Care and Adoptions Project, in operation from 1953 to 1958, was the first nationally coordinated effort to locate adoptive homes for African American children.[48] Some Urban League affiliates were blocked from participation because local agencies denied that black children in their jurisdictions needed services or refused the Urban League any role, however subordinate, in child welfare. In some cities where collaboration was attempted, such as Kansas City, black leaders were effectively excluded from the project, white social workers were insistent on applying identical standards to black and white families, and no progress was made.[49]

Adopt-A-Child was the next effort to promote African American and Puerto Rican adoption nationally during the postwar period, and it was more successful (figure 14).[50] Founded in January 1955 by fourteen New York adoption agencies and the National Urban League (which housed the project in its New York office), the program lasted five years before running out of money and closing its doors. It was supported by grants from the Field Foundation and the New York Fund for Children. Prominent individuals, including Justine Polier, served on its board. Dr. William S. Jackson left his job as program director for the Urban League of Greater New York to head the project. The campaign set out to "right a dreadful wrong" and "provide a home for every child who needs one."[51]

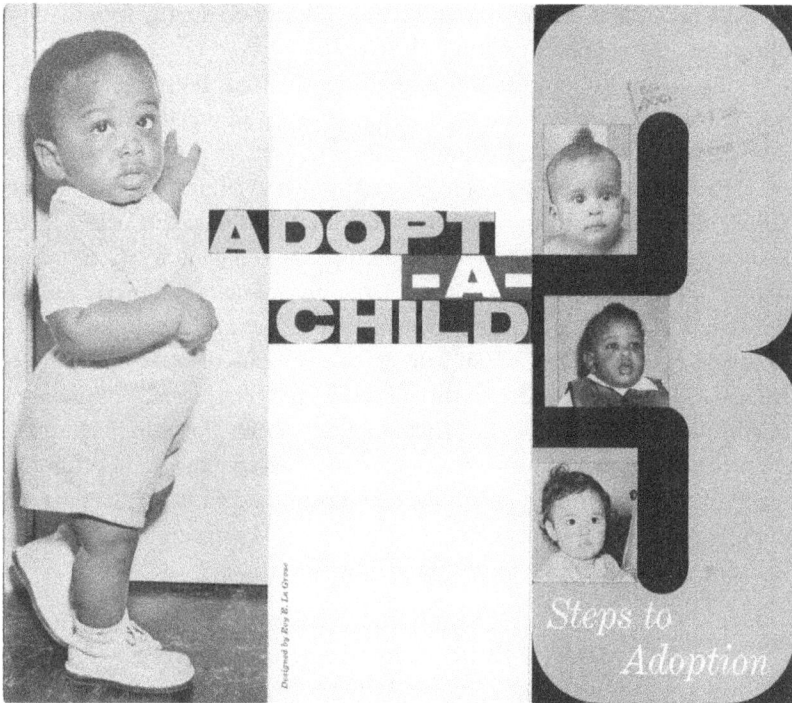

Figure 14. Adopt-A-Child was one of the first major efforts to recruit
African American and other minority adoptive parents in the 1950s.
Used by permission of the Child Welfare League of America.

Adopt-A-Child did what local citizens' committees around the country
did, but on a larger scale. It publicized (in Spanish and English) the need for
adopters on both radio and television, conducted research on the difficulties faced by minority adopters, and sponsored conferences and a speakers
bureau to disseminate information about methods for overcoming racial
bias. It sought to be "totally representative."[52] For example, at its first executive committee meeting, members passed a motion to redress a represen-
tational oversight and recruit a Puerto Rican into the project's leadership.[53]
It developed a clearinghouse that served as a model for adoption resource
exchanges (essential mechanisms for all "special needs" adoptions by the
late 1960s) by publishing monthly listings of waiting children and families.[54] But the primary goal of Adopt-A-Child was to boost applications and
coordinate referrals. The project received more than four thousand inquiries
from throughout the United States, Bermuda, Cuba, Puerto Rico, and the

Virgin Islands, and almost one thousand children eventually found adoptive homes through participating agencies.[55]

Considering the enthusiasm and effort involved, these results disappointed but did not surprise backers. Adopt-A-Child relied on agencies to oversee the adoptions and could not force them to jettison rigid policies that alienated applicants. The project did its best to cultivate diplomatic relationships with professionals, but its goal was to dislodge the racial bigotry and cultural bias that tarnished their services. A confidential report bluntly blamed white social workers. They failed to understand that blackness was not only a matter of skin color and hair texture but also a cultural and sociological identity. These social workers were confused by the spectrum of color—white to black and everything in between—that existed within many Puerto Rican families. They worried too much about "lowering" standards for black adopters when they really needed to accept "the socio-economic realities in which people must live, and where we find them."[56] And they rarely treated African American applicants as equal partners in family making, defensively guarding their own prerogatives instead.

Transracial Families in an Age of Matching

Adopt-A-Child assured members of minority communities that "you don't have to be rich to adopt a child" and insisted that age, education, and other requirements were flexible.[57] Adoption could identify a special child "who will blend into your family, grow happily in your home and may even look a little like you."[58] Adopt-A-Child was determined to increase the number of minority adoptions by recruiting minority parents, a goal premised on matching. It nevertheless received a substantial number of letters (20–25 percent of the total) from white couples interested in transracial adoption. These couples, most of whom were Jewish, worried that requests for African American children would be considered bizarre and rejected out of hand by conventional agencies.[59]

Such fears were well founded. The consensus against transracial adoptions was so complete before the 1960s that only two states—Texas and Louisiana—bothered to pass statutes explicitly prohibiting them, a stark contrast to antimiscegenation laws, which aggressively policed the color line in marriage.[60] Transracial adoptions were rare before the 1960s, but they did occur. The first case on record of an African American baby deliberately adopted by white parents took place in Minnesota in 1948 when his black social worker, Laura Gaskin, despaired of finding a black couple to adopt him and refused to place him in yet another foster home.[61] It is curious that matching was both paradigmatic and inconsistently applied, as if the naturalness of racial sameness was so incontrovertible that exceptions to it could barely be seen, no matter how visible they were.

Most children placed transnationally after 1945—from Asian countries including Japan, Korea, and Vietnam—were placed across lines that Americans understood to be "racial" even if those lines were not black and white. Indeed, Asian children placed in white families were the adoptees who made transracial adoption a conspicuous social issue for the first time. The context for transnational adoptions, as we have already seen, was hot and cold war, and they were spearheaded by military and civilian families who responded to humanitarian appeals by making foreign children (some of them fathered by members of the U.S. armed services) their own.[62]

The incorporation of American Indian children into non-Indian families constituted a kind of adoption that was at once transnational and transracial. Placing Native American children across lines of race was not the same as placing Korean children in white homes, but because tribes were dependent sovereign nations, neither was it entirely different. The Indian Adoption Project was funded by the Bureau of Indian Affairs and the USCB and was administered by the CWLA. Between 1958 and 1967, it deliberately placed 395 Native American children from reservations in sixteen western states with white families in Illinois, Indiana, New York, Massachusetts, Missouri, and other states in the East and Midwest.[63] Approximately half were under one year of age; more than half were "full-blooded Indian."[64] To date it was the most systematic violation of matching by the very professionals pledged to uphold the matching creed.

The Indian Adoption Project presented itself as a civil rights movement in the adoption world. Approximately fifty public and private adoption agencies around the country cooperated with the project. The largest number of children were placed by agencies that were already leaders in services to African American and mixed-race children: Louise Wise Services and Spence-Chapin Adoption Service (both of New York) and the Children's Bureau of Delaware. Agencies still nervous about their own ability to handle such sensitive placements gained confidence from their participation in the project. "Our whole agency has gone Indian," boasted a representative of the New England Home for Little Wanderers.[65]

The architects of the Indian Adoption Project knew they would face opposition. Arnold Lyslo, the project director, counseled agencies to be patient with tribes, whose willingness or unwillingness to see children adopted transracially was determined by "degree of acculturation"; some, like the Hopi and Navaho, were simply not ready to let children go.[66] He also denounced the white racism that frequently prevented the adoption of Native American children in their home states. And when potential parents were found at a geographic distance, agencies were told to probe their racial attitudes and "color tolerances" carefully.[67] Would they consider adopting a child from another minority group? Were they acquainted with any Indians? Would they permit the child's continued tribal membership if the birth mother thought this was important?[68] Peter, born in 1957 on a Montana reservation, was placed at age two with a Jewish couple in New York. The agency proudly noted that the child would remain an enrolled member of his tribe because "the adoptive father grew up in Canada and knows quite a bit about Indians."[69]

An outcome study, lasting from 1960 to 1968, followed almost one-third of the children adopted through the project. Most had adjusted well, a finding that author David Fanshel expected would decrease worry about transracial adoptions but leave unresolved the question of self-determination in Native American communities. "Even with the benign outcomes reported here," Fanshel noted prophetically, "it may be that Indian leaders would rather see their children share the fate of their fellow Indians than lose them in the white world."[70] An internal report on the project's accomplishments in 1967 ignored this dilemma and proudly declared that "one can no longer say that the Indian child is the 'forgotten child.'"[71] The heartwarming record of welcome into white families also made Native American birth mothers more willing to surrender children, "knowing that adoption may afford the child greater opportunity for a better life."[72] For project director Lyslo, this was progress.

Attitudes toward transracial adoptions were never uniform. They existed on a spectrum of more and less tolerable, reproducing the black-white binary that defined the historical color line in the United States. Many white parents who considered Native American children were unwilling to consider those whose backgrounds were "part Negro" because adopting children who were "red" or "yellow" or even "brown" was less transgressive than adopting children who were "black."[73] "Indian children and Oriental children were easy to place," commented Orv Garrison of the Boys and Girls Aid Society of Oregon. "They did not wait around very long. Black children or part-black children waited for months—years."[74] Studies showed that some white adopters would consider Native American or Latino children, but few found African American parentage acceptable, even around 1970, the moment of greatest openness toward black-white adoptions.[75]

Unlike transnational placement, which was never envisioned as a viable solution to the dire circumstances faced by children globally, the Indian Adoption Project was part of an ambitious experiment to remove an entire child population. By the early 1970s, one researcher estimated that 25–35 percent of all Indian children had been placed in adoption, foster care, or institutions and that 85–90 percent of all family placements were non-Indian.[76] In some states, such as Minnesota, almost one-quarter of all Indian children under the age of one were adopted, and the rates of child placement for Indian children in Montana, South Dakota, Washington, and Wisconsin were astronomically higher than for non-Indian children.[77]

The American Indian Movement denounced child placement as a genocidal policy while the Indian Adoption Project was still in existence. In 1974 the Association of American Indian Affairs began publishing *Indian Family Defense*, a newsletter concerned with the child welfare crisis, and organizations such as the National Indian Child Welfare Association worked to prevent the removal of Northwest Indian children. Beyond decimating tribes and reservations, placement in non-Indian homes caused children to experience abandonment, grief, and painful loss of identity, according to Native American activists. Adoption capped a history of tribe-, family-, and soul-destroying assimilationist efforts—including boarding schools, orphanages, and various Christianization campaigns—that aimed at nothing less than the eradication of Indianness itself.[78]

The Indian Child Welfare Act, passed by Congress in 1978, reversed these policies. It defined children as collective resources essential for tribal survival, gave tribal courts exclusive jurisdiction over many cases involving children, and augmented the ability of Indian authorities to pursue claims in state courts, even when Indian birth parents wished to place their children outside of tribal communities.[79] The act made the adoption of Native American children by non-Indian people extremely difficult, marking its departure from legal individualism as spectacular as it was exceptional. The law was defended as a necessary corrective to the harm done by the Indian Adoption Project. Child welfare leaders who had participated eagerly in the project less than two decades earlier confessed in 2001 that "it was wrong; it was hurtful; and it reflected a kind of bias that surfaces feelings of shame."[80] Equality in child welfare had been radically redefined.

The Indian Adoption Project expressed more complex realities than the antithesis between enlightenment and genocide suggested. It evoked the demographic, cultural, and political pressures that shaped race in postwar family making. The supply of healthy white infants declined because of more effective and accessible contraception and abortion, the sexual revolution corroded the stigma surrounding illegitimacy, and "ethnicity" became a favored group identity, more benign than "race" precisely because of its compatibility with whiteness.

Placing black children with white parents was the most controversial move in adoption because black-white families crossed the most stubborn racial line. Only tiny numbers of black children were adopted by white parents, even at their zenith around 1970–1971, when perhaps 2,500 were finalized each year, just 1.4 percent of all adoptions in the country.[81] In the years before 1975, there were probably no more than a total of twelve thousand black children adopted transracially, but these adoptions achieved a symbolic importance that overshadowed their statistical relevance. They defined the policy debate.

A few resolute white parents prevailed in adopting black children despite professional and community hostility. The Johnstons, a family in Kent, Washington (an overwhelmingly white community), took a black child into foster care in 1944, when she was only six weeks old. In 1953, when she was nine, they adopted her over the objections of their social worker and neighbors, who accused them of sacrificing the child's welfare to flatter their liberal ideals. Patty's white parents disagreed. "Our family believes it should be possible for an individual to live as a person among people, rather than a Negro among whites," Ann Johnston remarked.[82] Yet racial solidarity was also one of their goals. With the help of an African American friend, they took steps to ensure that Patty felt "proud of her people" and developed "poise and serenity as a young Negro woman."[83] The Johnstons' experience as a black-and-white family was unusual at the time, but they anticipated the multiculturalism of later years. It is telling that most black-white adoptions before the late 1960s took place in states such as Washington, which had a tiny African American population. Oregon, Minnesota, and Massachusetts were others.[84]

Determined would-be parents played key roles in the history of transracial adoption. They were adept at locating potentially sympathetic agencies. Adoption professionals who founded projects during the 1950s to increase the number of African American adoptions were astonished by the number of inquiries from whites. Although they considered same-race placements preferable, they realized that transracial placements were becoming imaginable, at least for children who would otherwise go parentless. Worn down by the challenges of recruiting parents who matched, some of these workers began to experiment gingerly with parents who did not match. In California, MARCH received "massive numbers" of applications from "Anglo-

Caucasians" even though it made no effort to recruit white parents.[85] Their applications were routinely rejected, generating "hostility" and "deep bitterness" among white applicants.[86] After making only fifty placements with minority parents in two and one-half years, MARCH finally placed five children with white parents in the late 1950s, all of whom had one "Anglo-Caucasian" birth parent.[87] By 1968, the Los Angeles County Bureau of Adoptions had placed one hundred children across racial lines.[88]

Agencies were defensive about reaching out to white families, and did so more out of desperation than commitment. Louise Wise Services set out to recruit white parents for its interracial program in 1963, after that program had already been in existence for more than a decade, and accurately predicted that doing so would be controversial (figure 15).[89] The agency "is fully aware of the questions raised by Negro-White adoptions," its director announced.[90] "Perhaps experience will prove us wrong, but we believe that some of these youngsters will gain more security and happiness in adoption by a white family than by never being adopted at all."[91] Other agencies that had arranged hundreds of interracial placements acknowledged that black-white adoptions were a last resort.[92]

In Illinois the Cook County Department of Public Aid began making transracial placements in 1965, so long as social workers were convinced that prospective adopters were independent minded and brave.[93] In Oregon the Boys and Girls Aid Society launched a transracial program as early as 1960; it was named "Opportunity" in 1967. When Oregonians Douglas and Gloria Bates applied to adopt in 1970, they found that "the state bureaucracy was not a slow train but a speeding locomotive."[94] "Neither of us had ever had a truly meaningful conversation with an African American," Douglas Bates recalled, and the couple had not seriously considered what transracial adoption might mean.[95] Yet by the age of twenty-five, they were the legal parents of two black daughters, Lynn and Liska, both scarred by abuse and impermanence early in life.

In Minnesota PAMY also inched toward transracial placements, but social workers anticipated problems with black-white adoptions that did not worry them when whites adopted Indian or Mexican children. They mistrusted parents' promises of color-blindness, doubted their ability to help children negotiate discrimination, and suspected that even the best intentions could not shield transracial families from hardships that might ruin lives. They knew about highly publicized disasters, such as that of Reverend David Cohen and his wife, Ann. The Cohens, veterans of civil rights campaigns in Mississippi and Alabama and parents of four, had adopted mixed-race David in infancy through the Los Angeles County Bureau of

Figure 15. Louise Wise Services established an Interracial Adoption Program in 1952.
Archives & Special Collections, Columbia University Health Sciences Library.
Used by permission.

Adoptions, only to give him up reluctantly at age two after intense harass-
ment and threats in their conservative community of Fullerton, California.[96] Reactions to other transracial adoptions were less violent but equally
hostile: local children were sometimes forbidden to play with the adoptees;
black children were banned from neighborhood swimming pools; and parents were taunted and called "nigger lovers" on the streets or in anonymous
phone calls. Thankfully, few such problems developed in the first twenty
transracial adoptions that PAMY oversaw. For these parents, the "motivation in adoption is based on love for a child, not on involvement with
racial problems," Harriet Fricke, the project coordinator, wrote in relief.[97]
Transracial placements were only a "little revolution."[98] "The reason we
did it," explained actor Beau Bridges, after adopting an African American
infant in 1969, "is we just kind of felt like it. We thought it would be fun,
it would be good, it would be nice."[99] Professionals were satisfied when
white parents considered their black children kin and not projects in racial
reconciliation.

For every agency that permitted the transracial adoption of black children, many more did not, and such placements were frequently contested
by public authorities.[100] Even in 1970 and 1971, the high-water mark for

transracial placements of African American children, knowledgeable professionals understood the circumstances of adoptable children of color to be so dire that they seriously discussed exporting these American children. "Why not make it possible for these babies to be adopted in Scandinavian countries where I am told there are many suitable homes and childless couples who have no hangups about skin color?" wrote Frederick Johnson to Trude Lash of the Citizens Committee for Children in New York.[101] Despite the much-discussed white baby shortage, most white adopters were never interested in adopting black children.

However rare, black-white families effectively challenged the equivalence between matching, nature, and realness. Skin-color differences betrayed the fact that adoption departed from nature. In addition, white families who took in black children before 1970 often did not conform to the model of infertile couples bent on making up families from scratch, "as if begotten." Families with children "made room for one more," a demographic pattern characteristic of many special-needs adoptions.[102] Whites who adopted transracially also tended to rank higher in education and occupation, depended less on their own families of origin, and expressed more humanitarian motives for adoption than those who adopted same-race children.[103] They approached agencies with confidence and spoke their minds. Because agencies needed them, the usual power relationship did not apply. "If they don't like our suggestions, they say so," commented the director of one minority adoption program. "And if they don't like us, they say so too."[104]

Jan and Joe Rigert, a white couple, encountered few obstacles to adopting black and mixed-race children after first adopting Douglas in 1962, even though they lived in Beaverton, Oregon, Olympia, Washington, and Minneapolis, Minnesota, cities with tiny minority populations. The Catholic couple made room for eight additional children after having one of their own. "Our family was not conceived or calculated to prove anything," Joe wrote, but "a multiracial family, by its very nature, is an experiment in human relationships."[105] The Rigerts affirmed the significance of the children's diverse backgrounds and deliberately prepared them to contend with racial hatred in the world outside their family. They also held fast to their belief in human commonality and relied on daily humor, recalling the sensibility of the Doss family.

Jan Rigert was a founding member of one of the new parent organizations that promoted adoptions of minority and other special-needs children. The Open Door Society of North America, founded in Montreal in 1959 by three white couples who had adopted black children, migrated to the United States from Canada. The Council on Adoptable Children, headquartered in Ann Arbor, Michigan, also emerged in the 1960s. By 1969 there were at least forty-seven organizations in the United States whose mission was to advocate for "waiting" children, most of whom had special needs, minority backgrounds, or both.[106] Many were local groups, such as Transracial Adoptive Parents in Illinois and Families for Inter-Racial Adoption in Boston.[107] Their vision of family heralded a significant shift in adoption culture, defying the claim that adoptive kinship had to be invisible to be authentic. This feature of the adoption world, in turn, reflected an even broader shift in conceptions of national belonging and citizenship as these moved toward explicitly acknowledging the country's multicultural and multiracial composition.

Difference, in Theory

The example of families forged across the borders of difference and the dilemmas of minority adoption served to redefine the meaning of authenticity in adoptive kinship. Eventually the paradigm that bound realness to sameness lost its hegemonic hold. This change had important consequences for all adoptions—most of which never crossed visible racial or national borders—because it announced the single most obvious fact about adoption. Kinship between strangers was made up socially and voluntarily. It was different by design.

H. David Kirk was the first person to elevate this commonsense observation to the level of sociological theory. From 1951 to 1961, Kirk directed the Adoption Research Project at McGill University, which eventually compiled data about the attitudes and experiences of two thousand families, most headed by infertile couples.[108] He and his wife adopted four children after becoming foster parents in 1950, and the interviews he conducted, as well as his own experience, taught him that "role handicap" was the cornerstone of adoptive parenthood. That is, infertile couples described feeling depressed and bitter about failing to meet normative expectations that they produce children of their own. To their surprise, adopting other people's children did not make their anguish disappear, nor did it dispel other people's pity and suspicion. Infertility was not a chapter that adoption closed.

Moreover, infertility not only compromised confidence but also placed equality beyond reach. Adopters were subjected to qualifying tests that natural parents never took. They also faced more discrimination from employers, insurers, and the Internal Revenue Service; less support from extended families; and indifference from a culture that did not dignify adoption with even a simple ritual parallel to the birthday. Two choices existed for handling the strain. Adoptive parents could conform to the culture of matching, pretend to be something they were not, and present themselves and their children to the world as exactly like other families. Or they could own up to their deprivations and differences and make common cause with their children and their children's birth parents.

Kirk termed these options "rejection-of-difference" and "acknowledgment-of-difference." Adopters who made the first choice—by insisting they were just like birth parents or neglecting to inform their children of their adoptive status—escaped the full force of social stigma and compensated themselves with a feeling of realness, but they abdicated their responsibility to empathize with their children. Adopters who made the second choice faced the penalty of perpetual challenges to their own authenticity, but they also allied themselves with children whose tenuous hold on belonging matched their own. Kirk's hypothesis was that adopters who had experienced the most severe losses and whose adoptions aspired to match most scrupulously would be most inclined toward rejection-of-difference. Couples who adopted after having children of their own, on the other hand, or even couples who adopted many children or older children, would find it easier to acknowledge difference because it was less threatening to their own claim to parental entitlement. Difference, Kirk argued, was the "shared fate" of adoptive parents and children. It unveiled "the shadow meanings behind . . . loving words about adoption."[109] Acknowledging it was less comfortable but far better for everyone involved.

Owning up to the difference that difference made, Kirk suggested, was the only real path to realness. Kirk's work mattered because it explicitly articulated the larger shift in authenticity strategies occurring within American adoption culture: from similarity to difference, from artifice to openness. As a new era of adoption reform dawned in the late 1960s, policies resting on the justification of benevolent naturalness came under scrutiny precisely for their denial of difference, which no longer seemed so natural. Arranging anonymous adoptions and sealing original birth records created the fiction of exclusivity and turned the fact that adoptees had more than one mother and father into an unspeakable secret. In a climate that venerated honesty as more authentic than simulation, matching appeared naive at best. Denying difference did not shield children and families from harm. It locked them into a confining adoption closet.

Postadoption services illustrate the shift from authenticity through similarity to authenticity through difference. Before the 1960s, help and information for adoptive parents and children after legalization was rarely if ever available. Casework and probationary periods from six to twelve months prior to legalization were nearly universal features of agency practice, but supervision ended promptly after adoptions were finalized.[110] Treating legally equivalent families differently violated matching. Offering adoptive families services because they were adoptive families, in other words, acknowledged the difference that design set out to erase.

The therapeutic logic associated with achieving authenticity through difference frequently equated difference with difficulty and damage. Yet Kirk, the primary theoretical exponent of bringing difference into the open, never did. Difference was a fact in adoption, and participants were certainly subjected to unique social pressures as a result, but Kirk objected to suggestions that adoption consequently led to developmental disadvantage, botched belonging, or spoiled selfhood.[111] Nor was he an advocate of "open adoptions," which aspired to ongoing contact between children and their natal relatives.[112] Realness resided in solidifying the social ground on which adoption rested, Kirk believed, not on granting its mediocrity in comparison to the real thing.

Racial Difference Reconsidered

Difference in adoption had many possible meanings. Kirk focused on the difference that all nonrelative adoptions had in common—their lack of biogenetic connection. In the 1960s and 1970s, at the point of transition from one authenticity strategy to another, researchers tracked the outcomes of special-needs, transracial, and transnational adoptions. The 1960–1968 follow-up on the Indian Adoption Project was exemplary. Such research indirectly assessed the cultural change that had made these adoptions possible in the first place.

Because positive outcomes were taken to be tacit endorsements of family making across lines of difference, and negative outcomes were presumed to show the folly of doing so, outcome studies were subject to heated debate. Most outcome research showed no significant differences between transracial and same-race adoptees in overall adjustment and found little evidence that either children or parents denied their differences, but a few studies revealed patterns of behavior and awareness that were interpreted both as proof of success (progress toward color-blindness) and failure (loss of racial consciousness). The controversy was (and is) most polarized in the case of black children adopted by white parents, where outcome research has invariably been used as ammunition in the policy war over transracial adoption itself.[113]

In the case of race, and especially blackness, the era of openness to difference that dawned in the adoption world of the late 1960s coincided with a powerful force moving in the opposite direction: a turn toward nationalism in the civil rights movement and an embrace of "roots" that reaffirmed the naturalness of sameness and continuity of identity. In 1972 the National Association of Black Social Workers (NABSW) issued a strongly worded statement that took "a vehement stand against the placements of black children in white homes for any reason," calling transracial adoption "unnatural," "artificial," "unnecessary," and proof that African Americans continued to be assigned to "chattel status."[114] It reiterated the charges of racial bias against white social workers and agencies that had animated the drive to recruit more African American and minority adopters in the 1950s, but did so more passionately and much less diplomatically. Transracial adoption was "an expedient for white folk."[115] Its boosters were hypocrites who claimed to care about civil rights but actually worked on behalf of white adults wanting unrestricted access to black children. This effort was more than arrogant and insulting. It was, according to an NABSW position paper, "a form of genocide" comparable to the slave trade.[116]

Instead of taking racial matching for granted, as most of the 1950s projects had done, the NABSW advanced an explicit theory of belonging and identity formation that tied same-race placements to the transmission of racial pride from African American parents to children. Severing this intergenerational bond was perilous not only for children but also for African American communities. The NABSW stated, "We affirm the inviolable position of black children in black families where they belong physically, psychologically and culturally in order that they receive the total sense of themselves and develop a sound projection of their future. . . . Black children in white homes are cut off from the healthy development of themselves as black people."[117]

Love was an insufficient condition for constructive growth, in other words. Transracial adoptions made the disastrous mistake of imagining that racial identity was something black children, surrounded by white relatives, could achieve all by themselves. They could not. Individualistic conceptions of how children grew up were luxuries associated with majority group membership, not accurate descriptions of the hurdles that black children faced in a racist society. Without same-race parents, black children would be left defenseless against bigotry; they would need "to be taught to do what comes naturally."[118] Instead of promoting their interests, transracial adoption made children even more vulnerable victims of racism.

Enough black adopters could be found, the NABSW insisted, with more effort and less bigotry, and these were the parents that black children desperately needed. White parents, on the other hand, were more injurious than life without any permanent kin. The organization's president, Cenie J. Williams, went so far as to declare that "black children should remain in foster homes and institutions rather than be placed in the homes of willing white families."[119] By 1972 the consensus on the attachment imperative in development was all but absolute, as was the conviction that a lack of permanent ties would result in permanent damage. The position that white parents were worse than no permanent parents at all was therefore extremely dramatic. It indicated that the threat race-mixing posed to community survival remained as or more powerful than the knowledge that healthy development required secure belonging. Racial fears among whites had always inhibited transracial adoptions, of course, and the number of African American children adopted by whites was never large. The NABSW statement slowed them to a trickle. In 1973, only 1,091 black children were adopted by white parents in the United States, a 30 percent decrease over the previous year; in 1974, only 747 such adoptions took place.[120]

In the wake of the 1972 statement by the NABSW, some agencies prohibited transracial adoption or limited it to couples whose racial credentials were deemed appropriate: they were aware of their own biases and free of stereotypes, lived in integrated neighborhoods, had social contacts across the color line, and expressed the desire to participate in ongoing support groups and counseling.[121] For thirty years, commentaries on transracial adoption have unfailingly identified the NABSW position paper as a powerful intervention in the debate and credited it with preventing adoptions that might have occurred otherwise. The 1972 controversy had other consequences. It encouraged the simplistic view that African Americans were monolithically opposed to transracial adoptions at a time when blacks were almost surely more tolerant of interracial families than whites.[122] It also affirmed the dominant skepticism about transracial placements that was already entrenched in the white child welfare establishment.[123] CWLA adoption standards, for example, had been revised in 1968 in a way that was slightly friendlier to transracial adoption, stipulating that "racial background in itself should not determine the selection of a home for a child."[124] In 1973 that standard was replaced with this one: "It is preferable to place children in families of their own racial background."[125] Same-race placements were almost always better because they facilitated easier integration into home and community, even if that home and community required relocating the child to another part of the country.

Among advocates of transracial adoption, few disagreed that race matching was preferable, and fewer still suggested that it was racist or illegal.[126]
Louise Wise Services, the agency whose Interracial Adoption Program had
been one of the first in the United States to make transracial placements,
observed that resistance to transracial adoptions in New York had increased
significantly by the late 1960s, and in 1972 the agency agreed that they should
not be prioritized, though neither should they be banned.[127] The agency's
point was pragmatic. Because the number of minority children needing
parents far exceeded the number of minority homes seeking children, ban-
ning transracial adoption meant that many children would grow up in the
foster care system, denied permanent belonging. This was far more damaging, in the agency's view, than identity confusion, which in any event was
a theoretical possibility, not yet a documented reality. In the tense racial
climate of the early 1970s, even the moderate argument that white parents
were better than none was not persuasive, however. In 1975 two prominent researchers declared that transracial adoption had "almost ceased to
exist."[128]

A number of new agencies were staffed entirely by African Americans,
energetically renewing the effort that had started in the late 1940s and
1950s to find black homes for black children. Examples included the Afro-
American Family and Community Services Agency in Chicago, Homes for
Black Children in Detroit, and Harlem-Dowling Children's Service in New
York (the brainchild of African American administrators at Spence-Chapin
Adoption Service). The NABSW also established an Adoption Counseling
and Referral Services of its own. These agencies reported considerable success with procedures sensitive to the historic experience of the African American community and applauded successful strategies, such as Baltimore's
outreach to members of Delta Sigma Theta sorority.[129] At Homes for Black
Children, applicants were greeted both on the phone and at the door by
black receptionists, applications were filled out in person rather than by
mail, motivation to adopt was not questioned, and the alienating word "investigation" was never used.[130] By 1975 the agency was placing all available
children and had a waiting list.[131]

The NABSW statement was influential, but its influence has been exaggerated. The NABSW was never able to translate its opposition to transracial
adoption into law as the Indian Child Welfare Act did in 1978. The decline
in whites adopting black children after 1972 may have had as much to do
with stubborn private preferences among would-be parents as with organized protest or policies that erected barriers to placements that crossed the
color line. The argument that transracial adoption spelled annihilation for

minority cultures was equally applicable, after all, to the adoption of racially different children born in other countries, whose removal from communities of descent deprived them of their native lands and languages along with their natal relatives. Yet transnational adoptions, a majority involving children from Asia, increased quite dramatically at just the moment when domestic transracial adoptions were becoming controversial.[132] In 1975, when the widely publicized "Operation Babylift" transported almost two thousand children away from Saigon on the eve of the U.S. evacuation of Vietnam, the Immigration and Naturalization Service reported that immigrant orphans admitted to the United States had increased 350 percent since 1968.[133] The number continued to accelerate rapidly throughout the 1970s, 1980s, and 1990s. Why did transnational adoptions increase? There are many reasons, but a simple one stands out. Most of these adoptions did not involve the specific kind of racial difference that had bothered Americans and had tortured their history most. Children adopted from overseas were not black.

The conviction that racial sameness was natural and necessary survived the sea change from denial of difference to acknowledgment of difference as a strategy for reaching authenticity in adoption. Many other ingredients of matching did not. Controversies about religious difference in families, for instance, had all but disappeared by the 1960s, supplanted by more vocal public debates about race and ethnicity. The therapeutic culture that flourished in the United States after 1945 also foregrounded psychological considerations in family making, such as emotional readiness, attachment, and "fit," demoting many types of physical likeness from essential necessities to superficial trivialities. The design of realness in adoptive kinship changed course to recognize which differences still made a difference.

The move from sameness to difference hinged on greater openness about the fact that adoptive kinship was achieved, not ascribed. It always had been, of course. But when parents and children did not resemble each other at all or when older children entered families, bringing with them memories that would never be shared by their legal kin, the fact that families were made up socially and purposefully, without the alchemy of blood, was inescapable. Adoptions that openly announced themselves on the basis of visible differences were only a small portion of adoptions in the United States, but they played a starring historical role. By displaying the face of difference, they made the difference that was inevitable in all nonrelative adoptions more thinkable, then more bearable, and eventually even honorable. No matter what they looked like, strangers who became kin were related by design.

CHAPTER EIGHT

Damaged Children, Therapeutic Lives

The struggle for realness in adoption was a struggle to manage the authenticity problems that difference caused. But what if adoption itself proved damaging? Perhaps the institution—and not merely the peculiar qualities, experiences, and motivations of its participants—harmed children. What were the prospects for reform if adoptive kinship thwarted the best efforts of regulatory, scientific, and therapeutic authority?

These questions exposed the enduring tension between design and authenticity. Families that were "made" were "clinically contrived" entities subject to ongoing intervention, their members destined to lead permanently therapeutic lives.[1] Surely this was an inescapable flaw at the heart of adoption, structurally precluding adoptive kinship from matching the psychological spontaneity of natural kinship. The labor-intensive projects of creating and maintaining authenticity contradicted the realness that members of adoptive families were so desperate to achieve. Authenticity could not be *made*. It had simply to *be*.

This chapter explores the historical career of one particular idea that gained currency in the early 1960s: that adoption per se placed children at risk for emotional disturbance and psychopathology. This idea may not seem like a novel proposition today. Trauma is a familiar term in many areas of post-Vietnam American culture. In the adoption world, the psychologically damaged adoptee is a stock figure. Many analysts invoke the need for recovery from the severing of "birth bonds," "primal wounds," and "adopted child syndromes."[2] Adoption was not always equated with attachment disorders, developmental disadvantage, or lifelong loss. The claim that adoptees' mental health might be jeopardized by virtue of their kinship arrangement alone was not widespread before the 1960s.

The equivalence between difference and damage triumphed during the 1960s for several reasons. First, risk was a factor deeply lodged in adoption history. Its affiliation with the institution—rather than with children's bad blood, parents' bad psychology, or the treacherous procedures that brought them together—was easily accomplished because danger and uncertainty were already familiar factors in adoption. Second, critics of matching and families formed transracially and transnationally succeeded in making difference a far more open issue in adoption debates by the 1960s, helped by the larger conversation about diversity and citizenship that accompanied the civil rights revolution. Finally, conceptualizing adoption as a risk factor was the logical culmination of interpretive practices in adoption, which originated in the World War I era, and the triumph of therapeutic culture at midcentury. It melded new clinical research, a newly popular sensibility, and new appreciation for the salience of identity with an old cultural fact: stigma.

Adoption, Psychopathology, and Mental Health

The issue of adoptees' mental health was multifaceted, but its bottom line was not. It reduced threats to normal development and secure identity to the absence of blood, a theme as old as nonbiological kinship itself. Long before significant numbers of clinicians and researchers wondered whether and why adoptees might be frequently referred for psychological treatment and disproportionately represented in clinical populations, individual mental health professionals speculated about the relationship between adoption and the problems presented by adoptees and adoptive families.

Before 1945, only scattered observations tied adoptive kinship itself to psychological disturbance, perhaps because significant numbers of children were placed in families at older ages and because it was apparent that many (if not all) of the difficulties they faced were traceable to histories of impermanence and worse that could hardly be blamed on adoption. Clinicians whose practices brought them into contact with adoptive families had their hands full helping older children adjust to lives apart from familiar people and surroundings and manage new (and typically more stringent) expectations for good grooming and behavior. For children whose early lives were filled with chaos and abuse, the prospect of adoption appeared to reduce many more risks than it created. Adoptees were considered lucky.

Occasionally, however, commentators hinted that adoption might cause problems. In the late 1930s, Edwina Cowan, a psychologist with the Wichita Child Welfare Research Laboratory, outlined a number of reasons why adoptees might be emotionally troubled. These factors included so-cioeconomic differences between natal and adoptive families. It was often challenging for children to negotiate the transition from precarious families where survival was a victory to families whose relative affluence imposed high behavioral and educational standards. More significant, however, was Cowan's theory that the difference inherent in adoption fueled children's tendency to believe that "all differences are for the worse."[3] On adoptive placement, even a previously happy and composed child might be shaken by the realization that "he differs from his companions in so important a matter as his relationship to his family."[4]

Compounding this blow was the deliberate "program of forgetting" favored by so many adoptive parents.[5] The expectation that children old enough to remember their earlier lives obliterate all their memories was, according to Cowan, "one of the most certain causes of emotional strain and maladjustment" in adopted children.[6] Many parents even associated the erasure of history with adoption success. "Rapid and apparently com-plete effacement of the past is accepted by foster parents as a condition of adjustment to the present," she noted.[7] No matter how well intended, the goal of psychological matching—the creation of new parent-child ties that were unitary and exclusive precisely because of their wholesale replacement of natal kin—placed children under pressure that seriously distorted their developing personalities and warranted stepped-up education and supervi-sion for adoptive families. "To be ashamed of one's parent is to be ashamed of one's self," Cowan noted, "because a parent is part of one's self."[8] The in-tegrity of personal history was simultaneously fundamental to development and disallowed in adoptions that idealized simulation and substitution. The psychological dilemma of the matching paradigm was that it simulta-neously promised and withheld what children and parents wanted most: the feeling that their kinship was complete and sufficient.

Freudian Family Romances

Psychoanalytic voices were prominent in the clinical debate about adop-tion. David Levy, of the New York Institute for Child Guidance, speculated about how and why adoption might prove corrosive to emotional security. Best known as a theorist of maternal overprotection, Levy suggested in 1937 that adoptees suffered from its opposite. Ill-timed separations from birth mothers led to "primary affect hunger" in many children. Denied emotional nurture at a crucial moment in their development, children suffered from "an emotional hunger for maternal love" that developed into a "deficiency disease of the emotional life" comparable to malnutrition or even starvation.[9] Later in life, this disease manifested as depression, troubled relationships, or both. The syndrome that Levy observed is now commonly termed "attachment disorder." It was a logical, historical outgrowth of the psychoanalytic theory that "object relations" —the critical interpersonal ties with parents through which human beings first internalized authority and love— decisively shaped personality and steered its future trajectory.

The cases recounted by Levy—all of them involving adoptees—were so drastic that neither restoration of maternal care nor psychotherapy could repair what amounted to permanent damage. These adoptions, Levy hypothesized, had severed children's earliest emotional attachments and "caused a situation similar to one in which the child could make no emotional attachment to start with."[10] The implication of this analysis was that children should be placed for adoption either shortly after birth or after the first few years of life, but not in between. Birth mothers who were unable to make final adoption plans, and who stayed in sporadic contact with young children placed in foster families, also injured their children by confounding their formative experiences of love and loss. Such mothers were frequently tortured by guilt, Levy admitted. They did not mean to hurt their children, but their equivocation denied children secure maternal love and the possibility of substituting a complete bond with an adoptive mother. Like kinship itself, real mother love was indivisible.

At the Menninger Clinic, probably the best-known psychoanalytic institution in the United States, psychiatrist Robert Knight was also intrigued by the emotional difficulties presented by adoptees and adoptive families. He attributed these problems to the delicate emotional management that was an inevitable part of adoption, a "complicated experiment in which a child who is *really* a 'little stranger' tries to live with two adults who are trying to understand, love and rear him."[11] Making children aware of their adopted status was a central task for both adults and children. Adoptive parents, eager to believe that children born to others were actually their "own," often inclined toward keeping the fact of adoption secret. This was a very bad idea, according to Knight, even in cases where children resembled their parents and had been adopted too early in life to know better. "Just as 'murder will out,' adoption also will out," he argued.[12]

Not telling was not good for parents either. Children who were never informed of their adoptions, discovered the fact accidentally, or were notified in adolescence were likely to resent or even hate their adoptive parents. Physician Sidney Tarachow studied six cases of too-late disclosure (five among "colored" boys) at the New York Training School for Boys in the mid-1930s.[13] Running away from home, he found, was a typical reaction. Adoptees who acted out angrily against parents and society were expressing understandable anguish over a violation of trust.

Freud's theory of "family romances" was never far below the surface in most of these clinical studies. Becoming an individual, Freud pointed out reasonably enough, required children to gradually free themselves from parental authority, a step that was necessary to successful development but painful. Fantasies that they were adopted—whether acted out in play, consciously articulated, or retrieved from the unconscious with the aid of psychoanalysis—were commonplace as children moved toward independence: "The child's imagination becomes engaged in the task of getting free from the parents of whom he now has such a low opinion and of replacing them by others, occupying, as a rule, a higher social station."[14] Freud observed that "family romances" followed a pattern in which children imagined their "real" parents to be much better, kinder, and more exalted than the imperfect people who were actually raising them. These fantasies served a useful purpose. Not only were they a vehicle for children's normal ambivalence about their parents. They also facilitated learning fundamental to healthy development over the long term. Parents were ordinary people, not gods who possessed magical powers.

The most important point about the adoption fantasies that Freud described was that they *were* fantasies. Because almost all children who daydreamed about being adopted were not, their fantasies were harmless, never causing real doubt about the permanence of parental love. But what about children who were adopted? What were the repercussions when "family romances" represented reality rather than fantasy? This was a key issue for psychoanalytically inclined clinicians, who agreed that the fact of abandonment and loss in adoptees' young lives was the fountainhead for all manner of childhood and adult problems with self-image and relationships. "There is a *real* element of mystery in the illegitimate child's background which makes such correction by reality either impossible or unconvincing," wrote social worker Mary Brisley in 1939."[15] Florence Clothier of the New England Home for Little Wanderers agreed: "For the adopted child, the second set of parents are obviously the unknown, lost real parents."[16] This meant that "correction of the foundling phantasy by reality is much less likely than in the own child."[17] Adoption denied an obvious truth about adopted children. They actually did have two sets of parents.

After 1960, analyses of adoptees' "family romances" grew more attentive to the timing of telling. The jumble of fantasy and reality for adoptees was compounded, many analysts believed, by an unfortunate coincidence with the oedipal crisis, a developmental landmark that Freud deliberately named after a mythical figure seeking to uncover the secret of his ancestry. (Oedipus concluded his family romance tragically, by unwittingly killing his father and marrying his mother.) "Genealogical bewilderment" (a phrase coined by H. J. Sants) could inhibit the parent-child identification that characterized this momentous turning point during which, according to Freud, children resolved their incestuous wishes and established their heterosexuality on the basis of similarity to the same-sex parent. As Sants suggested in a 1964 article, "Marked and peculiar differences in appearance and intelligence and skills" would certainly make negotiating the oedipal drama even more challenging.[18] The meeting of the American Psychoanalytic Association in December 1966 was the occasion for a wide-ranging discussion of adoption during which such prominent figures as Helene Deutsch weighed in on telling, identity problems, and the meaning of search.[19] In their 1975 discussion of adoptees' identity conflicts, Arthur Sorosky, Annette Baran, and Reuben Pannor argued that the "break in the continuity of life-through-the-generations" that adoption represented was especially consequential during late adolescence and early adulthood.[20]

Influenced by theorists such as Erik Erikson, who conceptualized development as a lifelong process rather than a feat accomplished once and for all during childhood, clinical interpretations of adoption's emotional meaning overstepped the boundaries of early experience and began to consider the entire life cycle. Sorosky and his colleagues were examples of this trend. For them, young adulthood was a moment when identity turned on mobilizing the past as a bridge to the future. Adoptees whose natal histories were missing or mysterious were literally prevented from moving forward into the adult phase of development. Agencies and parents who became "watchmen and censors of the truth" were condemning children to lifelong problems, no matter how much they claimed to love them.[21]

By the time Sorosky, Baran, and Pannor published their widely read book, *The Adoption Triangle*, in 1978, clinicians had started to advocate search and reunion—the antithesis of anonymity and confidentiality—on the basis of the very psychoanalytic perspectives that had earlier justified anonymity and confidentiality.[22] This change suggests that the view of adoption embedded in psychoanalytic narratives was pliable. On the one hand, adoption caused children's emotional difficulties because "roots in the natural family can never be severed without trace."[23] On the other hand, adoption might bring enduring parental love and authority to children who had never experienced either one. But how were children—or adult children for that matter—supposed to feel unconditionally loved when their kin ties were premised on an elemental act of rejection? Adoptees could never take belonging for granted precisely because they were adopted. They were haunted by the prospect that adoptive parents might repeat birth parents' decision to give them away.

Design and deliberation proved again to be at odds with realness. Love that was real was not made on purpose. It just was, and it could not be altered.

Attachment and Its Absence

Empirical studies of attachment and its absence in early life supplemented Freud's theory of "family romances" and clinical case histories in establishing a plausible link between adoption and psychopathology. Research on the behavioral and emotional difference that attachment made frequently used institutionalized populations, often comparing orphanage residents with children placed in families. This research tradition had dramatic implications for adoption policy and practice. It also reveals an important historical pattern in the relationship between research on children in the human sciences and a wide range of public policies. Investigations of abnormal conditions in abnormal environments produced knowledge about normality that applied to all children. The studies conducted by Harold Skeels, Marie Skodak, and their colleagues at the Iowa Child Welfare Station during the 1930s are perhaps the most famous examples.[24] By documenting the impact of environmental conditions on children in orphanages and foster homes, they turned the tide away from hereditarianism and emphasized the difference that early interventions could make in promoting healthy development. Children placed early enough and well enough would form attachments without difficulty.

According to historian Bernadine Barr, the psychological core of attachment was discernable only after Progressive reformers and researchers started to vanquish the material scourges of infant mortality, malnutrition, and poor sanitation.[25] As more children lived longer, psychopathologies became more evident. The focus of developmental science, in other words, changed over time from bodies to minds, and from the biomedical to the psychological, enshrining the salience of emotional growth to development only after serious threats to children's health and survival had diminished. In the 1910s, researchers began to focus on a syndrome they called "hospitalism." (The term was coined by German researcher L. F. Meyer in 1913.) Researchers first characterized the syndrome as digestive and respiratory problems with solutions related to bottle feeding and formula refinement but by the late 1930s concentrated on the behavioral and emotional consequences of institutional child care.[26] The failure of children to thrive in orphanages was dubbed "loneliness in infants" by pediatrician Harry Bakwin. Chicago physician Joseph Brennemann observed that children who were "nurse's pets" developed better and recommended that orphanage residents be regularly picked up and "mothered."[27] New technologies, such as incubators, and antiseptic protocols that had done so much to keep infants alive by protecting them from germs suddenly appeared as new toxins, isolating children from the stimulation and attachment that were building blocks of normal individuality. Sterilizing babies' physical care had unwittingly sterilized their emotional surroundings too.

Children needed all kinds of human contact, but mothering was the hinge on which attachment turned. Children who lived in orphanages and institutions were object lessons in maternal deprivation. They were robbed of an environmental asset that saturated normal development: intensive love from a single mother. By the 1930s, according to Barr, many orphanage researchers were Jewish orthopsychiatrists deeply influenced by the Freudian emphasis on early childhood; they pledged to deliver to impoverished orphanage residents the guidance and treatment services that middle-class children received. The earliest psychoanalytic report about orphanage children was made in 1935 by Samuel Orgel and Jacob Tuckman on the basis of work at the Hebrew Sheltering Guardian Society in Pleasantville, New York.[28] The first studies that blamed developmental and behavioral problems on either the absence of early attachment or problematic early attachment were conducted by psychiatrist Florence Powdermaker (who reorganized the Council Home for Jewish Girls in New York along psychoanalytic lines with her colleagues H. Turner Levis and G. Touraine) and David Levy of the New York Institute for Child Guidance.[29] Levy, a leading theorist of psychopathological maternity, consulted to the Free Synagogue Child Adoption Committee, where he observed firsthand what happened to children whose ties to caretakers during the first years of life were tenuous and unreliable.

Mass displacements during the World War II years also allowed clinicians to observe what happened when children of various ages were separated from their families and placed in institutions. In England, Anna Freud and Dorothy Burlingham carefully recounted the experience of Hampstead Nursery, one of three emergency facilities (two in London and one in Essex) financed by the Foster Parent Plan for War Children, an organization headquartered in New York.[30] Their report advanced the case against residential institutions and enshrined the mother-child tie as the wellspring of emotional development. Moved to nurseries for their own safety during the German onslaught, babies and young children were socialized largely by their peers. Freud and Burlingham noticed that many motherless children formed "artificial families" by affiliating themselves with staff members (who functioned as pseudo-parents) and establishing familylike groups (whose members functioned as pseudo-siblings). According to Freud and Burlingham, this effort to connect was "proof of the enormous strength of certain natural tendencies in the child."[31] The developmental logic of attachment was so inexorable that children gravitated toward it even in situations where the most crucial participant—the mother—was absent.

In the United States, émigré physician René Spitz furthered the growing consensus about attachment by pinpointing the moment when orphanage children began losing developmental ground. It occurred much earlier than anyone had previously suspected, with significant damage done during the first year of life. Like earlier research, the study Spitz reported in 1945 was psychoanalytic in its theoretical orientation and appeared in a psychoanalytic journal, but Spitz confined himself to reporting on observable behavior.[32] The study compared two institutions and involved a total of 164 children under the age of one. The first, called "Nursery," was a penal institution in which delinquent girls were sequestered and cared for their babies full-time. The second, called "Foundling Home," was an orphanage where all care was delivered by a paid staff. (Spitz also studied a control group of thirty-four children being raised by their parents at home.) These environments offered comparable material conditions: good hygiene, decent food, warm temperatures, clean clothing, and adequate medical care.

Determined to bring attention to the potential of infant psychiatry, a specialty that did not yet exist, Spitz criticized earlier institutional studies for focusing largely on older children. He tested and filmed children before they reached four months of age and again between the ages of eight and twelve months. He found that babies' developmental quotients remained stable, with the sole exception of those in the Foundling Home. The unlucky children who lived there experienced a precipitous drop in their average score and showed all the physical and mental symptoms of hospitalism and what Spitz also called anaclitic depression: eczema; eating disorders; disproportionate vulnerability to epidemic disease; and, in older children, significant delay in walking, talking, and toileting.

The difference, of course, was mothering. Children who had it, even in an institutional setting such as the Nursery, were protected from the worst ravages of hospitalism. Those who lacked it also lacked the bodily and psychic fortitude to develop normally. "Foundling Home does not give the child a mother, nor even a substitute mother," Spitz noted tersely, "but only an eighth of a nurse."[33] He also noted, "They suffer because their perceptual world is emptied of human partners . . . [and] their isolation cuts them off from any stimulation by any persons who could signify mother-representatives for the child at this age."[34] Institutions were bad for children not simply because family homes were better, as advocates had maintained for decades. They were bad for children because they actively derailed development. Without attachment to a mother, or some reasonable approximation of an individual who offered abundant and consistent care, children suffered permanent emotional harm. By the World War II era, "the right to a mother" was a new kind of psychological entitlement in any society that claimed to value children and mental health.[35]

Spitz's brand of research clearly reinforced the trend, already evident in adoption practice by 1945, to place children with adoptive parents earlier and with fewer stopovers in temporary care. To the extent that preadoptive placements were necessary, foster families were preferred over institutional nurseries. The goal was to ensure that children without birth mothers had substitute mothering as continuous, authentic, and permanent as possible. It was "in the interests of the adopted baby's mental health for him to be adopted soon after birth," concluded British psychiatrist John Bowlby.[36] Bowlby, who trained at the Boston Psychoanalytic Institute and worked in London's famous Tavistock Clinic after World War II, was closely associated with the origin and spread of attachment theory.[37] His theory, combined with the empirical studies of his colleague, Mary Ainsworth, became "probably the best supported theory of socioemotional development yet available."[38]

Unlike classical Freudians, for whom infant ties to the mother were secondary expressions of libido, Bowlby argued that attachment was instinctual, a primary life force whose function was to protect the growing organism.[39] Drawing on the ethological work of Konrad Lorenz, who had studied imprinting in ducks, Bowlby suggested that animals modeled the life-sustaining purpose of attachment that was also evident in systematic observations of how real children behaved. During the 1950s, animal studies comprised an important and visible part of the conversation about attachment, development, and motherhood. Harry Harlow's experiments with monkeys and mothering at the University of Wisconsin gained special notoriety.[40] During the pronatalist, baby boom years, these researchers did more than ratify the primacy of child-rearing in women's lives. They embodied the conviction, so crucial to the attachment consensus, that a true science of love had finally emerged. Its leading discovery was that mothering was a mandate from nature itself, an instinct required by the logic of evolution and not a mere social arrangement that could be reorganized at whim and without cost.[41]

Harlow's famous experiments separated infant rhesus monkeys from their mothers a few hours after birth.[42] These young animals were then "raised" by two kinds of surrogate monkey mother machines: half received milk from bare wire mesh forms and the other half received nourishment from wire mesh mothers cushioned with soft terry cloth. The point was to show that although both groups of monkeys drank equal amounts of milk and grew physically at the same rate, the two sorts of mothers were not psychologically equivalent. Infant-mother attachment was not a straightforward exercise in "drive reduction" or satisfaction of "innate needs."[43] Maternal labor was psychological labor. Mothers' contribution to emotional development, especially through soft body contact, was at least as important as the nourishment that nursing provided. It delivered assurance and security to infants, thereby keeping normal development on track.

The monkey experiments were designed to illuminate the developmental difference that emotional attachment made. Terry cloth mothers provided their young with the tactile comfort of cuddling, and this type of attachment proved decisive when the baby monkeys were confronted by strange, loud, and fear-inducing objects, such as mechanical teddy bears beating drums. In new and frightening situations, the monkeys raised by terry cloth mothers made contact with them, used them as a "psychological base of operations," and remained playful and inquisitive. Monkeys raised by wire mesh mothers, however, reacted by throwing themselves on the floor, clutching themselves, rocking back and forth, and screaming in terror. Lest the implication be lost on his audience, Harlow made it explicit: "Such activities closely resemble the autistic behavior seen frequently among neglected children in and out of institutions."[44] The awesome power of attachment to the mother could hardly have been performed more dramatically.

Harlow's monkeys also proved that "better late than never" was not a slogan applicable to attachment, a point René Spitz had already made. Monkeys raised for eight months in total isolation—denied contact with other infants or with either type of surrogate mother—were permanently damaged. Later experiments showed that no amount of exposure to peers or mothers after this period compensated for their emotional losses. "The long period of maternal deprivation had evidently left them incapable of forming a lasting affectional tie," Harlow reported.[45] This finding paralleled the clinical observation that "people who have been deprived of affection in infancy may have difficulty forming affectional ties in later life."[46] Harlow and his colleagues repeated their experiments, subjecting infant monkeys to varied periods of motherlessness. They showed that the impact of early maternal deprivation could be reversed if it had been brief. For monkeys, "brief" meant less than ninety days. The human equivalent, Harlow extrapolated, was six months.[47]

Attachment theory had direct and immediate implications for adoption. First, the experimental separation of biology from psychology that Harlow had achieved was a boon to a philosophy of kinship stressing love over blood. Even science now seemed to endorse the view that love and desire—not conception, birth, or lactation—were the quintessence of bonds between infants and mothers. Second, the "critical period" in early life when attachments were either formed or damaged meant that practices of lengthy or numerous temporary placements (earlier justified as a way to assess children's adoptability) caused psychological injuries that made it harder or impossible for children to adjust to family life.

Adoption researchers immediately appreciated the significance of general studies of attachment and maternal deprivation for the measurement of adoption outcomes. Several psychologists at Iowa State University in the late 1950s tried to correlate follow-up measures for children placed through the Iowa Children's Home Society with statistical summaries of their "noncontinuous mothering" experiences in infancy.[48] All the children had lived in an institutional setting for more than five months during the first year of life, after which they were placed temporarily in foster families before adoptive placement occurred at approximately age one.[49] By the time researchers tested the children and a set of matched controls, the subjects ranged from eight to seventeen years of age. The study was unable to pinpoint the "discriminable variations in personality during later childhood" that maternal deprivation was supposed to have caused.[50]

Not deterred, other researchers also set out to answer questions about placement timing as well as the particular qualities that were most desirable in adoptive mothers. Leon Yarrow, director of the Child Research Project at Child and Family Services of Washington, DC, was an advocate of the "critical-period hypothesis" suggested by Harlow's money experiments. Studies of adoptive kinship offered one of the only possibilities for testing this hypothesis in human beings, and Yarrow hoped to determine longitudinally whether separation from the mother was most traumatic and disturbing at particular moments in infancy. His research suggested that babies formed intense attachments between the ages of three and five months, so a policy aiming to conserve children's ability to form meaningful relationships would prioritize placement during the first two months of life. A related postulate was that the long-term consequences of separation and placement would depend on the particular developmental task that the change in mothers had interrupted.[51]

Yarrow and other adoption researchers amplified attachment theory by formulating a series of questions rooted in practical considerations. Were infants sensitive to the different meanings adults attributed to natural and adoptive motherhood? Did the qualities that made "good mothers" vary at different periods of development? What about the influence that children had on their parents? With a great deal of adoption research focused singlemindedly on selecting good parents, the power that children wielded over the behavior and attitudes of the adults who raised them was easily overlooked.

An Abnormal Psychology of Its Own

Studies exploring connections between adoption and increased incidence of psychopathology in children were offshoots of the attachment consensus of the 1940s and 1950s, but they also drew on the enduring rhetoric of risk in adoption history. If maternal deprivation and separation placed normal development in jeopardy, then it stood to reason that adoption was perilous, perhaps extremely so. "Especially because he is adopted, he needs to know that he is wanted, that he is acceptable, that the kind of person he is, is a good kind to be," Louise Raymond wrote in 1955.[52] Raymond added that children's adoption awareness could lead to a myriad of problems, from equating babysitters and summer camps with abandonment to extravagant grief on discovery that Santa Claus was not "real." Belonging was more important to adoptees than to nonadopted peers because their insecurity about belonging was a consequence of movement from one set of kin to another.

During the second half of the twentieth century, at least 150 studies probed the question of whether and why adoptees might be burdened with a uniquely abnormal psychology and vulnerable to problems that children living in natural families escaped.[53] Most of these studies focused on nonrelative adoptions because emotional risk was presumed to be greatest in these cases. (Relative adoptions were tabulated, if at all, for the purpose of excluding them from consideration.) The maternal transitions and deprivations shared by all adoptees, whether taken in by relatives or nonrelatives, were not equally consequential. Adoption by strangers posed far greater dangers.

Despite hints as early as the 1930s, it was a 1960 report in the *Archives of General Psychiatry* that galvanized the most attention and brought new scrutiny to the precarious mental health of adoptees.[54] Marshall Schechter, a psychiatrist in Beverly Hills, California, calculated that adoptees were one hundred times more likely to present a range of serious emotional problems than their numbers in the general population warranted. His data was drawn from 120 children seen in his private practice between 1948 and 1953: exactly sixteen (or 13.3 percent) had been adopted. Because he estimated that adoptees numbered less than 1/10 of 1 percent in the general population, Schechter concluded that adopted children were enormously overrepresented in his practice. Adoption, he boldly ventured, inflicted such "severe narcissistic injury" on children that no amount of reassurance that their adoptive parents loved and wanted them could make up for the damage.[55] Each and every one of his sixteen cases illustrated "how the idea of adoption had woven itself into the framework of the child's personality configuration," resulting in poorly integrated and unbounded identities.[56] By virtue of their separation from birth parents and placement with adoptive parents, children became neurotic and psychotic. Adoptive kinship stood squarely between them and knowledge of who they were.

Schechter's report was forcefully criticized, especially but not only on methodological grounds. Viola Bernard rejected his claim that "adoption is a kind of trauma" as a "mistake" that "can do great hardship to children" and pointed out that adoption meant the "gain of something" and not just the "loss of something."[57] Just as white clinicians had formerly thought about "our Negro patient and not our patient," she noted disapprovingly, they were similarly prone to distortions in adoption cases, where "you get an adopted child patient and it's an adopted child patient not a child patient."[58] The Division of Research at the USCB pointed out numerous errors in Schechter's calculations and advised child welfare professionals to wait for more reliable evidence before jumping to the conclusion that adoptees were at special risk for mental illness.[59] H. David Kirk, whose book *Shared Fate* had insisted on the central relevance of difference in adoption, also disparaged Schechter's tiny sample, crude statistics, and hopelessly flawed research design. The study was "spurious," Kirk charged, and reflected deep philosophical misunderstandings.[60]

Kirk maintained that adoption's disadvantage was social rather than natural, so the personality distortion Schechter treated as an inevitable derivative of adoption was in actuality a by-product of cultural attitudes and institutional arrangements that were subject to change. Schechter and three coauthors responded with a follow-up study based on more extensive empirical data that claimed to prove adoptees were disproportionately represented in a range of private and public clinical settings.[61] Their defensiveness turned out to be unnecessary. After 1960, studies of adoption psychopathology appeared at an increasing pace, and the notion that adoption was a risk factor spread. Today, half of all Americans still express the view that adoptive kinship is not equal to natural kinship, and very large numbers believe that adoptees are more inclined toward emotional, behavioral, medical, and academic problems; the numbers are even larger for children adopted from the public foster care system. Although two-thirds of Americans report "very favorable" opinions about adoption, risk remains a basic element in public perceptions of adoptive kinship in the early twenty-first century.[62]

Within a few years of Schechter's study, research on adoption and mental health was reported at the Staten Island Mental Health Center, the Children's Psychiatric Hospital of the University of Michigan Medical Center, Ohio's Columbus Children's Psychiatric Hospital, Jewish Hospital in St. Louis, and Langley Porter Neuropsychiatric Institute in San Francisco. These studies were more methodologically sophisticated than Schechter's and represented an epidemiological research tradition that eschewed case studies. They typically surveyed hundreds or even thousands of clinical records over a period of years, calculated the percentage of nonrelative adoptees in the sample, discussed diagnostic or other patterns that offered clues about the particular symptomatology of adoption psychopathology, and speculated about "causes."

One of the most reasonable explanations for the prevalence of adoptees in clinical populations identified socioeconomic, racial, and other demographic differences between adoptive and nonadoptive families—rather than adoption per se—as key variables. Adoptive parents brought their children to psychiatric clinics and hospitals not because the children were adopted but because the parents' higher-than-average ages and education and income levels inclined them to seek psychiatric help more frequently than other parents. They were also disproportionately likely to have daughters, whose problems often elicited speedier clinical intervention than sons. Adults who had adopted through agencies, two insightful commentators noted, scored unusually high on "help-proneness" because they had already had substantial contact with social and clinical service delivery and absorbed the lesson that willingness to accept aid was synonymous with emotional maturity.[63] Was it not probable that adopters sought help for children not only on a more frequent basis but also for less severe problems?

A study of children seen at the Staten Island Mental Health Center was conducted as a self-conscious "check" on the work of Marshall Schechter.[64] It urged adoption agencies alarmed by reports of high rates of psychiatric

illness in adoptees to "postpone their anxieties pending further investigations."[65] In this case, knowledge brought relief rather than risk. Influential
child welfare researcher Alfred Kadushin reviewed the literature on adoption and psychopathology in 1966. He noted that demographic differences
associated with adoptive families—adoptees were more likely to be first or
only children—made comparisons to nonadopted children chancy.[66] Even
if adoptees were overrepresented among children in psychiatric treatment,
perhaps their problems were far fewer than anyone had a right to expect,
given the personal deprivations and social stigma experienced by members
of adoptive families.

Several large clinical studies attempted to discern diagnostic patterns that
might be logically traceable to the fact of adoption. At the University of
Michigan Medical Center in Ann Arbor, Frances Menlove hypothesized that
problem behaviors would cluster around aggression and delinquency.[67]
Personality disorders related to adoptees' early break in object relations
would be more common than other diagnoses, she predicted, but she also
expected children adopted before six months of age to present fewer psychiatric symptoms. Menlove was disappointed in her quest for a distinctive
adoption syndrome and found that children adopted before and after six
months could barely be distinguished on the basis of their clinical profiles. Her study, however, confirmed that adoptees received treatment for
emotional disturbance out of proportion to their numbers. The fact that
the Michigan adoptees were brought to the hospital by their parents far
more often than nonadopted children (who were almost always referred by
schools and agencies) buttressed the theory that adoption psychopathology
might be an artifact of affluence and education rather than kinship.

Other researchers, such as Betty Ketchum, who studied cases at the Columbus Children's Psychiatric Hospital in 1962, found no evidence that
adoptive families were "treatment prone." In Columbus, unlike Ann Arbor, schools were more often the sources of adoptee referrals than parents,
and adoptive parents waited longer than natural parents to seek intervention. These findings prompted Ketchum to speculate that adoptive parents
might be more reluctant to seek clinical help for reasons ranging from the
insecurity associated with infertility to worries that their parental qualifications would be judged unfairly or their children removed.[68] In addition, the
study suggested that standard demographic variables—age of parents and
children, presence or absence of siblings, and even ordinal position in the
family—could not account for the disproportionate presence of adoptees in
the study sample. Ketchum's sample was very tiny: out of a total of 196 children ever treated by the hospital, 20 (or 10.7 percent) had been adopted.

On the basis of a close reading of these twenty records, Ketchum abandoned many of her initial hypotheses about where adoption psychopathology originated. The claim that independent adoptions had far worse results than those arranged by professional agencies was not borne out. Nor was it obvious that adoption itself had played a role in developmental difficulties. In the end, Ketchum emphasized the responsibility of adoptive parents. Adoptive mothers were highly perfectionistic and coercive, whereas adoptive fathers were punitive and remote.[69] "In every case these pathological attitudes were severe enough to account for the disturbance without any of the other factors present," she noted.[70] The Columbus study contradicted perceptions that adoptive families were open to clinical services in part because of their relative social and economic advantages. Adopters were hardly paragons of therapeutic virtue, according to Ketchum. In Ohio, they appeared to be carriers of "parental pathogens" who strengthened the case for better tools of prediction in adoption at the point of application and home study.

In Saint Louis, researchers who studied the records of adoptees seen at Jewish Hospital uncovered "a striking finding": incidence rates of psychiatric problems for adoptees were at least four times higher than the adoption rate in the surrounding community.[71] The pattern of personality disorders that Menlove had expected to find in Michigan (but did not) was more visible in Missouri. Researchers guessed that its cause might be adoptive parents' infertility. In particular, "conscious or preconscious hostility to the marriage partner who is held responsible for the inability to have children barely covers the unconscious hostility to the children."[72] Influenced by psychoanalytic perspectives on psychogenic sterility, this study concluded that aversion to parenthood (never expressed directly by adopters, of course, or detected by observers) was to blame for adoptees' emotional woes. Adults (especially women) who fancied themselves as rescuers, or who were perversely preoccupied by the dangers lurking in their children's genes, simply could not face the truth. Because they did not truly wish to be parents, they would do substantial psychological damage to children while attributing that damage to biological destiny.[73]

A San Francisco study reserved judgment on this point. At Langley Porter Neuropsychiatric Institute, researchers agreed that many adoptive parents had shown themselves to be uncooperative, defensive, rigid, and secretive clients whose habits included denial and projection.[74] They noted, however, that motives were notoriously difficult to evaluate. To attribute children's problems to their parents' psychological deficits might seem logical, but the same interpretations that caseworkers valued so highly as resources in therapeutic adoption were worthless as factual data in controlled studies. Hindsight was always better, the researchers admitted, but adoption workers, at the point of home study and placement, had only a tentative grasp on predicting which adults would function well or poorly as future parents.

The Telling Test of Telling

No issue represented adoption difference—or the fragile selfhood associated with it—more than "telling": the task of informing an adopted child of his or her adoptive status. Telling was both a momentous event and a conversation about adoption that continued over the course of childhood, even an entire lifetime. In contrast, nonadopted children were not typically "told" anything about their birth status. What could be more natural and less worthy of mention than being raised by one's own parents?

Telling was a paradoxical project. On the one hand, it promised to dignify and normalize adoptive kinship. On the other hand, telling starkly underlined the conflict that kinship by design attempted to manage, that is, the conflict between difference and authenticity. Encouraged to believe that their family was as real as real could be, telling reminded parents that their particular kinship was not only distinctive but also something less than completely natural and equal.

The potential of telling to simultaneously confer and deny realness was especially true for children adopted early in life. As long as no patently visible mismatching gave the fact of adoption away, the option of not telling always existed. Evidence suggests that many, and perhaps most, adoptive parents considered telling "a dreaded job."[75] It was such a constant source of distress that parents consistently requested advice about telling from social workers and government agencies, even while accusing agencies of imperiousness and intrusiveness.[76] The first how-to book on adoption, published in the 1930s, included a chapter titled "What to Tell the Adopted Child."[77] Telling has been a fixture of how-to literature on adoption since that genre's inception. It linked deliberate, emotional labor and the work of interpretation to the effective management of potentially damaging difference.

Despite widespread agreement among professionals that the shock of revelation would be more harmful to children than the fact of adoption itself, many parents postponed telling for years and sometimes never told at all. Living with secrets and lies was the price they paid to avoid the stigma that surrounded their families. A 1906 children's story described the anguish that simple knowledge of adoption inflicted on innocent children. Margaret overhears other children remarking on the fact that she is adopted.

"She had never been ashamed before, but she sat there a piteous little figure in the grip of it. . . . She could feel something burning on her forehead—it was 'Adopted,' branded there."[78] As it turns out, the conversation Margaret overheard was actually about another girl, Nelly. The story ends with a jubilant Margaret, relieved that she is not adopted and determined to make sure that Nelly never finds out.

Why should it be surprising that many parents wanted to spare their children such hurtful knowledge? The danger that telling might undermine the legitimacy of adoption and subject their children to ridicule was surely an important reason why so many parents regarded telling with trepidation. In the late-1950s, Henrietta Whitmore and her husband complied with the telling mandate but instantly regretted the anguish it caused their daughter. Even though not telling was "like advocating not saluting the American flag," Whitmore exhorted other adoptive parents not to make the same mistake. The powerful intuition among so many adoptive parents—"that *you are our child*"—was worth more than the advice of "wise people" and "experienced, intelligent authorities."[79]

There is no way of knowing exactly how many children grew up without knowledge that they were adopted, but the number may have been considerable, as many as half of all adoptees during the first several decades of the twentieth century.[80] One-third of adoptees followed in the classic 1924 outcome study, *How Foster Children Turn Out*, had never been told about their adoptions; most were placed as foundlings and grew up believing they were "own" children.[81] In 1936, C. C. Carstens observed that evasion of telling was still widespread among parents and constituted one of the major "pitfalls of adoption."[82] Some children were told during adolescence, on the eve of marriage, or even later in life. Many young draftees during the two world wars were surprised when the military's bureaucratic requirements, which included birth certificates, disclosed their adoptions.[83] After the New Deal programs went into effect, requests for Social Security and unemployment benefits also brought previously unknown adoptions to light. Adoptive parents were ultimately responsible for telling, but the growth of the state and its expanded functions in work, welfare, and war sometimes conveyed truths that parents withheld.

Throughout the twentieth century, professionals maintained that secrecy, misinformation, and deception between parents and children had no place in adoption. Those same social workers, however, frequently offered less than complete and honest information themselves. Rejecting adoptive applicants, for example, sometimes called for therapeutic lying. Many would-be parents were simply too lacking in insight to bear the reality of their own psychological defects, the professionals reasoned, so "telling the whole truth may, instead of being a virtue, actually be an act of the crassest cruelty."[84] Social workers also stopped short of full disclosure when children's backgrounds included such sensitive factors as racial mixture and illegitimacy. Adoption professionals were at their best when they grappled unflinchingly with the many uncertainties of making families, but uncertainty almost never applied to the mandate that children be told.

Resistance to telling buttressed the case for heightened therapeutic intervention. Adoptive parents who did not tell, many social workers believed, felt insecure about their entitlement to children. However understandable, their doubts suggested the need for more and better interpretation to prop up the authenticity of adoptive kinship. Collective advocacy on the part of adult adoptees was rare before the 1950s, but individuals did speak out. "Do you really believe that it is possible to found secure happiness for any family on so basic an untruth?" asked one adoptee in sharp rebuke to the suggestion that it might be preferable never to tell. "We would all like our children not to suffer, to shield them from hurt, but . . . each of us must learn to accept and to adjust to the circumstances and experiences that life brings."[85]

During the 1930s, a few frustrated agencies stopped pleading with adopters and became stricter, refusing to place children with parents who would not tell and routinely incorporating how-to-tell instructions into the adoption process.[86] By midcentury, most agencies required adopters to pledge in writing that they would tell and provided guidance on how to answer children's curious questions about their birth parents.[87] Telling strained the matching ideal by requiring extra effort of adoptive parents, effort that reminded them that the kinship they and their children forged could never be an exact match. Professionals tried to relieve adopters' anxiety by assuring them that telling was most important within the circle of immediate family. Children, immediate friends, and relatives needed to know, but the whole world did not need to be told.[88] Exiting the adoption closet too boldly could be as damaging as constructing it too tightly.

Various problems connected with not telling, tardy telling, and bungled telling received occasional notice early in the century. Ten young adults adopted around 1900 explained that adoptees were less happy and successful, on average, than natural children, but those who had been told early in life had far fewer problems than those told later on. "The successful ones among them today are those who in childhood were treated as rational beings who could safely be told that they were adopted, and not as mere emotional entities who had to be controlled by unthinking affection."[89]

By 1970, telling had emerged as a leading therapeutic issue in adoption. Not telling and telling were both associated with psychological trouble: the former amounted to lying, and the latter opened a Pandora's box of wrenching emotional dilemmas. "Being adopted means nothing unless it means that he is different from other children, and so the issue for him is what this difference consists of," Bruno Bettelheim wrote in 1970. "What is the solution?" he asked. "Maybe there is none. Maybe there are only problems that we must face without subterfuges. . . . There is no getting around telling him that his real mother just didn't appreciate him enough, which is a fact."[90]

Why Tell?

If telling was tantamount to reminding children of their original rejection by birth parents, why make it mandatory? The rationale for telling had less to do with honesty than it did with therapeutics. Parents were wise to tell children about their adoptions early on, before they learned the truth from unfeeling relatives, nosy neighbors, or cruel classmates. In 1930 *Children: The Magazine for Parents* urged telling because "tragedy may follow in the wake of concealment."[91] "Greater dangers . . . lie in wait for those who beg the question," warned *Ladies' Home Journal* in 1933.[92] Emotional inoculation against shock and stigma was the main reason for telling, according to the professional consensus. "Tell them it's OK. There's nothing to worry about," declared one twelve-year-old adoptee whose parents were apparently models of rectitude.[93] The fact that children born via donor insemination were not expected to be informed of this fact by their parents underscores that the reason for telling was not truth but the probability that adopted children would find out anyway. Helen and Carl Doss, in their adoption advice book, identified "artificial insemination" as an attractive alternative not only because a child who is "half theirs" may be better than "an adopted child who is a total stranger" but also because it did not involve the headache of telling.[94]

Trust between parents and children was a secondary benefit of telling that, conveniently, might console children wounded by the knowledge of their adoptions.[95] Intimacy was both the precondition for telling and its consequence, according to this way of thinking. Parents had nothing to fear because truthful information could not ruin parent-child relationships that were loving and secure. This reassuring message belied the tricky balancing act that telling entailed. Telling forced parents to navigate the distance between constructively emphasizing and destructively overemphasizing adoption. They were supposed to acknowledge that adoption was different, at least to their children, but also behave as if it were not. They were supposed to raise children who appreciated the momentousness of their adoptions, but did not ask probing questions about birth parents or seek to locate them.

Preoccupations with telling were inseparable from preoccupations with the power that parents—particularly mothers—wielded over children's development, especially characteristic of American culture during eras when parent education, Freudian psychology, and insistent domesticity were dominant themes. "You see," commented famous object relations theorist D. W. Winnicott about telling, "you are dealing with the child's mind."[96] Most parents were all too aware of their responsibilities for conserving children's mental well-being. Most took telling seriously and credited it with enormous import. Telling was a central adoption narrative. Like coming out for gay men and lesbians, it told a story about the adopted self that was simultaneously individual and social. Every child had a unique story, but the fact that something significant had to be revealed (or concealed) was common to all adoptive families, and that suffused adoption with effort and deliberation. If kinship by design aimed to narrow the gap between nature and artifice, telling merely emphasized the troublesome difference between them.

How and When to Tell?

How exactly were parents supposed to tell? Typical advice underscored the difficulty of acknowledging difference while containing the threat it posed to realness. Parents were urged to approach the explosive potential of adoption with an attitude of studied casualness. In 1929 Jessie Taft, an adoptive mother herself, compared telling to "sex instruction," another loaded topic. "It isn't something to be whispered about mysteriously, over-stressed emotionally, postponed to some more fitting time, or relegated to a formal occasion. It is a fact which should be breathed in naturally from the first where parents are secure in their love for each other and the child, and do not fear either past or future."[97] Benjamin Spock, the most trusted of all postwar child-rearing authorities, addressed telling in *The Common Sense Book of Baby and Child Care* (1946). He recommended that parents accept the fact of their child's adoption "as naturally as they accept the color of the child's hair," but suggested that adoption was anything but a neutral fact of this kind.[98] Adoption made children fearful and insecure to the point that "one threat uttered in a thoughtless or angry moment might be enough to destroy the child's confidence in them forever."[99] Adoption obviously mattered, but when telling was handled correctly, it was not supposed to seem that way.

The most popular advice about telling capitalized on the trend toward parents reading to their children.[100] Classic children's books about adoption, such as *The Chosen Baby* (1939) and *The Family That Grew* (1951), were only two examples from a burgeoning literature recommended by agency professionals and popular magazines.[101] Books provided handy aids that literally made adoption go down as easily as a bedtime story and relieved parents of always having to tell in their own words. Parents who wished to move beyond preformulated texts were urged to individualize storytelling rituals or supplement them with custom-made scrapbooks including photographs of landmark events: the day the child came home, the day adoption was finalized, and so on.[102] Occasionally, the strategy of allowing adoptees to "adopt" something themselves—usually pets—was advocated as an aid to telling. One fictional adoptee took in two kittens—one named Really and the other Truly—after a neighborhood child taunted him about his adoption and explicitly challenged his authenticity as a "really truly" member of his family.[103] As an activity with no guarantee of working out well (pets could misbehave, run away, or die), it had obvious disadvantages.

Detailed instructions about exact words, phrases, and sentences to use (or avoid) in telling underlined the power and peril of adoption as a factor in children's emotional development. Sample scripts were common.[104] Parents were tutored to use the words "chosen" and "adopted" interchangeably and only with a happy and relaxed tone of voice. Telling was supposed to happen early and often because children would assimilate their parents' feeling about adoption long before they could understand the meaning of the words. Any hint of anger of frustration could defeat the purpose of telling by betraying adoption's negative associations and substandard social status. "*Under no circumstances, ever,* should the child be reminded that he is adopted when the parent is feeling angry at him," admonished Robert Knight of the famous Menninger Clinic. "The adoption should *never be mentioned* except as a pleasant matter."[105]

Constructive government of children's emotional development was inseparable from strict government of parents' emotional expression. Parents who passed the telling test advantaged their children while proving they were real parents: mature, loving, able to prioritize their child's needs, and willing to acknowledge that adoption made their family both different and not different. Parents who failed betrayed doubts about their own authenticity. The same experts who maintained that there was no formula for how to tell also maintained that there were right and wrong ways to feel about telling. "If you yourselves have fully accepted your child's adoption," one wrote, "you will be able to make him accept it, fully and happily."[106] Inculcating the appropriate "feeling tone" and attitude in adults was a chief goal of the telling enterprise.[107]

Even with preverbal infants, verbal repetition promised to cement positive associations with phrases such as "my precious adopted daughter" and "my dear little adopted son."[108] The aim here was not only to boost children's self-esteem but also to prepare them for the inevitable encounter with adoption stigma. If a child's parents faithfully exclaimed, "How glad we are we picked you out!" then he was likely to absorb the lesson that "his parents chose him while most people have to take what nature sends to them."[109] Selection made adoption special, even superior.

Marshall Schechter's 1960 report on troubled adoptees, which did so much to pathologize them, also renewed debate about when to tell.[110] Schechter's recommendation that telling wait until post-oedipal children were firmly identified with their adoptive parents was seconded by psychoanalyst Lili Peller, who argued that revelation early in life "did considerable harm" by drawing adoption into "the whirlpool of the child's sexual and sadistic fantasies."[111] According to Schechter and Peller, telling early and often sabotaged parents' best intentions by reminding children that their belonging needed constant reinforcement. Schechter and Peller therefore opted for the school or even the teenage years as preferred times of revelation.

Few experts revised the telling timeline as radically as adolescent psychiatrist Joseph Ansfield, who stood virtually alone in suggesting that children never be told. His position, he admitted, "goes against practically all stated beliefs, opinions and policy of the past and present." "My strong belief," he wrote in 1971, "is that adopted children should not be told that they are adopted. They should not be told for a very good reason, that is, the knowledge will hurt them."[112] His lonely dissent made the comprehensive telling consensus all the more obvious.

Theoretically, too much emphasis on adoptive status could be as noxious as too little or none. The prospect that children might relish or even flaunt their adoptive status was alluring precisely because it was the opposite of what parents feared. "Am I a 'dopted child?" one worried little girl inquired in a 1929 story. "You certainly *are*," her mother replied, "but I wouldn't talk about it with the other children. It's not nice to boast."[113] Preoccupations with telling invariably centered on the damage that adoption awareness might do, not on the pleasure it would bring. Thus, most advice about telling stressed the theme of the "chosen child," repudiated by reformers after 1970 for sugarcoating painful realities.[114] Telling children they had been deliberately selected was supposed to reassure. It implied that relinquishment by birth parents had been equally deliberate while leaving that uncomfortable fact unspoken. As in so many dimensions of modern adoption history, design was the token of restitution for risk and loss.

What to Tell?

That children had been born to one set of parents and adopted by another was not the only fact at stake in telling. Adoptees' natal backgrounds frequently included poverty, alcoholism, mental illness, criminality, sexual immorality, incest, and other sordid details. What, if anything, should be disclosed about these? This question tormented parents. Advice givers emphasized that parents' emotional tone was more important than the substance of information conveyed. Whatever they shared, adopters should strive to talk about birth parents and relatives calmly and easily. Curiosity about the people who had given them life was inevitable in adoptees, and it was perfectly normal for them to ask questions, typically at the point when they were old enough to understand sex and reproduction.

The dilemma of what to say about birth parents symbolized the threat that unembellished information posed to adoptees' fragile personalities, much as the fact of adoption did. Children needed to be comfortable with whatever they were told about their "first" parents, advisors agreed, in order to sustain trust in their "second" and "real" parents.[115] In many cases, this involved highly censored communication, if not outright deception. Early studies that found high rates of telling also found that parents withheld background information.[116] A long-term follow-up of one hundred New York agency adoptions from the 1930s found that the vast majority of parents (90 percent) had told their children, scrupulously following instructions to tell early, often, and with the appropriate words and tenor. But no parents at all had given their children full and candid details about the reasons for their adoption.[117] Illegitimacy, for example, remained unmentionable through the 1960s. Many parents lied to their children, "killing off" birth parents rather than saying they had been unmarried.[118] To convey certain facts would publicize the moral failings of those parents and, by association, smear the children too.

One can understand why many parents withheld information they found embarrassing as well as menacing to their children. To prevent children from realizing too early that birth parents had been unable or unwilling to raise them, adoptive parents were told always to maintain that their children's original parents (particularly mothers) were good individuals who had made selfless decisions for their children's sake. The contradictory pressures built into telling were irreconcilable on this point. The same culture that demonized women who refused to mother, or to be "good" mothers, expected adoptive parents and children to consider surrender the result of maternal devotion—rather than desperation, coercion, or callous disregard. If some adults elected to become parents through adoption and dutifully reinforced the rhetoric of "chosen children," this reflected the powerlessness of others: birth mothers too poor and frightened and dependent to be endowed with choice-making authority of their own.[119]

Saying something to children about birth parents was important for therapeutic rather than legal or moral reasons. It was supposed to put children's minds at ease and comfort them with the thought that their birth parents were decent human beings. This was by no means an invitation to search. Prior to 1970 most advocates of telling were also advocates of confidentiality and anonymity. There was no contradiction, in their view, between the routine practice of telling children and the equally routine practice of keeping secrets about birth parents' identities and whereabouts. Well-known critics of matching and champions of legal protections for children, including Justine Wise Polier, denied that adoptees had rights to specific background information, arguing that "confidentiality is essential to a child's sinking his roots deep into his adoptive home."[120] After 1970 the Adoptees' Liberty Movement Association inaugurated a new push for adoption reform, galvanized by the compelling search narrative of its founder, Florence Fisher, and the thousands of adult adoptees and birth mothers who pleaded with agencies for help in finding lost relatives.[121] Adoption activism since then has increasingly targeted access to sealed birth records, demanded more openness, and championed reunions with natal kin.[122]

There had always been adoptees who searched for natal relatives, of course. Record-keeping reforms during the Progressive era were motivated partly by desires to create paper trails that would reunite birth relatives later in life, and many professionals during the early part of the century actively facilitated such reunions.[123] By midcentury, confidentiality (which kept records off-limits to nosy members of the public) had calcified into secrecy (which kept records off-limits to even the "parties of interest" themselves). The dramatic move away from disclosure can best be glimpsed in specific cases. In 1942, in an attempt to locate his natal relatives, one young adoptee serving in the armed forces wrote to the agency that had placed him. The director was assured by the agency's lawyer that disclosing identifying information was legal, but she refused on moral grounds, noting that "we are in grave danger if it should become known through any kind of publicity that we have revealed the whereabouts of natural parents."[124] The adoptee did not give up and wrote back repeatedly. "Again I must ask you to divulge more pertinent information as to the identity and present whereabouts of my blood relations. And that word is not singular, it is plural. I want to know also if I have any brothers or sisters." "I believe I have a decent right to know more," he explained. "I am no animal I am a man. . . . I'm more convinced than ever that it is a necessity and not curiosity that makes me make these requests."[125] Tragically, this young man died in China, his quest for reunion unfulfilled.[126]

Before the records wars of the 1970s, dominant views about telling emphasized that well-adjusted adoptees would not wish to find natal relatives. Jean Paton, for example, who founded the first adoptee search organization in the United States, Orphan Voyage, in 1953, formulated a "search hypothesis" in which the impulse to seek out natal relatives was calibrated to the security of the adoptive home.[127] Adoptees in normal, loving families, in other words, had no reason to search and probably would not. That a renegade early search advocate conceded such a direct relationship between insecurity and searching evidences not only Paton's experience as a trained social worker (her 1945 degree was from the University of Pennsylvania) but also the extent of agreement about what mental health looked like in adoptees: "the best-adjusted adopted child is the one who almost never thinks about the facts of his natural birth."[128] Michael, a teenager in 1965, had "been preoccupied since 5 with the past and with the true identity of his parents," a situation interpreted as evidence of "emotional disturbance" and need for help "away from his blind search for his mother to the more realistic approach of psychotherapy."[129] Children such as Michael, who dwelled on lost relatives, talked about them incessantly, or set out to locate them as adolescents or adults, needed psychiatric help. They were living proof of adoption's problems. Divided loyalties doomed the quest to authenticate adoption.

This situation put adoptive parents in a terrible bind. They were expected to talk honestly to their children about their birth parents, but they were also expected not to upset the children's emotional equilibrium or support search fantasies. Helen and Carl Doss, whose own transracial and transnational adoptions flouted matching, implied that the fact of having two sets of parents was an especially difficult difference to handle. They urged adoptive parents to "*forget everything that would not be helpful to your child.*"[130] Forgetting was the most poignantly revealing approach to the conflict between what parents knew about their children's natal backgrounds, the mandate to tell, and fears about what adoptees could bear. It diminished the danger of difference by disregarding knowledge of it.

"I don't know" was, ironically, the ideal answer to children's questions—and all the better if parents really did not. This approach explains why a remarkable number of parents between 1940 and 1970 did not want background information about the children they adopted and sometimes actively declined it during the adoption process. The possibility that communicating prejudicial facts might cause anguish also prompted agencies to ponder "whether or not to inform the adoptive parents of history which might be a cause of constant concern to them."[131] One scenario in which such anxiety was probable involved mixed-race children (or children suspected of being mixed) who might be able to pass for white; another involved family histories of mental illness.[132] Agency practices varied widely on this score. Some maintained they had moral obligations to convey what they knew; others suggested that adoptive parents be given no information at all. "Parents should be able to say truthfully that they do not know the reasons why the child was given up," reasoned one psychiatrist, and "this will enable the child to think that he comes from two loving parents who, by reason of some catastrophic event (the nature of which will be left to his own phantasy) could not keep him."[133]

One study of almost five hundred Florida adoptions between 1944 and 1947 found that 20 percent of adopters wished to know as much as possible about their children's birth parents and backgrounds, but a full 80 percent wanted little or no information.[134] Purposeful ignorance was a contorted way to preserve children's self-confidence and their own credibility, to be sure, but if everything worked out, children would take whatever they were told in stride. "If he knows in his mind he is adopted but feels in his heart that he belongs to his family," the adoptee would follow a course of normal mental and emotional development.[135] When telling was handled well—done for the right reasons, in the right ways, at the right times, and with the right information—children turned out to be real members of real families: nothing more, nothing less.

———

Considering the authenticity crises in adoption, it is not surprising that the simple dignity of realness turned out to be very difficult to achieve. By 1970 some researchers discovered that how children were told of their adoptions had little of the influence that previous generations of parents and professionals believed it did. Benson Jaffee and David Fanshel, for instance, were stunned to discover that how, when, and what children were told did not alter outcomes. This "rather challenging finding" "stands in sharp conflict with what has long been a fundamental working assumption in the field of adoption placement."[136] If children's mental health did not depend on how such explosive information was presented to them, had other differences associated with adoption been exaggerated or entirely misconstrued?

By 1970 the distinctive, abnormal psychology of adoption had already become an established part of adoption culture, with many professionals and family members persuaded that loss and attachment troubles were unavoidable dimensions of adoptive kinship. Outside of the adoption world, the civil rights revolution, nationalist mobilizations, massive new immigration, and cultural celebration of diversity within the American nation paralleled and reinforced the embrace of difference within it. Reform movements devoted to opening sealed records, promoting "open adoption," facilitating searches and reunions, and honoring transracial and transnational placements all pointed to difference as the heartbeat of a new adoption revolution. According to the difference paradigm, matching was a cruel hoax, and confidentiality was a lie. Honesty about difference—not efforts to hide or neutralize or minimize it—was the quintessence of authenticity. Getting to realness was still the point, but the way to get there had changed.

Differences associated with adoptive kinship were not defanged simply because they were more openly acknowledged after 1970. Difference and damage remained tightly intertwined. The spread of postadoption services since the 1960s offers an instructive example. That periods of observation and supervision were necessary safeguards for children and families was key to adoption standardization, regulation, and interpretation. Established early in the century, probationary periods from six to twelve months were all but universal features of agency practice by midcentury. Prior to the 1960s, however, supervision ended promptly after the new family's day in court.[137] Once the adoption was legalized, intervention into the adoptive family ceased in the interest of making it as autonomous and private as any other. The reasoning was that "adoptive parents should be made to feel that they are real parents—the child, as if born to them."[138]

Postadoption services hardly existed before the 1960s because differential treatment of legally equivalent families was a flagrant violation of a design for kinship in which simulation and sameness defined equality. With the emergence of the difference paradigm, postadoption services spread, along with their therapeutic logic.[139] It is ironic but true that greater public honesty about adoption multiplied the possibilities for instructing participants and governing their family lives.[140] The theory was that adoptive families did not cease to be distinctive simply because they were equal before the law and that adoption was not a process that ended when children and adults came together. Adoption had a "life cycle."[141] With phases that unfolded over the entire life course, adoptive kinship was an ongoing project, subject to perpetual regulation, study, and intervention. Difference was permanent, and so was its management.

Even as a new generation of reformers after 1970 worked to normalize adoption differences, the association between adoption and trauma became ever more fixed. In part, this was due to the enveloping language of trauma during this era in American cultural history. Trauma and its aftermath were institutionalized by Posttraumatic Stress Disorder (PTSD), a diagnosis added to the *Diagnostic and Statistical Manual* by the American Psychiatric Association in 1980. The architects of PTSD conceptualized the diagnosis as a response to horrific events outside the boundaries of ordinary experience—war, rape, torture, violent assaults, natural disasters, and life-threatening accidents—that injured selfhood and damaged relational ability. Gradually, trauma came to encompass more common psychological shocks related to family, work, and the stresses of daily life.

Adoption was one example. Nothing made this plainer than "Adopted Child Syndrome," a controversial defense used in a number of murder trials in the late 1980s to show that adoptees accused of killing their parents suffered from a mental illness similar to Multiple Personality Disorder.[142] According to its chief proponent, psychologist David Kirschner, the psychodynamics that led some adoptees to kill were poorly understood and unlikely to be recognized by either mental health or criminal justice professionals. The Adopted Child Syndrome could redress such ignorance by proving that "adoptees encounter psychological problems during childhood and adolescence unique to being adopted."[143] Typical problems, which included compulsive lying, stealing, fire setting, promiscuity, substance abuse, and running away, manifested the "toxic potential of adoption" and were simply an extreme version of something all adoptees felt: "a counterphobic defense against a repetition of the primal rejection."[144] Simply put, adoptee-murderers acted out of extreme dissociation, or splitting, encouraged by adoptive parents who denied that adoption might have anything to do with their children's problems. Prevented by pathological family dynamics from forming integrated identities, "bad" selves patterned after fantasies of "bad" birth parents committed homicide.

The difference associated with psychopathology existed on a continuum, to be sure. In most cases, difference damaged the self, whereas in cases of "adopted child syndrome," it proved lethal to others. Betty Jean Lifton, one of the most respected and widely read adoption activists of the post-1970 era, agreed that even the most "normal"-seeming adoptees had a "touch" of the syndrome and suggested that such notorious serial murderers as the

Son of Sam were full-blown victims of adoption secrecy and stigma.[145] If all adopted children were affected by "Post" or "Cumulative" Adoption Trauma, then adoption necessarily became a risk factor independent of any and all other variables affecting child and family life.[146]

The proliferation of adoption support services and groups has saturated the adoption world in recent years with a profoundly therapeutic sensibility. This certainly reflected broader cultural developments, that is, ongoing quests for community and the growth of small groups in an emphatically psychological post-1945 society.[147] But it also betrayed the belief that adoption was so flimsy and disadvantaged that the parties to it needed all the extra help they could get. Keen awareness of risk, unnaturalness, and inauthenticity were persistent characteristics of adoption history, not novel features of the postwar adoption world. Worries about "bad seeds" and disappointing outcomes were old too, along with suspicions that birth and adoptive parents were deeply flawed. Forever different, adopted children and all their parents were destined to be forever damaged as well.

Reckoning with Risk

How should kinship be designed? Who belongs in families? Which children and adults belong together? Between 1900 and 1975, answers to these questions changed. Children with physical and mental disabilities were reclassified from unadoptable to adoptable, reversing earlier policies that designated them as eugenic liabilities and radically expanding eligibility for family membership. The presumption that only heterosexual, married couples would adopt children, and then only children who shared their religious, racial, and national identities, was questioned, reflecting a sweeping reevaluation of sameness and difference in American life. Attitudes about premarital sexuality and single mothers underwent sharp reversals, as did attitudes about illegitimacy, infertility, orphanages, nature and nurture, secrecy, and various other issues with theoretical and practical implications for adoption. From matching to marriage, adoption rules once considered "only natural" were revised under historical pressure.

Not everything about adoption changed as old rules gave way, however. Successive waves of adoption reform—each one heralded as an enlightened advance over the benighted past—did not dislodge the consensus that adoption was full of risks. Those risks were repositioned over time. The prospect that adopters might take in children with disabilities, a common fear early in the twentieth century, was transmuted several decades later into the possibility that infertile adopters might turn out to be bad parents. Today, adoption is a "risk factor" that places children and birth parents "at risk" for a variety of problems. Throughout modern adoption history, the conviction that adoptive families were different, fragile, and prone to difficulty was the chief rationale for all the managerial, investigatory, and helping operations that transformed strangers into kin. Since the early twentieth century, demands that the state act to protect vulnerable members of the public from harm have turned adoption into a major social problem.

The history of modern adoption is the history of efforts to solve that problem by coming to terms with risk. This is the project I have called kinship by design. This book has emphasized those institutions and individuals who believed that rationalizing family making was the best approach to risk in adoption, from the USCB and the CWLA to Arnold Gesell, Jessie Taft, Viola Bernard, Justine Polier, and many others in psychology, social work, medicine, and law. Their campaign to improve adoptive family making was inextricably bound up with the professionalization of services to children and families, the philosophy of therapeutic government, and the institutional consolidation of the welfare state during the Progressive era, the New Deal, and World War II. Kinship by design was imbued with a managerial sensibility that relied on regulation, interpretation, standardization, and naturalization. These methods promised to minimize risk.

The first step toward making adoption modern was making it governable. We have seen that new forms of investigation, supervision, and record keeping mandated by adoption laws and consolidated as standards were simultaneously benevolent and burdensome. They subjected children and adults to inspection and interpretation that eventually transformed them into perpetual clients. These parties to adoption, in need of intensive instruction because of the proximity between difference, deviance, and damage, might achieve viable kinship with the help of design. Design promised beneficial interventions in exchange for participants' active cooperation in governing adoption. Design was nothing if not well-intentioned.

The goal of design's disciplinary operations was to avoid disasters and ensure that families were secure, satisfying, and free of stigma. The advocates of adoption modernization championed an ideology of public responsibility for child welfare and family protection, arguing that it was the business of government to plan, oversee, and monitor the quality of adoptive kinship. This ideology gained steady momentum during the first half of the twentieth century, but its backers were never entirely successful in transforming the adoption process, warranting its outcomes, or persuading the public of the rightness of their cause. Their earnest devotion to governing adoption angered those equally devoted to guaranteeing that family making remained as private and free of public interference as possible.

At least one animating principle of kinship by design was enormously influential nevertheless, that is, that families could and should be made for the explicit purpose of providing children and adults with opportunities for personal growth and happiness. By 1975 "love makes a family" was an ideology accepted all but universally by Americans, extending far beyond adoption to encompass marital companionship, sexual fulfillment, and a wide range of reproductive decisions. Modern kin ties were supposed to be exercises in reciprocal nurture, products of deliberation and careful planning that elevated achievement over ascription and choice over blood.

Choice has wielded special influence in the context of modern consumption, but it is hardly a new keyword in American political culture, where freedom and self-determination were as central to the country's eighteenth-century revolution as they have been to its twentieth- and twenty-first-century consumer culture.[1] More than 150 years ago, Alexis de Tocqueville observed that individualism was characteristic of democracies, unlike the selfishness that pervaded aristocratic regimes. Then, as now, individualism was cherished in America as a liberal value not only linked to choice but also emblematic of an optimistic, mobile, and egalitarian culture. The principle also contained disturbing shadow stories. The doctrine of individualism, Tocqueville pointed out, corroded the social bonds necessary to public life by convincing citizens that "their whole destiny is in their own hands. . . . Each man is forever thrown back on himself alone, and there is danger that he may be shut up within the solitude of his own heart."[2] Americans made choices as if they were making up their lives from scratch, leaving them with no social account of success or failure and no explanation for the absence of choice in so many lives.

To hold that children and families were products of individual choice was to concede that individuals might choose to change or leave their children and families, as of course they have done in significant numbers. (The rise in relative adoptions during the past half-century was, to a large degree, an artifact of the rise in divorce and remarriage.) The ambivalence that has surrounded this freedom of entry and exit from kinship surely reflects an analogous ambivalence about the voluntarism of American-style nationalism. If citizenship expressed nothing more exalted than personal preference, multiplied by millions, how satisfying or secure could Americanness be? How deep could it go? Family making and nation building manifested the same paradox. Solidarities that were socially achieved were idealized over solidarities that were naturally ascribed. But the fact that they might be made and unmade easily, even capriciously, filled them with risk and chance. So they paled in comparison.

Since 1975, adoption has become more visible than ever on the American scene, leading many observers to announce a sharp break with the past. But historical continuities are as instructive as more frequently noticed changes. Long-standing cultural commitments to conceiving of identity and

belonging as matters of personal choice have been encouraged by a vora-
cious, global consumer culture that has grown stronger, especially since the
end of the cold war. The numerical high point for adoptions was 1970,
when approximately 175,000 children were adopted in the United States
each year by strangers and relatives. That number decreased to 125,000 by
the late 1980s and has held fairly steady since then.

Why did adoption become easier to see at exactly the same time it became statistically rarer? There are two reasons. The first has to do with the
literal visibility of all kinds of "mixed" families. Growth in the proportion
of adoptions arranged internationally has boosted the numbers of foreign-
born children (most of them from Asia) growing up in white American
families. Families with children from China, Korea, India, and elsewhere
have put a tangible face on adoption that everyone around them can see
when attending church and synagogue, going to day care and school, watch-
ing television, surfing the Internet, and participating in the daily life of communities from coast to coast. In 2006 Americans adopted a total of 20,679
children from other countries, according to the Department of State, and
these represented approximately 17 percent of all adoptions by U.S. citizens.[3] Domestic transracial adoptions have remained comparatively few in
number, but African American children placed for adoption with white parents are the most visible of all transracial adoptees, no matter how few of
these families there are.[4]

The second reason that adoption has attracted attention since 1975 is because it stands as a longed-for symbol of national progress. Families made
across borders of difference ratify a triumphal narrative in which bright lines
separate the eras of Jim Crow and old-fashioned empire from our own age
of multiculturalism and postcolonialism. Adoption serves as a poignant re-
minder of the civil rights revolution as well as the complex of transnational
networks, migrations, wars, and occupations that shape today's world. Family making has become a more potent metaphor than ever for the problems
and possibilities of identity making, community making, nation making,
and world making. Adoption contrasts with virulently fundamentalist loyalties at home and abroad: religious, ethnic, national, and tribal. Pictures of
children and adults whose kinship is not obstructed by differences of color
and culture may be especially compelling precisely because they remain
exceptional.

Because adoption has become easier to see, many Americans believe that
it is far more common than it actually is. The tendency of adoption to represent, in microcosm, larger struggles to square difference with equality is
one reason why observers believe the United States is currently experienc-

ing another adoption revolution. Since the 1960s, vigorous reform movements have rocked the adoption world in the United States. Records reform has absorbed enormous energy, for instance, but yielded few institutional successes. The 1998 Oregon ballot measure that enacted that state's open-records law was an unusual victory.[5] States with full access to birth records currently include Alabama, Delaware, Maine, New Hampshire, North Carolina, Oregon, and Tennessee.[6] Approximately half the states in the country have opted for mutual consent registries, which allow contact between adult adoptees and birth parents only when all parties consent to it. U.S. states were comparatively early to enact adoption statutes in the nineteenth century, but they have been comparatively tardy to open records to adult adoptees: Scotland did so in 1930, and England and Wales opened theirs in 1975.

Although the attack on sealed records and the search-and-reunion movement have been slow to produce legislative results in the United States, they have attracted considerable public sympathy, suggesting that recent adoption revolutions have been more sweeping in culture than in either law or politics. The first support network for adoptees trying to locate natal kin, Orphan Voyage, was founded in 1953 by pioneering adoptee and social worker Jean Paton. Paton published a remarkable collection of life histories in 1954, *The Adopted Break Silence,* and called on adoptees to "look away from their paralyzing silences and their secrets."[7] Like its author, the book was well ahead of its time, and both remain obscure. Publicity for the search cause did not reach a national audience until the 1970s. In 1971 popular interest surged after the Adoptees' Liberty Movement Association was founded by Florence Fisher, an adoptee who spent twenty years searching for her birth mother in the face of strenuous opposition from officials and her adoptive family. She told her anguished story in *The Search for Anna Fisher,* a widely read 1973 memoir that doubled as an explanation for why birth records should be unconditionally opened to adult adoptees.[8] In 1975 the first voluntary mechanism for locating natal relatives, the International Soundex Reunion Registry, was founded by Emma May Vilardi in Carson City, Nevada.

During the past thirty years, published narratives, films, television dramas, and journalism have brought search and reunion to large audiences. Adult adoptees and birth mothers who surrendered children in the period between 1945 and 1973 have been the key actors in this drama, their storytelling saturated with the moral authority that accompanies emotionally wrenching and previously hidden truths.[9] Organizations such as Concerned United Birthparents (founded in 1976), the American Adoption Congress (founded in 1978), and Bastard Nation (founded in 1996) demanded that secrecy be dismantled and adoption practice changed. Not all advocacy groups agreed. The National Committee for Adoption, today known as the National Council for Adoption, was founded in 1980 to defend confidentiality and sealed records against attack, a goal it pursues to this day.

The exodus from the adoption closet was not limited to the blunt repudiation of "secrets and lies" that search and reunion represented.[10] Since the 1960s, advocates have explored the possibilities of "open adoption," in which contact between the child's two families is established as a condition of placement itself, typically declaring the arrangement to be a revolutionary break with the past while unwittingly restoring patterns that prevailed prior to the twentieth century. Open adoption reflects the growing power of birth mothers in adoption, especially since the legalization of abortion in 1973, and this change is noteworthy in light of the powerlessness that conditioned so many surrenders in the past. Today, few domestic adoptions occur without birth parents actively involved in decisions about how and with whom to place children, and this power has certainly increased pressures on many adoptive parents to consent to contact, both perfunctory and prolonged, with birth families.[11]

In practice, open adoptions exist on a wide spectrum. Some involve little more than occasional letters, e-mail, and pictures; this exchange of information may be all that is feasible when natal and adoptive kin are separated by geographic distance. Other open adoptions strive to realize in daily life the truth that adopted children indeed have more than one mother, father, and family. Open adoption agreements are not prohibited by state laws, but neither are they legally enforceable contracts. Open adoption is an index of how far the matching model of "as if begotten" families has declined. It grapples directly with the difference at the heart of adoption, makes "telling" irrelevant, and expresses the conviction that honesty is always better than the most natural-looking artifice.

It makes historical sense that the shift toward transparency unfolded in the years after 1970, when similar transformations were occurring elsewhere in American social and political life. In 1969 the Stonewall Riots in Manhattan launched a movement for gay and lesbian liberation that demanded an end to secrecy about homosexuality. Its chief aim was to abolish the "closet," a term denoting toxic secrecy that could only be redressed by "coming out," a strategy that pitted openness and publicity against shame and stigma. In 1971 the Pentagon Papers were leaked to the *New York Times*, exposing the gap between what the Department of Defense knew about the Vietnam War and what the public was told. The Watergate scandal unfolded between

1972 and 1974, eventually resulting in Richard Nixon's resignation, the first presidential resignation in U.S. history. At the time, Americans confronted governmental policies of official secrecy that facilitated systematic deception at the highest levels. Many citizens found themselves in a position parallel to that of adoptees facing sealed records. They knew they had been lied to, but they were powerless, as individuals, to do anything about it.

The angry revolt against secrets and lies has taken many forms during the past few decades. There has been the upsurge in testimonial and confessional forms of expression—from the revival of memoir as a literary genre to the popularity of Oprah Winfrey. These trends exhibited Americans' historic distrust of elites, elected and nonelected, while investing the evidence of experience with unparalleled truth value. In recent years, prominent journalists invented stories (Stephen Glass of the *New Republic*, Jayson Blair of the *New York Times*), best-selling authors embellished autobiographies (James Frey, *A Million Little Pieces*), and Pulitzer Prize–winning historians (Joseph Ellis) plagiarized their own life histories. The only thing more surprising than violations of first-person truth was the surprise that many Americans expressed to learn that stories of the self could be as easily fabricated, and discredited, as any others. Like adoption, these controversies illuminated the perpetual challenge of distinguishing fact from fiction. How do we know for sure what is "made up" and what is "real"?

The spread of therapeutic practices in American institutions—schools, courts, religious communities, and the Internet, as well as families—at the end of the twentieth century placed a premium on subjectivity.[12] This shifted the burden of proof in the battle over information, casting openness as the default position and secrecy as suspicious, rather than vice versa. In sum, there has been a sharp move away from policies that use design to hide adoption's distinctiveness by making it look like something other than what it is, and that move tracks broader trends in American politics and culture, at least domestically. Today's alarm about homeland security and programs of government concealment—from data mining to administrative detention and torture of terrorism suspects—clearly moves in the opposite direction, connecting secrecy to safety once again. September 11, 2001, changed many things, but the federal government's duty to protect the public by guarding information, classifying documents, and keeping secrets was not one of them. Secrecy was a fixture of the cold war national security state, and it is a fixture of today's war on terror.[13]

Other recent developments have the potential to move away from openness and restore policies that define kinship in more exclusive terms: *the family* in the singular rather than *families* in the plural. The political victories of conservatives since Ronald Reagan's election in 1980 are a case in point, based as they often have been on appeals to the "family values" of the "moral majority." Since *Roe v. Wade* legalized abortion in 1973, opponents of abortion have championed adoption as a laudable, prolife alternative, so it is not the case that liberals have been more enthusiastic about adoption than conservatives. Voices on the political left have continually pointed to the dramatic economic and racial inequalities that compromise adoption and argued that family preservation and support policies would be more compatible with social justice than adoption—not to mention benefit many more people. Although some feminists have seen a brief for voluntary motherhood in adoption, others have been highly sensitive to the coercive forces at play in reproductive decisions and have defended birth mothers. The result is a deep strain of skepticism about whether either surrender or adoption can be choices that women make freely.[14] Doubts about adoption linger among the feminists, liberals, and leftists who insist on women's right to abortion.

The child and family welfare policies favored by New Christian Right organizations, although favorable to adoption, have looked nostalgically for an imagined past when everyone understood exactly what a family was. In this sense, the rise of conservatism countered the trend toward expanding eligibility for family belonging so evident since the special-needs revolution at midcentury. Christian conservatives supported definitions of kinship and familial divisions of labor that were, in their view, "traditional": families centered on heterosexual marriages with stay-at-home mothers and breadwinning fathers who exercised patriarchal authority over children, especially sons. They have consequently campaigned to exclude singles and homosexuals from eligibility for adoption. Anita Bryant's "Save Our Children" campaign succeeded in 1977 in Florida, where gays and lesbians are, thirty years later, still prohibited from adopting (but not from becoming foster parents).[15]

The conflict between conservatives' vocal support for adoption and their stated desire to reinstate a strict legal and cultural hierarchy of acceptable families recalls important aspects of adoption modernization, which attempted to normalize adoption and all the parties to it by setting up qualifying tests for legitimate belonging. The campaign against same-sex marriage—which insists that heterosexuality be the prerequisite for marriage—is the most visible evidence that such tests are still supported by many Americans. Opposition to same-sex marriage is motivated by deep convictions that the point of marriage is reproduction and that children deserve to grow up with mothers and fathers rather than one or the other. The same-sex marriage debate is hardly limited to the rights and responsibilities of adult partners, important though these are. It is a debate about whether gay and lesbian citizens will be accorded equality as parents and their children considered members of "real" families.

Second-parent adoption, an innovative practice that allows two individuals of the same sex to simultaneously occupy roles as legal parents, circumvents one part of this debate because thousands of same-sex couples with children have already passed the test of second-parent adoption. They have secured recognition and protection for their parent-child relationships by convincing judges that legal access to the material benefits and resources of two parents is in children's best interest. Even for legal actors hostile to adult homosexuality, this was not a difficult call. Pioneered in Alaska in 1985, second-parent adoption has grown steadily. It exists as a possibility in approximately half the states in the country, authorized either by statute or by court decisions at the trial or appellate level.[16]

Continuities have been as striking as changes within the world of adoption. Expectations that science and technology can and should reduce risk are, if anything, higher today than in the past, and preadoption screening continues to take a variety of forms. For example, the American Academy of Pediatrics has recognized "adoption medicine" as a specialization devoted to preadoption assessment and counseling as well as postadoption evaluation. In clinics all over the United States, doctors examine potential adoptees from around the world on the basis of photos, medical records, and videos in advance of their adoptions.[17] Adoption-specific pediatrics has grown out of two parallel developments in the post-1975 era: the increase in adoptions of children from Romania, China, Guatemala, and other countries with inadequate systems of health care, and the increase in numbers of children in public foster care. Of the half-million children in the United States whose lives have been disrupted by foster care, only one-fifth are legally available for adoption; twenty thousand of them "age out" of the system annually without legal ties to any parents at all.[18] That foster children are significantly older and have more medical and psychological needs makes them symbols of how adoption has and has not changed. Many children whose chaotic lives and difficult behaviors are mired in domestic violence, substance abuse, and extreme disadvantage are free for adoption. Yet they are considered so challenging and difficult to place that the risks accompanying them (including the widespread prescription of psychoactive medications) require extensive assessment.

Such evaluations recapitulate historic efforts to use developmental diagnosis and measurement to certify the normality of adoptable children.

Because of the cultural divide that places us at arm's length from the era of vulgar eugenics and scientific racism, clinicians no longer advertise reliable methods of selecting desirable and excluding undesirable children. Rather, contemporary screeners pride themselves on providing would-be parents with as much information as possible in the interest of maximizing knowledge and facilitating fully informed decisions. Many adopters welcome this opportunity and seek as much information as they can obtain about the children they hope to adopt, unlike some of their counterparts in the past who considered ignorance of children's background an advantage in the quest for matching and realness. Like adopters in the past, however, today's would-be parents undoubtedly use the information they are given to choose the kinds of children they prefer to have. They may not admit that the goal of developmental scrutiny is to detect defects in children, preferring instead to couch decisions in terms of the "challenges" and "special needs" that particular individuals can and cannot handle. The renaissance of genetic science symbolized by the Human Genome Project only encouraged the popular eugenic thinking that has long existed, recalling the hereditarianism of the early twentieth century and reinforcing beliefs that problematic adoptees were "born that way."

In domestic adoptions, too, the trend is toward heightened scrutiny of children, with professionals and parents looking for signs of any and all problems, from fetal alcohol syndrome to autism spectrum disorders. Attorneys and facilitators enthusiastically point out that obtaining more detailed background information on children is an advantage of private adoption, much like greater choice and shorter waiting periods. Agencies whose difficult charge is to recruit families for children with special needs, including the thousands of children waiting in foster placements, publicize their desire to "screen in" potential parents rather than screen them out with selective criteria. (That these placements match less-desirable children and adults with one another is so axiomatic as to go unmentioned.) Preadoption training now typically includes an avalanche of facts and warnings about developmental problems such as attachment disorders and sexual abuse. Delivered at length in numerous training sessions, these screening procedures aim to help adults make intelligent decisions about entering into adoptive parenthood. The deliberation so characteristic of design remains deeply entrenched.

So too is the interpretive ethos, which evolved, as we have seen, as a key element of kinship by design over the course of the twentieth century. Today's adoption world is crowded with therapeutic language and teeming with therapeutic practices, from training groups for triad members to professional services that aim to diagnose and counter a host of problems associated with adoptive family formation.[19] Some of these interventions are directly related to recent innovations: support groups for families involved in "open adoption," for example. But the overwhelming emphasis on adoption-related losses and traumas, and the struggle to recover from them, reflects continuity between two eras in adoption history usually considered antithetical: the pre-1970 era of difference denial, on the one hand, and the post-1970 era of difference acknowledgment, on the other. Campaigns to reform spoiled selfhood in adoption reflect broader trends toward psychologizing childhood, intimate relationships, and identity in many spheres of social life.

Adoption commerce has always been a significant dimension of adoption history, deeply disturbing because of its implication that children are bought and sold as commodities. This practice echoes slavery, negates the pricelessness of modern childhood, and mocks the human values that modern social welfare supposedly represents. Adoption commerce, however, has endured historically. Not only has it persisted into the recent past, but it has also become more prominent, and far more global, during the past three decades. The regulatory impulse that characterized the entire New Deal era, from the Great Depression through the Great Society, from the 1930s through the 1960s, suffered serious setbacks with the post-1960s conservative ascendancy. The Reagan administration, in its drive to revive entrepreneurial freedoms it claimed were imperiled by the heavy yoke of bureaucratic control, enshrined deregulation in many areas of federal law and policy.

This move toward deregulation affected adoption no less than airlines. Since 1970, more responsibility for managing adoption has been located within the private rather than the public realm, shifting administration away from state actors and emphasizing the role of consumers whose preferences guide their market behavior. The number of adoptions arranged privately has grown steadily, as have "facilitators" who operate outside of licensed agencies. These middlemen, often but not always attorneys, broker adoptions by bringing together birth parents with adults interested in adopting. Facilitators are, at bottom, marketers, unregulated by state or federal law. When adoption markets cross national borders, as they increasingly have in the recent past, even widely publicized regulatory efforts, such as the 1993 Hague Convention on Intercountry Adoption, passed by the U.S. Congress in 2000, cannot effectively address the drastic disparities of wealth and power that make international placements possible.

In early 2001, the case of Tina Johnson publicized the nexus between facilitators, the adoption market, and the Internet in the post–cold war era.[20] Johnson, the founder of Caring Heart Adoption, an online facilitation service based in her San Diego home, arranged for the placement of twin girls with a California couple, Richard and Vicki Allen, who paid her a fee of $6,000. After two months, Johnson and the twins' birth mother, Tranda Wecker, requested a meeting with the adoptive parents. Because California law stipulates a ninety-day waiting period during which relinquishment may be rescinded, the Allens agreed. Johnson and Wecker promptly took the girls and placed them with a Welsh couple, Alan and Judith Kilshaw, who had paid a fee of $12,000 to Johnson and were waiting in a nearby hotel. After fleeing to Arkansas, where state law allowed them to adopt the twins quickly, the Kilshaws flew home to Great Britain, where the scandal came to light and received international attention. "Adoption in Britain is over-regulated and people are regarded as being unsuitable for silly reasons," Alan Kilshaw explained when asked by the BBC why he and his wife had gone all the way to the United States to adopt.[21] The twins ended up in state custody in Missouri, where they were born, and the rights of their birth parents were terminated in December 2002. In February 2003, Johnson was arrested and charged with multiple counts of wire fraud. Through Caring Heart Adoption, she had extracted adoptions fees from people in the United States and internationally over a five-year period, without ever once having completed an actual adoption. The charges against Johnson were dropped in 2005, and the twins have been in foster care for most of their lives.

The variability in state adoption laws that played a central role in the Johnson case is exactly the same phenomenon that invigorated efforts to govern adoption more strictly a century ago. The response has been similar. The California State Assembly legislated new requirements that facilitators register with the state and post a $25,000 bond because "recent accounts of fraudulent practices by adoption facilitators demonstrate that current regulations are not strict or extensive enough to safeguard birth parents and prospective adoptive parents from fraud."[22] Nationally as well, the campaign to promote a Uniform Adoption Act, most recently revived in 1994, represents at once the enduring appeal of regulation and standardization in adoption and the elusiveness of these goals. The Uniform Adoption Act, drafted by the National Conference of Commissioners on Uniform State Laws and supported by the American Bar Association, recommends a comprehensive overhaul of adoption procedures, especially those designed to prevent unlawful and blatantly commercial placements. Only a handful of states (Vermont, Montana, and Oklahoma among them) have enacted its provisions into law.[23] The rise of the Internet suggests how much technology has extended the marketing and brokering potential of adoption entrepreneurs.

The Internet also serves as a hub for decidedly noncommercial adoption-related communication. It provides a steady stream of information about the adoption process, tips about searching, outlets for political activism, and connections between people with shared experiences who would not otherwise meet. Bastard Nation, founded in 1996 by feisty activists devoted to open records and unfettered expression for adult adoptees, has relied heavily on creating a virtual community to spread its message and incite change.[24] The Vietnamese Adoptee Network and Adopted Vietnamese International were both founded in 2000—in the United States and Australia respectively—on the twenty-fifth anniversary of Operation Babylift, which, as noted earlier, transported more than two thousand children from Vietnam to the United States on the eve of the U.S. evacuation of Saigon.[25] Technological change has transformed adoption politics, culture, and communities in myriad ways, just as it has transformed adoption commerce. Electronic linkages make it possible to belong to an adoption diaspora that never before existed.

Adoption implies social mobility in one direction only—up. This is another historical constant reinforced by recent trends inseparable from the adoption market. Nowhere is this clearer than in the new world of international adoption, where children move from poorer to richer countries, just as domestic adoptions moved them from poorer to richer families. The potential for exploitation in exchanges that bring people with significant access to material resources and political power together with their opposites on the other side of the globe is obvious. In international adoptions, the result has been a spate of scandals that range from rumors that adoptions are fronts for murderous organ-stealing schemes (in Peru and Guatemala) to outright moratoria on adoption placements because of widespread baby selling and corruption (in Romania and Cambodia).[26] Like so many other things that circulate in the new global economy of the twenty-first century, the traffic in children follows commercial paths that are at once utterly innovative and deeply etched by the presence of the past.

Finally, the profound cultural equivalence between blood and belonging persists, suggesting yet another key continuity in adoption history. The idea that "blood is thicker than water" is no less stubborn in an era of new reproductive technologies that have reconfigured relationships between genes and gestation in ways that accentuate biology while subjecting it to previously unimaginable levels of human intervention. Technologies ranging from egg and embryo donation to sperm sorting have intensified the quest for "own" children and reinforced the allure of biogenetic connection even as they raise startling new questions about the meaning of family and nature.[27] Awareness that humans have aggressively manipulated and altered nature, placing it in serious jeopardy, has boosted its cultural power, as if acts of deference to all things natural could hide nature's fragility and the extent to which social designs already dominate our lives, bodies, and global environment.

Considering the allure of technological enhancements to flesh and blood, the self-congratulatory chorus equating adoption with enlightenment, multiculturalism, and nurture suggests halting progress, at best. There is every reason to believe that blood and biology have remained central cultural tributaries feeding adoption history during the second half of the twentieth-century and into the twenty-first. Talk of bad seed and bad blood has gone out of favor, to be sure, and the state policies (e.g., sterilization) that differentiated between more- and less-desirable citizens for a good part of the past century evoke apology and horror today. On the other hand, predictability and control are as attractive as ever. Efforts to make kinship knowable and manageable used to be visible chiefly in adoption, on the statistical margins of American kinship. Today, they extend to more reproductive decisions by more persons for more reasons than ever before.

Unlike adoption, new reproductive technologies are virtually unregulated by law and public policy, which does not mean that they are unregulated. In their case, design is negotiated by consumers expressing preferences in the medical marketplace rather than by agents of government whose standards and certification requirements determine who may have children and who may not. The pursuit of perfection through the design of better babies has grown more tempting and ethically charged with each technological advance. Opportunities to take advantage of this kind of kinship by design are (like opportunities to adopt privately) structured by the sharp socio-economic inequalities that stratify the United States at the beginning of the twenty-first century.[28]

The government of adoption lives in the historical shadow of blood. Kinship by design was a set of ideals and practices founded on a profoundly modern belief in the desirability of using social knowledge and action to achieve identity and solidarity rather than leaving either to blood or accident or fate. But it could not ultimately succeed in a culture where the safety, nature, and realness of family ties remained ascribed as well as achieved.

Kinship by design was an ideology of mastery in a world made simultaneously dangerous and controllable through knowledge. That is why adoption helps to illuminate a deep paradox in modern U.S. history. Why did problems of vulnerability and risk move to the center of historical experience and consciousness just as the technologies of government over individuals and institutions multiplied, grew more powerful, and extended their reach? These two developments were intimately related. Uncertainty became more intolerable as regulation, interpretation, standardization, and naturalization promised to control and compensate for it. The point of kinship by design was to determine the qualifications of children and adults, map the psychological damage of deprivation and loss, and predict how children and families would turn out. Kinship by design reckoned with risks by promising to make them more manageable, a sign of the optimism about permanent progress that charted a familiar path through American modernity.

For all that has been gained as a result of planning and reform, neither adoption nor modernity has been a straightforward story of improvement. The knowable is haunted by the specter of the inexplicable. Modern times marked a revolutionary break with the past, enhancing the potential of social knowledge to shape the world, but fundamental problems of value simply could not be decided on the basis of rational knowledge alone. What is a family? What are families for? How should families be made? Who will decide?

Uncertainty, like design, is inescapable in social and natural arrangements. If we can find the grace to accept what we do not know, perhaps it will be possible to reckon with risk differently. To concede limits on our rational control of ourselves and our world—including the fate of adopted children and adoptive kinship—is not to respond passively to change or meet threats with resignation. It does not sabotage agency, empty our ethical choices of positive meaning, or undermine the potential for democratic collective action. It certainly does not diminish our moral responsibility, as parents and citizens, to create families and communities that will allow all of our children to flourish. But balancing our desires for the sure thing with appreciation of luck, chance, and mystery might inject a welcome measure of humility into our private and public lives, reimagining an enchanted space between drift and mastery and transforming design into something that is as humane as it is human.

NOTES

Short titles are used for citations after their first mention within each chapter. Works and organizations frequently cited are identified by the following abbreviations:

AAC   Adopt-A-Child, National Urban League Papers, Library of Congress, Washington, DC
ALG   Arnold Lucius Gesell Papers, Library of Congress, Washington, DC
CC   Charities Collection, Simmons College Archives, Boston
CWLA   Child Welfare League of America
CWLA1   Child Welfare League of America Papers, University of Minnesota Library, Social Welfare History Archives (Call Number SW55), Minneapolis
CWLA2   Child Welfare League of America Papers, University of Minnesota Library, Social Welfare History Archives (Call Number SW55.1), Minneapolis
CWLAmicro   Microfilmed subset of CWLA Papers, University of Minnesota Library, Social Welfare History Archives, Minneapolis
DH   Dorothy Hutchinson Papers, Butler Library, Rare Books and Manuscripts, Columbia University, New York
ESD   Ethel Sturges Dummer Papers, Harvard University, Radcliffe Institute for Advanced Study, Schlesinger Library, Cambridge, MA
HCC   Hillcrest Children's Center Papers, Library of Congress, Washington, DC
ISSAB   International Social Service, American Branch Papers, University of Minnesota Library, Social Welfare History Archives, Minneapolis
JCRCGB   Jewish Community Relations Council of Greater Boston, American Jewish Historical Society
JT   Jessie Taft Papers, Butler Library, Rare Books and Manuscripts, Columbia University, New York
JWP   Justine Wise Polier Papers, Harvard University, Radcliffe Institute for Advanced Study, Schlesinger Library, Cambridge, MA
SP   Shad Polier Papers, American Jewish Historical Society, New York
USCB   U.S. Children's Bureau
USCB Papers U.S. Children's Bureau Papers, National Archives II, College Park, MD
VWB   Viola Wertheim Bernard Papers, Long Health Sciences Library, Archives and Special Collections, Columbia University, New York

INTRODUCTION

1. Unless otherwise noted, the term *adoption* refers to adoption by nonrelatives or "biological strangers." Adoptions by blood relatives were presumed to be natural and easy in comparison with nonrelative adoptions. During the twentieth century, a majority of adoptees were probably placed with nonrelatives, but there have always been a substantial number of adoptions by natal relatives and stepparents, as well as informal adoptions that are beyond the reach of law. The proportion of relative adoptions has increased since 1970 and represents approximately 50 percent of all adoptions today. Of these, stepparent adoptions are the most common.

2. The term *foster* denoted both temporary and permanent family placements until after 1945.

3. Wayne Carp tackled confidentiality in *Family Matters: Secrecy and Disclosure in the History of Adoption* (Cambridge, MA: Harvard University Press, 1998). By documenting the piecemeal establishment of sealed records, he exploded the myth that secrecy was more deeply lodged in adoption history than disclosure. In *Strangers and Kin: The American Way of Adoption* (Cambridge, MA: Harvard University Press, 2002), Barbara Melosh sensitively explored professionalization and matching, transracial and transnational placements, and significant but little-discussed issues, including adopters' uncommon preference for girls and the role of narratives in adoption activism. Julie Berebitsky, in *Like Our Very Own: Adoption and the Changing Culture of Motherhood, 1851–1950* (Lawrence: University Press of Kansas, 2000), pointed out that adoption could not be understood without also understanding motherhood, an argument equally applicable to child labor, orphanages, illegitimacy, infertility, and marriage, among other topics. For a survey of the field, see E. Wayne Carp, ed., *Adoption in America: Historical Perspectives* (Ann Arbor: University of Michigan Press, 2002). See also my Web site, The Adoption History Project, at http://www.uoregon.edu/~adoption/.

    On related topics, see Lori Askeland, ed., *Children and Youth in Adoption, Orphanages, and Foster Care: A Historical Handbook and Guide* (Westport, CT: Greenwood Press, 2006); Kenneth Cmiel, *A Home of Another Kind: One Chicago Orphanage and the Tangle of Child Welfare* (Chicago: University of Chicago Press, 1995); Nancy Cott, *Public Vows: A History of Marriage and the Nation* (Cambridge, MA: Harvard University Press, 2000); Ann Fessler, *The Girls Who Went Away: The Hidden History of Women Who Surrendered Children for Adoption in the Decades before Roe v. Wade* (New York: Penguin, 2006); Linda Gordon, *The Great Arizona Orphan Abduction* (Cambridge, MA: Harvard University Press, 1999); Timothy A. Hacsi, *Second Home: Orphan Asylums and Poor Families in America* (Cambridge, MA: Harvard University Press, 1998); Regina G. Kunzel, *Fallen Women, Problem Girls: Unmarried Mothers and the Professionalization of Social Work, 1890–1945* (New Haven, CT: Yale University Press, 1993); Margaret Marsh and Wanda Ronner, *The Empty Cradle: Infertility in America from Colonial Times to the Present* (Baltimore: Johns Hopkins University Press, 1996); Elaine Tyler May, *Barren in the Promised Land: Childless Americans and the Pursuit of Happiness* (New York: Basic Books, 1995); Rickie Solinger, *Wake Up Little Susie: Single Pregnancy and Race before Roe v. Wade* (New York: Routledge, 1992); Daniel Walkowitz, *Working with Class: Social Workers and the Politics of Middle-Class Identity* (Chapel Hill: University of North Carolina Press, 1999); Viviana A. Zelizer, *Pricing the Priceless Child: The Changing Social Value of Children* (New York: Basic Books, 1985), chap. 6.

4. Recent analyses include Elizabeth Bartholet, *Nobody's Children: Abuse and Neglect, Foster Drift, and the Adoption Alternative* (Boston: Beacon Press, 1999); Naomi Cahn

and Joan Heifetz Hollinger, eds., *Families by Law: An Adoption Reader* (New York: New York University Press, 2004); Sara K. Dorow, *Transnational Adoption: A Cultural Economy of Race, Gender, and Kinship* (New York: New York University Press, 2006); Hawley Fogg-Davis, *The Ethics of Transracial Adoption* (Ithaca, NY: Cornell University Press, 2002); Sally Haslanger and Charlotte Witt, eds., *Adoption Matters: Philosophical and Feminist Essays* (Ithaca, NY: Cornell University Press, 2005); Randall Kennedy, *Interracial Intimacies: Sex, Marriage, Identity, and Adoption* (New York: Pantheon Books, 2003); Marianne Novy, ed., *Imagining Adoption: Essays on Literature and Culture* (Ann Arbor: University of Michigan Press, 2001); Dorothy Roberts, *Shattered Bonds: The Color of Child Welfare* (New York: Basic Books, 2002), 149–72; Barbara Katz Rothman, *Weaving a Family: Untangling Race and Adoption* (Boston: Beacon Press, 2005); Kathy Shepherd Stolley and Vern L. Bullough, eds., *The Praeger Handbook of Adoption*, 2 vols. (Westport, CT: Praeger, 2006); Jane Jeong Trenka, Julia Chinyere Oparah, and SunYung Shin, eds., *Outsiders Within: Racial Crossings and Adoption Politics* (Cambridge, MA: South End Press, 2006); Toby Volkman, ed., *Cultures of Transnational Adoption* (Durham, NC: Duke University Press, 2005); Katarina Wegar, ed., *Adoptive Families in a Diverse Society* (New Brunswick, NJ: Rutgers University Press, 2006); Katarina Wegar, *Adoption, Identity and Kinship: The Debate over Sealed Birth Records* (New Haven, CT: Yale University Press, 1997). Documentaries have been important: "Daughter from Danang" (Berkeley, CA: Interfaze Educational Productions, 2002); "First Person Plural" (San Francisco: ITVS, 1999); "Secret Daughter" (Boston: WGBH, 1996); "That's a Family" (San Francisco: Women's Educational Media, 2000).

5. Statistics on domestic adoptions are unreliable. A national reporting system existed only between 1945 and 1975, when the U.S. Children's Bureau and the National Center for Social Statistics collected data supplied voluntarily by states and territories. Total adoptions increased steadily after 1945, reached a zenith of 175,000 annually in 1970, and then began decreasing. Most likely a pattern of steady increase also held from 1900 to 1945. Totals obscure significant trends: numbers of children adopted by relatives or nonrelatives, independently or by agencies, as babies or at older ages, transracially and transnationally. Statistical data for international placements are much better. Adoptions of foreign-born children have increased, tripling since 1990; virtually all have been nonrelative adoptions. But nonrelative adoption represented only slightly more than half of all adoptions during the twentieth century, and relative adoptions increased after 1970. Transracial adoptions have attracted much attention, but they are more symbolically than statistically significant. The largest number of domestic transracial adoptions occurred around 1970, perhaps a few thousand annually. One of the only national surveys of black children adopted documented 4,336 in 1969, 6,474 in 1970, and 7,420 in 1971, of which almost one-third were transracial. See Opportunity, "Adoption of Black Children in 1969," ISSAB, Box 26, Folder: "Oregon—Adoption," and Opportunity, "National Survey of Black Children Adopted in 1972," Viola Wertheim Bernard Papers, Columbia University, Long Health Sciences Library, Archives and Special Collections (hereafter cited as VWB), Box 162, Folder 7. Finally, independent placements decreased after 1945 from more than 50 percent of nonrelative placements to a low of 21 percent in 1970 and 1971, with agency placements increasing correspondingly during these years. For the period for which statistical data are best, see Penelope L. Maza, "Adoption Trends: 1944–1975," Child Welfare Research Notes No. 9 (U.S. Children's Bureau, August 1984), table 1, Child Welfare League of America Papers, University of Minnesota Library, Social Welfare History Archives (Call Number SW55.1) (hereafter cited as

CWLA2), Box 65, Folder: "Adoption—Research—Reprints of Articles," and Kathy S. Stolley, "Statistics on Adoption in the United States," *Future of Children* 3, no. 1 (Spring 1993): 26–42. For more recent data, see Evan B. Donaldson Adoption Institute, http://www.adoptioninstitute.org (accessed December 17, 2007); Anjani Chandra et al., "Adoption, Adoption Seeking, and Relinquishment for Adoption in the United States," *Advance Data from Vital and Health Statistics of the Centers for Disease Control and Prevention/National Center for Health Statistics*, no. 306 (May 11, 1999); Victor E. Flango and Mary M. Caskey, "Adoptions, 2000–2001," *Adoption Quarterly* 8 (2005): 23–43; U.S. Department of State, "Immigrant Visas Issued to Orphans Coming to the U.S.," http://www.travel.state.gov (accessed December 17, 2007). The trend toward fewer total adoptions and a higher proportion of international placements appears equally prevalent in Canada, Western Europe, and Australia.

6.   U.S. Census Bureau, "Census 2000 Special Reports, Adopted Children and Stepchildren: 2000" (Washington DC: U.S. Department of Commerce, Economics and Statistics Administration, August 2003).

7.   Stephanie Coontz, *The Way We Never Were: American Families and the Nostalgia Trip* (New York: Basic Books, 1992).

8.   Elizabeth Frazer, "We Have Done It!" *Saturday Evening Post*, June 21, 1930, 59.

9.   "Adoption Country," *New Yorker*, May 10, 1993, 8.

10. Adam Pertman, *Adoption Nation: How the Adoption Revolution Is Transforming America* (New York: Basic Books, 2000).

11. David M. Schneider, *American Kinship: A Cultural Account,* 2nd ed. (Chicago: University of Chicago Press, 1980).

12. David A. Hollinger, *Postethnic America: Beyond Multiculturalism* (New York: Basic Books, 1995).

13. Rogers M. Smith, *Civic Ideals: Conflicting Visions of Citizenship in U.S. History* (New Haven, CT: Yale University Press, 1997).

14. Michel Foucault, *Discipline and Punish: The Birth of the Prison* (New York: Vintage Books, 1979); Michel Foucault, *Madness and Civilization: A History of Insanity in the Age of Reason* (New York: Vintage Books, 1965).

15. Gerald N. Grob, *The Mad among Us: A History of the Care of America's Mentally Ill* (New York: Free Press, 1994), 48.

16. Christopher Lasch, *Haven in a Heartless World: The Family Besieged* (New York: W. W. Norton, 1977).

17. Ibid., xx.

18. Jacques Donzelot, *The Policing of Families* (New York: Pantheon Books, 1979).

19. Theodore Porter, *The Rise of Statistical Thinking, 1820–1900* (Princeton, NJ: Princeton University Press, 1986); Peter Wagner, "Social Science and Social Planning during the Twentieth Century," in *The Cambridge History of Science*, vol. 7, *The Modern Social Sciences*, ed. Theodore M. Porter and Dorothy Ross (New York: Cambridge University Press, 2003), 591–607. Ambitious, state-directed social engineering programs were equally significant in authoritarian societies. See James C. Scott, *Seeing Like a State: How Certain Schemes to Improve the Human Condition Have Failed* (New Haven, CT: Yale University Press, 1998).

20. U.S. Census Bureau, *Measuring America: The Decennial Censuses from 1790 to 2000* (Washington, DC: U.S. Department of Commerce, 2002); U.S. Census Bureau, *200 Years of Census Taking: Population and Housing Questions, 1790–1990* (Washington, DC: Department of Commerce, 1989).

21. William Graebner, *The Engineering of Consent: Democracy and Authority in Twentieth-Century America* (Madison: University of Wisconsin Press, 1987); Ellen Herman, *The Romance of American Psychology: Political Culture in the Age of Experts* (Berkeley and Los Angeles: University of California Press, 1995); Sarah E. Igo, *The Averaged American: Surveys, Citizens, and the Making of a Mass Public* (Cambridge, MA: Harvard University Press, 2007); Walter A. Jackson, *Gunnar Myrdal and America's Conscience: Social Engineering and Racial Liberalism, 1938–1987* (Chapel Hill: University of North Carolina Press, 1990); Rebecca Lemov, *World as Laboratory: Experiments with Mice, Mazes, and Men* (New York: Hill and Wang, 2005); Alice O'Connor, *Poverty Knowledge: Social Science, Public Policy, and the Poor in Twentieth-Century U.S. History* (Princeton, NJ: Princeton University Press, 2001); Diana Selig, *Americans All: The Cultural Gifts Movement* (Cambridge, MA: Harvard University Press, 2008); Ethan G. Srivnick, "Rehabilitating Child Welfare: Children and Public Policy, 1945–1980" (Ph.D. diss., University of Virginia, 2007).

22. Virginia Postrel, *The Future and Its Enemies: The Growing Conflict over Creativity, Enterprise, and Progress* (New York: Free Press, 1998).

23. Estelle B. Freedman, *Maternal Justice: Miriam Van Waters and the Female Reform Tradition, 1887–1974* (Chicago: University of Chicago Press, 1996), chap. 8.

24. Barbara Young Welke, *Recasting American Liberty: Gender, Race, Law, and the Railroad Revolution, 1865–1920* (New York: Cambridge University Press, 2001).

25. Jackson Lears, *No Place of Grace: Antimodernism and the Transformation of American Culture, 1880–1920* (New York: Pantheon, 1981); Jackson Lears, *Fables of Abundance: A Cultural History of Advertising in America* (New York: Basic Books, 1994); Jackson Lears, *Something for Nothing: Luck in America* (New York: Viking, 2003). For an overview, see Michael Saler, "Modernity and Enchantment: A Historiographic Review," *American Historical Review* 111, no. 3 (June 2006): 692–716.

26. "BJ Lifton Booted from Adoption Conference; Offensive Language Cited," Daily Bastardette (blog), September 5, 2006, bastardette.blogspot.com.

CHAPTER ONE

1. Joseph Ben-Or, "The Law of Adoption in the United States: Its Massachusetts Origins and the Statute of 1851," *New England History and Genealogical Registry* 130 (1976): 266.

2. Mississippi passed an adoption law first, in 1846, followed by Alabama, Texas, and Vermont, but the Massachusetts law was more comprehensive and characterized adoption as a procedure devoted to child welfare rather than adult interests. See Ben-Or, "Law of Adoption"; Yasuhide Kawashima, "Adoption in Early America," *Journal of Family Law* 20 (1981–82): 677–96; Stephen B. Presser, "The Historical Background of the American Law of Adoption," *Journal of Family Law* 11 (1971–72): 443–516; Jamil Shaheen Zainaldin, "The Origins of Modern Legal Adoption: Child Exchange in Boston, 1851–93" (Ph.D. diss., University of Chicago, 1976); Jamil S. Zainaldin, "The Emergence of a Modern American Family Law: Child Custody, Adoption, and the Courts, 1796–1851," *Northwestern University Law Review* 73 (1979): 1038–89.

3. For a sample of international and comparative perspectives, see Jamila Bargach, *Orphans of Islam: Family, Abandonment, and Secret Adoption in Morocco* (Lanham, MD: Rowman and Littlefield, 2002); John Boswell, *The Kindness of Strangers: The Abandonment of Children in Western Europe from Late Antiquity to the Renaissance* (New York: Pantheon, 1988); Agnès Fine and Claire Neirinck, eds., *Parents de Sang, Parents Adoptifs: Approches Juridiques et Anthropologiques de L'adoption, France, Europe, USA,*

Canada (Paris: Librarie L.G.D.J., 2000); Kristin Elizabeth Gager, *Blood Ties and Fictive Ties: Adoption and Family Life in Early Modern France* (Princeton, NJ: Princeton University Press, 1996); Kerry O'Halloran, *The Politics of Adoption: International Perspectives on Law, Policy and Practice* (Dordrecht, The Netherlands: Springer, 2006); Veronica Strong-Boag, *Finding Families, Finding Ourselves: English Canada Encounters Adoption from the Nineteenth Century to the 1990s* (Don Mills, Ontario: Oxford University Press, 2006); Ann Beth Waltner, *Getting an Heir: Adoption and the Construction of Kinship in Late Imperial China* (Honolulu: University of Hawaii Press, 1990); Arthur P. Wolf and Chieh-shan Huang, *Marriage and Adoption in China, 1854–1945* (Stanford, CA: Stanford University Press, 1980).

4. Sophie van Senden Theis, *How Foster Children Turn Out*, Publication No. 165 (New York: New York State Charities Aid Association, 1924), 127.

5. Informal adoptions move children between adults and households without legal oversight and are impossible to document statistically. Such adoptions were very common forms of child care before institutional and public services were widely available and remained common throughout the twentieth century, especially in minority and poor communities. Carol B. Stack, *All Our Kin: Strategies for Survival in a Black Community* (New York: Harper, 1974).

6. *Proceedings of the Conference on the Care of Dependent Children Held at Washington, DC,* 60th Cong., 2nd sess., 1909, S. Doc. 721 (Washington, DC: Government Printing Office, 1909), 9.

7. Matthew A. Crenson, *Building the Invisible Orphanage: The Prehistory of the American Welfare System* (Cambridge, MA: Harvard University Press, 1998), 42; Marian J. Morton, "Surviving the Great Depression: Orphanages and Orphans in Cleveland," *Journal of Urban History* 26 (May 2000): 441.

8. Sophie van Senden Theis, "The Passing of the Orphanage," *New York Times Magazine*, January 18, 1953, 16; Bernadine Barr, "Spare Children, 1900–1945: Inmates of Orphanages as Subjects of Research in Medicine and in the Social Sciences in America" (Ph.D. diss., Stanford University, 1992), 32, fig. 2.2.

9. See Kenneth Cmiel, *A Home of Another Kind: One Chicago Orphanage and the Tangle of Child Welfare* (Chicago: University of Chicago Press, 1995).

10. In 1927 twelve states still allowed indenture for children in public care: Wisconsin, Illinois, Michigan, Indiana, Kansas, Pennsylvania, Arkansas, Maryland, Rhode Island, Virginia, West Virginia, and Nebraska.

11. U.S. Children's Bureau (hereafter cited as USCB), *Children Indentured by the Wisconsin State Public School*, Bureau Publication No. 150 (Washington, DC: Government Printing Office, 1925), 16.

12. Sophie van Senden Theis and Constance Goodrich, *The Child in the Foster Home, Part 1: The Placement and Supervision of Children in Free Foster Homes, A Study Based on the Work of the Child-Placing Agency of the New York State Charities Aid Association* (New York: New York School of Social Work, 1921), 31.

13. One national study showed that for children in family placements in 1930, 72 percent of the children had their board paid for, 19 percent were in free homes, and 6 percent were self-supporting (the remaining 3 percent were simply identified as "under other type of care"), and wide regional variations existed. USCB, *Care of Dependent and Neglected Children*, Bureau Publication No. 209, Part 2: *Social Statistics in Child Welfare and Related Fields—Annual Report for the Registration Area for the Year 1930* (Washington, DC: Government Printing Office, 1932), 15, table 10.

14. Albert H. Stoneman, "The Work of a State-Wide Child-Placing Organization" in USCB, *Foster-Home Care for Dependent Children*, Bureau Publication No. 136 (Washington, DC: Government Printing Office, 1926), 96.

15. W. H. Slingerland, *Child-Placing in Families: A Manual for Students and Social Workers* (New York: Russell Sage Foundation, 1919), chap. 12.

16. Marilyn Irvin Holt, *The Orphan Trains: Placing Out in America* (Lincoln: University of Nebraska Press, 1992); Stephen O'Connor, *Orphan Trains: The Story of Charles Loring Brace and the Children He Saved and Failed* (Boston: Houghton Mifflin, 2001).

17. Bruce Bellingham, "Little Wanderers: A Socio-Historical Study of the Nineteenth Century Origins of Child Fostering and Adoption Reform, Based on Early Records of the New York Children's Aid Society" (Ph.D. diss., University of Pennsylvania, 1984); Clay Gish, "Rescuing the 'Waifs and Strays' of the City: The Western Emigration Program of the Children's Aid Society," *Journal of Social History* 33 (Fall 1999): 121–41; Tim Hacsi, "From Indenture to Family Foster Care: A Brief History of Child Placing," in *A History of Child Welfare*, ed. Eve P. Smith and Lisa A. Merkel-Holguín (New Brunswick, NJ: Transaction Publishers, 1996), 155–73. Helen Cole, who directed the Foster Care Department of the Children's Aid Society after Brace's son Robert retired in 1930, wrote that "our Trustees have no idea of how poor some of our former placing was. They still believe that a majority of the placements were highly successful." Helen Cole to Katharine Lenroot, March 24, 1932, U.S. Children's Bureau Papers, National Archives II, College Park, MD (hereafter cited as USCB Papers), Box 406, Folder 7-3-3-3, "Boarding Homes."

18. Mrs. M. H. Hache to Mrs. Brown, October 1, 1901, Hillcrest Children's Center Papers, Library of Congress, Washington, DC (hereafter cited as HCC), Box 2, Folder: "Applications for Admission, 1908–23."

19. All comments found on completed forms. See "Application for Admission of Children to the Washington City Orphan Asylum," HCC, Box 2, Folder: "Applications for Admission, 1908–23."

20. I. A. Nicholson to the Board of Managers, November 2, 1916, HCC, Box 2, Folder: "Reference Ltrs. re: Admission of Children, 1901–."

21. A. W. Sprinkle to Mrs. M. L. Squires, May 30, 1918, June 15, 1918, and June 20, 1918, HCC, Box 3, Folder: "Return of Children to Parents, 1918."

22. E. E. Richardson to Dear Madam, March 12, 1912, HCC, Box 3, Folder: "Indentures, Adoptions, Court Orders 1870–1923, 1941."

23. Mary Tinney, "An Interpretation of Three Thousand Placements by the New York Catholic Home Bureau," *Proceedings of the National Conference of Catholic Charities* (Washington, DC: Catholic University, 1916), 190.

24. April 21, 1910, indenture and subsequent letter from Earnest requesting a change of placement, HCC, Box 3, Folder: "Indentures, Adoptions, Court Orders 1870–1923, 1941."

25. Neva R. Deardorff, "Bound Out," *Survey* 56 (July 15, 1926): 458. See also Paul L. Benjamin, "The 'Home Boy' in Delaware: Conditions of Child Life in a State Which Still Legalizes the Binding Out System," *Survey* 46 (April 16, 1921): 81–82.

26. Lawrence C. Cole, "A Study of Adoptions in Cuyahoga County," *Family* (1926): 261; Helen Lucile Pearson, "Child Adoption in Indiana" (M.A. thesis, Indiana University, 1925), 43–44.

27. Ida R. Parker, *Fit and Proper? A Study of Legal Adoption in Massachusetts* (Boston: Church Home Society, 1927), 86.

28. Neva R. Deardorff, "'The Welfare of the Said Child . . .'" *Survey Midmonthly* 53 (January 15, 1925): 458.
29. Case 6, "Study of the Practice of Adoption in Philadelphia County," in *Report of the Commission Appointed to Study and Revise the Statutes of Pennsylvania Relating to Children, Part 1*, in Robert H. Bremner, ed., *Children and Youth in America: A Documentary History, vol. 2, 1866–1932* (Cambridge: Harvard University Press, 1971), 142.
30. Case 8, "Study of the Practice of Adoption in Philadelphia County," in *Report of the Commission Appointed to Study and Revise the Statutes of Pennsylvania Relating to Children*, 142.
31. Tinney, "Interpretation," 192. In her study of family violence in Boston, Linda Gordon found that 29 percent of the incest cases handled by agencies involved step-, foster-, and adoptive fathers. See Linda Gordon, *Heroes of Their Own Lives: The Politics and History of Family Violence* (New York: Viking, 1988), 211, table 7.
32. Viviana A. Zelizer, *Pricing the Priceless Child: The Changing Social Value of Children* (New York: Basic Books, 1985).
33. Clara M. Curran to Ladies, November 30, 1913, HCC, Box 3, Folder: "Applications for Adoption, 1906–1913."
34. Emily McA to USCB, December 9, 1920, USCB Papers, Box 67, Folder 7-3-4-3, "Adoption."
35. Mrs. S. K. Jackson (of NC) to USCB, May 7, 1922, USCB Papers, Box 211, Folder 7-3-4-2-1, "Boarding Homes for Babies and Children" and 7-3-4-3, "Adoption."
36. E. L. Armstrong to USCB, February 28, 1928, USCB Papers, Box 294, Folder 7-3-4-3, "Adoption."
37. For one example, see USCB, *Adoption Laws in the United States: A Summary of the Development of Adoption Legislation and Significant Features of Adoption Statutes, with the Text of Selected Laws*, Bureau Publication No. 148, ed. Emelyn Foster Peck (Washington, DC: Government Printing Office, 1925), 4. "The adoption acts of the various States show a gradual development from a transaction of contractual character toward a procedure in which human values are carefully considered and the supervisory duty of the State is recognized."
38. One study of Alameda County, California, found that only 297 adoptions took place between 1890 and 1910, with 66 percent conforming to the "as if begotten" family that came to define the modern adoption ideal. See Chris Guthrie and Joanna L. Grossman, "Adoption in the Progressive Era: Preserving, Creating, and Re-Creating Families," *American Journal of Legal History* 43 (July 1999): 235–53.
39. J. Prentice Murphy, "The Foster Care of Neglected and Dependent Children," *Annals of the American Academy of Political and Social Science* 77 (May 1918): 121.
40. J. Prentice Murphy, "Mothers and–Mothers," *Survey* 42 (May 3, 1919): 176.
41. *Proceedings of the Conference on the Care of Dependent Children Held at Washington, DC*, 140.
42. Slingerland, *Child-Placing in Families*, 167.
43. Lawrence Cole, "The Need of the Case Work Method in Dealing with Illegitimacy," *Hospital Social Service* 13 (May 1926): 435, 433.
44. A. H. Stoneman, "Safeguarding Adoptions, Legally and Socially," *Proceedings of the National Conference of Social Work* (Chicago: University of Chicago Press, 1924), 148.
45. Parker, *Fit and Proper*, 58.
46. *Little Wanderers' Advocate* 59 (June 1923): 20.
47. "Case Work Problems on Illegitimacy," *Proceedings of the National Conference of Charities and Correction* (Boston: George H. Ellis, 1915), 126.

48. Martha J. Megee, "The Problems of Children as a Child Placing Agency Sees Them," *Annals of the American Academy of Political and Social Science* 121 (September 1925): 159–63. See also Marion E. Kenworthy, "The Mental Hygiene Aspects of Illegitimacy," *Mental Hygiene* 5 (July 1921): 499–508. Regina Kunzel argues that the reconsideration of adoption among social workers did not occur until at least the 1920s; Wayne Carp disputes this chronology and maintains that professionals considered adoption a viable solution to illegitimacy earlier. See Regina G. Kunzel, *Fallen Women, Problem Girls: Unmarried Mothers and the Professionalization of Social Work, 1890–1945* (New Haven, CT: Yale University Press, 1993), and E. Wayne Carp, "Professional Social Workers, Adoption, and the Problem of Illegitimacy, 1915–1945," *Journal of Policy History* 6 (1994): 161–84.

49. Jacob A. Riis, *How the Other Half Lives: Studies among the Tenements of New York* (New York: Hill and Wang, 1971), 142.

50. Mrs. Standard to Julia Lathrop, January 21, 1916, USCB Papers, Box 67, Folder 7-3-4-2, "Placing Out."

51. W. H. Sullivan to Gentlemen, April 27, 1918, USCB Papers, Box 67, Folder 7-3-4-3, "Adoption."

52. Mr. Chas Benthall to USCB, n.d., but January 1933, USCB Papers, Box 458, Folder 7-3-3-4, "Adoption 1934 & 33."

53. Mr. and Mrs. Otho Holmes to USCB, November 17, 1928, USCB Papers, Box 294, Folder 7-3-4-3, "Adoption."

54. Quoted in Suzanne Morton, "'To Take an Orphan': Gender and Family Roles following the Halifax Explosion," in *Gendered Pasts: Historical Essays in Femininity and Masculinity in Canada*, ed. Kathryn McPherson, Cecilia Morgan, and Nancy M. Forestell (Don Mills, Ontario: Oxford University Press, 1999), 112.

55. "Our Adopted Baby," *Woman's Home Companion*, April 1916, 68.

56. For an unusual narrative from an adoptive father, see Elizabeth Frazer, "We Have Done It!" *Saturday Evening Post*, June 21, 1930.

57. "Adopted Mother by Herself," *Scribner's* 97 (January 1935): 56–57. The first of her adoptions took place around 1920.

58. "Our Greatest Experience," *Scribner's* 103 (January 1938): 61–62.

59. Ibid., 62.

60. Ibid.

61. Honoré Willsie, "The Adopted Mother," *Century*, September 1922, 657.

62. Ibid., 662.

63. Ibid., 660.

64. Sherri Maxine Broder, "Politics of the Family: Political Culture, Moral Reform, and Family Relations in Gilded Age Philadelphia" (Ph.D. diss., Brown University, 1988), 168. See also Sherri Broder, *Tramps, Unfit Mothers, and Neglected Children: Negotiating the Family in Nineteenth-Century Philadelphia* (Philadelphia: University of Pennsylvania Press, 2002).

65. See the case of "Dorothy" in Pearson, "Child Adoption in Indiana," 42–43.

66. George Walker, *The Traffic in Babies: An Analysis of the Conditions Discovered during an Investigation Conducted in the Year 1914* (Baltimore: Norman, Remington Co., 1918), 3.

67. Mary Boyle O'Reilly, "The Daughters of Herod: A Plea for Child-Saving Legislation in New Hampshire," *New England Magazine*, October 1910, 140.

68. Riis, *How the Other Half Lives*, 144.

69. Caroline Jean Acker, *Creating the American Junkie* (Baltimore: Johns Hopkins University Press, 2002); Andrea Friedman, *Prurient Interests: Gender, Democracy, and Obscenity*

in New York City, 1909–1945 (New York: Columbia University Press, 2000); Kathy Peiss, *Cheap Amusements: Working Women and Leisure in Turn-of-the-Century New York* (Philadelphia: Temple University Press, 1986).

70. Richard A. Meckel, *Save the Babies: American Public Health Reform and the Prevention of Infant Mortality, 1850–1929* (Baltimore: Johns Hopkins University Press, 1990); Alexandra Minna Stern and Howard Markel, eds., *Formative Years: Children's Health in the United States, 1880–2000* (Ann Arbor: University of Michigan Press, 2002), esp. pt. 1.

71. Quoted in Rael Jean Isaac, "Children Who Need Adoption: A Radical View," *Atlantic*, November 1963, 50.

72. USCB, *The Welfare of Infants of Illegitimate Birth in Baltimore: As Affected by a Maryland Law of 1916 Governing the Separation from Their Mothers of Children under 6 Months Old*, Bureau Publication No. 144, Part 1: "Mortality among Infants Born Out of Wedlock in 1915 and 1921," by Rena Rosenberg, and Part 2: "Effect of the Law on the Policies and Work of Social Agencies," by A. Mardorah Donahue (Washington, DC: Government Printing Office, 1925), 2.

73. Arthur Alden Guild, "Baby Farms in Chicago: An Investigation Made for the Juvenile Protective Association," 1917, 7–9, Child Welfare League of America Papers, University of Minnesota Library, Social Welfare History Archives (Call Number SW55), Minneapolis (hereafter cited as CWLA1), Box 44, Folder 4. See also "Some Facts about the Survey of Uncertified Homes Where Children Are Boarded Apart from Their Parents," April 6, 1917, USCB Papers, Box 67, Folder 7349.1, "Baby Farms."

74. Walker, *Traffic in Babies*, 27.

75. Riis, *How the Other Half Lives*, 142.

76. Theda Skocpol, *Protecting Soldiers and Mothers: The Political Origins of Social Policy in the United States* (Cambridge, MA: Harvard University Press, 1992), 9, table 1.

77. E. Wayne Carp and Anna-Leon Guerrero, "When in Doubt, Count: World War II as a Watershed in the History of Adoption," in E. Wayne Carp, ed., *Adoption in America: Historical Perspectives* (Ann Arbor: University of Michigan Press, 2002), 181–217.

78. Linda Gordon, *Pitied but Not Entitled: Single Mothers and the History of Welfare, 1890–1935* (New York: Free Press, 1994); Molly Ladd-Taylor, *Mother-Work: Women, Child Welfare, and the State, 1890–1930* (Urbana: University of Illinois Press, 1994); Skocpol, *Protecting Soldiers and Mothers*.

79. Memorandum for Miss Lathrop, July 22, 1918, regarding Sunshine Nursery, 4, USCB Papers, Box 60, Folder 7349.1, "Baby Farms."

80. Mary Boyle O'Reilly, "The Daughters of Herod II," *New England Magazine*, October 1910, 279.

81. Leopold Katscher to USCB, May 14, 1914, and "Infanticide and Children Traffic in America," USCB Papers, Box 60, Folder 7346, "Adoption."

82. Walker, *Traffic in Babies*, 36, 39.

83. Memorandum for Miss Lathrop, July 22, 1918, re Sunshine Nursery, 3.

84. O'Reilly, "Daughters of Herod II," 283.

85. Broder, "Politics of the Family," 203.

86. Leopold Katscher to USCB and "Infanticide and Children Traffic in America."

87. "Some Facts about the Survey of Uncertified Homes Where Children Are Boarded Apart from Their Parents."

88. Guild, "Baby Farms in Chicago." For a summary of the Chicago investigation, see also "Boarding and Sale Homes for Babies," *Survey* 39 (January 5, 1918): 403–7.

89. Broder, "Politics of the Family," 203. Twenty years later, maternity homes in Pennsylvania were still charging surrender fees of $50 to $250. See USCB, *A Study of Mater-*

nity Homes in Minnesota and Pennsylvania, Bureau Publication No. 167 (Washington, DC: Government Printing Office, 1926), 63.

90. Walker, *Traffic in Babies*, 98.
91. Ibid.
92. Helen Schaefer to Katharine Lenroot, August 26, 1933, USCB Papers, Box 543, Folder 7-3-1-1, "Traffic in Children."
93. "Giving Babies Away," *Social Service Review* 20 (1946): 566–67.
94. USCB to Louise Cothell, September 29, 1933, USCB Papers, Box 548, Folder 7-3-3-4, "Adoption 1934 & 33."
95. O'Reilly, "Daughters of Herod,"139–40, emphasis in original.
96. *Brooklyn Eagle* ad, March 1948, Shad Polier Papers, American Jewish Historical Society, New York (hereafter cited as SP), Box 8, Folder: "Child Adoption Committee—Correspondence since 1946."
97. USCB, *Child-Welfare Conditions and Resources in Seven Pennsylvania Counties*, Bureau Publication No. 176, ed. Neva R. Deardorff (Washington, DC: Government Printing Office, 1927), 261.
98. *Boston Globe* ad, quoted in Carrington Howard, "Adoption by Advertisement," *Survey* 35 (December 11, 1915).
99. O'Reilly, "Daughters of Herod," 138, emphasis in original. See also the condemnation of adoption ads in Riis, *How the Other Half Lives*, 145.
100. Howard, "Adoption by Advertisement."
101. Pearson, "Child Adoption in Indiana," 45.
102. "A Baby a Day Given Away," New York State Charities Aid Association, 1922, CWLA1, Box 44, Folder 3.
103. E. H. Bartlett to USCB, October 28, 1919, USCB Papers, Box 67, Folder 7-3-3-1, "Traffic in Children (Baby Farms)."
104. L. A. Halbert to Grace Abbott, March 7, 1930, USCB Papers, Box 407, Folder 7-4-3-1-1, "Maternity Homes."
105. *Willows Magazine*, March–April, 1930.
106. Ibid.
107. Ibid.
108. Ibid.
109. "A Baby a Day Given Away."
110. Hastings Hart, *Preventative Treatment of Neglected Children* (New York: Charities Publication Committee, Russell Sage Foundation, 1910), 229.
111. Ewing Galloway, "He Likes Babies," *Collier's*, June 20, 1914, 23.
112. Ibid., 23–24.
113. Ibid., 24.
114. Lawrence F. Abbott, "A Unique Memorial," *Outlook*, February 6, 1924, 214–15.
115. Charles Gilmore Kerley, "The Adoption of Children," *Outlook*, January 12, 1916, 107.
116. Peter Romanofsky, "The Early History of Adoption Practices" (Ph.D. diss., University of Missouri-Columbia, 1969), and Peter Romanofsky, "Professional versus Volunteers: A Case Study of Adoption Workers in the 1920's," *Journal of Voluntary Action Research* 2 (April 1973): 95–101. Susan Porter has shown that the female founders of nineteenth-century orphanages anticipated sentimental adoption. See Susan Porter, "A Good Home: Indenture and Adoption in Nineteenth-Century Orphanages," in Carp, *Adoption in America*, 27–50.
117. Spence Alumni Society, 1916 Annual Report, 2, CWLA2, Box 7, Folder: "Adoption 1925–1966."

118. Alice Chapin Adoption Nursery, 1928 Annual Report, CWLA2, Box 7, Folder: "Adoption 1925–1966."

119. Henry Dwight Chapin, "Babies Wanted," *Review of Reviews* 78 (August 1926): 183.

120. "Training Babies for the 'Golden Spoon,'" *Literary Digest*, April 8, 1916, 1020.

121. Laura Crozer, "Clearing House for Babies," *Illustrated World*, February 1916, 763–64.

122. Kerley, "Adoption of Children," 106.

123. Ibid.

124. Julie Berebitsky, *Like Our Very Own: Adoption and the Changing Culture of Motherhood, 1851–1950* (Lawrence: University Press of Kansas, 2000), chap. 2.

125. Louise Waterman Wise, "Mothers in Name," *Survey* 43 (March 20, 1920): 780.

126. "Training Babies for the 'Golden Spoon,'" 1020.

127. Ibid., 1022.

128. Rickie Solinger, *Wake Up Little Susie: Single Pregnancy and Race before Roe v. Wade* (New York: Routledge, 1992), esp. chap. 5; Barbara Melosh, *Strangers and Kin: The American Way of Adoption* (Cambridge, MA: Harvard University Press, 2002), chap. 3.

129. The evidence conflicts on whether it was her sister or a friend. The Cradle's Web site identifies the person as Walrath's sister; see http://www.cradle.org. Also see Neil M. Clark, "Filling Empty Arms," *American Magazine*, September 1930, 24–25; Eleanor Garrigue Gallagher, *The Adopted Child* (New York: Reynal and Hitchcock, 1936), 222–37; Milton MacKaye, "The Cradle," *Saturday Evening Post*, April 9, 1938, 12–13; Paula F. Pfeffer, "Homeless Children, Childless Homes," *Chicago History* 16 (Spring 1987): 51–65. There are many stories about replacing babies who were stillborn or died in early infancy, suggesting that the practice was not uncommon. See, for example, Barbara Stoddard Burks, "What Makes Jack a Bright Boy—Home or Heredity?" *North American Review* 228 (November 1929): 601.

130. Quoted in Clark, "Filling Empty Arms," 25. A similar comment can be found in A. S. Chapman, "Homes for Babies, Babies for Homes," *Hygeia* (December 1932): 1107.

131. MacKaye, "Cradle," 12.

132. Excerpt from *Chicago Sun Times*, June 17, 1948, USCB Papers, Box 157, Folder 7-3-3-4, "Adoptions 11/48."

133. Memo, "Report on the Cradle," April 27, 1945, USCB Papers, Box 158, Folder 7-3-3-4, "Adoptions, May 1948."

134. Clark, "Filling Empty Arms," 25.

135. Chapman, "Homes for Babies, Babies for Homes," 1106–9. The Cradle published *Aseptic Nursery Technique as Used at the Cradle* (1941) and made a 1947 film to promote the Dick technique.

136. Memo, "Report on the Cradle," 3.

137. Albert H. Stoneman, "Adoption of Illegitimate Children: The Peril of Ignorance," *CWLA Bulletin* 5 (February 15, 1926): 8.

138. MacKaye, "Cradle," 98.

139. Chapman, "Homes for Babies, Babies for Homes," 1108.

140. Memorandum from Miss Shepperson to Dr. Elliot, February 24, 1944, 1, USCB Papers, Box 169, Folder 7-3-3-4, "Adoption." See also the critical report in Katharine F. Lenroot to Eleanor Roosevelt, March 4, 1944, USCB Papers, Box 169, Folder 7-3-3-4, "Adoption."

141. Elizabeth Harral Carlton, "An Adoption Agency Looks at Fees," *CWLA Bulletin* 23 (February 1944): 4–5, 9; Eilene F. Crosier, *Fee Charging for Adoption Service* (New York: Child Welfare League of America, 1949); Sybil Foster, "Fees for Adoption Service," *Proceedings of the National Conference of Social Work* (New York: Columbia

University Press, 1948), 344–50; Minutes of the Free Synagogue Child Adoption Committee, October 26, 1949, 1–2, VWB, Box 155, Folder 1.

142. Memo, "Report on the Cradle," 5.

143. Quoted in Romanofsky, "Early History of Adoption Practices," 13, 19.

144. Michael Grossberg, *A Judgment for Solomon: The D'Hauteveille Case and Legal Experience in Antebellum America* (New York: Cambridge University Press, 1996); Mary Ann Mason, *From Father's Property to Children's Rights: The History of Child Custody in the United States* (New York: Columbia University Press, 1994).

145. Tinney, "Interpretation," 181.

146. John O'Grady, *Catholic Charities in the United States: History and Problems* (Washington, DC: National Conference of Catholic Charities, 1994); Susan S. Walton, *To Preserve the Faith: Catholic Charities in Boston, 1870–1930* (New York: Garland Publishing, 1993).

147. James Sullivan, "Institutional Care of Children," *Proceedings of the First National Conference of Catholic Charities* (Washington, DC: Catholic University, 1910), 285.

148. Theis, *How Foster Children Turn Out*, 133.

149. Ibid., 61.

150. Roberta Star Hirshson, in collaboration with Clifford W. Falby, *"There's Always Someone There . . .": The History of the New England Home for Little Wanderers* (Boston: New England Home for Little Wanderers, 1989).

151. New England Home for Little Wanderers superintendent Frederic Knight, quoted on dedicating the Study Home, in *Little Wanderers' Advocate* 51 (August 1915): 12. See also Florence Clothier, "The Role of the Study Home in Child Guidance," *Mental Hygiene* 28 (1944): 64–76.

152. Rose S. Hardwick, "The Stanford-Binet Intelligence Examination Re-Interpreted with Special Reference to Qualitative Differences" (Ph.D. diss., Radcliffe, 1924), 17.

153. Slingerland, *Child-Placing in Families*, 120, 142, 41, 48.

154. H. Ida Curry to Commonwealth Fund, November 26, 1919, microfilmed subset of CWLA Papers, University of Minnesota, Social Welfare History Archives, Minneapolis (hereafter cited as CWLAmicro), reel 1.

155. Draft letter to the Commonwealth Fund, August 1920, CWLAmicro, reel 1.

156. See Mary S. Doran and Bertha C. Reynolds, *The Selection of Foster Homes for Children: Principles and Methods Followed by the Boston Children's Aid Society with Illustrative Cases* (New York: New York School of Social Work, 1919) and Theis and Goodrich, *Child in the Foster Home.*

157. Theis and Goodrich, *Child in the Foster Home*, 76–77.

158. Hart, *Preventative Treatment of Neglected Children*, 236.

159. Brian Paul Gill, "The Jurisprudence of Good Parenting: The Selection of Adoptive Parents, 1894–1964" (Ph.D. diss., University of California, Berkeley, 1997), chap. 3; Joan H. Hollinger, "Introduction to Adoption Law and Practice" in *Adoption Law and Practice*, vol. 1, ed. Joan H. Hollinger (New York: Matthew Bender, 1994), 1-24–1-47.

160. Rollin Lynder Hartt to Helen L. Sumner, May 10, 1915, USCB Papers, Box 60, Folder 7346, "Adoption"; Howard, "Adoption by Advertisement."

161. Virginia P. Robinson, "Analysis of Processes in the Records of Family Case Working Agencies," *Family* 2 (July 1921): 101.

162. Jessie Taft, "Relation of Personality Study to Child Placing," *Proceedings of the National Conference of Social Work* (Chicago: University of Chicago Press, 1919), 64.

163. Jessie Taft, "Comment on 'the Underlying Philosophy of Social Case Work,'" *Proceedings of the National Conference of Social Work* (New York: Columbia University Press,

1941), 5, emphasis in original; Jessie Taft Papers, Butler Library, Rare Books and Manuscripts, Columbia University, New York (hereafter cited as JT), Box 2.

164. John H. Ehrenreich, *The Altruistic Imagination: A History of Social Work and Social Policy in the United States* (Ithaca, NY: Cornell University Press, 1985); Daniel Walkowitz, *Working with Class: Social Workers and the Politics of Middle-Class Identity* (Chapel Hill: University of North Carolina Press, 1999).

165. Abraham Flexner, "Is Social Work a Profession?" *Proceedings of the National Conference on Charities and Correction* (Boston: George H. Ellis, 1915), 588.

166. Katherine P. Hewins, "The Child in the Foster Home," *Survey* 47 (March 18, 1922): 963.

167. Kunzel, *Fallen Women, Problem Girls*, chap. 5; Walkowitz, *Working with Class*, chap. 3.

168. Honoré Willsie, "Are You Afraid to Adopt a Child?" *Delineator*, August 1919, 25.

169. Helen D. Sargent, "Is It Safe to Adopt a Child?" *Parents*, October 1935, 26.

CHAPTER TWO

1. James C. Scott, *Seeing Like a State: How Certain Schemes to Improve the Human Condition Have Failed* (New Haven, CT: Yale University Press, 1998).

2. Minimum standards for food, housing, and wages offer instructive parallels. See Dana Jean Simmons, "Minimal Frenchmen: Science and Standards of Living, 1840–1960" (Ph.D. diss., University of Chicago, 2004).

3. Douglas A. Thom, "Adoptions," *Journal of Pediatrics* 15 (August 1939): 258.

4. Ibid., 259.

5. Molly Ladd-Taylor, *Mother-Work: Women, Child Welfare, and the State, 1890–1930* (Urbana: University of Illinois Press, 1994); Kriste Lindenmeyer, *"A Right to Childhood": The U.S. Children's Bureau and Child Welfare, 1912–46* (Urbana: University of Illinois Press, 1997); Robyn Muncy, *Creating a Female Dominion in American Reform, 1890–1935* (New York: Oxford University Press, 1991); Alice Boardman Smuts, *Science in the Service of Children, 1893–1935* (New Haven, CT: Yale University Press, 2006), chaps. 5 and 13.

6. Elinor Nims, *The Illinois Adoption Law and Its Administration* (Chicago: University of Chicago Press, 1928), 75–76.

7. Edmond J. Butler, "Standards of Child Placing and Supervision," in USCB, *Standards of Child Welfare: A Report of the Children's Bureau Conferences, May and June 1919* (Washington, DC: Government Printing Office, 1919), 353.

8. Edmond J. Butler, "Standards of Child Placing and Supervision," *Proceedings of the Sixth National Conference of Catholic Charities* (Washington, DC: Catholic University, 1920), 92.

9. Rollin Lynder Hartt to Helen L. Sumner, May 10, 1915, and memo from E. O. Lundberg to Miss Lathrop, May 22, 1915, USCB Papers, Box 60, Folder 7346.

10. Mrs. L. A. Parkhurst to USCB, September 3, 1919, USCB Papers, Box 67, Folder 7-3-4-3, "Adoption."

11. Mr. and Mrs. Arthur Wilston to USCB, December 12, 1924, USCB Papers, Box 211, Folder 7-3-4-2-1, "Boarding Homes for Babies and Children," and 7-3-4-3, "Adoption."

12. Lundberg to Lathrop, May 22, 1915.

13. *Standards for Adoption Service* was revised in 1968, 1973, 1978, and 1988. The newest revision is Child Welfare League of America (hereafter cited as CWLA), *Standards of Excellence for Adoption Services*, rev. ed. (Washington, DC: CWLA, 2000).

14. Ellen C. Potter, "State Supervision of Placing-Out Agencies," in USCB, *Foster-Home Care for Dependent Children*, Bureau Publication No. 136 (Washington, DC: Government Printing Office, 1926), 181.

15. USCB, *Laws Relating to Interstate Placement of Dependent Children*, Bureau Publication No. 139 (Washington, DC: Government Printing Office, 1924), 6.

16. CWLA Constitution, adopted June 1921, CWLAmicro, reel 1.

17. Hartt to Sumner, May 10, 1915, and Lundberg to Lathrop, May 22, 1915.

18. Minutes, May 14, 1916, CWLAmicro reel 1; C. C. Carstens, "Report of the Director to the Executive Committee," February 28, 1921, CWLAmicro reel 1.

19. "Brief Summary of Plans for Providing Apprenticeship Training and Training in Practice for Children's Case Workers," n.d., but probably 1926, 1, CWLAmicro reel 1.

20. Ibid.

21. Minutes, May 14, 1916, 1; Carstens, "Report of the Director to the Executive Committee."

22. "Executive Director's Report, Submitted at Meeting of Board of Directors of the League, October 29, 30 and 31, 1928," 5, CWLAmicro reel 1.

23. Butler, "Standards of Child Placing and Supervision," in *Standards of Child Welfare*, 355–56.

24. Julie Berebitsky, *Like Our Very Own: Adoption and the Changing Culture of Motherhood, 1851–1950* (Lawrence: University Press of Kansas, 2000), chap. 4. On men adopting, see Sophie van Senden Theis and Constance Goodrich, *The Child in the Foster Home, Part 1: The Placement and Supervision of Children in Free Foster Homes, A Study Based on the Work of the Child-Placing Agency of the New York State Charities Aid Association* (New York: New York School of Social Work, 1921), 56–57. For a professional woman who adopted on her own, see "I Just Adopted a Baby," *Ladies' Home Journal*, August 1937, 14. For fictional representations of single adoptive mothers, see Claudia Nelson, *Little Strangers: Portrayals of Adoption and Foster Care in America, 1850–1929* (Bloomington: Indiana University Press, 2003), 124–32, and Claudia Nelson, "Nontraditional Adoption in Progressive-Era Orphan Narratives," *Mosaic* 34 (June 2001): 181–97.

25. Linda Gordon, *The Great Arizona Orphan Abduction* (Cambridge, MA: Harvard University Press, 1999); Ellen Herman, "The Difference Difference Makes: Justine Wise Polier and Religious Matching in Twentieth-Century Child Adoption," *Religion and American Culture* 10 (Winter 2000): 57–98.

26. "Resolutions on Standards Relating to 'Children in Need of Special Care,'" in *Minimum Standards for Child Welfare: Adopted by the Washington and Regional Conferences on Child Welfare, 1919*, Conference Series No. 2, Bureau Publication No. 62, ed. USCB (Washington, DC: Government Printing Office, 1919), 11–12.

27. Neva R. Deardorff, "Bound Out," *Survey* 56 (July 15, 1926): 459.

28. Ruth W. Lawton and J. Prentice Murphy, "A Study of Results of a Child-Placing Society," *Proceedings of the National Conference of Charities and Correction* (Boston: George H. Ellis, 1915), 164–74.

29. Chris Guthrie and Joanna L. Grossman, "Adoption in the Progressive Era: Preserving, Creating, and Re-Creating Families," *American Journal of Legal History* 43 (July 1999): 242.

30. In 1891, Michigan called on judges to "investigate" before entering final adoption decrees, but did not detail standards or authorize judges to have third parties conduct investigations. In contrast, the 1917 Minnesota law directed the state "to verify the allegations of the petition, to investigate the conditions and antecedents of the child for the purpose of ascertaining whether he is a proper subject for adoption, and to make appropriate inquiry to determine whether the proposed foster home is a suitable home for the child." The inquiry was to be conducted by the state welfare

department, a licensed children's agency, a court social worker, or another qualified investigator, with results to be submitted in writing with a specific recommendation. For more on the Minnesota statute, see USCB, *Adoption Laws in the United States: A Summary of the Development of Adoption Legislation and Significant Features of Adoption Statutes, with the Text of Selected Laws*, Bureau Publication No. 148, ed. Emelyn Foster Peck (Washington, DC: Government Printing Office, 1925), 27–28. The Minnesota law was also the first to require the sealing of all records in adoption proceedings. The 1921 Ohio statute can be found on pp. 32–34. As important as investigation itself was the deference Minnesota courts eventually showed to recommendations by the State Board of Control. Between 1918 and 1922, Minnesota courts still granted adoptions to 22 percent of petitioners who had been disapproved; by 1924 that number had decreased to 8 percent. See Elinor Nims, "Experiments in Adoption Legislation," *Social Service Review* 1 (1927): 242–43. Another study of all adoptions of illegitimate children in Minnesota during the decade after the law's passage confirmed the difference that regulation made. Only 33 adoptive homes disapproved by investigations had been approved by courts, and only 159 cases (out of 2,414 total) had escaped investigation. See Alice Leahy, "Some Characteristics of Adoptive Parents," *American Journal of Sociology* 38 (January 1933): 548–63. In Ohio, a study of 311 adoptions in 1922 and 1923 found that reports were frequently nonexistent despite the legal mandate to investigate. See Lawrence C. Cole, "A Study of Adoptions in Cuyahoga County," *Family* (1926): 260.

31. Agnes K. Hanna, "Some Problems of Adoption," *Child* 1 (December 1936): 4. See also Carl A. Heisterman, "A Summary of Legislation on Adoption," *Social Service Review* 9 (1935): 270–75.

32. Mazie Hough, "'To Conserve the Best of the Old': The Impact of Professionalization on Adoption in Maine," *Maine History* 40, no. 3 (Fall 2001): 213.

33. *Social Work Year Book*, vols. 1–10 (New York: Russell Sage Foundation, 1929–1949); *Social Work Year Book*, vols. 11–12 (New York: American Association of Social Workers, 1951–1954); *Social Work Year Book*, vols. 13–14 (New York: National Association of Social Workers, 1957–1960); *Encyclopedia of Social Work*, vols. 15–19 (New York: National Association of Social Workers, 1965–1995). The *Social Work Year Book* (renamed the *Encyclopedia of Social Work* in 1965) was a comprehensive reference guide to the varied activities of social work professionals. Entries on adoption, which began in 1929, mark the expansion of adoption regulation. In addition see entries on child welfare, dependent and neglected children, and family services. See also USCB, *Essentials of Adoption Law and Procedure*, Bureau Publication No. 331 (Washington, DC: Government Printing Office, 1949).

34. "Outline for Measuring the Work of Child-Placing Agencies," n.d., but probably 1928, CWLAmicro reel 1.

35. Dortha Diller to USCB, May 1926, and Katharine Lenroot to Dortha Diller, May 22, 1926, USCB Papers, Box 294, Folder 7-3-4-3, "Adoption."

36. Georgia G. Ralph, *Elements of Record Keeping for Child-Helping Organizations* (New York: Russell Sage Foundation, 1915), 4.

37. Elizabeth J. Samuels, "The Idea of Adoption: An Inquiry into the History of Adult Adoptee Access to Birth Records," *Rutgers Law Review* (Winter 2001): 367–436.

38. Dortha Diller to USCB, May 1926, and Katharine Lenroot to Dortha Diller, May 22, 1926; James E. Stuart to Mrs. Miller, January 30, 1926, HCC, Box 4, Folder: "Genealogical Data, Legal Adoption, 1876–1942"; Dorothy Swisshelm to Mr. Ralph A. Ricketts, February 19, 1940, HCC, Box 4, Folder: "Genealogical Data, Legal Adoption,

1876–1942." Wayne Carp has provided evidence that, in Washington, disclosure was not replaced by confidentiality until 1940. See E. Wayne Carp, *Family Matters: Secrecy and Disclosure in the History of Adoption* (Cambridge, MA: Harvard University Press, 1998).

39. Jennie Specter to Dear Madam, undated, and Superintendent to Jennie Specter, May 11, 1940, HCC, Box 3, Folder: "Letters from Children, 1871–1941."

40. E. L. Beckwith to Grace Abbott, June 21, 1931, USCB Papers, Box 406, Folder 7-3-3-2, "Foster Home Care, Placing Out."

41. Elizabeth Lee to Miss Katharine F. Lenroot, August 6, 1931, USCB Papers, Box 548, Folder 7-3-3-2, "Foster Home Care."

42. Ralph, *Elements of Record Keeping,* 5.

43. Minutes of the Meeting of the Executive Committee, January 21–23, 1926, 9–10, CWLAmicro reel 1.

44. Sophie van Senden Theis, *How Foster Children Turn Out,* Publication No. 165 (New York: New York State Charities Aid Association, 1924), esp. chap. 1.

45. C. C. Carstens, "Report of the Director" to the CWLA annual meeting, June 23, 1921, CWLAmicro reel 1.

46. "The First Child Welfare Case Record Exhibit," *CWLA Bulletin* (June 1941), CWLA2, Box 35, Folder: "Reprints 1939–53."

47. CWLA2, Box 18 contains most files included in the CWLA's Case Record Exhibit.

48. USCB, *The ABC of Foster-Family Care for Children,* Bureau Publication No. 216 (Washington, DC: Government Printing Office, 1933), 40.

49. Heisterman, "Summary of Legislation on Adoption," 289.

50. Leila Zenderland, *Measuring Minds: Henry Herbert Goddard and the Origins of American Intelligence Testing* (New York: Cambridge University Press, 1998), chap. 5.

51. Henry H. Goddard, "Wanted: A Child to Adopt," *Survey* 27 (October 14, 1911): 1003–9.

52. Henry Herbert Goddard, "The Elimination of Feeble-Mindedness," *Annals of the American Academy of Political and Social Science* 37 (March 1911): 262.

53. Henry H. Goddard, "The Basis for State Policy," *Survey* 27 (March 2, 1912): 1853.

54. Ibid., 1854.

55. Goddard, "Elimination of Feeble-Mindedness," 505–15.

56. W. H. Slingerland, *Child-Placing in Families: A Manual for Students and Social Workers* (New York: Russell Sage Foundation, 1919), 103. He also makes this point, in slightly different words, on p. 69.

57. A. H. Stoneman, "Safeguarding Adoptions, Legally and Socially," *Proceedings of the National Conference of Social Work* (Chicago: University of Chicago Press, 1924), 145.

58. Theis and Goodrich, *Child in the Foster Home, Part 1,* 104.

59. Theis, *How Foster Children Turn Out,* 12.

60. Paul Popenoe, *Practical Applications of Heredity* (Baltimore: Williams and Wilkins Co., 1930), 106.

61. Florence Clothier, "Some Aspects of the Problem of Adoption," *American Journal of Orthopsychiatry* 9 (July 1939): 604.

62. R. L. Jenkins, "On Adopting a Baby: Rules for Prospective Adoptive Parents," *Hygeia* (December 1935): 1068.

63. Catherine S. Amatruda and Joseph V. Baldwin, "Current Adoption Practices," *Journal of Pediatrics* 38 (February 1951): 208.

64. Cole, "Study of Adoptions in Cuyahoga County," 260.

65. Helen Lucile Pearson, "Child Adoption in Indiana" (M.A. thesis, Indiana University, 1925), 42.

66. "Adoption II," 1–2, Justine Wise Polier Papers, Harvard University, Radcliffe Institute for Advanced Study, Schlesinger Library, Cambridge, MA (hereafter cited as JWP), Box 18, Folder 207.

67. Cole, "Study of Adoptions in Cuyahoga County," 260; Nims, *Illinois Adoption Law*, 41–42.

68. Ruth F. Brenner, Annual Report to the Free Synagogue, 1944, from the Child Adoption Committee, January 28, 1945, 3, 5, VWB, Box 154, Folder 4.

69. Theis and Goodrich, *Child in the Foster Home, Part 1*, 17. The amateur founders of the first specialized adoption agencies also emphasized grooming. See Lawrence F. Abbott, "A Unique Memorial," *Outlook*, February 6, 1924, 215.

70. Minutes of the Free Synagogue Child Adoption Committee, March 29, 1944, VWB, Box 155, Folder 1.

71. Alexandra Minna Stern, "Beauty Is Not Always Better: Perfect Babies and the Tyranny of Paediatric Norms," *Patterns of Prejudice* 36 (2002): 68–78.

72. "Report on Mental Examination from September 1, 1915 to March 31, 1916," *Little Wanderers' Advocate* 52 (May 1916): 17. This piece has no byline, but it was probably written by Rose Hardwick.

73. All information and quotations in this paragraph are from Theis and Goodrich, *Child in the Foster Home, Part 1*, 30.

74. All information and quotations in this paragraph are from ibid., 27–28.

75. Ralph, *Elements of Record Keeping*, 19.

76. Ibid., chap. 4.

77. USCB, *ABC of Foster-Family Care for Children*, 4.

78. See Mary S. Doran and Bertha C. Reynolds, *The Selection of Foster Homes for Children: Principles and Methods Followed by the Boston Children's Aid Society with Illustrative Cases* (New York: New York School of Social Work, 1919), 11.

79. Theis and Goodrich, *Child in the Foster Home, Part 1*, 30.

80. Pearson, "Child Adoption in Indiana," 9.

81. Doran and Reynolds, *Selection of Foster Homes for Children*, 18–23.

82. Ibid., 28.

83. Theis and Goodrich, *Child in the Foster Home, Part 1*, 33.

84. Ibid., 59.

85. All information and quotations in this and the next paragraph are from ibid., 49–54.

86. Butler, "Standards of Child Placing and Supervision," in *Standards of Child Welfare*, 357.

87. Albert H. Stoneman, "Report of the Committee on Standards of Membership, October 29, 1926," CWLAmicro reel 1. Stoneman notes that supervision should be "bona fide and efficient" even in cases of very lengthy foster care. "It is dangerous to assume that with the passing years there will not occur changes in the circumstances of the foster family which cannot be foreseen or forestalled. Since the agency continues as legal guardian of the child, it has a moral as well as legal obligation to know and keep in record his actual situation and condition." In contrast, Edmond Butler described cases so like adoption, except for their legal status, that it was desirable for agencies to cease supervision so that visits would not reveal the children's status to them. Butler, "Standards of Child Placing and Supervision" (paper), 97.

88. Theis, *How Foster Children Turn Out*, 136, table 36.

89. Theis and Goodrich, *Child in the Foster Home, Part 1*, 61–63.

90. "A Study of Board Rates," Special Bulletin, January 1942, 3, CWLAmicro reel 3. The difficulties of securing foster care during the war years led some professionals to ac-

cept "the validity of the money motive." See Henrietta L. Gordon, "Recent Developments in Home Finding," *CWLA Bulletin* 21 (September 1942): 11.

91. This assumption plagued foster care and hindered subsidized adoptions, which used economic incentives to move children toward permanence. New York was the first to experiment with subsidies in 1968. Other states followed quickly, but no federal law existed until the Adoption Assistance and Child Welfare Act of 1980. See Gloria Waldinger, "Subsidized Adoption: How Paid Parents View It," *Social Work* (November 1982): 516–21.

92. "Study of Board Rates," 3; Waldinger, "Subsidized Adoption," 516; Weltha M. Kelley, "The Boarding Parents Apply to Adopt—A Dilemma," *CWLA Bulletin* 26 (December 1947): 2.

93. Beth Roberts, "Foster Home," *Survey* 61 (January 1, 1929): 421–22.

94. "Adoption Practices, Procedures and Problems, Report on Workshop Material and Proceedings of the Adoption Conference Held May 19–21, 1948 in New York City," compiled by Henrietta L. Gordon, 29–31, CWLAmicro reel 3.

95. Theis and Goodrich, *Child in the Foster Home, Part 1*, 62.

96. Kelley, "Boarding Parents Apply to Adopt," 2.

97. Theis and Goodrich, *Child in the Foster Home, Part 1*, 79.

98. Sophie van Senden Theis, "Social Aspects of Child Adoption" (paper presented at the Eastern Regional Conference of the CWLA, New York, May 1, 1937), 8. Typescript from CWLA in possession of author.

99. Frances Lockridge and Sophie van Senden Theis, *Adopting a Child* (New York: Greenberg, 1947), 114; Carl Doss and Helen Doss, *If You Adopt a Child: A Complete Handbook for Childless Couples* (New York: Henry Holt, 1957), 138, emphasis in original.

100. USCB, *When You Adopt a Child*, rev. ed. (Washington, DC: Government Printing Office, 1958), 19. "On approval" appeared in quotation marks, indicating disapproval of comparing children to merchandise while using a familiar commercial practice to clarify the logic of probation.

101. Louise Raymond, *Adoption . . . and After* (New York: Harper and Brothers, 1955), 59.

102. Theis and Goodrich, *Child in the Foster Home, Part 1*, 99.

103. Lee M. Brooks and Evelyn C. Brooks, *Adventuring in Adoption* (Chapel Hill: University of North Carolina Press, 1939), 40, 45.

104. Theis and Goodrich, *Child in the Foster Home, Part 1*, 100.

105. Surveys in New York and California in the 1920s showed that half to two-thirds of children adopted before age five were kept ignorant of their status. See Paul Popenoe, "The Foster Child," *Scientific Monthly*, September 1929, 244. A follow-up study of Minnesota adoptions between 1918 and 1928 found that 50 percent of children studied (all between the ages of five and fourteen) had been told. Because fear that the child's adoption would be revealed was a common reason that parents refused to participate in the study, it is likely that an accurate figure would be higher. See Alice M. Leahy, "Nature-Nurture and Intelligence," *Genetic Psychology Monographs* 17 (August 1935): 264. The first major outcome study, *How Foster Children Turn Out*, found that 34 percent of adoptees had never been told (Theis, *How Foster Children Turn Out*, 124, 231, table 60). The few studies that found high rates of "telling" before 1945 found that parents were not likely to provide children with specific details about their backgrounds. See Georgina D. Hotchkiss, "Adoptive Parents Talk about Their Children: A Follow-Up Study of Twenty-Four Children Adopted through a Child Placing Agency" (M.S. thesis, Simmons College, 1950), 42–48.

106. Theis and Goodrich, *Child in the Foster Home, Part 1*, 91.

107. Lawton and Murphy, "Study of Results of a Child-Placing Society," 170.

108. Children's Home Society of Washington, *A Century of Turning Hope into Reality: A 100-Year Retrospect of Children's Home Society in Washington State* (Seattle: Children's Home Society of Washington, 1996), 19; Patricia S. Hart, "A Nation's Need for Adoption and Competing Realities: The Washington Children's Home Society, 1895–1915," in E. Wayne Carp, ed., *Adoption in America: Historical Perspectives* (Ann Arbor: University of Michigan Press, 2002), 151.

109. Iris Ruggles Macrae, "An Analysis of Adoption Practices at the New England Home for Little Wanderers" (M.S. thesis, Simmons College, School of Social Work, 1937), 82; Florence Clothier, "The Problem of Frequent Replacement of the Young Dependent Child," *Mental Hygiene* 21 (October 1937): 553.

110. Betty Hannigan, "Those Who Came Back," *Catholic Charities Review* 40 (April 1956): 8–12.

111. Theis and Goodrich, *Child in the Foster Home, Part 1,* 116.

112. All case details in this and the following two paragraphs are from ibid., 129–46.

113. Neva R. Deardorff, "'The Welfare of the Said Child . . .'" *Survey Midmonthly* 53 (January 15, 1925): 457.

114. Neva R. Deardorff, "Scrutinizing Adoption," *Catholic Charities Review* 10 (January 1926): 6–7; Deardorff, "'Welfare of the Said Child,'" 458.

115. Deardorff, "Scrutinizing Adoption," 7.

116. Deardorff, "'Welfare of the Said Child,'" 457, 459.

117. Ibid., 457.

118. Margaret Bourne, "A Pioneer Job in Court Adoptions," *CWLA Bulletin* (May 1940): 3; Deardorff, "Scrutinizing Adoption," 4.

119. Cole, "Study of Adoptions in Cuyahoga County," 259–64.

120. Nims, *Illinois Adoption Law,* 75.

121. Pearson, "Child Adoption in Indiana," 36.

122. Ida R. Parker, *Fit and Proper? A Study of Legal Adoption in Massachusetts* (Boston: Church Home Society, 1927), 26. The USCB conducted a field study in Massachusetts in 1914 and reached the same conclusion. See USCB, *Illegitimacy as a Child-Welfare Problem, Part 2: A Study of Original Records in the City of Boston and in the State of Massachusetts,* by Emma O. Lundberg and Katharine F. Lenroot, Dependent, Defective, and Delinquent Classes Series No. 10, Bureau Publication No. 75 (Washington, DC: Government Printing Office, 1921), chap. 3.

123. Parker, *Fit and Proper,* 69.

124. Ibid.

125. Mrs. J. S. Milliken to USCB, July 16, 1927, USCB Papers, Box 292, Folder 7-3-2, "Causes of Neglect and Dependency."

126. In the 1930s the USCB was still pushing volunteer and untrained child placers toward professional standards. See USCB, *ABC of Foster-Family Care for Children.*

127. Nims, *Illinois Adoption Law,* 97.

CHAPTER THREE

1. David M. Schneider, *American Kinship: A Cultural Account,* 2nd ed. (Chicago: University of Chicago Press, 1980). See also Joan Heifetz Hollinger, "Authenticity and Identity in Contemporary Adoptive Families," *Journal of Gender Specific Medicine* 3 (November–December 2000): 23–26.

2. The literature is vast. For example, see Robert N. Bellah et al., *Habits of the Heart: Individualism and Commitment in American Life* (New York: Harper and Row, 1985);

Francesca Cancian, *Love in America: Gender and Self-Development* (New York: Cambridge University Press, 1987); Christopher Lasch, *The Minimal Self: Psychic Survival in Troubled Times* (New York: W. W. Norton, 1984); Robert Jay Lifton, *The Protean Self: Human Resilience in an Age of Fragmentation* (New York: Basic Books, 1993); James Miller, *"Democracy Is in the Streets": From Port Huron to the Siege of Chicago* (New York: Simon and Schuster, 1987); Miles Orvell, *The Real Thing: Imitation and Authenticity in American Culture, 1880–1940* (Chapel Hill: University of North Carolina Press, 1989); Doug Rossinow, *The Politics of Authenticity: Liberalism, Christianity, and the New Left in America* (New York: Columbia University Press, 1998); Warren I. Susman, "'Personality' and the Making of Twentieth-Century Culture," in *Culture as History: The Transformation of American Society in the Twentieth Century* (New York: Pantheon, 1984), 271–85; Charles Taylor, *The Ethics of Authenticity* (Cambridge, MA: Harvard University Press, 1991); Robert Wuthnow, *Sharing the Journey: Support Groups and America's New Quest for Community* (New York: Free Press, 1994).

3. "Quotable Quotes" from adopting parents, Dorothy Hutchinson Papers, Butler Library, Rare Books and Manuscripts, Columbia University, New York (hereafter cited as DH).

4. Bernice F. Seltz, "Interpreting Good Adoption Practice," *Child Welfare* (October 1950): 16–17.

5. Peter N. Stearns, *Battleground of Desire: The Struggle for Self-Control in Modern America* (New York: New York University Press, 1999).

6. Alice Boardman Smuts, *Science in the Service of Children, 1893–1935* (New Haven, CT: Yale University Press, 2006).

7. Julia Grant, *Raising Baby by the Book: The Education of American Mothers* (New Haven, CT: Yale University Press, 1998); Kathleen W. Jones, *Taming the Troublesome Child: American Families, Child Guidance, and the Limits of Psychiatric Authority* (Cambridge, MA: Harvard University Press, 1999).

8. David M. Levy, "Clinical Evidence of Changing Attitudes," *Child Study* 6 (October 1928): 9.

9. Estelle B. Freedman, *Maternal Justice: Miriam Van Waters and the Female Reform Tradition, 1887–1974* (Chicago: University of Chicago Press, 1996); Molly Ladd-Taylor, *Mother-Work: Women, Child Welfare, and the State, 1890–1930* (Urbana: University of Illinois Press, 1994); Sonia Michel, *Children's Interests, Mothers' Rights: The Shaping of America's Child Care Policy* (New Haven, CT: Yale University Press, 1999); Robyn Muncy, *Creating a Female Dominion in American Reform, 1890–1935* (New York: Oxford University Press, 1991); Theda Skocpol, *Protecting Soldiers and Mothers: The Political Origins of Social Policy in the United States* (Cambridge, MA: Harvard University Press, 1992).

10. Ethel Dummer to Jessie Taft, December 4, 1921, Ethel Sturges Dummer Papers, Harvard University, Radcliffe Institute for Advanced Study, Schlesinger Library, Cambridge, MA (hereafter cited as ESD), Box 36, Folder 776.

11. Hamilton Cravens, *Before Head Start: The Iowa Station and America's Children* (Chapel Hill: University of North Carolina Press, 1993).

12. Dennis Raymond Bryson, *Socializing the Young: The Role of Foundations, 1923–1941* (Westport, CT: Bergin and Garvey, 2002).

13. Lawrence K. Frank, "Childhood and Youth," in *Recent Social Trends in the United States*, ed. President's Research Committee on Social Trends (New York: McGraw-Hill, 1933), 798.

14. Ibid., 800.

15. Viola W. Bernard, "Marion E. Kenworthy, M.D.: Trailblazer for Psychiatric Social Work," in *Women Physicians in Leadership Roles*, ed. Leah J. Dickstein and Carol C. Nadelson (Washington, DC: American Psychiatric Press, 1986), 79–85; "Marion Kenworthy, A Psychiatrist, Dies," *New York Times*, June 27, 1980, VWB, Box 59, Folder 7. Viola Bernard, Justine Wise Polier, and David Levy were Kenworthy's close colleagues; Charlotte Towle was her student and lifelong friend; Jessie Taft explicitly acknowledged Kenworthy's influence. See Minutes of the Free Synagogue Child Adoption Committee, December 10, 1940, VWB, Box 155, Folder 1.

16. Dorothy Hutchinson, "Child Welfare, Yesterday, Today, Tomorrow," in *Cherish the Child: Dilemmas of Placement*, ed. Maude von P. Kemp (Metuchen, NJ: Scarecrow Press, 1972), 24.

17. Leslie B. Alexander, "Social Work's Freudian Deluge: Myth or Reality?" *Social Service Review* 46 (December 1972): 517–38; John H. Ehrenreich, *The Altruistic Imagination: A History of Social Work and Social Policy in the United States* (Ithaca, NY: Cornell University Press, 1985), chap. 2; Martha Heineman Field, "Social Casework Practice during the 'Psychiatric Deluge,'" *Social Service Review* 54 (December 1980): 482–507; Elizabeth Lunbeck, *The Psychiatric Persuasion: Knowledge, Gender, and Power in Modern America* (Princeton, NJ: Princeton University Press, 1994), 35–42.

18. Viola W. Bernard, "Application of Psychoanalytic Concepts to Adoption Agency Practice," in *Readings in Adoption*, ed. I. Evelyn Smith (New York: Philosophical Library, 1963), 432.

19. Virginia P. Robinson, ed., *Jessie Taft: Therapist and Social Work Educator, A Professional Biography* (Philadelphia: University of Pennsylvania Press, 1962), 36.

20. Jessie Taft, "The Woman Movement from the Point of View of Social Consciousness" (Ph.D. diss., University of Chicago, 1916).

21. Robinson, *Jessie Taft*, 37.

22. Ibid., 30.

23. Ibid., 33.

24. Ethel Dummer to Jessie Taft and Virginia Robinson, February 18, 1925, ESD, Box 36, Folder 776. Other child welfare professionals who adopted included penologist Miriam van Waters and attorney Mabel Walker Willebrandt. Frances Ilg, who wrote the syndicated column "Parents Ask" and directed the Gesell Institute in the 1950s, adopted a child in Sweden. Gertrude Battles Lane, editor of *Woman's Home Companion*, adopted a World War I orphan. Adelaide Hasse, a well-known New York librarian, adopted two boys. Writer Edith Hamilton adopted the nephew of her partner, Doris Reid. Educator Elisabeth Irwin adopted at least one child to raise with Katherine Anthony, her partner. Health reformers Harriet Johnson and Harriet Forbes raised an adopted daughter together. On the marriage and family patterns for highly educated women during this era, see Nancy F. Cott, *The Grounding of Modern Feminism* (New Haven, CT: Yale University Press, 1987), 147–48, Linda Gordon, "Black and White Visions of Welfare: Women's Welfare Activism, 1890–1945," *Journal of American History* 78 (September 1991): 574–75, and Carroll Smith-Rosenberg, *Disorderly Conduct: Visions of Gender in Victorian America* (New York: Oxford University Press, 1985), 253. On "Boston marriages," see John D'Emilio and Estelle B. Freedman, *Intimate Matters: A History of Sexuality in America* (New York: Harper and Row, 1988), 190–94.

25. David R. Contosta, *Philadelphia's Progressive Orphanage: The Carson Valley School* (University Park: Pennsylvania State University Press, 1997), 75–78. Other members of the Flourtown community also adopted children: Elizabeth Roemer adopted a boy

named Merle, and Elsa Ueland and Catherine ("Kate") Tucker adopted Carl (who died in the influenza epidemic of 1918), Robert, and Tucker's niece by marriage, Yvonne.

26. Jessie Taft to Ethel Dummer, April 3, 1923, ESD, Box 36, Folder 776.
27. Roy J. deCarvalho, "Otto Rank, The Rankian Circle in Philadelphia, and the Origins of Carl Rogers' Person-Center Psychotherapy," *History of Psychology* 2 (May 1999): 132–48.
28. JT, Box 2, Folders: "The Organization of the Self," "Theories of Personality Development," and "Growth, Learning, and Change in the Development of the Individual."
29. Jessie Taft, "Comment on the Death of Otto Rank," 1–2, JT, Box 2, Folder: "Comment on the Death of Otto Rank."
30. "Problems of Helper," February 18, 1947, JT, Box 2, Folder: "Case Material on Supervision, 1946–47."
31. Jessie Taft, "A Philosophy of Helping in Social Work," talk given to school counselors, January 8, 1947, JT, Box 2, Folder: "A Philosophy of Helping in Social Work"; Carl L. Rogers, *Client-Centered Therapy: Its Current Practice, Implications, and Theory* (Boston: Houghton Mifflin, 1951), 10. For Rogers's background in child guidance, see Carl R. Rogers, "A Good Foster Home: Its Achievements and Limitations," *Mental Hygiene* 17 (January 1933): 21–40.
32. The exceptions are Mary Jo Deegan, "The Clinical Sociology of Jessie Taft," *Clinical Sociology Review* 4 (1986): 30–45; James Livingston, "The Strange Career of the 'Social Self,'" *Radical History Review* 76 (Winter 2000): 53–79; Rosalind Rosenberg, *Beyond Separate Spheres: Intellectual Roots of Modern Feminism* (New Haven, CT: Yale University Press, 1982), chap 5; Charlene Haddock Seigfried, "Introduction to Jessie Taft, 'The Woman Movement from the Point of View of Social Consciousness,'" *Hypatia* 8 (Spring 1993): 215–18. A complete bibliography of Taft's writings can be found in Robinson, *Jessie Taft*, 371–84.
33. Taft did not merit a single mention in the most celebrated recent book on pragmatism: Louis Menand, *The Metaphysical Club: A Story of Ideas in America* (New York: Farrar, Straus and Giroux, 2002).
34. Jessie Taft, "Relation of Personality Study to Child Placing," in *Proceedings of the National Conference of Social Work* (Chicago: University of Chicago Press, 1919), 64, emphasis in original.
35. Ibid., 64.
36. Susman, "'Personality' and the Making of Twentieth-Century Culture," 271–85.
37. Taft, "Relation of Personality Study to Child Placing," 67.
38. Ibid., 67.
39. Jessie Taft, "The Need for Psychological Interpretation in the Placement of Dependent Children," *CWLA Bulletin* 6 (April 1922): 14.
40. Jessie Taft, "The Home Has Lost Its Halo," *Survey Graphic* (December 1927): 287.
41. Jessie Taft, "The Spirit of Social Work," *Family* 9 (June 1928): 105.
42. Ibid., 106.
43. Jessie Taft, "The Adjustment of Our Emotional Lives," *Hygeia* (December 1926): 673.
44. Jessie Taft, "Bringing Up Children," *Iowa Children's Home Herald* 28 (October–December 1923): 5; JT, Box 3, Folder: "Printed—(1)."
45. Taft, "Spirit of Social Work," 105.
46. Jessie Taft, "A Changing Psychology in Child Welfare," *Annals of the American Academy of Political and Social Science* 151 (September 1930): 123.

47. Jessie Taft, "Qualifications of the Psychiatric Social Worker," *Mental Hygiene* 3 (July 1919): 428.
48. Ibid., 429–30.
49. Jessie Taft, "The Function of a Mental Hygienist in a Children's Agency," n.d., but probably 1927, 5, JT, Box 2, Folder: "The Function of a Mental Hygienist in a Children's Agency."
50. Elizabeth E. Bissell, "The Effect of Foster Home Placement on the Personality of Children," *Family* 9 (July 1928): 161.
51. Ibid., 162.
52. Taft, "Home Has Lost Its Halo," 287.
53. Jessie Taft, "Concerning Adopted Children," *Child Study* 6 (January 1929): 87.
54. Florence Clothier, "The Psychology of the Adopted Child," *Mental Hygiene* 27 (April 1943): 222.
55. Ibid., 223.
56. Dorothy Hutchinson, "Re-examination of Some Aspects of Case Work Practice in Adoption," *Child Welfare* 25 (November 1946): 4.
57. Dorothy Hutchinson, *In Quest of Foster Parents: A Point of View on Homefinding* (New York: Columbia University Press, 1943), 91.
58. Ibid., 52.
59. Suggested Psychiatric Consultation and In-Service Training Program for the Professional Staff of the F.S.C.A.C., for 1949–50, March 18, 1949, VWB, Box 157, Folder 3.
60. Amey Eaton Watson, "The Illegitimate Family," *Annals of the American Academy of Political and Social Science* 77 (May 1918): 103.
61. Kenworthy, "Mental Hygiene Aspects of Illegitimacy,"503.
62. Henry C. Schumacher, "The Unmarried Mother: A Socio-Psychiatric Viewpoint," *Mental Hygiene* 11 (October 1927): 775.
63. Charlotte Lowe, "Intelligence and Social Background of the Unmarried Mother," *Mental Hygiene* 11 (October 1927): 783–94; W. E. McClure and Bronett Goldberg, "Intelligence of Unmarried Mothers," *Psychological Clinic* 18 (May–June 1929): 119–27; W. E. McClure, "Intelligence of Unmarried Mothers, II," *Psychological Clinic* 20 (October 1931): 154–57.
64. Alice M. Leahy, "A Study of Certain Selective Factors Influencing Prediction of the Mental Status of Adopted Children or Adopted Children in Nature-Nurture Research," *Journal of Genetic Psychology* 41 (1932): 294–327. For mental testing of birth mothers, see the 1946 case of M, "Report of Psychological Examination," DH, Box 1, Folder 7. (All names in case records located in the Dorothy Hutchinson Papers have been abbreviated. Case materials from other archival sources are treated differently.)
65. Mabel Higgins Mattingly, "The Unmarried Mother and Her Child: A Fact Finding Study of Fifty-Three Cases of Unmarried Mothers Who Kept Their Children" (M.S. thesis, Western Reserve University, June 1928), 72.
66. Ibid., 72–73.
67. Michael T. Khlentzos and Mary A. Pagliaro, "Observations from Psychotherapy with Unwed Mothers," *American Journal of Orthopsychiatry* 35 (July 1965): 780.
68. Mary S. Brisley, "Parent-Child Relationships in Unmarried Parenthood," *Proceedings of the National Conference of Social Work* (New York: Columbia University Press, 1939), 439.
69. Florence Clothier, "The Unmarried Mother of School Age as Seen by a Psychiatrist," *Mental Hygiene* 39 (October 1955): 640.

70. Florence Clothier, "Problems of Illegitimacy as They Concern the Worker in the Field of Adoption," *Mental Hygiene* 25 (October 1941): 579.
71. Memo, Viola Bernard to Florence Brown, July 12, 1961, 2–3, VWB, Box 157, Folder 8.
72. Hutchinson, "Re-examination of Some Aspects," 6.
73. Some of the cases in Hutchinson's files included sections titled "Psychosocial Diagnosis." For example, see the case of Miss L, DH, Box 2, Folder 24. In others, diagnostic information was incorporated into the narrative describing contacts with birth mothers and adopters.
74. Case of S, 5, DH, Box 1, Folder 3.
75. Ibid., 6.
76. Ibid., 7.
77. Case of G, 5, DH, Box 1, Folder 3.
78. Ibid., 10.
79. Case of M, 35, DH, Box 1, Folder 7.
80. Ibid., 31.
81. Ibid., n.p., emphasis in original.
82. Dorothy Hutchinson to Ruth Koehler, April 30, 1947, Case of M.
83. Dorothy Hutchinson, "Report for Joint Planning Services," April 1953, 10, DH, Box 4, Folder: "Home Finding."
84. Ibid., 11.
85. Case of Miss L, 7.
86. Hutchinson, "Report for Joint Planning Services," 1, 2, 3, 5.
87. "Adoption Practices," talk given at Annual Meeting, Episcopal Service for Youth, February 13, 1947, 4, emphasis in original, DH, Box 1, Folder 7.
88. For example, see Joan Younger, "The Unwed Mother," *Ladies' Homes Journal*, June 1947, 44.
89. Leontine Young, *Out of Wedlock: A Study of the Problems of the Unmarried Mother and Her Child* (New York: McGraw-Hill, 1954). See also Leontine R. Young, "Personality Patterns in Unmarried Mothers" and "The Unmarried Mother's Decision about Her Baby," in *Understanding the Psychology of the Unmarried Mother* (New York: Family Service Association of America, 1945–1947), 7–13, 13–20.
90. Memo on difficulties of home finding from New York State Department of Social Welfare, 1954, 3, DH, Box 4, Folder: "Home Finding."
91. Dorothy Hutchinson, "The Request for Placement Has Meaning," *Family* 25 (June 1944): 128.
92. Dorothy Hutchinson, "Competence and Conscience in Homefinding," *Journal of Social Casework* 36 (1955): 368.
93. Dorothy Hutchinson, "The Placement Worker and the Child's Own Parents" in *Cherish the Child* (see note 16), 62.
94. Hutchinson, *In Quest of Foster Parents*, 4.
95. Dorothy Hutchinson, "Teaching Notes—Foster Home Finding," in *Cherish the Child* (see note 16), 79.
96. Hutchinson, *In Quest of Foster Parents*, 135.
97. Ibid., 133. See also Dorothy Hutchinson, "What It Means to Be a Foster Parent," in *Cherish the Child* (see note 16), 87–93.
98. Hutchinson, "Child Welfare, Yesterday, Today, Tomorrow," 18.
99. Memo on the difficulties of home finding from New York State Department of Social Welfare, 1. See also Minutes of the Free Synagogue Child Adoption Committee, March 23, 1949, 2, VWB, Box 151, Folder 1.

100. Mattingly, "Unmarried Mother and Her Child, 73.
101. Florence Clothier, "The Social Worker in the Field of Adoption," *Mental Hygiene* 24 (April 1940): 212.
102. Eleanor W. Gordon, "The Child Welfare Worker and Adoption" (State of New Jersey, Department of Institutions and Agencies, Board of Child Welfare, Trenton, 1958), 10.
103. Clothier, "Social Worker in the Field of Adoption," 215.
104. Dorothy Hutchinson, "Homefinding Trends," in *Social Work in Adoption: Collected Papers*, ed. Robert Tod (London: Longman, 1971), 32.
105. Hutchinson, "Request for Placement Has Meaning," 131.
106. Sarabelle McCleery, "The Adoption Worker's Role and His Personality in the Professional Adoption Process," *Child Welfare* 31 (October 1952): 3.
107. "Summary, Orientation Course in Social Casework for Volunteer Social Work Aides," November 30, 1954, 1, emphasis in original, DH, Box 4, Folder: "Home Finding."
108. Ibid., emphasis in original.
109. Ibid., 2–3, emphasis in original.
110. Viola W. Bernard, "Psychiatric Consultation in the Social Agency," *Child Welfare* 33 (November 1954): 3.
111. American Association for the History of Medicine, Sigerist Circle, "Viola W. Bernard, Pioneer in Social Psychiatry, Dead at 91," March 25, 1998, circulated on the Cheiron ListServ, March 30, 1998, document in possession of author.
112. Justine Wise Polier to Viola Bernard, March 15, 1961, VWB, Box 157, Folder 8.
113. Jessie Taft, ed., *The Role of the Baby in the Placement Process* (Philadelphia: Pennsylvania School of Social Work, 1946). See also Leontine Young, "Placement from the Child's Viewpoint," *Social Casework* 31 (1950): 250–55.
114. Jessie Taft, "Foster Home Care for Children," *Annals of the American Academy of Political and Social Science* 212 (November 1940): 181.
115. Taft, *Role of the Baby in the Placement Process*, 104.
116. Ibid., 105.
117. J. Kasanin and Sieglinde Handschin, "Psychodynamic Factors in Illegitimacy," *American Journal of Orthopsychiatry* 11 (January 1941): 83.
118. Lilian Ripple, "Social Work Studies of Unmarried Parenthood as Affected by Contemporary Treatment Formulations: 1920–1940" (Ph.D. diss., University of Chicago, 1953), 109.
119. Maud Morlock, "Social Treatment of the Unmarried Mother Separated from Her Child," *Hospital Social Service* 6 (August 1922): 68–75.
120. Maud Morlock, "Foster-Home Care for Unmarried Mothers," *Child* 3 (September 1938): 55.
121. Maud Morlock, "Better Homes," address at the Fifty-sixth Florence Crittenton Conference, Boston, May 23, 1939, 7, CWLA1, Box 49, Folder 1.
122. Ibid., 5.
123. Young, *Out of Wedlock*, chap. 8.
124. Maud Morlock, "The Fathers of Children Born out of Wedlock," 1939, 3, CWLA1, Box 47, Folder 9.
125. Kathleen d'Olier, "Case Work with the Unmarried Father," *Proceedings of the Twenty-third National Conference of Catholic Charities* (Washington, DC: Catholic University, 1937), 127.
126. Norman Reider, "The Unmarried Father," *American Journal of Orthopsychiatry* 18 (April 1948): 230–37.
127. Draza Kline, *Casework with Foster Parents* (New York: CWLA, 1956), 6.

128. CWLA, *Standards for Adoption Service* (New York: CWLA, 1958), 32.

129. Ibid.

130. Helen Harris Perlman, "Charlotte Towle: An Appreciation," in *Helping: Charlotte Towle on Social Work and Social Casework*, ed. Helen Harris Perlman (Chicago: University of Chicago Press, 1969), 10.

131. At issue was Towle's book *Common Human Needs*. She used the term "socialized state," which offended the conservative American Medical Association, whose leaders equated it with "socialism" and charged Towle with subversion. The federal government, which had sponsored the book as an aid to social workers in public agencies, destroyed all remaining copies when the controversy erupted. Towle's incensed colleagues at the American Association of Social Workers reprinted the book, which was translated into ten languages and remains in print to this day.

132. Perlman, "Charlotte Towle," 20.

133. Ibid., 19.

134. Charlotte Towle, "The Evaluation of Homes in Preparation for Child Placement," *Mental Hygiene* 11 (July 1927): 461.

135. Ibid.

136. Charlotte Towle, "How to Know a Foster Family, Part 1," *CWLA Bulletin* 7 (April 1928): 2.

137. Towle, "Evaluation of Homes," 479, emphasis in original.

138. Charlotte Towle, "The Evaluation and Management of Marital Situation in Foster Homes," *American Journal of Orthopsychiatry* 1 (April 1931): 271–83.

139. Charlotte Towle, "The Psychiatric Approach in Home Finding," *Social Worker* 8 (June 1931): 11.

140. Charlotte Towle, "Evaluating Motives of Foster Parents," in *Helping* (see note 130), 155.

141. Towle, "Psychiatric Approach in Home Finding," 13.

142. Towle, "Evaluation of Homes," 467.

143. Ibid., 470.

144. Ibid., 471.

145. Ibid., 475, 477.

146. Ibid., 477.

147. The sole exception involved couples who risked serious hereditary illness, such as hemophilia and Tay-Sachs. See Minutes of Dr. Bernard's Seminar, April 8, 1952, VWB, Box 161, Folder 5, and Minutes of Dr. Bernard's Seminar, June 14, 1954, VWB, Box 161, Folder 6.

148. Maurice J. Barry, "Emotional Transactions in the Pre-Adoptive Study" in *Social Work in Adoption* (see note 104), 52.

149. Frederick M. Hanson and John Rock, "The Effect of Adoption on Fertility and Other Reproductive Functions," *American Journal of Obstetrics and Gynecology* 59 (1950): 311–20; Margaret Marsh and Wanda Ronner, *The Empty Cradle: Infertility in America from Colonial Times to the Present* (Baltimore: Johns Hopkins University Press, 1996), chap. 5; Eugene A. Weinstein, "Adoption and Infertility," *American Sociological Review* 27 (June 1962): 408–12; H. F. Perkins, "Adoption and Fertility," *Eugenical News* 21 (September–October 1936): 95–101.

150. Helen Fradkin, *The Adoption Home Study* (Trenton, NJ: Bureau of Children's Services, 1963), 11.

151. Bernard, "Application of Psychoanalytic Concepts," 420–21; Free Synagogue Child Adoption Committee, Staff Meeting with Dr. Bernard, January 20, 1943, and "Confidential Medical Report on Fertility Status of Prospective Adoptive Couple," n.d.,

but early 1940s; VWB, Box 157, Folder 1. Other terms in vogue included "psycho-somatic" and "functional." See Richard Frank, "What the Adoption Worker Should Know about Infertility" in Michael Schapiro, *A Study of Adoption Practice*, vol. 2, *Selected Scientific Papers Presented at the National Conference on Adoption, January, 1955* (New York: CWLA, 1956), 113–18.

152. "Report to the Board of the Free Synagogue Child Adoption Committee of One Year's Intake Service to Prospective Adoptive Parents, December 1, 1942–December 1, 1943," 4, VWB, Box 157, Folder 1.

153. Ernest Cady and Frances Cady, *How to Adopt a Child* (New York: Whiteside and William Morrow and Co., 1956), 41.

154. "Report to the Board of the Free Synagogue Child Adoption Committee," 4.

155. Fradkin, *Adoption Home Study*, 49.

156. Referral suggestion, November 8, 1953, VWB, Box 157, Folder 4.

157. Case of Benjamin and Rose K, 4, VWB, Box 160, Folder 4. (All names in case records located in the Viola Wertheim Bernard Papers were abbreviated in the original documents. Case materials from other archival sources are treated differently.)

158. Frieda M. Kuhlmann and Helen P. Robinson, "Rorschach Tests as a Diagnostic Tool in Adoption Studies," *Social Casework* 32 (January 1951): 15–22.

159. Case of Mr. and Mrs. W, 1947, 12, emphasis in original, DH, Box 2, Folder 17.

160. Ibid., 13.

161. Psychological examination, July 2, 1958, Mrs. R, 4, VWB, Box 160, Folder 4.

162. Ibid., 3.

163. Minutes of Dr. Bernard's Seminar, April 19, 1954, VWB, Box 161, Folder 6.

164. Viola W. Bernard, "First Sight of the Child by Prospective Parents as a Crucial Phase in Adoption," *American Journal of Orthopsychiatry* 15 (April 1945): 236.

165. Douglass W. Orr, "Pregnancy following the Decision to Adopt," *Psychosomatic Medicine* 3 (October 1941): 445.

166. H. David Kirk, "Nonfecund People as Parents—Some Social and Psychological Considerations," *Fertility and Sterility* 14 (May–June 1963): 312.

CHAPTER FOUR

1. Lorraine Daston and Fernando Vidal, eds., *The Moral Authority of Nature* (Chicago: University of Chicago Press, 2004).

2. Judith S. Modell, *Kinship with Strangers: Adoption and Interpretations of Kinship in American Culture* (Berkeley and Los Angeles: University of California Press, 1994).

3. Donna J. Haraway, "Universal Donors in a Vampire Culture: It's All in the Family; Biological Kinship Categories in the Twentieth-Century United States," in *Uncommon Ground: Toward Reinventing Nature*, ed. William Cronon (New York: W. W. Norton, 1995), 321–66. Haraway refers to the "Sacred Image of the Same" as a fixture in liberal and scientific descriptions of kinship throughout the twentieth century, especially at midcentury.

4. W. H. Slingerland, *Child-Placing in Families: A Manual for Students and Social Workers* (New York: Russell Sage Foundation, 1919), 125.

5. Arno Dosch, "Not Enough Babies to Go Around," *Cosmopolitan* September 1910, 433–35.

6. USCB, *Adoption Laws in the United States: A Summary of the Development of Adoption Legislation and Significant Features of Adoption Statutes, with the Text of Selected Laws*, Bureau Publication No. 148, ed. Emelyn Foster Peck (Washington, DC: Government Printing Office, 1925), 28.

7. Legal inequality persisted, especially in inheritance. Until midcentury, references in wills to "children" or "heirs" did not include adoptees unless they were explicitly named. After midcentury, legal reforms automatically included adoptees unless they were explicitly excluded. Complexities persist in inheritance to this day. See Naomi Cahn, "Inheritance and Adoption," in *The Praeger Handbook of Adoption*, vol. 1, ed. Kathy Shepherd Stolley and Vern L. Bullough, 326–29, and Joan H. Hollinger, "Introduction to Adoption Law and Practice" in *Adoption Law and Practice*, vol. 1, ed. Joan H. Hollinger (New York: Matthew Bender, 1994), 1-24–1-47.

8. Case of S, 5, DH, Box 1, Folder 3. (All names in case records located in the Dorothy Hutchinson Papers have been abbreviated. Case materials from other archival sources are treated differently.)

9. Sample, "Application for Child for Adoption," n.d., but marked 1940, CWLA1, Box 15, Folder 5. This particular form included blanks for hair, eyes, skin, height, and weight.

10. Home Investigation of Mr. and Mrs. A, 1, DH, Box 1, Folder 3.

11. Case of Benjamin and Rose K, 1, VWB, Box 160, Folder 4. (All names in case records located in the Viola Wertheim Bernard Papers were abbreviated in the original documents. Case materials from other archival sources are treated differently.)

12. Quoted in Linda Gordon, *The Great Arizona Orphan Abduction* (Cambridge, MA: Harvard University Press, 1999), 17.

13. "Memorandum in Regard to Wendall Macauliffe," September 29, 1925, Arnold Lucius Gesell Papers, Library of Congress, Washington, DC (hereafter cited as ALG), Box 45, Folder: "Adoption, 1923, 1932 [Agencies]."

14. Case of Mr. and Mrs. G, DH, case notes, June 7, 1947, Box 1, Folder 7.

15. Case of J, DH, case notes, April 21, 1948, Box 1, Folder 7.

16. Case of Mr. and Mrs. H, 1946–1947, 6, DH, Box 1, Folder 11.

17. Case of David and Sylvia B, June 20, 1944, 2A, 9A, VWB, Box 160, Folder 4.

18. Case of Mr. and Mrs. F, from Children's Aid and Protective Society in Orange, NJ, 1946, DH, Box 2, Folder 24.

19. Case of F, 1946, Home Study of Mr. and Mrs. M, 6, DH, Box 1, Folder 10.

20. Ruth Carson, *So You Want to Adopt a Baby*, 6th ed. (New York: CWLA, Public Affairs Committee, 1957), 18. See also Robert C. Cook, "Genetics and Adoption Practices" in Michael Schapiro, *A Study of Adoption Practice*, vol. 2, *Selected Scientific Papers Presented at the National Conference on Adoption, January, 1955* (New York: CWLA, 1956), 59–65.

21. Case memo on JM, March 4, 1952, DH, Box 1, Folder 2.

22. Florence Clothier, "Placing the Child for Adoption," *Mental Hygiene* 26 (April 1942): 268–69.

23. A. S. Chapman, "Homes for Babies, Babies for Homes," *Hygeia* (December 1932): 1108.

24. Clothier, "Placing the Child for Adoption," 270.

25. Hollinger, "Introduction to Adoption Law and Practice," 1-24–1-47.

26. Edmond J. Butler, "Standards of Child Placing and Supervision," in USCB, *Standards of Child Welfare: A Report of the Children's Bureau Conferences, May and June 1919* (Washington, DC: Government Printing Office, 1919), 356, and "Minimum Standards for Boarding and Permanent Homes," Children's Bureau, State Board of Control, St. Paul, MN, adopted September 2, 1924, 12, CWLA1, Box 44, Folder 4.

27. USCB, *The Work of Child-Placing Agencies*, Bureau Publication No. 171 (Washington, DC: Government Printing Office, 1927), 64–65.

28. Brian Paul Gill, "The Jurisprudence of Good Parenting: The Selection of Adoptive Parents, 1894–1964" (Ph.D. diss., University of California, Berkeley, 1997), chaps. 2–4.

29. For example, *Purinton v. Jamrock*, 195 Mass. Reports 187, 80 N.E. (1907).

30. Gordon, *Great Arizona Orphan Abduction*.

31. Louise Waterman Wise, "Mothers in Name," *Survey* 43 (March 20, 1920): 780; Dennis R. Young, revised draft of a case study of Louise Wise Services, January 1980, 3, JWP, Box 33, Folder 418.

32. Fragment of letter from Louise Wise, probably 1917, JWP, Box 20, Folder 233.

33. "Orphans' Home," *B'nai B'rith Messenger*, March 25, 1910, n.p. Thanks to Bill Toll for sharing this document with me.

34. Boston Children's Aid Society, Fifty-first Annual Report, 1915, 13, Charities Collection, Simmons College Archives, Boston (hereafter cited as CC). See also Minnie F. Low to Julia Lathrop, June 3, 1921, USCB, Box 211, Folder 7-3-4-2, "Placing Out."

35. Jessie P. Condit to Ellen Potter, November 25, 1941, USCB, Box 165, Folder 7-3-1-3, "Transportation of Dependents—Juvenile, Immigration, Etc."; Ruth Brenner to Mary Ruth Colby, June 25, 1942, and Ruth Brenner to Mary Ruth Colby, July 23, 1942, USCB, Box 169, Folder 7-3-3-4, "Adoption"; Mary Ruth Colby to Howard Hopkirk, November 5, 1942, USCB, Box 169, Folder 7-3-3-4, "Adoption"; Alan Kohn, "Demand for Babies to Adopt Far Exceeds Small Supply," *National Jewish Post*, August 19, 1955, Jewish Community Relations Council of Greater Boston, American Jewish Historical Society (hereafter cited as JCRCGB), Box 42, Folder: "Adoption 8/55–12/55."

36. "A Memorandum concerning Child Adoption across Religious Lines: Background for Discussion of a Policy for Jewish Religious Bodies and Jewish Community Relations Agencies, Based on Presentations by Judge Justine Wise Polier and Florence Brown at a Meeting of the Executive Committee of the National Community Relations Advisory Council" (draft), 2, JWP, Box 18, Folder 207. See the final version of this document in JCRCGB, Box 42, Folder: "Adoption, 8/55–12/55."

37. Karen A. Balcom, "The Traffic in Babies: Cross-Border Adoption, Baby-Selling and the Development of Child Welfare Systems in the United States and Canada, 1930–1960" (Ph.D. diss., Rutgers University, 2002).

38. "Case Record No. 109," 1959, 2, CWLA2, Box 18, Folder: "CWLA—Adoption Case Records Nos. 113–14; 120–124."

39. Ibid., 6.

40. Ellen Herman, "The Difference Difference Makes: Justine Wise Polier and Religious Matching in Twentieth-Century Child Adoption," *Religion and American Culture* 10 (Winter 2000).

41. Matthew Frye Jacobson, *Whiteness of a Different Color: European Immigrants and the Alchemy of Race* (Cambridge, MA: Harvard University Press, 1998).

42. Jessie Taft, "The Home Has Lost Its Halo," *Survey Graphic* (December 1927): 287.

43. Lawrence Cole, "The Need of the Case Work Method in Dealing with Illegitimacy," *Hospital Social Service* 13 (May 1926): 433.

44. Mrs. Brenner to Viola Bernard, February 13, 1945, VWB, Box 160, Folder 4.

45. Charles W. Chesnutt, *The Quarry* (Princeton, NJ: Princeton University Press, 1999).

46. Ibid., 32, 51.

47. Carrington Howard, "Adoption by Advertisement," *Survey* 35 (December 11, 1915): 285.

48. H. L. Shapiro, "Anthropology and Adoption Practice" in Schapiro, *Study of Adoption Practice*, 2:34–38.

49. Justine Wise Polier to Florence Kreech, October 19, 1978, JWP, Box 33, Folder 417.
50. Nina Bernstein, *The Lost Children of Wilder: The Epic Struggle to Change Foster Care* (New York: Pantheon Books, 2001), 149; Louise Wise Services, Minutes of the Child Adoption Committee, March 7, 1956, 2, VWB, Box 155, Folder 2.
51. Quoted in Randall Kennedy, *Interracial Intimacies: Sex, Marriage, Identity, and Adoption* (New York: Pantheon Books, 2003), 6, 3.
52. Pearl S. Buck, *Children for Adoption* (New York: Random House, 1964), 115; Sheldon C. Reed, "Skin Color," in *Counseling in Medical Genetics* (Philadelphia: W. B. Saunders Company, 1955), 153–62; Louise Wise Services, Minutes of the Child Adoption Committee, October 8, 1958, 2, VWB, Box 155, Folder 3.
53. Sheldon C. Reed, "Normal Traits," in *Counseling in Medical Genetics*, 3rd ed. (New York: Alan R. Liss, 1980), 175.
54. Phyllis Dunne, "Placing Children of Minority Groups for Adoption," *Children* (March–April 1958): 44.
55. "Case Record No. 122," 1958, 3, CWLA2, Box 18, Folder: "CWLA—Adoption Case Records Nos. 113–14; 120–124."
56. Justine Wise Polier, *Juvenile Justice in Double Jeopardy: The Distanced Community and Vengeful Retribution* (Hillsdale, NJ: Lawrence Erlbaum Associates, 1989), 145.
57. Minutes of Adoptive Staff Meeting, May 13, 1963, VWB, Box 161, Folder 11.
58. Mrs. Ryo Suzuki and Mrs. Marilyn Horn, Follow-up Study on Negro-White Adoptions, VWB, Box 65, Folder 5. This study of transracial placements by the Los Angeles County Bureau of Adoptions between 1956 and 1964 found that "matching was a factor in the Bureau's placement of these Negro and part-Negro children, even though this appears to be a contradiction in Negro-Caucasian adoptions" (11).
59. Sheldon Reed to R. T. Wilbur, November 26, 1957, International Social Service, American Branch Papers, University of Minnesota Library, Social Welfare History Archives, Minneapolis (hereafter cited as ISSAB), Box 10, Folder: "Adoption Plans of Racially Mixed Children 1954–1965."
60. Sheldon C. Reed and Esther B. Nordlie, "Genetic Counseling: For Children of Mixed Racial Ancestry," *Eugenics Quarterly* 8 (September 1961): 157–63, and Esther B. Nordlie and Sheldon C. Reed, "Follow-up on Adoption Counseling for Children of Possible Racial Admixture," *Child Welfare* 41 (September 1962): 297–304, 327.
61. Louise Wise Services, Minutes of the Child Adoption Committee, March 7, 1956, 2. For an independent adoption in which a white couple took in a baby who looked white as a newborn, but darkened considerably over time, see Stanley Gordon, "A Rare Lesson about Love," *Look*, March 23, 1965, 33–36.
62. Reed, "Skin Color," 160.
63. Ibid., 153–62.
64. Suzuki and Horn, Follow-up Study on Negro-White Adoptions, 2, emphasis in original.
65. Reed and Nordlie, "Genetic Counseling," 163.
66. Bernadine Barr, "Spare Children, 1900–1945: Inmates of Orphanages as Subjects of Research in Medicine and in the Social Sciences in America" (Ph.D. diss., Stanford University, 1992); Anna Freud and Dorothy Burlingham, *Infants without Families: The Case for and against Residential Nurseries* (New York: International University Press, 1944): Harry F. Harlow, "Love in Infant Monkeys," *Scientific American*, June 1959, 68–74; Harry F. Harlow and Robert R. Zimmermann, "Affectional Responses in the Infant Monkey," *Science* 130 (August 21, 1959): 421–32; Harry F. Harlow and Margaret Kuenne Harlow, "Social Deprivation in Monkeys," *Scientific American*, November 1962, 136–46.

67. John Bowlby, *Maternal Care and Mental Health: A Report Prepared on Behalf of the World Health Organization as a Contribution to the United Nations Programme for the Welfare of Homeless Children* (Geneva: World Health Organization, 1952), 113–14.
68. Louise Raymond, *Adoption . . . and After* (New York: Harper and Brothers, 1955), 87.
69. Diane Eyer, *Mother-Infant Bonding: A Scientific Fiction* (New Haven, CT: Yale University Press, 1992), chap. 3; Michael Schapiro, *A Study of Adoption Practice*, vol. 1, *Adoption Agencies and the Children They Serve* (New York: CWLA, 1956), 61–62.
70. Ernest Cady and Frances Cady, *How to Adopt a Child* (New York: Whiteside and William Morrow and Co., 1956), 69.
71. Joseph Goldstein, Anna Freud, and Albert J. Solnit, *Beyond the Best Interests of the Child* (New York: Free Press, 1973).
72. C. C. Carstens to Alice Leahy, March 11, 1936, CWLA2, Box 1, Folder: "Correspondence—C. C. Carstens, 1932–38."
73. "Adoptions, A Statement of the Problem," November 5–6, 1937, 2, CWLA1, Box 15, Folder 5.
74. Ibid., 2.
75. C. C. Carstens to CWLA members, June 22, 1936, CWLA1, Box 15, Folder 5.
76. C. C. Carstens, "Safeguards in Adoption," *CWLA Bulletin* (April 1936): 4.
77. Publicity brochure, ALG, Box 45, Folder: "Subject File: Adoption [Memoranda]."
78. "Adoptions, A Statement of the Problem," 1.
79. "Minimum Safeguards in Adoption," approved by the CWLA Board of Directors on November 5, 1938, CWLA1, Box 15, Folder 5. These safeguards were published under the title "A Program in Education," *CWLA Bulletin* 17 (November 1938): 4–5.
80. "Adoptions, A Statement of the Problem," 4, 2.
81. "Some Poor Adoptions," May 4, 1939, ALG, Box 45, Folder: "Adoption [Memoranda]." See also "Regarding Adoptions," March 1937, CWLA Special Bulletin, 1–4, CWLAmicro reel 3.
82. Vera Connolly, "Bargain-Counter Babies," *Pictorial Review*, March 1937, 17.
83. John Janney, "One Man's Gilt-Edge Investments," *American Magazine*, May 1939, 32–33. For adoption's popularity during the Depression, see Dorothy Dunbar Bromley, "Demand for Babies Outruns the Supply," *New York Times Magazine*, March 3, 1935, 9.
84. John C. Murdock, "Dividends," *American Magazine*, October 1935, 74–76.
85. Iris Ruggles Macrae, "An Analysis of Adoption Practices at the New England Home for Little Wanderers" (M.S. thesis, Simmons College, School of Social Work, 1937), 23.
86. Viviana A. Zelizer, *Pricing the Priceless Child: The Changing Social Value of Children* (New York: Basic Books, 1985).
87. Elizabeth Frazer, "The Baby Market," *Saturday Evening Post*, February 1, 1930, 25; Connolly, "Bargain-Counter Babies," 17ff.
88. Frazer, "Baby Market," 85–86. On the challenge of assessing adopters' gender preferences, see Ruth F. Brenner, *A Follow-Up Study of Adoptive Families* (New York: Child Adoption Research Committee, March 1951), 35–43. H. David Kirk offered a sociological explanation: girls were a compromise between wives' desires to adopt and husbands' loyalty to patriarchal definitions of lineage. See H. David Kirk, *Shared Fate: A Theory of Adoption and Mental Health* (New York: Free Press of Glencoe, 1964), chap 8. For a historical perspective, see Barbara Melosh, *Strangers and Kin: The American Way of Adoption* (Cambridge, MA: Harvard University Press, 2002), 55–69.

89. Bromley, "Demand for Babies Outruns the Supply," 9. For a description of an adoption display room, see "We Adopt a Child," *Atlantic Monthly*, March 1940, 316–23.
90. Frazer, "Baby Market," 86.
91. Edith M. H. Baylor and Elio D. Monachesi, *The Rehabilitation of Children: The Theory and Practice of Child Placement* (New York: Harper and Brothers, 1939), 33.
92. "Regarding Adoptions." 8.
93. Florence Clothier, "Adoption Procedure and the Community," *Mental Hygiene* 25 (April 1941): 196–209; Evelyn Seeley, "Agencies Share Blame for Baby Black Market," *PM* 7 (December 1946): 9; Catherine Donnell, "Financial Assistance in an Adoption Agency," *Social Casework* 31 (1950): 28–33. Donnell describes a one-year experiment by the Free Synagogue Child Adoption Committee to provide financial assistance to birth mothers. The agency launched this controversial program to decrease the number of independent placements, but it worried that the plan would place undue pressure on women to surrender babies and that it would create public relations problems.
94. Bromley, "Demand for Babies Outruns the Supply," 9, 16.
95. Unless otherwise noted, all references and quotations in this paragraph are drawn from "A Study of the Adoption Situation of New York City as It Relates to Protestant Children," January–April 1938, CWLAmicro reel 3. For a brief published summary, see Mary Frances Smith, "Adoption as the Community Sees It," in *Social Case Work with Children: Studies in Structure and Process*, ed. Jessie Taft (Philadelphia: Pennsylvania School of Social Work, 1940), 6–16.
96. Frances Lockridge and Sophie van Senden Theis, *Adopting a Child* (New York: Greenberg, 1947), 12.
97. James W. Cook, *The Arts of Deception: Playing with Fraud in the Age of Barnum* (Cambridge, MA: Harvard University Press, 2001); Miles Orvell, *The Real Thing: Imitation and Authenticity in American Culture, 1880–1940* (Chapel Hill: University of North Carolina Press, 1989).
98. Mona Gardner, "Traffic in Babies," *Collier's*, September 16, 1939, 14.
99. Ibid.
100. Frazer, "Baby Market," 85, 86.
101. Anne Higonnet, *Pictures of Innocence: The History and Crisis of Ideal Childhood* (New York: Thames and Hudson, 1998).
102. Virginia Reid, "Black Market Babies," *Woman's Home Companion*, December 1944, 30.
103. Gardner, "Traffic in Babies," 44.
104. Anonymous letter from Salem, Oregon, March 13, 1958, USCB, Box 882, Folder 7-3-1-1, "Traffic in Children, Baby Farms."
105. Ibid.
106. Dorothy Thompson, "Fit for Adoption," *Ladies' Home Journal*, May 1939, 4; Agnes Sligh Turnbull, "The Great Adventure of Adopting a Baby," *American Magazine*, May 1929, 44.
107. Frederick G. Brownell, "Why You Can't Adopt a Baby," *Reader's Digest*, September 1948, 55–59; Albert Q. Maisel, "Why You Can't Adopt a Baby," *Woman's Home Companion*, March 1950.
108. "We Bought a Black-Market Baby," *McCall's*, November 1952, VWB, Box 161, Folder 1.
109. Maisel, "Why You Can't Adopt a Baby," 31.
110. Rael Jean Isaac, "Children Who Need Adoption: A Radical View," *Atlantic*, November 1963, 47.

111. Ibid., 50.
112. A major outcome study of independent adoptions in Florida found that less than 1 percent of adopters considered adopting an unhealthy child a serious risk. See Helen L. Witmer et al., *Independent Adoptions: A Follow-Up Study* (New York: Russell Sage Foundation, 1963), 105, 129.
113. Dorothy Barclay, "Adoption Problems," *New York Times Magazine*, April 2, 1950, 48.
114. Barbara Raymond, *The Baby Thief: The Untold Story of Georgia Tann, the Baby Seller Who Corrupted Adoption* (New York: Carroll and Graff, 2007).
115. "Adoption Practices, Procedures and Problems," 5, CWLA1, Box 15, Folder 6.
116. "Brief Summary of Adoption Conference Called by the CWLA in New York City, May 19–20," 1948, 3, CWLA1, Box 15, Folder 5.
117. Seeley, "Agencies Share Blame for Baby Black Market," 9. See also Ruth Latimer, "How to Wreck the Baby Racket," *American Monthly*, September 1957, 19–22.
118. Catherine S. Amatruda and Joseph V. Baldwin, "Current Adoption Practices," *Journal of Pediatrics* 38 (February 1951): 211, 210, table 2. See also Marguerite Bengs, "Study of Independent Adoptions in Connecticut since Passage of Adoption Law," *Social Service Review* 20 (1946): 392, table 1. This study of 673 Connecticut adoptions between October 1944 and October 1945 showed that not a single agency placed children before six months of age, whereas almost one-third of independent adoptions involved infants less than six months old.
119. Witmer et al., *Independent Adoptions*, 77, table 2.
120. Ibid., 77.
121. Schapiro, *Study of Adoption Practice*, 1:71.
122. Case of Mr. and Mrs. H, 1946–1947, 6.
123. Schapiro, *Study of Adoption Practice*, 1:61. See also the numerous letters on the question of infant placements in CWLA1, Box 15, Folder 6.
124. Helen Fradkin and Dorothy Krugman, "A Program of Adoptive Placement for Infants under Three Months," *American Journal of Orthopsychiatry* 26 (July 1956): 577–93; Louise Wise Services, Minutes of Child Adoption Committee, February 20, 1952, 2, VWB, Box 155, Folder 2.
125. Dorothy Hutchinson, "Adoption Practices," talk given at Annual Meeting, Episcopal Service for Youth, February 13, 1947, 6, DH, Box 1, Folder 7.
126. Sylvia Oshlag, "Direct Placement in Adoption," *Journal of Social Casework* 27 (October 1946): 229–38.
127. Schapiro, *Study of Adoption Practice*, 1:128.
128. Address by Marshall Field to the National Conference on Adoptions, January 26, 1955, 2, CWLA1, Box 16, Folder 8.
129. Ibid., 4.
130. Memo to member agencies from Mr. Reid, January 24, 1955, CWLA1, Box 16, Folder 8.
131. Michael Schapiro, *A Study of Adoption Practice*, 3 vols. (New York: CWLA, 1956). A great deal of additional material related to the conference can be found in CWLA1, Box 16, Folders 7–11, and CWLA2, Box 1, Folder: "Speeches—Joseph Reid, 1952, 1955" and Box 10, "Adoption—National Conference on Adoption, 1955."
132. Schapiro, *Study of Adoption Practice*, 1:9.
133. Three questionnaires (on agency practices, special-needs placements, and fee policies) were sent to all 503 U.S. agencies involved in making adoption placements; 270 responses represented well over half of all agencies involved in adoption as of 1953. The survey was not limited to CWLA members.

134. Schapiro, *Study of Adoption Practice*, 1:101.

135. Ibid., 8.

136. Ibid., 10.

137. Ibid., 113.

138. William D. Schmidt, "The Community and the Adoption Problem," *Child Welfare* (May 1952): 3–7, and Bernice F. Seltz, "Interpreting Good Adoption Practice," *Child Welfare* (October 1950): 16–17.

139. Percentages calculated on the basis of Schapiro, *Study of Adoption Practice*, 1:28, table 1.

140. Ibid., 64.

141. Ibid., 67–68, 70, table 4.

142. Ibid., 87.

143. "Adoption Practices, Procedures and Problems," 60. The survey conducted prior to this conference can be found in CWLA, Special Bulletin: A Preliminary Report of a Study of Policies and Practices in Adoption," comp. Henrietta L. Gordon, April 1948, CWLA1, Box 15, Folder 5. A follow-up survey and conference took place in 1951. See CWLA, *Adoption Practices, Procedures and Problems: A Report of the Second Workshop Held in New York City under the Auspices of the Child Welfare League of America, May 10–12, 1951* (New York: CWLA, 1952).

144. Penelope L. Maza, "Adoption Trends: 1944–1975," Child Welfare Research Notes No. 9 (U.S. Children's Bureau, August 1984), table 1, CWLA2, Box 65, Folder: "Adoption—Research—Reprints of Articles."

145. *Brooklyn Eagle* ad, March 1948, SP, Box 8, Folder: "Child Adoption Committee—Correspondence since 1946."

146. Military metaphors were common in the war against independent adoption. See USCB, *Protecting Children in Adoption: Report of a Conference Held in Washington, June 27 and 28, 1955* (Washington, DC: Government Printing Office, 1955).

147. Dorothy Hutchinson, "Supervision of Foster Homes," in *Cherish the Child: Dilemmas of Placement*, ed. Maude von P. Kemp (Metuchen, NJ: Scarecrow Press, 1972), 100. On adoption challenges during the war, see Henrietta L. Gordon, "Current Trends in Adoption," *CWLA Bulletin* 24 (February 1945): 11–15.

148. Press release dated April 15, 1955, 2, CWLA1, Box 12, Folder 10; "Proposal of Special Project for Development of Child Welfare Standards," September 1, 1954, 2, CWLA1, Box 12, Folder 10.

149. Memo dated April 29, 1955, "To All Member Agencies of the Child Welfare League of America," CWLA1, Box 12, Folder 10. In addition to adoption, the CWLA issued standards for homemaker services, foster family care, child protection, services to unmarried parents, day care, group care, services to children in their own homes, residential treatment, community planning and organization of child welfare services, administration and organization of child welfare services, and state child welfare services.

150. Senate Committee on the Judiciary, Subcommittee to Investigate Juvenile Delinquency, *Hearings on Interstate Adoption Practices*, 84th Cong., 1st sess., July 15–16, 1955, 2, 3.

151. "Annual Report, Standard Project," May 1956, 5, CWLA1, Box 12, Folder 10.

152. "Working Committee on Adoption Standards," December 16, 1955, CWLA1, Box 13, Folder 7. Private and public agencies were represented. Committee members also included a physician, a psychiatrist, and individuals appointed to represent researchers and social work educators. Geographically, the committee was limited. No state west of Pennsylvania was represented, nor were any rural constituencies included.

Most committee appointees came from New York (six), Washington, DC (six), Baltimore (three), Richmond (three), and Philadelphia (two).

153. Zitha R. Turitz, "The Standards Project: A Progress Report, November 1960," 2, CWLA1, Box 12, Folder 10; Zitha R. Turitz, "Follow-up Report, Use of Child Welfare League of America Standards, May 1963," CWLA1, Box 12, Folder 10. Brian Gill illustrates that *Standards for Adoption Service* was cited by judges and used by state officials to shut down noncompliant agencies. See Gill, "Jurisprudence of Good Parenting," chap. 2.

154. CWLA, *Standards for Adoption Service* (New York: CWLA, 1958), 14.

155. Bernice R. Brower, "What Shall I Do with My Baby?" *Child* 12 (April 1948): 166–69. In one early study (1926–35), the ideology of professional neutrality coexisted with an increase in the number of surrenders by unmarried mothers. See Macrae, "Analysis of Adoption Practices," 54–59; Ellen Herman, *The Romance of American Psychology: Political Culture in the Age of Experts* (Berkeley and Los Angeles: University of California Press, 1995).

156. Mary S. Brisley, "Parent-Child Relationships in Unmarried Parenthood," *Proceedings of the National Conference of Social Work* (New York: Columbia University Press, 1939), 436, 437–38.

157. Case of Miss L, DH, Box 2, Folder 24, 17.

158. CWLA, *Standards for Adoption Service* (1958), 19, emphasis in original.

159. Ibid., 27. For an illustration of the confusion this standard caused, see Gertrude Sandgrund to Viola Bernard, December 16, 1963, VWB, Box 158, Folder 1.

160. E. Wayne Carp, *Family Matters: Secrecy and Disclosure in the History of Adoption* (Cambridge, MA: Harvard University Press, 1998).

161. Margaret A. Thornhill, "Unprotected Adoptions," *Children* 2 (September–October 1955): 183.

162. CWLA, *Standards for Adoption Service* (1958), 38.

163. Ibid., 38–39.

164. See the American Medical Association's Rating Sheet for Prospective Parents, which replicated CWLA standards. Alfred Kadushin, "Substitute Care: Adoption," in *Child Welfare Services* (New York: Macmillan, 1967), 445, table 10-1. For tension between the CWLA and the AMA, see Joseph Reid to Norman V. Lourie, January 10, 1964, marked "Personal and Confidential," CWLA2, Box 65, Folder: "CWLA—Joseph H. Reid, adoption."

165. CWLA, *Standards for Adoption Service* (1958), 35, 37.

166. Ibid., 37.

167. Ibid., 19–20 (on children of mixed racial background), 24 (on the advantages of racial matching), 25–26 (on religious matching). The CWLA consulted the National Urban League when it revised the 1958 standards. That organization argued that race should not be singled out as a determining factor in child placement, but agreed that transracial adoptions should not be encouraged. See Zitha R. Turitz memo, October 2, 1963, "Discussion with National Urban League of Revision of Adoption Standards," CWLA1, Box 13, Folder 7. The result was an awkward compromise. Zitha R. Turitz, "A New Look at Adoption: Current Developments in the Philosophy and Practice of Adoption" (paper presented at CWLA Eastern Regional Conference, February 19, 1965), 6–7, CWLA1, Box 16, Folder 1.

168. CWLA, *Standards for Adoption Service* (1958), 32.

169. Ibid., 6.

170. Frieda M. Kuhlmann and Helen P. Robinson, "Rorschach Tests as a Diagnostic Tool in Adoption Studies," *Social Casework* 32 (January 1951): 18. Louise Wise Services

charged only $25 for the Rorschach test. See Fee Schedule B (Fiscal Year 7/1/49–6/30/50), VWB, Box 157, Folder 3.

171. Kuhlmann and Robinson, "Rorschach Tests as a Diagnostic Tool," 21.

172. Ibid., 19.

173. Ibid.

174. Ibid., 17–18. This quotation can also be found in Case of Mr. and Mrs. W, 1947, 4, DH, Box 2, Folder 17.

175. Case of Mr. and Mrs. W, 10.

176. All details and quotations in this paragraph are from Helen Fradkin, *The Adoption Home Study* (Trenton, NJ: Bureau of Children's Services, 1963). The case record, which ends with approval, is presented on pp. 106–27, but chapter 5, "Psychiatric Factors in Adoption," explains why Mr. and Mrs. W should have been rejected as adoptive parents.

177. Sigmund Freud, "Family Romances," in *Collected Papers*, ed. James Strachey (New York: Basic Books, 1959), 5:74–78.

178. Marshall D. Schechter, "Observations on Adopted Children," *Archives of General Psychiatry* 3 (July 1960): 29. See also Bernice T. Eiduson and Jean B. Livermore, "Complications in Therapy with Adopted Children," *American Journal of Orthopsychiatry* 23 (October 1953): 795–802.

179. Schechter, "Observations on Adopted Children," 31. Others disagreed with this view. For example, see H. David Kirk, "Are Adopted Children Especially Vulnerable to Stress? A Critique of Some Recent Assertions," *Archives of General Psychiatry* 14 (March 1966): 291–98.

180. Leontine R. Young, "The Unmarried Mother's Decision about Her Baby," in Family Service Association of America, *Understanding the Psychology of the Unmarried Mother* (New York: Family Service Association of America, 1945–1947), 14.

181. Robert P. Knight, "Some Problems in Selecting and Rearing Adopted Children," *Bulletin of the Menninger Clinic* 5 (May 1941): 65–74.

182. For example, see Joseph Reid's comments in USCB, *Protecting Children in Adoption*, 28.

183. "Connecticut Outlaws Independent Placements," *Social Service Review* 31 (1957): 323–24.

184. John Carson, "The Science of Merit and the Merit of Science: Mental Order and Social Order in Early Twentieth-Century France and America," in *States of Knowledge: The Co-Production of Science and Social Order*, ed. Sheila Jasanoff (New York: Routledge, 2004), 181–205.

CHAPTER FIVE

1. Barbara Stoddard Burks, "What Makes Jack a Bright Boy—Home or Heredity?" *North American Review* 228 (November 1929): 607.

2. Lee M. Brooks and Evelyn C. Brooks, *Adventuring in Adoption* (Chapel Hill: University of North Carolina Press, 1939), 12.

3. Genevieve Parkhurst, "Standing in the Place of Mother," *Good Housekeeping*, May 1939, 23.

4. John Carson, *The Measure of Merit: Talents, Intelligence, and Inequality in the French and American Republics, 1750–1940* (Princeton, NJ: Princeton University Press, 2006).

5. Michael M. Sokal, ed., *Psychological Testing and American Society, 1890–1930* (New Brunswick, NJ: Rutgers University Press, 1987); Leila Zenderland, *Measuring Minds: Henry Herbert Goddard and the Origins of American Intelligence Testing* (New York: Cambridge University Press, 1998).

6. F. Allan Hanson, *Testing Testing: Social Consequences of the Examined Life* (Berkeley and Los Angeles: University of California Press, 1993); Ellen Herman, "Mental and Intelligence Testing," *Encyclopedia of American Studies* (Grolier), 2001, available at http://eas-ref.press.jhu.edu (accessed December 17, 2007).

7. Lawrence Cole, "The Need of the Case Work Method in Dealing with Illegitimacy," *Hospital Social Service* 13 (May 1926): 433.

8. For a detailed description of overplacement, see Ira S. Wile, *The Challenge of Childhood: Studies in Personality and Behavior* (New York: Thomas Seltzer, 1925), 254–59.

9. W. H. Slingerland, *Child-Placing in Families: A Manual for Students and Social Workers* (New York: Russell Sage Foundation, 1919), 73.

10. Ibid., 69.

11. Quoted in ibid., 118.

12. Paul Popenoe, "The Foster Child," *Scientific Monthly*, September 1929, 248.

13. Lucille J. Grow and Deborah Shapiro, *Black Children—White Parents: A Study of Transracial Adoption* (New York: CWLA, 1974), 133–34, 236–37.

14. Leila Zenderland, "The Debate over Diagnosis: Henry Herbert Goddard and the Medical Acceptance of Intelligence Testing" in Sokal, *Psychological Testing* (see note 5), 65 n. 67.

15. Rose S. Hardwick, "The Stanford-Binet Intelligence Examination Re-Interpreted with Special Reference to Qualitative Differences" (Ph.D. diss., Radcliffe, 1924), 17. Hardwick described 175 tests administered between June 1918 and October 1923.

16. Form No. 9A, "Personal Record of Child," in Georgia G. Ralph, *Elements of Record Keeping for Child-Helping Organizations* (New York: Russell Sage Foundation, 1915), 45.

17. A study of 852 adoptions in Massachusetts between 1922 and 1925 found that few involved mental examinations prior to placement and that more than 70 percent were arranged independently. These deplorable facts made the case for reform. See Ida R. Parker, *Fit and Proper? A Study of Legal Adoption in Massachusetts* (Boston: Church Home Society, 1927), 29, 96.

18. Honoré Willsie, "The Adopted Mother," *Century*, September 1922, 660.

19. Popenoe, "Foster Child," 245.

20. Henry H. Goddard, "Wanted: A Child to Adopt," *Survey* 27 (October 14, 1911): 1006.

21. Ruth W. Lawton and J. Prentice Murphy, "A Study of Results of a Child-Placing Society," *Proceedings of the National Conference of Charities and Correction* (Boston: George H. Ellis, 1915), 168.

22. Ibid., 167.

23. Goddard, "Wanted: A Child to Adopt," 1006.

24. Amey Eaton Watson, "The Illegitimate Family," *Annals of the American Academy of Political and Social Science* 77 (May 1918): 103.

25. Ibid., 113.

26. Ibid., 103.

27. Iris Ruggles Macrae, "An Analysis of Adoption Practices at the New England Home for Little Wanderers" (M.S. thesis, Simmons College, School of Social Work, 1937), 67.

28. Ibid.

29. Sophie van Senden Theis, *How Foster Children Turn Out*, Publication No. 165 (New York: New York State Charities Aid Association, 1924), 167.

30. Marie Wilson Peters, "What the Social Worker Expects from the Psychologist," *Family* 15 (October 1934): 181.

31. Lawton and Murphy, "Study of Results," 169.

32. Alice M. Leahy, "Nature-Nurture and Intelligence," *Genetic Psychology Monographs* 17 (August 1935): 250.

33. Georgina D. Hotchkiss, "Adoptive Parents Talk about Their Children: A Follow-Up Study of Twenty-Four Children Adopted through a Child Placing Agency" (M.S. thesis, Simmons College, 1950), 32–34.

34. Macrae, "Analysis of Adoption Practices," 36, 37, table 12.

35. Willsie, "Adopted Mother," 658.

36. Eleanor Garrigue Gallagher, *The Adopted Child* (New York: Reynal and Hitchcock, 1936), 96.

37. Douglas A. Thom, "Aid of Science in Child Adoption," *CWLA Bulletin* 16 (February 1937): 2.

38. Douglas A. Thom, "Adoptions," *Journal of Pediatrics* 15 (August 1939): 259.

39. "Hell Is Paved with Good Intentions," n.d., but 1944, VWB, Box 160, Folder 8.

40. "Adopted Mother by Herself," *Scribner's* 97 (January 1935): 57.

41. Louis Hooper to Grace Abbott, April 28, 1931, USCB, Box 406, Folder 7-3-3-4, "Adoption."

42. "We Adopt a Child," *Atlantic Monthly*, March 1940, 318, 322.

43. Katherine Kinkead, "Our Son," *New Yorker*, March 4, 1950, 38.

44. Brooks and Brooks, *Adventuring in Adoption*, 17.

45. For one such story, see Elizabeth Frazer, "We Have Done It!" *Saturday Evening Post*, June 21, 1930, 59.

46. Mary Tinney, "An Interpretation of Three Thousand Placements by the New York Catholic Home Bureau," *Proceedings of the Fourth National Conference of Catholic Charities* (Washington, DC: Catholic University, 1916), 185; Sophie van Senden Theis and Constance Goodrich, *The Child in the Foster Home, Part 1: The Placement and Supervision of Children in Free Foster Homes, A Study Based on the Work of the Child-Placing Agency of the New York State Charities Aid Association* (New York: New York School of Social Work, 1921), 121, 126, 127.

47. C. Ray Jeffery, "Social Class and Adoption Petitioners," *Social Problems* 9 (Spring 1962): 354–58.

48. Edmund V. Mech, "Trends in Adoption Research," in *Perspectives on Adoption Research*, ed. CWLA (New York: CWLA, 1965), 9.

49. Henry S. Maas, "The Successful Adoptive Parent Applicant," *Social Work* 5 (January 1960): 14–20. This article summarizes Henry S. Maas and Richard E. Engler, Jr., *Children in Need of Parents* (New York: Columbia University Press, 1959).

50. Thyra Samter Winslow, "Certified Babies," *Technical World*, February 1915, 829–32.

51. Ellen Herman, "Families Made by Science: Arnold Gesell and the Technologies of Modern Adoption," *Isis* 92 (December 2001): 684–715.

52. Arnold Gesell, "The Psychological Welfare of Adopted and Foster Children," October 26, 1937, 3, ALG, Box 45, Folder: "Subject File: Adoption."

53. Arnold Gesell, "Psychoclinical Guidance in Child Adoption" in USCB, *Foster-Home Care for Dependent Children*, Bureau Publication No. 136 (Washington, DC: Government Printing Office, 1926), 204.

54. Gesell, "Psychological Welfare," 3; Arnold Gesell, *The Pre-School Child from the Standpoint of Public Hygiene and Education* (Boston: Houghton Mifflin, 1923), 139–41.

55. Arnold Gesell, "Is It Safe to Adopt an Infant?" n.d., 2, ALG, Box 45, Folder: "Subject File: Adoption [Law]"; Raymond Stephens to Gesell, January 16, 1958, and Gesell to Raymond Stephens, January 21, 1958, ALG, Box 45, Folder: "Subject File: Adoption."

56. Gesell, "Is It Safe," 11.

57. For example, see "Adoption," Memorandum re: Child Welfare League of America Program, June 7, 1939, ALG, Box 45, Folder: "Subject File: Adoption [Law]"; Maud Morlock to Arnold Gesell, July 22, 1944, and Arnold Gesell to Maud Morlock, July 27, 1944, ALG, Box 45, Folder: "Subject File: Adoption, 1939–56"; Memorandum re: Child Adoption, January 30, 1939, ALG, Box 45, Folder: "Subject File: Adoption [Memoranda]"; Memorandum re: Meeting of Committee, CWLA, June 9, 1939, ALG, Box 45, Folder: "Subject File: Adoption, 1939 [CWL of America]."

58. Ann Hulbert, *Raising America: Experts, Parents, and a Century of Advice about Children* (New York: Alfred A. Knopf, 2003), chap. 6.

59. Alice Boardman Smuts, *Science in the Service of Children, 1893–1935* (New Haven, CT: Yale University Press, 2006), chap. 10. When Gesell retired in 1948, Yale abandoned its sponsorship of the clinic, and colleagues founded an independent organization, the Gesell Institute of Child Development.

60. Arnold Gesell and Helen Thompson, *Infant Behavior: Its Genesis and Growth* (New York: McGraw-Hill, 1934), 327.

61. Gesell, *Pre-School Child*, 137. For Cobb's original research report, see Margaret Evertson Cobb, "The Mentality of Dependent Children," *Journal of Delinquency* 7 (May 1922): 132–40.

62. Arnold Gesell, *The Mental Growth of the Pre-School Child: A Psychological Outline of Normal Development from Birth to the Sixth Year, Including a System of Developmental Diagnosis* (New York: Macmillan, 1926), 428. Chapter 36 is titled "Clinical Phases of Child Adoption."

63. Gesell, "Psychoclinical Guidance in Child Adoption," 193.

64. Arnold Gesell, "Child Adoption in Connecticut," 3, address delivered to the quarterly meeting of the probate judges of Connecticut, May 17, 1939, ALG, Box 45, Folder: "Subject File: Adoption."

65. Brooks and Brooks, *Adventuring in Adoption*, 89.

66. Louise B. Heathers to Arnold Gesell, September 17, 1946, and attached manuscript, "Psychologists Look at Adoption," ALG, Box 45, Folder: "Subject File: Adoption."

67. Avis Carlson, "To Test a Baby," *Atlantic*, June 1940, 829–32.

68. Vera Connolly, "Bargain-Counter Babies," *Pictorial Review*, March 1937, 96; Edith F. Symmes, "An Infant Testing Service as an Integral Part of a Child Guidance Clinic," *American Journal of Orthopsychiatry* 3 (October 1933): 409–30. Symmes reported on two hundred children referred by New York agencies in the late 1920s for preadoption workups. The Gesell scale was administered to them all, along with the Buhler Test, the Merrill-Palmer Performance Scale, and the Kuhlmann-Binet.

69. Dorothy K. Hallowell, "Stability of Mental Test Ratings for Preschool Children," *Pedagogical Seminary and Journal of Genetic Psychology* 40 (1932): 406.

70. Marie Skodak and Harold M. Skeels, "A Final Follow-Up Study of One Hundred Adopted Children," *Journal of Genetic Psychology* 75 (September 1949): 94.

71. Hallowell, "Stability of Mental Test Ratings," 409.

72. Hotchkiss, "Adoptive Parents Talk about Their Children," 30. For a published report, see Hazel S. Morrison, "Research Study in an Adoption Program," *Child Welfare* (July 1950): 7–9, 12–13.

73. Sibylle Escalona, "The Use of Infant Tests for Predictive Purposes," *Bulletin of the Menninger Clinic* 14 (July 1950): 117–28.

74. Frances Lockridge and Sophie van Senden Theis, *Adopting a Child* (New York: Greenberg, 1947), chap. 6; see Mrs. Brenner memo to Dr. Bernard, March 19, 1946, VWB, Box 157, Folder 2.

75. Mazie Hough, "'To Conserve the Best of the Old': The Impact of Professionalization on Adoption in Maine," *Maine History* 40, no. 3 (Fall 2001): 202–6.

76. Simon H. Tulchin, "Psychological Testing in Social Welfare," in *Social Work Year Book* (New York: Russell Sage Foundation, 1947), 368; Abraham Joseph Simon, "Social Agency Adoption; A Psycho-Sociological Study in Prediction" (Ph.D. diss., Washington University, St. Louis, 1953), 88.

77. Children's Aid Society of Western Pennsylvania, "Procedures and Practices in Adoption," 6, n.d., penciled in 1955, CWLA1, Box 18, Folder 8.

78. Arnold Gesell, *Infancy and Human Growth* (New York: Macmillan, 1928), 21, emphasis in original.

79. Arnold Gesell, "The Social Significance of a Science of Child Development," May 15, 1943, 7, ALG, Box 146, Folder: "Speech, Article, Book File: Address, The Social Significance of a Science of Child Development, 1943."

80. Arnold Gesell, "Reducing the Risks of Child Adoption," *CWLA Bulletin* 6 (May 15, 1927): 2.

81. Arnold Gesell and Catherine S. Amatruda, *Developmental Diagnosis: Normal and Abnormal Child Development, Clinical Methods and Practical Applications* (New York: Paul B. Hoeber, 1941), 3.

82. Gesell, *Infancy and Human Growth*, 13.

83. Ibid., 362, 373.

84. Esther Thelen and Karen E. Adolph, "Arnold Gesell: The Paradox of Nature and Nurture," in *A Century of Developmental Psychology*, ed. Ross D. Parke et al. (Washington, DC: American Psychological Association, 1994), 357–87.

85. Gesell, *Pre-School Child*, 138.

86. Arnold Gesell, "Adoption" radio talk, November 3, 1930, 2, ALG, Box 45, Folder: "Subject File: Adoption [Law]."

87. See any number of cases in Theis and Goodrich, *Child in the Foster Home, Part 1;* Minutes of the Free Synagogue Child Adoption Committee, March 29, 1944, VWB, Box 155, Folder 1.

88. Symmes, "Infant Testing Service," 427 (case 2, Jack).

89. Case of Mr. and Mrs. W, 1947, 31, DH, Box 2, Folder 17.

90. Supplementary Memorandum for Child Welfare Association, Re: Rebecca Nearing, November 16, 1923, ALG, Box 45, Folder: "Subject File: Adoption, 1923 [Cases]." (All names in clinical case records located in the Arnold Gesell Papers have been changed. Case materials from other archival sources are treated differently.)

91. Arnold Gesell, untitled draft, n.d., 1, ALG, Box 45, Folder: "Subject File: Adoption [Law]."

92. Gesell, "Psychological Welfare," 2.

93. Charlotte Lowe, "Intelligence and Social Background of the Unmarried Mother," *Mental Hygiene* 11 (October 1927): 783–94; W. E. McClure and Bronett Goldberg, "Intelligence of Unmarried Mothers," *Psychological Clinic* 18 (May–June 1929): 119–27; W. E. McClure, "Intelligence of Unmarried Mothers, II," *Psychological Clinic* 20 (October 1931): 154–57; Lilian Ripple, "Social Work Studies of Unmarried Parenthood as Affected by Contemporary Treatment Formulations: 1920–1940" (Ph.D. diss., University of Chicago, 1953). Alice Leahy theorized the reverse, suggesting that the intelligence of children born to unmarried mothers would be higher than average because "the economic inadequacy of unmarried parents is frequently associated with youth, while the economic inadequacy of married parents generally arises from intellectual and personality deficiencies" (Leahy, "Nature-Nurture and

Intelligence," 254). Leahy's study of Minnesota adoptions also found that birth mothers who placed children for adoption had more education and higher IQs than birth mothers who kept their children or placed them in either temporary family or institutional care. See Alice Leahy Shea, "Family Background and the Placement of Illegitimate Children," *American Journal of Sociology* 93 (July 1937): 103–4; Alice M. Leahy, "A Study of Certain Selective Factors Influencing Prediction of the Mental Status of Adopted Children or Adopted Children in Nature-Nurture Research," *Journal of Genetic Psychology* 41 (1932): 294–327.

94. Gesell, untitled draft, 3, 2. Gesell believed in sealing the original birth records of young adoptees, but also thought they should be given identifying information about birth parents on reaching adulthood.

95. Ibid., 3.

96. Gesell, *Pre-School Child*, 138.

97. Arnold Gesell, "The Nursery School Movement," *School and Society* 20 (November 22, 1924): 648. Thanks to Ben Harris for sharing this reference with me.

98. Bernadine Barr, "Spare Children, 1900–1945: Inmates of Orphanages as Subjects of Research in Medicine and in the Social Sciences in America" (Ph.D. diss., Stanford University, 1992); Inge Bretherton, "The Origins of Attachment Theory: John Bowlby and Mary Ainsworth," in *Century of Developmental Psychology* (see note 84), 431–71; John Bowlby, *Maternal Care and Mental Health: A Report Prepared on Behalf of the World Health Organization as a Contribution to the United Nations Programme for the Welfare of Homeless Children* (Geneva: World Health Organization, 1952); Diane Eyer, *Mother-Infant Bonding: A Scientific Fiction* (New Haven, CT: Yale University Press, 1992); Joseph Goldstein, Anna Freud, and Albert J. Solnit, *Beyond the Best Interests of the Child* (New York: Free Press, 1973).

99. Arnold Gesell, "Adoption" draft manuscript, n.d., 2, ALG, Box 45, Folder: "Subject File: Adoption [Law]."

100. Gesell, "Psychological Welfare," 1.

101. Index card describing Sarah's case, emphasis in original, ALG, Box 45, Folder: "Subject File: Adoption, 1957."

102. Gesell, untitled draft, 1.

103. Gesell, "Adoption" draft manuscript, 1.

104. Adoption timing was a problem often featured in the popular press. See Honoré Willsie, "When Is a Child Adoptable?" *Delineator* 95 (December 1919): 35.

105. Hallowell, "Stability of Mental Test Ratings," 419.

106. E. J. Mandeville to Yale Psycho-Clinic, July 11, 1940, ALG, Box 45, Folder: "Subject File: Adoption, 1923–43 [cases, with individuals concerning]."

107. On the difficulty of racial determination, see Arnold Gesell, "Child Adoption," June 29, 1937, ALG, Box 45, Folder: "Subject File: Adoption" and fragment: "case 6," n.d., ALG, Box 45, Folder: "Subject File: Adoption [Memoranda]."

108. List of children recommended and not recommended for adoption, 1934–35, ALG, Box 45, Folder: "Subject File: Adoption [Law]."

109. Arnold Gesell, "Clinical Aspects of Child Adoption" in Arnold Gesell and Catherine S. Amatruda, *Developmental Diagnosis: Normal and Abnormal Child Development, Clinical Methods and Practical Applications*, 2nd ed., rev. (New York: Harper and Row, 1947), 341.

110. Gesell, "Psychoclinical Guidance in Child Adoption," 200–201.

111. Clinical Memorandum in Regard to Rose, November 13, 1923, ALG, Box 45, Folder: "Subject File: Adoption, 1923 [Cases]." For another case where a psychologist de-

clared that a normal-looking baby really was not, see "A Baby in Your Arms," *CWLA Bulletin* (December 1937): 2.

112. September 1939 correspondence from Alice Taylor includes test schedules and scoring sheets for Matilda; see ALG, Box 60, Folder: "Subject File: Clinical Records, Matilda, [Adoption case–Penn.], 1938."

113. Hallowell, "Stability of Mental Test Ratings," 407.

114. C. V. Williams, "Before You Adopt a Child," *Hygeia* 2 (1924): 424.

115. Elizabeth Comeau to Arnold Gesell, June 29, 1950, ALG, Box 45, Folder: "Subject File: Adoption."

116. Thurston Blodgett to Yale Psycho-Clinic, n.d., but probably late 1920s, ALG, Box 45, Folder: "Subject File: Adoption, 1923, 1932 [Agencies]."

117. E. J. Mandeville to Yale Psycho-Clinic.

118. Ralph P. Winch to Department of Human Relations, Yale Medical School, March 29, 1939, ALG, Box 45, Folder: "Subject File: Adoption, 1923–43 [cases, with individuals concerning]."

119. Gesell, "Is It Safe to Adopt an Infant," 82.

120. Gesell to D. Oberteuffer, September 25, 1937, ALG, Box 45, Folder: "Subject File: Adoption, 1923–43 [cases, with individuals concerning]."

121. Gesell, "Psychoclinical Guidance in Child Adoption," 199.

122. Mary Douglas, *Risk and Blame: Essays in Cultural Theory* (New York: Routledge, 1992), chaps. 1–4; Ian Hacking, *The Taming of Chance* (New York: Cambridge University Press, 1990); T. J. Jackson Lears, "What If History Was a Gambler?" in *Moral Problems in American Life: New Perspectives on Cultural History*, ed. Karen Halttunen and Lewis Perry (Ithaca, NY: Cornell University Press, 1998), 309–29.

123. *Adoption Quarterly* regularly reports such studies. See also the research database of the Evan B. Donaldson Adoption Institute at http://adoptioninstitute.org/.

124. Ruth F. Brenner, *A Follow-Up Study of Adoptive Families* (New York: Child Adoption Research Committee, March 1951), 18.

125. Kurt Danziger, *Constructing the Subject: Historical Origins of Psychological Research* (New York: Cambridge University Press, 1990), esp. chap. 5; Theodore M. Porter, *Trust in Numbers* (Princeton, NJ: Princeton University Press, 1995).

126. Caroline Jean Acker, *Creating the American Junkie* (Baltimore: Johns Hopkins University Press, 2002); Ellen Fitzpatrick, *Endless Crusade: Women Social Scientists and Progressive Reform* (New York: Oxford University Press, 1990), chap. 5.

127. CWLA, ed., *Quantitative Approaches to Parent Selection* (New York: CWLA, 1962); Mech, "Trends in Adoption Research," 7; Paul V. Carlson, "Methodological Problems in Adoption Research," in *Perspectives on Adoption Research* (see note 48), 43.

128. Theis, *How Foster Children Turn Out.*

129. Lawton and Murphy, "Study of Results," 166.

130. A. H. Stoneman, "Safeguarding Adoptions, Legally and Socially," *Proceedings of the National Conference of Social Work* (Chicago: University of Chicago Press, 1924), 148.

131. Theis, *How Foster Children Turn Out*, 6.

132. Ibid., 25, table 3, 161–64.

133. Ibid., 23.

134. Ibid.

135. Ibid., 170.

136. Ibid.

137. Ibid.

138. Ibid.
139. The study schedule is reprinted in ibid., 172–79.
140. A summary table can be found in ibid., 214–15, table 45.
141. Ibid., 53, table 6. In comparison, only 4 percent came from "predominantly good" family backgrounds, and 4 percent came from "good–unknown" family backgrounds.
142. Ibid., 50.
143. Popenoe, "Foster Child," 245.
144. Ibid.
145. Ibid.
146. Theis, *How Foster Children Turn Out*, 113, table 24.
147. Ibid., 117 (multiple placements), 116, table 26 (schooling), 114, table 25 (social adjustment).
148. Ibid., 117.
149. Ibid., 118.
150. Ibid., 121, table 29, 120, table 28.
151. Ibid., 122, table 31, 123.
152. Ibid., 128.
153. Ibid., 127.
154. Ibid., 163–64.
155. Ibid., 164.
156. Willsie, "Adopted Mother," 666.
157. Ibid.
158. J. Richard Wittenborn, *The Placement of Adoptive Children* (Springfield, IL: Charles Thomas, 1957), 178.
159. Macrae, "Analysis of Adoption Practices," 92–93. This did not necessarily mean that children were told, but simply that social workers consistently told parents to tell.
160. Ibid., 96, 97.
161. Lucie K. Browning, "A Private Agency Looks at the End Results of Adoptions," *CWLA Bulletin* 21 (January 1942): 3.
162. Ibid.
163. Ruth Medway Davis and Polly Bouck, "Crucial Importance of Adoption Home Study," *Child Welfare* 34 (March 1955): 21.
164. Ibid.
165. Hotchkiss, "Adoptive Parents Talk about Their Children." A published summary of this study can be found in Morrison, "Research Study in an Adoption Program" (see note 72), 7–9, 12–13.
166. Hotchkiss, "Adoptive Parents Talk about Their Children," 16.
167. Ibid., 25–30.
168. Ibid., 23.
169. Ibid., 39.
170. Ibid., 30–34.
171. Ibid., 39.
172. Ibid., 3.
173. Benson Jaffee and David Fanshel, *How They Fared in Adoption: A Follow-up Study* (New York: Columbia University Press, 1970).
174. Ibid., 14.
175. Ibid.
176. Ibid., 16.

177. Ibid., 41.
178. Ibid., 141, 217.
179. Ibid., 72.
180. Families with adoption secrets had disincentives to participate in adoption research, so this figure is inflated. Even in the 1960s, many adoptees were never told of their adoptions. See Louise Wise Services, Board Minutes, March 5, 1975, 5, VWB, Box 155, Folder 5.
181. Jaffee and Fanshel, *How They Fared in Adoption*, 129, 133.
182. Ibid., 138, table 7-6.
183. Ibid., chap. 14.
184. Ibid., 286–90.
185. Ibid., 12. See also note 2 on pp. 348–50 for a detailed exposition of their statistical method.
186. Catherine S. Amatruda and Joseph V. Baldwin, "Current Adoption Practices," *Journal of Pediatrics* 38 (February 1951): 208–12; Fern Marja, "Gray Market Babies Sent to 'Bad' Homes," *New York Post Home News*, February 17, 1949, VWB, Box 160, Folder 8; Mary Beth Weinstein, "The Markets—Black and Gray—in Babies," *New York Times Magazine*, November 27, 1955, 12.
187. Amatruda and Baldwin, "Current Adoption Practices," 212.
188. Catherine Amatruda, notes from a talk given at the Annual Meeting of the Connecticut Welfare Association, May 1948, 1, VWB, Box 160, Folder 8.
189. Helen L. Witmer et al., *Independent Adoptions: A Follow-Up Study* (New York: Russell Sage Foundation, 1963), 77, table 2.
190. Ibid., 91, table 15.
191. Ibid., 108, table 20, 101–2, table 17, 139, 269.
192. Ibid., 277.
193. Alfred Kadushin, "Substitute Care: Adoption," in *Child Welfare Services* (New York: Macmillan, 1967), 482–83, table 10-2.
194. Wittenborn, *Placement of Adoptive Children*, 58.
195. Michael Schapiro, *A Study of Adoption Practice*, vol. 1, *Adoption Agencies and the Children They Serve* (New York: CWLA, 1956), 32. Volume 2 includes additional material on mental measurement in adoption.
196. Schapiro, *Study of Adoption Practice*, 1:56.
197. Ibid., 84, table 7. One agency that studied its own testing practices in almost one hundred adoptive placements concluded in 1945 that "no baby has changed enough [in IQ] to say that it has been misplaced." Minutes of the Free Synagogue Child Adoption Committee, May 25, 1945, VWB, Box 155, Folder 1; Psychological Research during the Years 1941 to 1945 (Reexamination of 95 Children in Their Adoptive Homes), Free Synagogue Child Adoption Committee, report submitted by Marguerite Wetmore, VWB, Box 157, Folder 2.
198. National Conference of Catholic Charities, *Adoption Practices in Catholic Agencies* (Washington, DC: National Conference of Catholic Charities, 1957), 96, table A-24, 100, table A-29. See also "Draft of Adoption Study," Box 89, Folder: "Adoption Study Drafts (1)," National Conference of Catholic Charities/Catholic Charities USA Records, Archives of the Catholic University of America, Washington, DC. The National Conference of Catholic Charities conducted this national survey in part because of its conflict with the CWLA over religious matching. The following statement appears on page 4 of the adoption study draft but not in its final published form: "Although it seldom happens, we would rather keep a child in a Catholic foster

home, or even in a Catholic institution, over a long period of time than to have him placed in a home of a different religious faith."

199. Kathy S. Stolley, "Statistics on Adoption in the United States," *Future of Children* 3, no. 1 (Spring 1993): 30–31, fig. 3, and Penelope L. Maza, "Adoption Trends: 1944–1975," Child Welfare Research Notes No. 9 (U.S. Children's Bureau, August 1984), table 3, fig. 2, CWLA2, Box 65, Folder: "Adoption—Research—Reprints of Articles."

CHAPTER SIX

1. Percy Maddux to Justine Wise Polier, June 23, 1944, JWP, Box 18, Folder 205.

2. Michael Schapiro, *A Study of Adoption Practice*, vol. 1, *Adoption Agencies and the Children They Serve* (New York: CWLA, 1956), 33. Five percent also refused service to children from certain national backgrounds (see p. 54). See also Michael Schapiro, *A Study of Adoption Practice*, vol. 3, *Adoption of Children with Special Needs* (New York: CWLA, 1956), 11.

3. Schapiro, *Study of Adoption Practice*, 1:33.

4. Ibid., 3:10, table 1. The number of independent placements of "Negro" children was minuscule.

5. Ibid., 11–12.

6. Dorothy E. Reinhart, "Reader's Forum: Adoption of Negro Children," *Child Welfare* 28 (December 1948): 11; "Proposed Research Project on Negro Adoption," n.d., but penciled in is 1959, CWLA1, Box 15, Folder 7; David Fanshel, *A Study in Negro Adoption* (New York: CWLA, 1957), 9–10.

7. Schapiro, *Study of Adoption Practice*, 3:45.

8. Alfred Kadushin, "A Study of Adoptive Parents of Hard-to-Place Children," *Social Casework* 43 (May 1962): 230; Schapiro, 1:85.

9. David Fanshel, *Far from the Reservation: The Transracial Adoption of American Indian Children* (Metuchen, NJ: Scarecrow Press, 1972). Fanshel found adopting families quite varied in their political orientation, gender ideology, and demographic profile. Only 20 percent of the couples who adopted through the Indian Adoption Project actively sought to adopt an Indian child.

10. Ibid., 84.

11. Ibid., 92.

12. Ibid., 120–21, table V-5, and 166–67, table VI-5.

13. "Case Record No. 109, Fisher, Adoption, Study of a 4-Year-Old Adopted Girl for Whom a Second Adoption Is Being Considered," 1959, and "Case Record No. 122, Mrs. L., Adoptive Home Study, Home Study of a Middle Aged Couple for the Adoption Placement of a 10 Months old Eurasian girl," 1958, CWLA2, Box 18, Folder: "CWLA—Adoption Case Records Nos. 102–104; 107–112." Case 109 describes how a child adopted as a newborn was returned several years later because of her half–African American appearance. Case 122 describes a couple willing to adopt a mixed-race child as long as they were reassured that the child would appear white.

14. Memo from Zelma Felton to Joseph Reid, December 5, 1955, describing children difficult to place for adoption, CWLA2, Box 1, Folder: Speeches—Joseph Reid, 1952, 1955.

15. Minutes, Adoption Committee, March 10, 1959, 1, VWB, Box 161, Folder 11.

16. Lucille J. Grow and Deborah Shapiro, *Black Children—White Parents: A Study of Transracial Adoption* (New York: CWLA, 1974), 191; Minutes of Dr. Bernard's Seminar, March 6, 1951, VWB, Box 161, Folder 5.

17. Schapiro, *Study of Adoption Practice*, 3:13; Staff Meeting of Adoption Department, October 16, 1961, VWB, Box 161, Folder 11.

18. Bernice J. Daniels, "Significant Considerations in Placing Negro Infants for Adoption," *Child Welfare* (January 1950): 8–9, 11.

19. Schapiro, *Study of Adoption Practice*, 1:85.

20. Ibid., 49–51, 3:11.

21. "Hard-to-Place Children, Part 2: Illegitimate Negro Children, Kansas City, Missouri, 1954" (Kansas City, MO: Community Studies, March 1956), 41–42.

22. See Rickie Solinger, *Wake Up Little Susie: Single Pregnancy and Race before Roe v. Wade* (New York: Routledge, 1992), and Rickie Solinger, *Beggars and Choosers: How the Politics of Choice Shapes Adoption, Abortion, and Welfare in the United States* (New York: Hill and Wang, 2001).

23. Alice Lake, "Babies for the Brave," *Saturday Evening Post*, July 31 1954, 26.

24. Martha May Eliot, "Adoption as a National Problem," address at the Committee on Adoptions Panel Discussion at the 25th Annual Meeting of the American Academy of Pediatrics, New York City, October 8, 1956, 5, Martha May Eliot Papers, Harvard University, Radcliffe Institute for Advanced Study, Schlesinger Library, Cambridge, MA, Box 8, Folder 108.

25. Schapiro, *Study of Adoption Practice*, 1:35–36.

26. Address by Marshall Field to the National Conference on Adoptions, January 26, 1955, 4, CWLA1, Box 16, Folder 8.

27. For the argument that ordinary people embraced special-needs children before professional social workers did, see Julie Berebitsky, *Like Our Very Own: Adoption and the Changing Culture of Motherhood, 1851–1950* (Lawrence: University Press of Kansas, 2000), 154–65.

28. Schapiro, *Study of Adoption Practice*, 1:56.

29. Ibid., 84, table 7. Only one agency reported that intellectual matching was unimportant, whereas ten designated race and thirteen designated religion as unimportant.

30. Ibid., 45.

31. Differential treatment of married and unmarried birth fathers was hardly new. See Kathleen d'Olier, "Case Work with the Unmarried Father," *Proceedings of the Twenty-third National Conference of Catholic Charities* (Washington, DC: Catholic University, 1937), 120–28.

32. Susan K. Ginsburg, "Suggestions for Practice with Respect to the Rights of Unmarried Fathers: The Aftermath of *Stanley v. Illinois*," August 4, 1975, CWLA2, Box 10, Folder: "*Stanley vs. Illinois*, 1972–1975."

33. Ner Littner, "The Natural Parents," in Schapiro, *Study of Adoption Practice*, 2:23.

34. Ann Fessler, *The Girls Who Went Away: The Hidden History of Women Who Surrendered Children for Adoption in the Decades before Roe v. Wade* (New York: Penguin, 2006); Solinger, *Wake Up Little Susie.*

35. Schapiro, *Study of Adoption Practice*, 1:47.

36. Littner, "Natural Parents," 21–33; Family Service Association of America, *Understanding the Psychology of the Unmarried Mother* (New York: Family Service Association of America, 1945–1947); Lilian Ripple, "Social Work Studies of Unmarried Parenthood as Affected by Contemporary Treatment Formulations: 1920–1940" (Ph.D. diss., University of Chicago, 1953). For the opposite view, see Clark E. Vincent, "Unwed Mothers and the Adoption Market: Psychological and Familial Factors," *Marriage and Family Living* 22 (May 1960): 112–18.

37. Schapiro, *Study of Adoption Practice*, 1:45–47.
38. Ibid., 72.
39. Ibid., 78.
40. Typescript by Ruth F. Brenner, "Supervision after Adoptive Placement of a Child or Post Placement Counselling," n.d., but June 6, 1950, is penciled in, paper presented at Mid-West CWLA conference, June 6, 1950, CWLA1, Box 15, Folder 6.
41. Ruth F. Brenner, "Selection of Adoptive Parents: A Casework Responsibility," *CWLA Bulletin* 25 (December 1946): 1.
42. Ibid., 2.
43. Schapiro, *Study of Adoption Practice*, 1:72–81. See also Florence G. Brown, "What Do We Seek in Adoptive Parents?" *Social Casework* 32 (April 1951): 155–61.
44. Schapiro, *Study of Adoption Practice*, 1:77; Minutes of the Free Synagogue Child Adoption Committee, January 27, 1943, VWB, Box 155, Folder 1.
45. Schapiro, *Study of Adoption Practice*, 1:75, table 6; Richard Frank, "What the Adoption Worker Should Know about Infertility" in Schapiro, *Study of Adoption Practice*, 2:113–18.
46. Claudia Nelson, "Nontraditional Adoption in Progressive-Era Orphan Narratives," *Mosaic* 34 (June 2001): 181–97.
47. Ethel Branham, "One Parent Adoptions," *Children* 17, no. 3 (May–June 1970): 103–7.
48. Charles E. Brown, "Agency Seeks Homes for Negro Kids, Single Persons May Adopt," 1966, unidentified newspaper clipping, VWB, Box 64, Folder 7.
49. Walter A. Jackson, *Gunnar Myrdal and America's Conscience: Social Engineering and Racial Liberalism, 1938–1987* (Chapel Hill: University of North Carolina Press, 1990).
50. Gunnar Myrdal, *An American Dilemma: The Negro Problem and Modern Democracy* (New York: Harper and Brothers, 1944), xlviii.
51. Ruth Feldstein, *Motherhood in Black and White: Race and Sex in American Liberalism, 1930–1965* (Ithaca, NY: Cornell University Press, 2000), and Peggy Pascoe, "Miscegenation Law, Court Cases, and Ideologies of 'Race' in Twentieth-Century America," *Journal of American History* 83 (June 1996): 44–69.
52. Joyce A. Ladner, *Mixed Families: Adopting across Racial Boundaries* (Garden City, NY: Anchor Press, Doubleday, 1977), 59–60.
53. Lynn Gilbert and Gaylen Moore, *Particular Passions: Talks with Women Who Have Shaped Our Times* (New York: Clarkson N. Potter, 1981), 124–25.
54. Horace Kallen to Mr. [Morris B.] Abram, January 19, 1973, JWP, Box 1, Folder 6.
55. "A Battling Judge Retires to Aid Minority Children," *New York Times*, February 3, 1973, JWP, Box 1, Folder 6.
56. Gilbert and Moore, *Particular Passions*, 121.
57. Polier told this story repeatedly. See "Adoption II," JWP, Box 18, Folder 207; "Adoption Black Practices Must Be Outlawed," Annual Meeting of Spence-Chapin Adoption Service, January 9, 1947, 5, JWP, Box 45, Folder 558; untitled draft describing risks of commercial adoption, August 1947, JWP, Box 45, Folder 558.
58. Polier's thinking about the role of professionals in adoption changed over time. See "Professional Abuse of Children," American Orthopsychiatric Association, Fifty-second Annual Meeting, March 22, 1975, JWP, Box 47, Folder 591.
59. "Treatment Services of the Psychiatric Clinic of the Manhattan Children's Court," June 14, 1943, in JWP, Box 6, Folder 63. Additional information on the court clinic is located in Box 6, Folder 64.
60. She followed the work of the Iowa Child Welfare Research Station and knew of H. David Kirk's work before it was published. See "Adoption Aids Minds of Imbeciles'

Waifs," *New York Times*, January 25, 1938, JWP, Box 24, Folder 294, and summary of David Kirk dissertation, "Community Sentiments in Relation to Child Adoption," JWP, Box 18, Folder 207.

61. "Adoption 1," 2–3, n.d., but probably 1947, JWP, Box 18, Folder 207.

62. Justine Wise Polier, "Attitudes and Contradictions in Our Culture," *Child Welfare* 39 (November 1960): 2.

63. Marian J. Morton, "Institutionalizing Inequalities: Black Children and Child Welfare in Cleveland, 1859–1998," *Journal of Social History* 343 (Fall 2000): 141–62.

64. Justine Wise Polier to Lawrence B. Buttenweiser, January 29, 1974, JWP, Box 21, Folder 254.

65. Justine Wise Polier, oral history, 15, JWP, Box 1, Folder 3.

66. Fragment describing 1956 case of L. D., JWP, Box 28, Folder 356. The record does not indicate how this case was resolved.

67. *Matter of Santos*, 278 App. Div. Rep., S. Ct. New York 373 (1951); *Matter of Santos*, 279 App. Div., S. Ct. New York 578 (1951); *Matter of Santos* 304 Ct. App. New York 483 (1952). For more, see SP, Boxes 2–5.

68. "Summary on the Southern Case, FSCAC," by Florence Brown, January 15, 1952, 2, 5, SP, Box 2, Folder: "Summary of Southern Case."

69. Untitled document, 1938, JWP, Box 22, Folder 256.

70. Court transcript re: Ana Marie, James, Brenda, Peter, Francis, June 30, 1959, 2, JWP, Box 19, Folder 228.

71. Rachel Nash, "Justine Wise Polier: The Conscience of the Juvenile Court" (senior honors thesis, Harvard College, 1998), 67.

72. Justine Wise Polier, *Juvenile Justice in Double Jeopardy: The Distanced Community and Vengeful Retribution* (Hillsdale, NJ: Lawrence Erlbaum Associates, 1989), 148.

73. New York City Commission for the Foster Care of Children, Staff Statement on Proposed Adoption Service in the Department of Welfare, January 7, 1955, JWP, Box 18, Folder 207.

74. Press release regarding New York City's establishment of public adoption services, January 15, 1957, JWP, Box 18, Folder 206.

75. Justine Wise Polier, "Religion and Child-Care Services," *Social Service Review* 30 (June 1956): 134. She made the same comment in Justine Wise Polier, "Adoption and Law," *Pediatrics* 20 (August 1957): 377.

76. Nina Bernstein, *The Lost Children of Wilder: The Epic Struggle to Change Foster Care* (New York: Pantheon Books, 2001). Polier's pivotal role in the *Wilder* class action case is also documented in JWP, Box 21, Folders 251–54, and Box 22, Folder 255.

77. Memo from Justine Wise Polier to Alvin Schorr, March 18, 1975, JWP, Box 22, Folder 255.

78. Memo from Florence Brown to Justine Wise Polier, April 6, 1965, JWP, Box 33, Folder 415; "Memorandum on Louise Wise Services," 1978, 7, JWP, Box 18, Folder 208.

79. "Contributions from Federation, July 1969–June 1976," JWP, Box 33, Folder 417; "Memorandum on Louise Wise Services," 1978, 8, 11. By 1978–79, Louise Wise Services received less than $57,000 from the federation out of a budget of almost $2 million.

80. Polier, "Religion and Child-Care Services," 135.

81. "Adoption," White House Conference, Subcommittee Discussion, October 15, 1959, 2, JWP, Box 46, Folder 570.

82. Polier, "Attitudes and Contradictions in Our Culture," 2.

83. Ibid.

84. Ibid.

85. This line of thinking has been recently championed by Elizabeth Bartholet and Randall Kennedy. See Elizabeth Bartholet, "Where Do Black Children Belong," *Reconstruction* 1 (1992): 22–55, and Randall Kennedy "How Are We Doing with Loving? Race, Law and Intermarriage," *Boston University Law Review* 77 (October 1997): 815.

86. Peter Conn, *Pearl S. Buck: A Cultural Biography* (New York: Cambridge University Press, 1996).

87. Pearl S. Buck, "I Am the Better Woman for Having My Two Black Children," *Today's Health,* January 1972, 22.

88. Pearl S. Buck, "The Child Who Never Grew," *Ladies' Home Journal,* May 1950, 34. A longer version of the article was published in book form in September 1950.

89. Personal communication, Peter Conn, November 22, 2002.

90. "Pearl S. Buck Will Adopt Negro-Japanese Child," *New York Herald Tribune,* October 29, 1957.

91. Pearl S. Buck, "Should White Parents Adopt Brown Babies?" *Ebony,* June 1958, 28.

92. Pearl S. Buck, "Welcome House," *Reader's Digest,* July 1958, 47–50; Pearl S. Buck, *Children for Adoption* (New York: Random House, 1964), chap. 4; Pearl S. Buck, *My Several Worlds* (New York: John Day Co., 1954), 362–66.

93. Conn, *Pearl S. Buck,* 313.

94. Buck, "Welcome House," 48.

95. Buck, *Children for Adoption,* 90, 91.

96. Ibid., 238.

97. Ibid., 212.

98. Mary L. Dudziak, *Cold War Civil Rights: Race and the Image of American Democracy* (Princeton, NJ: Princeton University Press, 2000).

99. Helen Doss, *The Family Nobody Wanted* (Boston: Northeastern University Press, 2001). The narrative first appeared in magazine form: Helen Doss, "Our 'International Family,'" *Reader's Digest,* August 1949, 55–59; "*Life* Visits a One-Family U.N.," *Life,* November 12, 1951, 157–59.

100. Doss, *Family Nobody Wanted,* 3.

101. Ibid., 15. Her earlier description made it sound more trying: "We waited more than three years on two waiting lists to get our first baby, a sturdy little boy the spit'n' image of his new daddy" ("Our 'International Family,'" 55).

102. Doss, *Family Nobody Wanted,* 30, emphasis in original.

103. Helen Doss, *The Really Real Family* (Boston: Little, Brown, 1959), 164.

104. Doss, *Family Nobody Wanted,* 186.

105. Doss, *Really Real Family.*

106. Doss, *Family Nobody Wanted,* 92.

107. Ibid., 185.

108. Ibid., 188.

109. Ibid., 188, emphasis in original.

110. Ibid., 191, emphasis in original.

111. Pearl S. Buck, "The Children Waiting: The Shocking Scandal of Adoption," *Woman's Home Companion,* September 1955, 132.

112. Joseph Reid to Paul Smith, September 15, 1955, CWLA1, Box 15, Folder 7.

113. Ibid.

114. Joseph Reid to Pearl Buck, September 15, 1955, CWLA1, Box 15, Folder 7.

115. "400,000 Babies Left Behind," *U.S. News and World Report,* September 23, 1955, 53–54; Norman M. Lobsenz, "The Sins of the Fathers," *Redbook,* April 1956, 22. Lobsenz

reported 85,000 children in Germany (of whom 10,000 were fathered by African Americans), 35,000 in England, and up to 300,000 in Asia.

116. Lobsenz, "Sins of the Fathers," 22.

117. As of 1956, only two thousand American servicemen had acknowledged fathering any of the eighty-five thousand children left in West Germany, and military officials had never replied to inquiries from the German agency charged with responsibility for illegitimate children. See ibid., 83–84.

118. Armed Forces Information and Education, *Manual on Intercountry Adoption for Use in Guidance of U.S. Service Couples Seeking to Adopt a Foreign Child* (Washington, DC: Department of Defense, 1959).

119. Lobsenz, "Sins of the Fathers," 85–86. For the stigma facing German children with African American fathers, see Ika Hügel-Marshall, *Invisible Woman: Growing Up Black in Germany*, trans. Elizabeth Gaffney (New York: Continuum, 2001).

120. Susan Pettiss to Rosalind Giles, April 5, 1957, ISSAB, Box 10, Folder: "Adoption Plans of Racially Mixed Children, 1954–1965."

121. Laura Briggs, "Mother, Child, Race, Nation: The Visual Iconography of Rescue and the Politics of Transnational and Transracial Adoption," *Gender and History* 15 (2003): 179–200; Ann Laura Stoler, *Carnal Knowledge and Imperial Power: Race and the Intimate in Colonial Rule* (Berkeley and Los Angeles: University of California Press, 2002).

122. John C. Caldwell, *Children of Calamity* (New York: John Day, 1957); Tobias Hübinette, *Comforting an Orphaned Nation: Representations of International Adoption and Adopted Koreans in Korean Popular Culture* (Seoul: Jimoondang, 2006), chap. 2; Christina Klein, *Cold War Orientalism: Asia in the Middlebrow Imagination, 1945–1961* (Berkeley and Los Angeles: University of California Press, 2003), chap. 4; Arissa Oh, "A New Kind of Missionary Work: Christians, Christian Americanists, and the Adoption of Korean GI Babies, 1955–1961," *Women's Studies Quarterly* 33 (Fall/Winter 2005): 161–88.

123. Kirsten Lovelock, "Intercountry Adoption as a Migratory Practice: A Comparative Analysis of Intercountry Adoption and Immigration Policy and Practice in the United States, Canada and New Zealand in the Post WWII Period," *International Migration Review* 34 (Fall 2000): 907–49.

124. Karen A. Balcom, "The Traffic in Babies: Cross-Border Adoption, Baby-Selling and the Development of Child Welfare Systems in the United States and Canada, 1930–1960" (Ph.D. diss., Rutgers University, 2002).

125. Memo, December 3, 1957, Subject: Telephone Calls concerning Adoption, ISSAB, Box 12, Folder: "Group Consultation Meetings." This memo notes that 90 percent of the calls received by the ISSAB were from Jews.

126. Department of Foreign Affairs, Adoption Policy Files, quoted in Moira J. Maguire, "Foreign Adoptions and the Evolution of Irish Adoption Policy, 1945–52," *Journal of Social History* 36 (Winter 2002): 390.

127. "400,000 Babies Left Behind," 53.

128. Charles Lanius, "We Found a Baby Bonanza in West Germany," *Woman's Day*, November 1954, 43.

129. Margaret A. Thornhill, "Unprotected Adoptions," *Children* 2 (September–October 1955): 180.

130. Susan T. Pettiss to Mabel Hill Souvaine, November 16, 1954, ISSAB, Box 15, Folder 6.

131. Balcom, "Traffic in Babies," chaps. 1–2, and League of Nations Advisory Committee on Social Problems, *The Placing of Children in Families*, 2 vols. (Geneva: League of Nations, 1938).

132. Lovelock, "Intercountry Adoption as a Migratory Practice." The U.S. signed no international convention until 1993, when it endorsed the Hague Convention on the Protection of Children and Co-Operation in Respect to Intercountry Adoption (approved by the U.S. Senate in 2000).

133. Laurin Hyde and Virginia P. Hyde, "A Study of Proxy Adoptions," Child Welfare League of America and International Social Service (American Branch), June 1958, and Ernest A. Mitler, "Report on Inter-Country Adoptions," n.d., but first page is stamped December 28, 1959, CWLA1, Box 17, Folder 1. See also pamphlet by International Social Service, "Adoption Agencies Fight Mail Order Baby Racket" and "Statement of Ernest A. Mitler for Senate Immigration Committee, Re: Intercountry Adoption Legislation" in CWLA2, Box 10, Folder: "Study on Proxy Adoptions 1957–1958" (1 of 2 and 2 of 2).

134. "The Alien Child: A Symposium," Social Casework 41 (1960): 123–27; International Social Service, Adoption of Oriental Children by American White Families (New York: CWLA, May 1960); Susan T. Pettiss, "Cultural Factors in Adoption of Immigrant Children," Social Work 7 (October 1962): 22–25; Memo, December 2, 1954, Subject: Interracial Placement of Children for Adoption, ISSAB, Box 12, Folder: "Group Consultation Meetings."

135. International Social Service, American Branch, "Practical Hints about Your Child from Hong Kong," November 1958, CWLA2, Box 10, Folder: "Study on Proxy Adoptions 1957–1958" (1 of 2).

136. International Social Service, "Adoption of Oriental Children," 61; Letitia DiVirgilio, "Adjustment of Foreign Children to Their Adoptive Homes," Child Welfare 35 (November 1956): 15–21.

137. Susan T. Pettiss, "Adoption by Proxy," Child Welfare 34 (October 1955): 20.

138. Arnold Lyslo, "A Few Impressions on Meeting the Harry Holt Plan, the 'Flying Tiger,' Which Arrived in Portland, Oregon, December 27, 1958," 4, ISSAB, Box 10, Folder: "Children—Independent Adoption Schemes, Holt, Harry, vol. 2, 1958–1959."

139. Ibid.

140. Jeanne Jewett to Carl Adams, August 30, 1957, ISSAB, Box 10, Folder: "Children—Independent Adoption Schemes, Holt, Harry, vol. 1, 1955–1957."

141. Katherine B. Oettinger, Statement on Legislation Re Intercountry Adoption, May 20, 1959, 8, USCB (Information File), Box 132, Folder 7-3-1-3 Oe8. See also Katherine B. Oettinger, "Supplementary Information on Legislative Proposals on Intercountry Adoptions," February 12, 1959, and "Selected Summaries of Proxy Adoptions Reported to the Children's Bureau," n.d., but probably 1959, USCB, Box 883, Folder 7-3-1-2, "Non-Resident Problems (Include Juvenile Immigrant, Transient Boys)." Professionals believed the surge in transnational placements originated with the domestic baby shortage. See, for example, confidential memo from Wells C. Klein to Travelers Aid–International Social Service of America (TAISSA) Board of Directors, October 18, 1972, ISSAB, Box 18, Folder: "Casework Statistics."

142. Katherine B. Oettinger, Statement on Legislation Re Intercountry Adoption, 6.

143. For criticism of the Holts, see ISSAB, Box 10.

144. Excerpt from Congressional Record, July 30, 1955, ISSAB, Box 10, Folder: "Children—Independent Adoption Schemes, Holt, Harry, vol. 1, 1955–1957."

145. "Dear Friends" form letter from Harry Holt and form for "Family Information," ISSAB, Box 10, Folder: "Children—Independent Adoption Schemes, Holt, Harry, vol. 1, 1955–1957."

146. Elizabeth Campbell to Bessie Irvin, n.d., but stamped April 4, 1956, ISSAB, Box 10, Folder: "Children—Independent Adoption Schemes, Holt, Harry, vol. 1, 1955–1957."

147. Buck, *Children for Adoption*, 152–67.

148. Henry F. Pringle and Katharine Pringle, "Babies for Sale," *Saturday Evening Post*, December 22, 1951, 12. See also Robert Holman, "New Ways to Select Foster Parents," *New Society*, March 26, 1964, 20.

149. Carol S. Prentice, *An Adopted Child Looks at Adoption* (New York: D. Appleton-Century, 1940), chaps. 4 and 5. Prentice argued that heterosexual marriage was essential for normal family life and that adoption by single women or female couples exposed children to psychological danger. Pearl Buck believed that "no experience is more heart-breaking for an adult couple, warm-hearted and mature, than to realize that their fate depends upon a young woman with little or no experience of life" (Buck, *Children for Adoption*, 208–9).

150. Florida legislative hearing testimony quoted in Helen L. Witmer et al., *Independent Adoptions: A Follow-Up Study* (New York: Russell Sage Foundation, 1963), 48.

151. Ibid., 50, 97.

152. Daniel G. Grove, "Independent Adoption: The Case for the Gray Market," *Villanova Law Review* 13 (Fall 1967): 136.

153. "A Study of the Adoption Situation of New York City as It Relates to Protestant Children," January–April 1938, CWLAmicro reel 3.

154. Senate Committee on the Judiciary, Subcommittee to Investigate Juvenile Delinquency, *Hearings on Interstate Adoption Practices*, 84th Cong., 1st sess., July 15–16, 1955, 44.

155. Ibid., 87, 85–86.

156. Ernest Mitler, "Outline of Report," May 4, 1960, 1, CWLA1, Box 17, Folder 12.

157. "Report No. 1, Submitted by Investigator Pat Sax," February 5, 1960, CWLA1, Box 18, Folder 1.

158. William Trombley, "Babies without Homes," *Saturday Evening Post*, February 16, 1963, 20.

159. Quoted in ibid.

160. Alice Lake, "Why Young Girls Sell Their Babies," *Cosmopolitan*, December 1956, 44.

161. Witmer et al., *Independent Adoptions*, 93.

162. Ibid., 92.

163. Ibid., 93.

164. They still do. Desire to forge exclusive parent-child bonds may be a major factor in increasing transnational adoptions, where anonymity is far more likely than in domestic adoptions.

165. Quoted in Trombley, "Babies without Homes," 20.

166. Thomas S. Kuhn, *The Structure of Scientific Revolutions*, 2nd ed. (Chicago: University of Chicago Press, 1962); Rachel Carson, *Silent Spring* (New York: Houghton Mifflin, 1962). For a discussion of what the shift in thinking about nature implies for kinship, see Marilyn Strathern, *After Nature: English Kinship in the Late Twentieth Century* (Cambridge: Cambridge University Press, 1992).

CHAPTER SEVEN

1. Andrew Billingsley and Jeanne M. Giovannoni, *Children of the Storm: Black Children and American Child Welfare* (New York: Harcourt, Brace, Jovanovich, 1972), 72.

2. "Hard-to-Place Children, Part 2: Illegitimate Negro Children, Kansas City, Missouri, 1954" (Kansas City, MO: Community Studies, March 1956), 39–42; National Council on Illegitimacy, "Comments on Incidence of Illegitimacy among NonWhites,"

prepared by Mazy O. Yurdin, June 1969, CWLA1, Box 48, Folder 3. For a general discussion, see Rickie Solinger, *Wake Up Little Susie: Single Pregnancy and Race before Roe v. Wade* (New York: Routledge, 1992).

3. For example, *Matter of Bonez*, 48 Misc. N.Y. 2d 900 (1966), and *Matter of Bess P.*, Misc. N.Y. 2d 528 (1966); Nina Bernstein, *The Lost Children of Wilder: The Epic Struggle to Change Foster Care* (New York: Pantheon Books, 2001).
4. "Special Searchers—1901–1931," *CWLA Bulletin* 10 (September 1931): 5, JT, Box 3.
5. C. C. Carstens, "Annual Report of the Director of the Child Welfare League of America, Year 1922–23" and "Report of the Executive Director for the Year Ending September 30, 1926," CWLAmicro reel 1.
6. Leopold Katscher to USCB, May 14, 1914, and "Infanticide and Children Traffic in America," USCB Papers, Box 60, Folder 7346, "Adoption."
7. Billingsley and Giovannoni, *Children of the Storm*, 51–55.
8. Marian J. Morton, "Cleveland's Child Welfare System and the 'American Dilemma,' 1941–1964," *Social Service Review* 72 (March 1998): 115.
9. W. E. Burghardt DuBois, ed., *Efforts for Social Betterment among Negro Americans* (Atlanta: Atlanta University Press, 1909), 11.
10. Charles S. Johnson, *Shadow of the Plantation* (Chicago: University of Chicago Press, 1934), 65.
11. Mildred Arnold to Ethel Branham, December 22, 1948, USCB, Box 157, Folder 7-3-3-4, "Adoptions 11/48."
12. "Report of the Executive Director for the Year Ending September 30, 1927," CWLAmicro reel 1.
13. Marian J. Morton, "Institutionalizing Inequalities: Black Children and Child Welfare in Cleveland, 1859–1998," *Journal of Social History* 343 (Fall 2000): 141–62; Morton, "Cleveland's Child Welfare System," 123.
14. Lucile Tompkins Lewis, *What about Adoption for Me?* (New York: CWLA, 1952).
15. Lisa N. Nobe, "The Children's Village at Manzanar: The World War II Eviction and Detention of Japanese American Orphans," *Journal of the West* 38 (April 1999): 65–71.
16. Mildred Arnold to Ethel Branham, December 22, 1948.
17. Sophie van Senden Theis, *How Foster Children Turn Out*, Publication No. 165 (New York: New York State Charities Aid Association, 1924), 235, table 67.
18. Billingsley and Giovannoni, *Children of the Storm*, 115; CWLA, *Child Care Facilities for Dependent and Neglected Negro Children in Three Cities: New York City, Philadelphia, Cleveland* (New York: CWLA, 1945), 55.
19. Rita Dukette and Thelma G Thompson, *Adoptive Resources for Negro Children: The Use of Community Organization and Social Casework in Recruitment and Development* (New York: CWLA, 1959).
20. "Homes Needed for 10,000 Brown Orphans," *Ebony*, October 1948, 19.
21. Annie Lee Davis, Memorandum, Adoptive Homes for Negro Children in Kansas, November 10, 1948, USCB, Box 157, Folder 7-3-3-4, "Adoptions 11/48"; Adopt-A-Child, Minutes of the Executive Committee, May 16, 1955, Adopt-A-Child, Natural Urban League Papers, Library of Congress, Washington, DC (hereafter cited as AAC), Box 1, Folder: "Adopt-A-Child Minutes and Agenda, 1955."
22. Adopt-A-Child Clearance Bulletin, March 1958, AAC, Box 1, Folder: "Adopt-A-Child, Minutes and Agenda, 1957–June 1958."
23. Walter A. Heath, "Mass Communication Methods in Recruiting Minority Group Adoptive Homes," *Public Welfare* (July 1955): 112.

24. "Sample Letter to Enlist Support of Ministers" and other sample documents, CWLA1, Box 17, Folder 10.
25. Mildred Hawkins, "Negro Adoptions—Challenge Accepted," in *Readings in Adoption,* ed. I. Evelyn Smith (New York: Philosophical Library, 1963), 212.
26. July 1, 1957, memo from Victor Weingarten, Public Relations to Child Welfare Agencies, CWLA1, Box 40, Folder 1. See also *Adoptive Placement of Minority Group Children in the San Francisco Bay Area: A Study of MARCH* (San Francisco: MARCH, 1959), 9. Other film projects included the following. *Your Very Own* (1956) showed how an agency placed a child with a young African American couple; the film was produced by the University of Southern California for the California Department of Social Welfare, Bureau of Adoptions. *A Minority Problem* and *Response to a Minority Problem* (televised in 1962 to promote transracial adoptions) were made by PAMY. *Not Asked For* was produced in 1957 for Arlene Francis's *Home Show* on NBC; it showed how agencies worked together to find homes for hard-to-place, mixed-race children. *Angel by the Hand* was produced by the Los Angeles County Bureau of Adoptions in 1964, with the help of actress Jane Russell, to promote special-needs adoptions. *Run, Jimmy, Run* was a 1968 documentary made by KOIN-TV in Portland, Oregon, about two white couples who adopted African American children. See *PAMY's Progress: Report of Recruitment Campaign Conducted by Parents-to-Adopt-Minority-Youngsters* (St. Paul, MN: PAMY, June 1963), 7, and "Description of Films," VWB, Box 162, Folder 2.
27. Annie Lee Sandusky et al., *Families for Black Children: The Search for Adoptive Parents, 2. Programs and Projects* (Washington, DC: U.S. Department of Health, Education, and Welfare, Office of Child Development, Children's Bureau, 1972). MARCH published one of the most detailed reports to come out of these projects. See *Adoptive Placement of Minority Group Children.*
28. Heath, "Mass Communication Methods," 114; Charles E. Brown, "Agency Seeks Homes for Negro Kids, Single Persons May Adopt," 1966, unidentified newspaper clipping, VWB, Box 64, Folder 7; Walter A. Heath to Viola Bernard, March 29, 1972, VWB, Box 65, Folder 5. For an analysis of these early single-parent placements, see Ethel Branham, "One Parent Adoptions," *Children* 17, no. 3 (May–June 1970): 103–7. PAMY also considered accepting applications from singles as a way to recruit homes for nonwhite children. See *PAMY's Progress,* 17–18.
29. *Adoptive Placement of Minority Group Children,* 7–8 n. 1.
30. Theodora Allen to Hazel Hendricks, February 7, 1941, USCB, Box 176, Folder 7-4-3-3-3, "Boarding and Foster Home Care."
31. E. Wayne Carp and Anna-Leon Guerrero, "When in Doubt, Count: World War II as a Watershed in the History of Adoption," in *Adoption in America: Historical Perspectives,* ed. E. Wayne Carp (Ann Arbor: University of Michigan Press, 2002), 195; Patricia M. Collmeyer, "From 'Operation Brown Baby' to 'Opportunity': The Placement of Children of Color at the Boys and Girls Aid Society of Oregon (1944–1977)," in *A History of Child Welfare,* ed. Eve P. Smith and Lisa A. Merkel-Holguín (New Brunswick, NJ: Transaction Publishers, 1996), 235–56.
32. Elizabeth Shepherd, "Adopting Negro Children: White Families Find It Can Be Done," *New Republic,* June 20 1964, 10–12; *PAMY's Progress.*
33. Lois Wildy, "Letter on Negro Adoptions," *Child Welfare* (January 1949): 10.
34. Francis Haight, "The Development of an Interracial Program," *Child Welfare* 32 (May 1953): 11–12.
35. Davis, Memorandum.

36. Martha Perry, "An Experiment in Recruitment of Negro Adoptive Parents," *Social Casework* 39 (1958): 292. Catholic Social Service in San Francisco did the same thing. See Phyllis Dunne, "Placing Children of Minority Groups for Adoption," *Children* (March–April 1958): 46.

37. Dorothy E. Reinhart, "Adoption of Negro Children," *Child Welfare* 22 (December 1948): 11.

38. Hawkins, "Negro Adoptions," 211.

39. *PAMY's Progress.*

40. Bernice J. Daniels, "Significant Considerations in Placing Negro Infants for Adoption," *Child Welfare* (January 1950): 9.

41. Randall Kennedy, *Interracial Intimacies: Sex, Marriage, Identity, and Adoption* (New York: Pantheon Books, 2003), 523–24 n. 8.

42. Mrs. Joseph Samuel to USCB, October 28, 1948, USCB, Box 159, Folder 7-3-3-4-1, "Appeals from People Wishing Children for Adoption."

43. Virginia G. Beaton to USCB, October 28, 1948, USCB, Box 159, Folder 7-3-3-4-1, "Appeals from People Wishing Children for Adoption."

44. Mrs. Thomas Jones to Social Welfare Department, n.d., but stamped September 22, 1948, USCB, Box 159, Folder 7-3-3-4-1, "Appeals from People Wishing Children for Adoption."

45. David Fanshel, *A Study in Negro Adoption* (New York: CWLA, 1957). See also "Proposed Research Project on Negro Adoption," n.d., but penciled in is 1959, CWLA1, Box 15, Folder 7; Frances Jerome Woods and Alice Cunningham Lancaster, "Cultural Factors in Negro Adoptive Parenthood," *Social Work* 7 (October 1962): 14–21. Researchers did not investigate the experience of Latino or Asian adopters, but evidence suggests that they would have faced similar obstacles. See Dunne, "Placing Children of Minority Groups," 46–47.

46. One of the earliest proposals to subsidize adoption recognized that potential African American adopters were working-class, experienced parents rather than middle-class, childless couples. See Irving A. Fowler, "The Urban Middle-Class Negro and Adoption: Two Series of Studies and Their Implications for Action," *Child Welfare* 45 (November 1966): 522–25.

47. Elizabeth A. Lawder et al., *A Study of Black Adoption Families: A Comparison of a Traditional and a Quasi-Adoption Program* (New York: CWLA, 1971). Louise Wise Services began experimenting with subsidies for black families in the late 1950s on a case-by-case basis at the point of legal adoption. See Louise Wise Services, Board Minutes, June 10, 1959, VWB, Box 157, Folder 7.

48. Billingsley and Giovannoni, *Children of the Storm*, 141–57.

49. Ibid., 143–57.

50. Ibid., 157–70.

51. "Children Who Wait," Adopt-A-Child Conference, November 19, 1955, JWP, Box 45, Folder 566.

52. Adopt-A Child, Minutes of the Board of Directors, April 25, 1955, 4, AAC, Box 1, Folder: "Adopt-A-Child Minutes and Agenda, 1955."

53. Adopt-A-Child, Minutes of the Executive Committee, February 10, 1955, AAC, Box 1, Folder: "Adopt-A-Child Minutes and Agenda, 1955."

54. Adopt-A-Child Clearance Bulletin, March 1958, and "Procedure for Adoption Clearance of Children and Families by Adoption Agencies of Metropolitan New York," February 28, 1956, with blank forms, AAC, Box 1, Folder: "Adopt-A-Child, Misc."

For more on the early thinking behind adoption exchanges, which began on the state level, see Zelma Felten, "Use of Adoption Resource Exchanges" (paper presented at the New England Regional Conference of CWLA, March 1958), CWLA1, Box 18, Folder 3. A version was published as "Adoption Resource Exchanges," *Pediatrics* 23 (February 1959): 365–68.

55. Final Report of Adopt-A-Child, January 1, 1955–December 31, 1959, 2, appendix A, JWP, Box 18, Folder 206. This document can also be found in AAC, Box 1, Folder: "Adopt-A-Child, Reports." The project's final report noted 927 adoptions, but that included the year 1954, which was one year before Adopt-A-Child began. Children placed for adoption between 1955 and 1959 numbered 812.

56. Confidential Report, "Problems Encountered by Adopt-A-Child in Its Relationships with the Affiliated Adoption Agencies," December 19, 1955, 3, AAC, Box 1, Folder: "Adopt-A-Child, Reports."

57. Spot Announcements for Radio and Television, attached to memo dated May 15, 1956, AAC, Folder: "Adopt-A-Child, Misc."

58. Pamphlet for Adopt-a-Child, CWLA1, Box 17, Folder 10.

59. Adopt-A Child, Minutes of the Allocation Committee, May 26, 1955, 3–4, AAC, Box 1, Folder: "Adopt-A-Child Minutes and Agenda, 1955"; Memo from Justine Wise Polier to Mrs. Naomi Levine, November 21, 1955, JWP, Box 18, Folder 207.

60. Texas stated that "no white child can be adopted by a negro person nor can a negro child be adopted by a white person," a law declared unconstitutional in 1967 by *In re Gomez*, 424 SW 2d 656 (Tex. Cir. Ct. App. 1967). Louisiana limited qualified parties to adults and children of the same race; its law was struck down in 1972 by *Compos v. McKeithen*, 341 F. Suppl. 264 (E.D. La. 1972). See also "Federal Court Voids a Law Prohibiting Biracial Adoptions," *New York Times*, March 25, 1972; Kennedy, *Interracial Intimacies*, 387–89.Two other states—Kentucky and Missouri—protected white couples who unintentionally adopted nonwhite children. Their statutes allowed for annulment up to five years following the adoption if the child developed traits revealing a racial background different from the adopting parents.

61. Joyce A. Ladner, *Mixed Families: Adopting across Racial Boundaries* (Garden City, NY: Anchor Press, Doubleday, 1977), 59–60.

62. One study of 779 adoptions from Japan between 1946 and 1955 found that almost none of the adopters had Japanese ancestry, but many had served in the armed forces in Japan. See Lloyd B. Graham, "Children from Japan in American Adoptive Homes," *Casework Papers* (1957): 130–44.

63. The National Adoption Resource Exchange (NARE, later renamed the Adoption Resource Exchange of North America, or ARENA) was founded in 1966. It placed Native American children with white adoptive parents until the early 1970s. See "Indian Adoption Project, Annual Report–1972," report submitted by Barbara Lewis Roberts, director, Adoption Resource Exchange of North America, CWLA1, Box 17, Folder 4. The Canadian episode known as the "Sixties Scoop" was similar. Canadian government statistics for 1971–1981 show that the percentage of Native American children adopted by non–Native American parents ranged from a high of 84.9 percent in 1972 to a low of 71.4 percent in 1975. See Patrick Johnston, *Native Children and the Child Welfare System* (Toronto: James Lorimer, 1983), 57, table 32, chap. 2; Suzanne Fournier and Ernie Crey, *Stolen from Our Embrace: The Abduction of First Nations Children and the Restoration of Aboriginal Communities* (Vancouver: Douglas and McIntyre, 1997), 81–114.

64. "The Indian Adoption Project—1958 through 1967, Report of Its Accomplishments, Evaluation and Recommendations for Adoption Services to Indian Children," submitted by Arnold Lyslo, April 1, 1968, 1, CWLA1, Box 16, Folder 2.

65. Ibid., 8.

66. Arnold Lyslo, "The Indian Adoption Project: An Appeal to Catholic Agencies to Participate," *Catholic Charities Review* 48 (May 1964): 13. In 1960 the Navajo Nation advocated adoption by tribal members and condemned the removal of Navajo children from the reservation. See "Resolution of the Navajo Tribal Council: Tribal Policy on Adoption of Navajo Orphans and Abandoned or Neglected Children," in Steven Unger, ed., *The Destruction of American Indian Families* (New York: Association on American Indian Affairs, 1977), 85–86.

67. "Guideline for Use in Submitting Adoptive Studies to the Indian Adoptive Project," May 1, 1963, CWLA1, Box 17, Folder 4.

68. "Suggested Criteria to Evaluate Families to Adopt American Indian Children through the Indian Adoption Project," December 1962, 5, CWLA1, Box 17, Folder 3.

69. Minutes, Adoption Committee Meeting, January 12, 1960, 2, VWB, Box 161, Folder 11.

70. David Fanshel, *Far from the Reservation: The Transracial Adoption of American Indian Children* (Metuchen, NJ: Scarecrow Press, 1972). 342.

71. "Indian Adoption Project—1958 through 1967," 6.

72. Ibid.

73. Staff Meeting of Adoption Department, January 20, 1964, VWB, Box 158, Folder 1.

74. David Peterson Del Mar, *Through the Eyes of a Child: The First 120 Years of the Boys and Girls Aid Society of Oregon* (Portland, OR: Boys and Girls Aid Society of Oregon, 2005), 156. Thanks to David Del Mar for sending me a copy of this book.

75. Bernice Q. Madison and Michael Schapiro, "Black Adoption—Issues and Policies: Review of the Literature," *Social Service Review* 47 (1973): 540–41.

76. William Byler, "The Destruction of American Indian Families" in Unger, *Destruction of American Indian Families*, 1.

77. Ibid.

78. K. Tsianina Lomawaima, *They Called It Prairie Light: The Story of Chilocco Indian School* (Lincoln: University of Nebraska Press, 1994); Marilyn Irvin Holt, *Indian Orphanages* (Lawrence: University Press of Kansas, 2001); Sondra Jones, "'Redeeming' the Indian: The Enslavement of Indian Children in New Mexico and Utah," *Utah Historical Quarterly* 67 (1999): 220–41.

79. Indian Child Welfare Act, http://www.law.cornell.edu/. See also Joan Heifetz Hollinger, "Beyond the Best Interests of the Tribe: The Indian Child Welfare Act and the Adoption of Indian Children," *University of Detroit Law Review* 66 (1989): 451–501.

80. Shay Bilchik, "Working Together to Strengthen Supports for Indian Children and Families: A National Perspective" (paper presented at the National Indian Child Welfare Association, Anchorage, AK, April 24, 2001), 3. A work of fiction offered the most chilling indictment. See Sherman Alexie, *Indian Killer* (New York: Warner Books, 1996).

81. Estimates of the numbers of black children adopted by white parents for the years 1968 through 1974 are as follows: 1968—733; 1969—1,447; 1970—2,284; 1971—2,574; 1972—1,569; 1973—1,091; and 1974—747. See Opportunity, "Adoption of Black Children in 1969," ISSAB, Box 26, Folder: "Oregon—Adoption"; Opportunity, "National Survey of Black Children Adopted in 1972," VWB, Box 162, Folder 7; Dawn Day, *The Adoption of Black Children* (Lexington, MA: Lexington Books, 1979), 93, table 6-1; Madison and Schapiro, "Black Adoption," 539–40, table 1; Rita James

Simon and Howard Alstein, *Transracial Adoption* (New York: Wiley, 1977), 10–11. As of 1970, no transracial adoptions had yet taken place in Alabama, Arkansas, Louisiana, Mississippi, and South Carolina. See Ladner, *Mixed Families*, 68.

82. Ann Johnston, "Our Negro Daughter," *Ebony*, May 1960, 67.

83. Ibid., 75.

84. Opportunity, "Adoption of Black Children in 1969."

85. *Adoptive Placement of Minority Group Children*, 23.

86. Ibid., 60.

87. Ibid., 50–55. White couples were primarily interested in "Spanish-American" children. None inquired about adopting African American or part African American children. MARCH generated 801 total inquiries, but the number of placements in June 1958 was only 49. The report optimistically predicted that up to 100 children would eventually be placed as a result of MARCH (ibid., 37, 65).

88. Billingsley and Giovannoni, *Children of the Storm*, 198; Mrs. Ryo Suzuki and Mrs. Marilyn Horn, Follow-up Study on Negro-White Adoptions, VWB, Box 65, Folder 5.

89. "Whites Are Urged to Adopt Negroes," *New York Times*, November 14, 1963, VWB, Box 162, Folder 7.

90. Louise Wise Services press release, November 12, 1963, 2, VWB, Box 162, Folder 7.

91. Florence Brown to Staff, November 26, 1963, 1, Box 162, Folder 7.

92. "Transracial Adoptions—When a Good Family Is Not Good Enough," Discussion by Ethel E. Branham, Speaker: Judd Marmor, n.d., but mid-1960s, 2, VWB, Box 162, Folder 7.

93. Madison and Schapiro, "Black Adoption," 540.

94. J. Douglas Bates, *Gift Children: A Story of Race, Family, and Adoption in a Divided America* (New York: Ticknor and Fields, 1993), 29.

95. Ibid., 14.

96. "Phone Calls Force Whites to Give Up Adopted Negro Waif," *New York Times*, March 24, 1966; Ladner, *Mixed Families*, 211; Mignon Krause, memo, April 14, 1966, VWB, Box 162, Folder 7. A fictionalized version is John Neufeld, *Edgar Allan* (New York: S. G. Phillips, 1968).

97. Harriet Fricke, "Interracial Adoption: The Little Revolution," *Social Work* 10 (July 1965): 96. For more on PAMY's transracial placements, see *PAMY's Progress*, 25–31.

98. Fricke, "Interracial Adoption," 92–97.

99. Joan Barthel, "Of Father, Sons and Love," *Life*, May 15, 1970, 68.

100. Ruth Abram to Viola Bernard, July 14, 1965; "State Trying to Take Couple's Negro Baby," *Miami Herald*, April 30, 1965; Anton, Antoinette, and Joel to Dear Friends, December 1965, VWB, Box 65, Folder 5.

101. Frederick Johnson to Trude Lash, February 9, 1971, ISSAB, Box 26, Folder: "New York City Adoptions."

102. Louise Wise Services, "The Interracial Adoption Program," VWB, Box 154, Folder 1.

103. Laurence L. Falk, "A Comparative Study of Transracial and Inracial Adoptions," *Child Welfare* 49 (February 1970): 82–88, and "Identity and the Trans-Racially Adopted Child," *Lutheran Social Welfare* 9 (Summer 1969): 18–25. Falk reported on 205 children adopted transracially by 186 families. Most adoptees (111, or 54 percent) were classified as Indian or Indian-Caucasian, with 73 (36 percent) classified as Negro or Negro-Caucasian. Results did not distinguish between the families who had adopted Indian versus African American children.

104. *PAMY's Progress*, 22.

105. Joe Rigert, *All Together: An Unusual American Family* (New York: Harper and Row, 1973), 153.
106. Madison and Schapiro, "Black Adoption," 539; description of the First International Conference on Transracial Adoption, Montreal, May 30–June 1, 1969, VWB, Box 162, Folder 7.
107. Madison and Schapiro, "Black Adoption," 539 n. 8, 540.
108. The culmination of this project was H. David Kirk, *Shared Fate: A Theory of Adoption and Mental Health* (New York: Free Press of Glencoe, 1964).
109. H. David Kirk, *Looking Back, Looking Forward: An Adoptive Father's Sociological Testament* (Indianapolis, IN: Perspective Press, 1995), 11.
110. Michael Schapiro, *A Study of Adoption Practice*, vol. 1, *Adoption Agencies and the Children They Serve* (New York: CWLA, 1956), 65.
111. H. David Kirk, "Are Adopted Children Especially Vulnerable to Stress? A Critique of Some Recent Assertions," *Archives of General Psychiatry* 14 (March 1966): 291–98.
112. Kirk, *Looking Back, Looking Forward*.
113. Elizabeth Bartholet, "Where Do Black Children Belong," *Reconstruction* 1 (1992): 22–55; Ruth-Arlene W. Howe, "Redefining the Transracial Adoption Controversy," *Duke Journal of Gender Law and Policy* 2 (1995): 131–64. Outcome studies of black children adopted by whites (and summaries of outcome research) from the late 1960s and 1970s include the following: Falk, "Comparative Study of Transracial and Inracial Adoptions"; Falk, "Identity and the Trans-Racially Adopted Child," 18–25; William Feigelman and Arnold R. Silverman, "The Long-Term Effects of Transracial Adoption," *Social Service Review* 58 (1984): 588–602; Lucille J. Grow and Deborah Shapiro, *Black Children—White Parents: A Study of Transracial Adoption* (New York: CWLA, 1974); Madison and Schapiro, "Black Adoption," 531–60; Ruth G. McRoy and Louis A. Zurcher, Jr., *Transracial and Inracial Adoptees: The Adolescent Years* (Springfield, IL: Charles C. Thomas, 1983); Charles H. Zastrow, "Outcome of Black Children–White Parents Transracial Adoptions" (San Francisco: R and E Research Associates, 1977). Rita James Simon and Howard Alstein conducted the most sustained research, focusing largely (but not exclusively) on African American children adopted by white parents. They began in 1972 and conducted follow-ups in 1979 and 1984. See Rita James Simon and Howard Alstein, *Transracial Adoption: A Follow-Up* (Lexington, MA: Lexington Books, 1981), and *Transracial Adoptees and Their Families: A Study of Identity and Commitment* (New York: Praeger, 1987).
114. National Association of Black Social Workers Statement, 1972, in Robert H. Bremner, ed., *Children and Youth in America: A Documentary History*, vol. 3, *1933–1973* (Cambridge, MA: Harvard University Press, 1974), 777, 779–80. The National Association of Black Social Workers has reiterated its opposition to transracial adoption since 1972. See National Association of Black Social Workers, "The Case against Transracial Adoption," *Focal Point* 10 (Spring 1996): 18–20, and "Position Statement: Preserving African American Families," Detroit, Michigan, April 1994, document in possession of author. For a recent summary, see Madelyn Freundlich, *The Role of Race, Culture, and National Origin in Adoption*, vol. 1, *Adoption and Ethics* (Washington, DC: CWLA, 2000). Other statements of opposition to transracial adoption are John A. Brown, "Transracial Adoptions: An Organizational Analysis of a Questionable Practice," *Catholic Charities Review* 57 (January 1973): 10–17; Leon Chestang, "The Dilemma of Biracial Adoption," *Social Work* 17 (May 1972): 100–105; Amuzie Chimezie, "Transracial Adoption of Black Children," *Social Work* 20 (July 1975): 296–301.

115. National Association of Black Social Workers Statement (see note 114), 778.
116. "Position Paper Developed from Workshops concerning Trans-Racial Adoption" (National Association of Black Social Workers' Conference, Nashville, Tennessee, April 4–9, 1972). The terminology of this position paper is close to the more frequently quoted 1972 statement, but that document did not include the word "genocide."
117. National Association of Black Social Workers Statement (see note 114), 777–78.
118. Ibid., 779.
119. Judy Klemesrud, "Furor over Whites Adopting Blacks," *New York Times*, April 12, 1972, 38.
120. Simon and Alstein, *Transracial Adoption*, 10–11. Also see note 81.
121. In June 1973 the Illinois Department of Children and Family Services prohibited transracial placements in response to pressure from black social workers. See Simon and Alstein, *Transracial Adoption*, 22. For an example of a study that recommended restricting transracial placements to white families with special characteristics, see McRoy and Zurcher, *Transracial and Inracial Adoptees*, chap. 11.
122. George Gallup, "Tolerance of Mixed Marriages Increases," *Washington Post*, November 19, 1972; Alicia Howard, David D. Royse, and John A. Skerl, "Transracial Adoption: The Black Community Perspective," *Social Work* (May 1977): 186; Day, *Adoption of Black Children*, 103–4; Ladner, *Mixed Families*, 202–3.
123. Randall Kennedy, "Orphans of Separatism: The Painful Politics of Transracial Adoption," *American Prospect*, no. 17 (Spring 1994): 38–45.
124. CWLA, *Standards for Adoption Service*, rev. ed. (New York: CWLA, 1968), 34.
125. Ibid., 92.
126. Recent arguments have gone much further. See Richard Banks, "The Color of Desire: Fulfilling Adoptive Parents' Racial Preferences through Discriminatory State Action," *Yale Law Journal* 107 (1998): 875–964. For an analysis that seeks to resolve the tension between race consciousness and principled nondiscrimination, see Hawley Fogg-Davis, *The Ethics of Transracial Adoption* (Ithaca, NY: Cornell University Press, 2002).
127. Louise Wise Services, Board Minutes, April 19, 1972, 3–4, VWB, Box 155, Folder 5.
128. Simon and Alstein, *Transracial Adoption*, 10.
129. Billingsley and Giovannoni, *Children of the Storm*, chap. 7. For a description of the ABCD project in Baltimore (Adopt a Black Child through Delta and Maryland Conference), see Edmond D. Jones, "On Transracial Adoption of Black Children," *Child Welfare* 51 (1972): 161.
130. Clarence D. Fischer, "Homes for Black Children, Part 2," *Lutheran Social Welfare* 10 (Fall 1970).
131. Ladner, *Mixed Families*, 225.
132. John E. Adams and Hyung Bok Kim, "A Fresh Look at Intercountry Adoptions," *Children* 18 (November–December 1971): 216, table 1, 217, table 2.
133. Gloria Emerson, "Operation Babylift," *New Republic*, April 26, 1975, 8–10; Arthur R. Silverman and William Feigelman, "Some Factors Affecting the Adoption of Minority Children," *Social Casework* 58 (November 1977): 555 n. 7.

CHAPTER EIGHT
1. Donald Brieland, "Adoption Research: An Overview," in *Perspectives on Adoption Research*, ed. CWLA (New York: CWLA, 1965), 61.
2. Barbara Taylor Blomquist, *Insight into Adoption: What Adoptive Parents Need to Know about the Fundamental Differences between a Biological and an Adopted Child—and Its*

Effect on Parenting (Springfield, IL: Charles C. Thomas, 2006); Heather Carlini, *Adoptee Trauma: A Counseling Guide for Adoptees* (Saanichton, British Columbia: Morning Side Publishing, 1993); Karen J. Foli and John R. Thompson, *The Post-Adoption Blues: Overcoming the Unforeseen Challenges of Adoption* (Emmaus, PA: Rodale, 2004); Judith S. Gediman and Linda P. Brown, *BirthBond: Reunions between Birthparents and Adoptees—What Happens After . . .* (Far Hills, NJ: New Horizon Press, 1991); Kathleen Hushion, Susan B. Sherman, and Diana Siskind, eds., *Understanding Adoption: Clinical Work with Adults, Children, and Parents* (Lanham, MD: Jason Aronson, 2006); Ruth G. McRoy, Harold D. Grotevant, and Louis A. Zurcher, Jr., *Emotional Disturbance in Adopted Adolescents: Origins and Development* (New York: Praeger, 1988); Joyce Maguire Pavao, *The Family of Adoption* (Boston: Beacon Press, 1998); Elinor B. Rosenberg, *The Adoption Life Cycle: The Children and Their Families through the Years* (New York: Free Press, 1992); Joe Soll, *Adoption Healing: A Path to Recovery* (Baltimore: Gateway Press, 2000); Joe Soll and Karen Wilson Butterbaugh, *Adoption Healing . . . A Path to Recovery for Mothers Who Lost Children to Adoption* (Baltimore: Gateway Press, 2003); Nancy Newton Verrier, *The Primal Wound: Understanding the Adopted Child* (Baltimore: Gateway Press, 1993); Robin C. Winkler et al., *Clinical Practice in Adoption* (New York: Pergamon Press, 1988).

3. Edwina A. Cowan, "Some Emotional Problems Besetting the Lives of Foster Children," *Mental Hygiene* 22 (July 1938): 455.

4. Ibid.

5. Ibid., 456.

6. Ibid.

7. Ibid.

8. Ibid., 455.

9. David M. Levy, "Primary Affect Hunger," *American Journal of Psychiatry* 94 (November 1937): 643–44.

10. Ibid., 647.

11. Robert P. Knight, "Some Problems in Selecting and Rearing Adopted Children," *Bulletin of the Menninger Clinic* 5 (May 1941): 65, emphasis in original.

12. Ibid., 70. In the early 1960s, another Menninger clinician, Povl W. Toussieng, estimated that one-tenth to one-third of all outpatients seen at the clinic were adoptees. See Povl W. Toussieng, "Thoughts Regarding the Etiology of Psychological Difficulties in Adopted Children," *Child Welfare* (February 1962): 59; private communication from Toussieng in Marshall D. Schechter, "Observations on Adopted Children," *Archives of General Psychiatry* 3 (July 1960): 21.

13. Sydney Tarachow, "The Disclosure of Foster-Parentage to a Boy: Behavior Disorders and Other Psychological Problems Resulting," *American Journal of Psychiatry* 94 (September 1937): 401–12.

14. Sigmund Freud, "Family Romances," in *Collected Papers*, ed. James Strachey (New York: Basic Books, 1959), 5:76.

15. Mary S. Brisley, "Parent-Child Relationships in Unmarried Parenthood," *Proceedings of the National Conference of Social Work* (New York: Columbia University Press, 1939), 439, emphasis in original.

16. Florence Clothier, "The Psychology of the Adopted Child," *Mental Hygiene* 27 (April 1943): 230.

17. Ibid.

18. H. J. Sants, "Genealogical Bewilderment in Children with Substitute Parents," *British Journal of Medical Psychology* 37 (1964): 136. The psychiatric significance of genealog-

ical confusion was noticed earlier. See E. Wellisch, "Children without Genealogy—A Problem of Adoption," *Mental Health* 13 (1952): 41–42.

19. "Psychoanalytic Theory as It Relates to Adoption," reported by Marshall D. Schechter, *Journal of the American Psychoanalytic Association* 15 (July 1967): 695–708.

20. Arthur D. Sorosky, Annette Baran, and Reuben Pannor, "Identity Conflicts in Adoptees," *American Journal of Orthopsychiatry* 45 (January 1975): 24.

21. Ibid., 25.

22. Arthur D. Sorosky, Annette Baran, and Reuben Pannor, *The Adoption Triangle: Sealed or Opened Records: How They Affect Adoptees, Birth Parents, and Adoptive Parents* (San Antonio, TX: Corona Publishing, 1978).

23. Sants, "Genealogical Bewilderment," 140.

24. Hamilton Cravens, *Before Head Start: The Iowa Station and America's Children* (Chapel Hill: University of North Carolina Press, 1993), and Alice Boardman Smuts, *Science in the Service of Children, 1893–1935* (New Haven, CT: Yale University Press, 2006), chap. 7.

25. Bernadine Barr, "Spare Children, 1900–1945: Inmates of Orphanages as Subjects of Research in Medicine and in the Social Sciences in America" (Ph.D. diss., Stanford University, 1992), esp. chap. 4. Much of my analysis here is indebted to Barr's excellent study.

26. Observations that institutionalization impaired normal development appeared before empirical confirmation. See *Proceedings of the Conference on the Care of Dependent Children Held at Washington, DC*, 60th Cong., 2nd sess., 1909, S. Doc. 721 (Washington, DC: Government Printing Office, 1909), 141.

27. Barr, "Spare Children," 147 (Bakwin quotation), 146 (Brennemann quotation).

28. Ibid., 276.

29. Florence Powdermaker, H. Turner Levis, and G. Touraine, "Psychopathology and Treatment of Delinquent Girls," *American Journal of Orthopsychiatry* 7 (January 1937): 58–71, and Levy, "Primary Affect Hunger," 643–52.

30. Anna Freud in collaboration with Dorothy Burlingham, *Infants without Families: Reports on the Hampstead Nurseries, 1939–1945* (New York: International Universities Press, 1973); Anna Freud and Dorothy Burlingham, *Infants without Families: The Case for and against Residential Nurseries* (New York: International University Press, 1944); Anna Freud and Dorothy T. Burlingham, *War and Children* (New York: Medical War Books, 1943). Some of this material overlaps.

31. Freud and Burlingham, *Infants without Families: The Case for and against Residential Nurseries*, 69.

32. René A. Spitz, "Hospitalism: An Inquiry into the Genesis of Psychiatric Conditions in Early Childhood," *Psychoanalytic Study of the Child* 1 (1945): 65 n. 9.

33. Ibid., 65.

34. Ibid., 68.

35. Margaret A. Ribble, *The Rights of Infants: Early Psychological Needs and Their Satisfaction* (New York: Columbia University Press, 1943).

36. John Bowlby, *Maternal Care and Mental Health: A Report Prepared on Behalf of the World Health Organization as a Contribution to the United Nations Programme for the Welfare of Homeless Children* (Geneva: World Health Organization, 1952), 101.

37. Inge Bretherton, "The Origins of Attachment Theory: John Bowlby and Mary Ainsworth," in *Century of Developmental Psychology*, ed. Ross D. Parke et al. (Washington, DC: American Psychological Association, 1994), 431–71.

38. John Bowlby, "Attachment and Loss: Retrospect and Prospect," *American Journal of Orthopsychiatry* 52 (October 1982): 669.

39. John Bowlby, *Attachment and Loss*, vol. 1, *Attachment* (New York: Basic Books, 1969), chap 1, chap. 12, 361–78.

40. Donna Haraway, *Primate Visions: Gender, Race, and Nature in the World of Modern Science* (New York: Routledge, 1989), chap. 9.

41. Diane Eyer, *Mother-Infant Bonding: A Scientific Fiction* (New Haven, CT: Yale University Press, 1992); Maria Margarita Vicedo-Castello, "The Maternal Instinct: Mother Love and the Search for Human Nature" (Ph.D. diss., Harvard University, 2005).

42. Harry F. Harlow, "Love in Infant Monkeys," *Scientific American*, June 1959, 68–74; Harry F. Harlow and Robert R. Zimmermann, "Affectional Responses in the Infant Monkey," *Science*, August 21, 1959, 421–32.

43. Harlow and Zimmermann, "Affectional Responses," 421–32.

44. Harlow, "Love in Infant Monkeys," 72.

45. Ibid., 74.

46. Ibid., 73.

47. Harry F. Harlow and Margaret Kuenne Harlow, "Social Deprivation in Monkeys," *Scientific American*, November 1962, 136–46.

48. Bruce Gardner, Glenn R. Hawkes, and Lee G. Burchinal, "Noncontinuous Mothering in Infancy and Development in Later Childhood," *Child Development* 32 (1961): 225–34.

49. Ibid., 227, table 2.

50. Ibid., 233.

51. Leon J. Yarrow, "Theoretical Implications of Adoption Research," in *Perspectives on Adoption Research* (see note 1), 45–57.

52. Louise Raymond, *Adoption . . . and After* (New York: Harper and Brothers, 1955), 87.

53. Mary D. Howard, "The Adoptee's Dilemma: Obstacles in Identity Formation," in *Adoption Resources for Mental Health Professionals*, ed. Pamela V. Grabe (New Brunswick, NJ: Transaction Publishers, 1990), 245–46. See also Katarina Wegar, "Adoption and Mental Health: A Theoretical Critique of the Psychopathological Model," *American Journal of Orthopsychiatry* 65 (October 1995): 540–48.

54. In addition to the clinical studies described in this chapter, a number of others appeared before 1960. In chronological order, they are as follows: Elsie S. Stonesifer, "The Behavior Difficulties of Adopted and Own Children," *Smith College Studies in Social Work* 13 (December 1942): 161; Houston McKee Mitchell, "Adopted Children as Patients of a Mental Hygiene Clinic," *Smith College Studies in Social Work* 15 (1944): 122–23; Bernice T. Eiduson and Jean B. Livermore, "Complications in Therapy with Adopted Children," *American Journal of Orthopsychiatry* 23 (October 1953): 795–802; Portia Holman, "Some Factors in the Aetiology of Maladjusted Children," *Journal of Mental Science* 99 (1953): 654–88; National Association for Mental Health, *A Survey Based on Adoption Case Records* (London: National Association for Mental Health, 1954). Stonesifer was the only one to conclude that nothing significantly distinguished the clinical profiles of adopted and nonadopted children.

55. Schechter, "Observations on Adopted Children," 31.

56. Ibid., 29.

57. Meeting of Psychiatric Consultants on Telling the Child of His Adoption, July 10, 1962, 21–22, VWB, Box 162, Folder 6.

58. Ibid., 25.

59. USCB Division of Research, "Psychiatric Problems among Adopted Children," *Child Welfare* 43 (March 1964): 137–39.

60. H. David Kirk, "Are Adopted Children Especially Vulnerable to Stress? A Critique of Some Recent Assertions," *Archives of General Psychiatry* 14 (March 1966): 292.

61. Marshall D. Schechter et al., "Emotional Problems in the Adoptee," *Archives of General Psychiatry* 10 (February 1964): 109–18.

62. Princeton Survey Research Associates, "Benchmark Adoption Survey: Report on the Findings" (New York: Evan B. Donaldson Adoption Institute, 1997), 1, 8; Dave Thomas Foundation for Adoption in cooperation with the Evan B. Donaldson Adoption Institute, "National Adoption Attitudes Survey," June 2002, 5–8, 20–21, http://www .adoptioninstitute.org (accessed December 17, 2007).

63. Edgar F. Borgatta and David Fanshel, *Behavioral Characteristics of Children Known to Psychiatric Outpatient Clinics with Special Attention to Adoption Status, Sex, and Age Groupings* (New York: CWLA, 1965), 33.

64. Viola Bernard to Trudy Festinger, dictated April 16, 1967, VWB, Box 59, Folder 2.

65. Jerome D. Goodman, Richard M. Silberstein, and Wallace Mandell, "Adopted Children Brought to Child Psychiatric Clinic," *Archives of General Psychiatry* 9 (November 1963): 456.

66. Alfred Kadushin, "Adoptive Parenthood: A Hazardous Adventure?" *Social Work* (July 1966): 30–39.

67. Frances L. Menlove, "Acting Out Behavior in Emotionally Disturbed Adopted Children" (Ph.D. diss., University of Michigan, 1962); Frances L. Menlove, "Aggressive Symptoms in Emotionally Disturbed Adopted Children," *Child Development* 36 (June 1965): 519–32.

68. Betty K. Ketchum, "Reports on Study of Adopted Children," *Child Welfare* 43 (May 1964): 249; Betty K. Ketchum, "An Exploratory Study of the Disproportionate Number of Adopted Children Hospitalized at Columbus Children's Psychiatric Hospital" (master's thesis, Ohio State University, 1962), 10–11.

69. Ketchum, "Exploratory Study," 27, 28, table 7. See also appendix A on page 46 for definitions of "parental pathogens."

70. Ibid., 37.

71. Nathan M. Simon and Audrey G. Senturia, "Adoption and Psychiatric Illness," *American Journal of Psychiatry* 122 (February 1966): 863.

72. Ibid.

73. An influential statement of this position was Helene Deutsch, "Adoptive Mothers," in her work *The Psychology of Women* (New York: Grune and Stratton, 1945), 393–433. Its influence is apparent in Ethel D. Walsh and Frances S. Lewis, "A Study of Adoptive Mothers in a Child Guidance Clinic," *Journal of Social Casework* 50 (December 1969): 587–94.

74. Shirley A. Reece and Barbara Levin, "Psychiatric Disturbances in Adopted Children: A Descriptive Study," *Social Work* (January 1968): 107–8.

75. Carl Doss and Helen Doss, *If You Adopt a Child: A Complete Handbook for Childless Couples* (New York: Henry Holt, 1957), 28.

76. M. Mueller to USCB, May 29, 1930, USCB, Box 406, Folder 7-3-3-4, "Adoption"; "A Study of the Adoption Situation of New York City as It Relates to Protestant Children," January–April 1938, 13–17, CWLAmicro reel 3; Louise Wise Services, Questions for Discussion at Group Meetings, n.d., but mid-1950s, VWB, Box 157, Folder 6; First Group Meeting, April 19, 1955, VWB, Box 161, Folder 10.

77. Eleanor Garrigue Gallagher, *The Adopted Child* (New York: Reynal and Hitchcock, 1936), chap. 6.

78. Annie Hamilton Donnell, "The Adopted," *Harper's Monthly*, November 1906, 930.

79. Henrietta Sloane Whitmore, "I Wish I Hadn't Told You," *McCalls*, September 1959, 67, emphasis in original.
80. See note 105 in chapter 2.
81. Sophie van Senden Theis, *How Foster Children Turn Out*, Publication No. 165 (New York: New York State Charities Aid Association, 1924), 157.
82. C. C. Carstens, "The Pitfalls of Adoption," *CWLA Bulletin* 15 (1936): 4.
83. For one story, see Eda Houwink, "An Adopted Child Seeks His Own Mother," *CWLA Bulletin* 22 (April 1943): 1–4.
84. Howard G. Aronson, "The Problem of Rejection of Adoptive Applicants," *Child Welfare* 39 (October 1960): 23. See also Minutes of Seminar with Dr. Bernard, November 28, 1950, VWB, Box 157, Folder 4, and Summary for Dr. Bernard's Seminar, November 29, 1950, case of Norman and Anne S, VWB, Box 161, Folder 5.
85. Martha Miller (pseudonym in original) to Herbert R. Hayes, September 14, 1959, VWB, Box 63, Folder 6.
86. Gallagher, *Adopted Child*, 115–16; Iris Ruggles Macrae, "An Analysis of Adoption Practices at the New England Home for Little Wanderers" (M.S. thesis, Simmons College, School of Social Work, 1937), 94.
87. Raymond, *Adoption . . . And After*, 63.
88. Some advice-givers suggested sending cards "announcing the blessed event," locating adoption-friendly pediatricians, and having annual adoption day celebrations. Most were more cautious. See Resume of Group Meetings with Adoptive Parents, May 31, 1955, VWB, Box 161, Folder 10.
89. Martha Vansant, "The Life of the Adopted Child," *American Mercury* 28 (1933): 216.
90. Bruno Bettelheim, "What Adoption Means to a Child," *Ladies' Home Journal*, October 1970, 18.
91. "Tell the Child the Truth," excerpted in USCB, Box 406, Folder 7-3-3-4, "Adoption."
92. Marion L. Faegre, "Shall I Tell My Child He Is Adopted?" *Ladies' Home Journal*, June 1933, 32.
93. Frances Lockridge and Sophie van Senden Theis, *Adopting a Child* (New York: Greenberg, 1947), 153.
94. Doss and Doss, *If You Adopt a Child*, 46, 49. On donor insemination, see Margaret Marsh and Wanda Ronner, *The Empty Cradle: Infertility in America from Colonial Times to the Present* (Baltimore: Johns Hopkins University Press, 1996), 167, and Jill Morawski, "Imaginings of Parenthood: Artificial Insemination, Experts, Gender Relations, and Paternity," in *Believed-In Imaginings: The Narrative Construction of Reality*, ed. Joseph de Rivera and Theodore R. Sarbin (Washington, DC: American Psychological Association, 1998), 229–46.
95. "Problems in Adoption Must Be Faced Squarely," *Hygeia* (August 1933): 757.
96. D. W. Winnicott, "On Adoption," in *The Child and the Family: First Relationships*, ed. Janet Hardenberg (London: Tavistock, 1957), 128.
97. Jessie Taft, "Concerning Adopted Children," *Child Study* 6 (January 1929): 87.
98. Benjamin Spock, *The Common Sense Book of Baby and Child Care* (New York: Duell, Sloan and Pearce, 1946), 506.
99. Ibid., 507.
100. Anne Scott MacLeod, *American Childhood: Essays on Children's Literature of the Nineteenth and Twentieth Centuries* (Athens: University of Georgia Press, 1994), 114–26.
101. Valentina P. Wasson, *The Chosen Baby* (New York: J. B. Lippincott, 1939); Florence Rondell and Ruth Michaels, *The Adopted Family*, Book 2, *The Family That Grew* (New York: Crown Publishers, 1951); "How-What to Tell an Adopted Child," *Social Service*

Review 21 (1947): 251–52. For evidence that agencies encouraged book reading, see Ruth F. Brenner, *A Follow-Up Study of Adoptive Families* (New York: Child Adoption Research Committee, March 1951), chap. 5. One Vermont agency found 100 percent reliance on book reading as a telling method. See Julia E. Hatch, "Telling Children about Adoption," *Child Welfare* 43 (July 1964): 365–66. Poems were less prominent than stories. For an example, see Polly Lindquist and Prudence Lyle, "The Adoption Story," DH, Box 1, Folder 9.

102. Florence Rondell and Ruth Michaels, *The Adopted Family*, Book 1, *You and Your Child: A Guide for Adoptive Parents* (New York: Crown Publishers, 1951). This guide, which accompanied these authors' *The Family That Grew*, advised parents on how to read that book to children. See also Doss and Doss, *If You Adopt a Child*, 189; Raymond, *Adoption . . . And After*, 58. "Life books" are frequently presented as recent innovations, dating to the 1970s or 1980s, when they actually have a longer history. See Kristina A. Backhaus, "Life Books: Tool for Working with Children in Placement," *Social Work* (November–December 1984): 551–54.

103. Carolyn Haywood, *Here's a Penny* (New York: Harcourt, Brace and Co., 1944), chaps. 1–2.

104. Doss and Doss, *If You Adopt a Child*, 186–89; Spock, *Common Sense Book*, 503–7. For a contemporary version, see Linda Bothun, *Dialogues about Adoption: Conversations between Parents and Their Children* (Chevy Chase, MD: Swan Publications, 1994).

105. Knight, "Some Problems,"71, emphasis in original.

106. Raymond, *Adoption . . . And After*, 85.

107. Meeting of Psychiatric Consultants on Telling the Child.

108. Gallagher, *Adopted Child*, 116.

109. Lee M. Brooks and Evelyn C. Brooks, *Adventuring in Adoption* (Chapel Hill: University of North Carolina Press, 1939), 67.

110. Louise Wise Services, Minutes of the Child Adoption Committee, May 4, 1966, 3–7, VWB, Box 155, Folder 4.

111. Lili Peller, "About 'Telling the Child' of His Adoption," *Bulletin of the Philadelphia Association for Psychoanalysis* 11 (December 1961): 145.

112. Joseph G. Ansfield, *The Adopted Child* (Springfield, IL: Charles C. Thomas, 1971), 35–36.

113. Agnes Sligh Turnbull, "The Great Adventure of Adopting a Baby," *American Magazine*, May 1929, 182, emphasis in original.

114. Reformers have hardly abandoned children's books and stories. For example, see Betty Jean Lifton, *Tell Me a Real Adoption Story* (New York: Alfred A. Knopf, 1993).

115. Doss and Doss, *If You Adopt a Child*, 187; Raymond, *Adoption . . . And After*, 76; Rondell and Michaels, *The Adopted Family*, Book 1, *You and Your Child*, 30.

116. Georgina D. Hotchkiss, "Adoptive Parents Talk about Their Children: A Follow-Up Study of Twenty-Four Children Adopted through a Child Placing Agency" (M.S. thesis, Simmons College, 1950), 42–48.

117. Benson Jaffee and David Fanshel, *How They Fared in Adoption: A Follow-up Study* (New York: Columbia University Press, 1970), 129.

118. Joan Lawrence, "The Truth Hurt Our Adopted Daughter," *Parents' Magazine*, January 1963, 44, and First Group Meeting, April 19, 1955.

119. Rickie Solinger, *Beggars and Choosers: How the Politics of Choice Shapes Adoption, Abortion, and Welfare in the United States* (New York: Hill and Wang, 2001).

120. Quoted in Curtis J. Sitomer, "What to Tell an Adopted Child," *Christian Science Monitor*, July 25,1974, 7.

368 / Notes to Pages 278–282

121. Florence Fisher, *The Search for Anna Fisher* (New York: Arthur Fields Books, 1973).
122. E. Wayne Carp, *Family Matters: Secrecy and Disclosure in the History of Adoption* (Cambridge, MA: Harvard University Press, 1998), chaps. 5–6.
123. Ibid., chap. 3. See also Carp's "Adoption and Disclosure of Family Information: A Historical Perspective," *Child Welfare* 74 (January/February 1995): 217–39, and "The Sealed Adoption Records Controversy in Historical Perspective: The Case of the Children's Home Society of Washington, 1895–1988," *Journal of Sociology and Social Welfare* 19 (June 1992): 27–57.
124. Ruth Brenner to Viola Bernard, June 13, 1942, VWB, Box 160, Folder 6; Ruth Brenner to L, October 25, 1943, VWB, Box 160, Folder 6.
125. L to Ruth Brenner, October 5, 1943, VWB, Box 160, Folder 6. See also L to Mrs. Brenner, November 6, 1943, VWB, Box 160, Folder 6. Birth parents also sought information from agencies about their children. See Dorothy Scherl to Mr. and Mrs. Meyer S, April 15, 1946, Mrs. Nettie S to Dorothy Scherl, April 30, 1946, and Memo to Mrs. Brenner from D. S., May 2, 1946, VWB, Box 160, Folder 6.
126. Minutes of the Free Synagogue Child Adoption Committee, October 24, 1945, VWB, Box 155, Folder 1.
127. Jean M. Paton, *The Adopted Break Silence* (Philadelphia: Life History Study Center, 1954), 114.
128. Ernest Cady and Frances Cady, *How to Adopt a Child* (New York: Whiteside and William Morrow and Co., 1956), 118.
129. Summary of B Case, July 16, 1965, VWB, Box 162, Folder 5.
130. Doss and Doss, *If You Adopt a Child*, 191, emphasis in original.
131. Minutes of the Free Synagogue Child Adoption Committee, April 28, 1943, 2, VWB, Box 155, Folder 1.
132. Louise Wise Services, Minutes of the Child Adoption Committee, March 7, 1956, 3; Florence Brown to Viola Bernard, February 19, 1958, VWB, Box 157, Folder 7; Gertrude Sandgrund to Viola Bernard, December 16, 1963, VWB, Box 158, Folder 1; Staff Meeting of Adoption Department, January 20, 1964, VWB, Box 161, Folder 1; Minutes of Adoption Dept. Staff Meeting, October 30, 1961, VWB, Box 161, Folder 11.
133. Seminar with Dr. Annamarie Weil, May 9, 1957, Summary of Discussion, 1, VWB, Box 157, Folder 6.
134. Helen L. Witmer et al., *Independent Adoptions: A Follow-Up Study* (New York: Russell Sage Foundation, 1963), 93.
135. Doss and Doss, *If You Adopt a Child*, 204, emphasis in original.
136. Jaffee and Fanshel, *How They Fared in Adoption*, 311, 275.
137. Michael Schapiro, *A Study of Adoption Practice*, vol. 1, *Adoption Agencies and the Children They Serve* (New York: CWLA, 1956), 65.
138. Ibid., 89.
139. Barbara Jordan Bache-Wiig, "Adoption Insights: A Course for Adoptive Parents," *Children Today* 4 (January–February 1975): 22–25.
140. Nancy G. Janus, "Adoption Counseling as a Professional Specialty Area for Counselors," *Journal of Counseling and Development* 75 (March–April 1997): 266–75.
141. Rosenberg, *Adoption Life Cycle*.
142. Many experts regard "adopted child syndrome" as pseudoscientific folklore; it is not listed in the current *Diagnostic and Statistical Manual*. It nevertheless dramatically summarizes the consensus that adoptees are "at risk" for a wide range of mental health problems. For an argument against adopted child syndrome, see Jerome Smith, "The Adopted Child Syndrome: A Methodological Perspective," *Families in*

Society: The Journal of Contemporary Human Services 82 (September–October 2001): 491–97. For lists and discussions of the murder cases in which Kirschner consulted, see David Kirschner, "Understanding Adoptees Who Kill," *International Journal of Offender Therapy and Comparative Criminology* 36 (1992): 323–33, and David Kirschner and Linda Nagel, "Catathymmic Violence, Dissociation, and Adoption Pathology: Implications for the Mental Status Defense," *International Journal of Offender Therapy and Comparative Criminology* 40 (1996): 204–11.

143. David Kirschner, "Adoption Psychopathology and the 'Adopted Child Syndrome,'" in *Hatherleigh Guide to Child and Adolescent Therapy* (New York: Hatherleigh Press, 1996), 103.

144. David Kirschner and Linda S. Nagel, "Antisocial Behavior in Adoptees: Patterns and Dynamics," *Child and Adolescent Social Work* 5 (Winter 1988): 312; David Kirschner, "The Adopted Child Syndrome: Considerations for Psychotherapy," *Psychotherapy in Private Practice* 8 (1990): 97.

145. Betty Jean Lifton, *Journey of the Adopted Self: A Quest for Wholeness* (New York: Basic Books, 1994), 101–4. In the acknowledgments, Lifton extends special thanks to "David Kirschner, who with great integrity and courage has taken on the difficult task of educating the public on the psychodynamics of the deeply troubled adoptee" (p. 301). See also Betty Jean Lifton letter to the *New York Times*, "Adoptees Ignorant of Their Roots," November 7, 1979, VWB, Box 64, Folder 3.

146. Betty Jean Lifton, "The Formation of the Adopted Self," *Psychotherapy in Private Practice* 8 (1990): 86; Lifton, *Journey of the Adopted Self*, 92–93.

147. Robert N. Bellah et al., *Habits of the Heart: Individualism and Commitment in American Life* (New York: Harper and Row, 1985); Ellen Herman, *The Romance of American Psychology: Political Culture in the Age of Experts* (Berkeley and Los Angeles: University of California Press, 1995); Robert Wuthnow, *Sharing the Journey: Support Groups and America's New Quest for Community* (New York: Free Press, 1994).

EPILOGUE

1. David Steiegerwald, "All Hail the Republic of Choice: Consumer History as Contemporary Thought," *Journal of American History* 93, no. 2 (September 2006): 385–403.

2. Alexis de Tocqueville, *Democracy in America*, vol. 2 (New York: Harper and Row, 1969), 508.

3. "Immigrant VISAs Issued to Orphans Coming to the U.S," http://travel.state.gov (accessed December 17, 2007).

4. The number of these adoptions may have recently started to rise. See Lynette Clementson, "Overcoming Adoption's Racial Barriers," *New York Times*, August 17, 2006.

5. E. Wayne Carp, *Adoption Politics: Bastard Nation and Ballot Initiative 58* (Lawrence: University Press of Kansas, 2004).

6. Specific provisions vary from state to state. Massachusetts, for example, recently passed a law allowing access only for adoptees born on or before July 14, 1974, or on or after January 1, 2008. Alaska and Kansas never sealed records. See Evan B. Donaldson Adoption Institute E-Newsletter, September 2007, http://www.adoptioninstitute.org (accessed December 17, 2007).

7. Jean M. Paton, *The Adopted Break Silence* (Philadelphia: Life History Study Center, 1954), 3.

8. Florence Fisher, *The Search for Anna Fisher* (New York: Arthur Fields Books, 1973).

9. Ann Fessler, *The Girls Who Went Away: The Hidden History of Women Who Surrendered Children for Adoption in the Decades before Roe v. Wade* (New York: Penguin, 2006);

Barbara Melosh, "Adoption Stories: Autobiographical Narrative and the Politics of Identity," in *Adoption in America: Historical Perspectives,* ed. E. Wayne Carp (Ann Arbor: University of Michigan Press, 2002), 218–45.

10. *Secrets and Lies* was a critically acclaimed 1996 film by Mike Leigh about a British adoptee's search for her birth mother.

11. Lisa Belkin, "Now Accepting Applications for My Baby," *New York Times Magazine,* April 5, 1998, 58–62; Lincoln Caplan, *An Open Adoption* (New York: Farrar, Straus and Giroux, 1990). The growth of domestic openness may be a factor in increasing international adoptions, where birth parents are invariably powerless and unknown.

12. Jonathan B. Imber, ed., *Therapeutic Culture: Triumph and Defeat* (Somerset, NJ: Transaction Publishers, 2004).

13. Francis Fukuyama, "The American Way of Secrecy," *New York Times,* October 8, 2006. See also Daniel Patrick Moynihan, *Secrecy: The American Experience* (New Haven, CT: Yale University Press, 1998).

14. Dorothy Roberts, *Shattered Bonds: The Color of Child Welfare* (New York: Basic Books, 2002); Rickie Solinger, *Beggars and Choosers: How the Politics of Choice Shapes Adoption, Abortion, and Welfare in the United States* (New York: Hill and Wang, 2001).

15. On the conflict over Florida's policy, see *We Are Dad* (Los Angeles: Tavroh Films, 2005). Restrictions on gays and lesbians adopting have been passed recently in Michigan, Mississippi, Nebraska, North Dakota, Oklahoma, and Utah. For issue maps regarding adoption laws and foster parent regulations, see National Gay and Lesbian Task Force, http://www.thetaskforce.org/ (accessed December 17, 2007).

16. Issue map for second-parent adoption at National Gay and Lesbian Task Force, http://www.thetaskforce.org (accessed December 17, 2007).

17. Jane Gross, "Seeking Doctors' Advice in Adoptions from Afar," *New York Times,* January 3, 2006, http://www.nytimes.com (accessed December 17, 2007). The American Academy of Pediatrics Web site includes a directory of adoption medicine specialists; see http://www.aap.org/ (accessed December 17, 2007).

18. Adoption and Foster Care Analysis and Reporting System, "Trends in Foster Care and Adoption—FY2000–FY2005," http://www.acf.hhs.gov/programs/cb/stats_research/index.htm; CWLA, "Quick Facts about Foster Care," http://www.cwla.org/programs/fostercare/factsheet.htm (both sites accessed December 17, 2007).

19. The Center for Family Connections, founded by Dr. Joyce Pavao, author of *The Family of Adoption,* is a leader in the field; see http://www.kinnect.org (accessed December 17, 2007).

20. Other cases of Internet adoption fraud include Tender Hearts Adoption Facilitation Services, through which adoption facilitator Sonya Furlow scammed forty-four couples between 1993 and 1997. See Amanda Ripley, "The Empty Crib," *Time,* July 17, 2000, http://www.time.com (accessed December 17, 2007).

21. "Couple Vow to Keep Internet Twins," *BBC World Service,* January, 16, 2001, http://news.bbc.co.uk (accessed December 17, 2007).

22. California State Assembly, SB 1758, introduced February 24, 2006, signed into law on September 29, 2006, http://www.leginfo.ca.gov (accessed December 17, 2007).

23. Joan Heifetz Hollinger, "Uniform Adoption Act of 1994: Proposed UUA" in *The Praeger Handbook of Adoption,* ed. Kathy Shepherd Stolley and Vern L. Bullough (Westport, CT: Praeger, 2006), 2:653–56.

24. Bastard Nation, http://www.bastards.org/ (accessed December 17, 2007).

25. The Vietnamese Adoptee Network, http://www.van-online.org/; Adopted Vietnamese International, http://www.darlo.tv/indigo/VVietnam2.html (both sites accessed December 17, 2007).

26. United States Information Agency, "The 'Baby Parts' Myth: The Anatomy of a Rumor," May 1996, http://usinfo.state.gov; Kathleen Hunt, "The Romanian Baby Bazaar," *New York Times Magazine*, March 24, 1991; Marc Lacey, "Guatemala System Is Scrutinized as Americans Rush In to Adopt," *New York Times*, November 5, 2006, A1, http://nytimes.com (all sites accessed December 17, 2007).

27. See Richard Lewontin, *It Ain't Necessarily So: The Dream of the Human Genome and Other Illusions* (New York: New York Review of Books, 2000); President's Council on Bioethics, *Reproduction and Responsibility: The Regulation of New Biotechnologies* (March 2004), www.bioethics.gov (accessed December 17, 2007); Dorothy Roberts, *Killing the Black Body: Race, Reproduction, and the Meaning of Liberty* (New York: Pantheon Books, 1997); Arlene Skolnick, "Solomon's Children: The New Biologism, Psychological Parenthood, Attachment Theory, and the Best Interests Standard," in *All Our Families: New Policies for a New Century*, ed. Mary Ann Mason, Arlene Skolnick, and Stephen D. Sugarman, 236–55 (New York: Oxford University Press, 1998); Charis Thompson, *Making Parents: The Ontological Choreography of Reproductive Technologies* (Cambridge, MA: MIT Press, 2005). The profound impact of the new biologism on adoption is illustrated in Jill Bialosky and Helen Schulman, eds., *Wanting a Child: Twenty-Two Writers on Their Difficult but Mostly Successful Quests for Parenthood in a High-Tech Age* (New York: Farrar, Straus and Giroux, 1998).

28. Michael J. Sandel, *The Case against Perfection: Ethics in the Age of Genetic Engineering* (Cambridge, MA: Harvard University Press, 2007).

INDEX

Page numbers in italics refer to figures.

Abbott, Edith, 59, 110
Abbott, Grace, 59
abortion, 5, 28, 37, 242, 290, 292
Addams, Jane, 92, 205
adjustment (of personality), 13, 16, 89–94,
  96, 101–13, 117
adoptability. *See* eligibility criteria, for children; eligibility criteria, for parents
Adopt-A-Child, 236–38, *237*, 357n55
Adopted Break Silence, The (1954), 289
Adopted Child, The (1936), 162
Adopted Child Syndrome, 253, 282,
  368–69n142
Adopted Vietnamese International, 297
Adoptees' Liberty Movement Association
  (ALMA), 278, 289
adoption advertising, 2, 37–39, 40, 130,
  140, 147, 226, 311n99
adoption agencies, first specialized, 31,
  39–45, 205, 318n69
adoption facilitators, 296
adoption market. *See* commercial adoption
adoption medicine, 293, 370n17
adoption research. *See* clinical studies; field
  studies; nature-nurture studies; outcome
  studies
Adoption Research Project (McGill University), 246
adoption resource exchanges, 237,
  356–57n54, 357n63
adoption subsidies, 236, 319n91, 356n46,
  356n47
Adoption Triangle, The (1978), 258

African American children, 6, 17, 22,
  42, 58, 130–33, 196–99, 204, 206,
  208, 211, 215, 229–39, *237*, 242–46,
  249–52, 288, 303n5, 346n13, 351n115,
  351n119, 355n26, 356n46, 358n81,
  359n87, 359n103, 360n113
Afro-American Family and Community
  Services Agency (Chicago), 251
Ainsworth, Mary, 262
Alice Chapin Nursery, 40, 45
Amatruda, Catherine, 188
American Adoption Congress, 289
American Academy of Child Psychiatry, 88
American Association of Social Workers, 52
American Indian Movement, 241
American Institute of Family Relations, 66
American Jewish Congress, 40, 205
American Joint Committee for Assisting
  Japanese-American Orphans, 217
American Medical Association, 150,
  327n151
American Psychiatric Association, 282
American Psychoanalytic Association, 88,
  90, 258
American Statistical Association, 63
anonymity, 211, 226–27, 247, 258, 278,
  353n164
Ansfield, Joseph, 276
antimiscegenation laws, 6, 205, 238
anti-Communism, 210, 212
attachment, 3, 17, 88, 106, 133–34, 172,
  250, 252, 253, 256, 259–65, 281, 294
authenticity. *See* realness

www.ingramcontent.com/pod-product-compliance
Lightning Source LLC
Chambersburg PA
CBHW072102040426
42334CB00042B/2125